Pragmatic and Discourse Disorders: A Workbook

An essential study-aid for students of speech and language pathology, this highly practical workbook includes short-answer questions and data analysis exercises, which help students to test and improve their knowledge of pragmatic and discourse disorders. The book contains a detailed examination of the causes, and language and cognitive features of these disorders, and includes frequently encountered clinical populations and conditions that are overlooked by other texts. The use of actual linguistic data provides readers with an authentic insight into the clinical setting.

Features:

- 200 short-answer questions help students to develop and test their knowledge of pragmatic and discourse disorders.
- 68 data analysis exercises provide readers with real-life clinical scenarios.
- Fully worked answers are provided for all exercises, saving the lecturer time, and allowing the reader to self-test and improve understanding.
- A detailed glossary of terms makes the text a self-contained reference tool.
- Carefully selected suggestions for further reading are provided for each chapter.

Louise Cummings is Professor of Linguistics at Nottingham Trent University. She is a member of the Royal College of Speech and Language Therapists, and is registered with the Health and Care Professions Council in the UK.

Pragmatic and Discourse Disorders

A Workbook

LOUISE CUMMINGS

CAMBRIDGE
UNIVERSITY PRESS

CAMBRIDGE
UNIVERSITY PRESS

University Printing House, Cambridge CB2 8BS, United Kingdom

Cambridge University Press is part of the University of Cambridge.

It furthers the University's mission by disseminating knowledge in the pursuit of education, learning and research at the highest international levels of excellence.

www.cambridge.org
Information on this title: www.cambridge.org/9781107491960

First published 2015

Printed in the United Kingdom by TJ International Ltd. Padstow Cornwall

A catalogue record for this publication is available from the British Library

Library of Congress Cataloguing in Publication data
Cummings, Louise, author.
Pragmatic and discourse disorders : a workbook / Louise Cummings.
    pages   cm
Includes bibliographical references and index.
ISBN 978-1-107-09920-3 (hardback)
1. Speech disorders.   2. Pragmatics.   3. Language disorders.   I. Title.
RC423.C866   2015
616.85'506 – dc23   2015012664

ISBN 978-1-107-09920-3 Hardback
ISBN 978-1-107-49196-0 Paperback

Additional resources for this publication at www.cambridge.org/9781107491960

Contents

Preface   *page* vii

Acknowledgements   ix

List of data analysis exercises   x

1   Introduction to pragmatic and discourse disorders   1
    Section A: Short-answer questions   3
        1.1   Pragmatics and discourse in human communication   3
        1.2   Disorders of pragmatics and discourse   5
        1.3   Clinical distinctions   8
    Section B: Clinical scenarios   10
        1.4   Pragmatics and discourse in human communication   10
        1.5   Disorders of pragmatics and discourse   13
        1.6   Clinical distinctions   15
    Suggestions for further reading   17

2   Developmental pragmatic and discourse disorders   18
    Section A: Short-answer questions   20
        2.1   Pragmatic language impairment   20
        2.2   Intellectual disability   22
        2.3   Autism spectrum disorder   25
        2.4   Childhood traumatic brain injury   27
        2.5   Epileptic syndromes   28
        2.6   Childhood cancer   30
    Section B: Data analysis exercises   33
        2.7   Pragmatic language impairment   33
        2.8   Intellectual disability   59
        2.9   Autism spectrum disorder   64
        2.10 Childhood traumatic brain injury   81
        2.11 Epileptic syndromes   85
        2.12 Childhood cancer   91
    Suggestions for further reading   93

3   Acquired pragmatic and discourse disorders   95
    Section A: Short-answer questions   97
        3.1   Acquired aphasia   97
        3.2   Right-hemisphere language disorder   99
        3.3   Traumatic brain injury   101
        3.4   Dementias   103

	3.5	Neurodegenerative disorders	105
	3.6	Central nervous system infections	106
Section B: Data analysis exercises			108
	3.7	Acquired aphasia	108
	3.8	Right-hemisphere language disorder	126
	3.9	Traumatic brain injury	131
	3.10	Dementias	139
	3.11	Neurodegenerative disorders	150
	3.12	Central nervous system infections	153
Suggestions for further reading			155

4 Mental health and pragmatic and discourse disorders — **156**

Section A: Short-answer questions			158
	4.1	Schizophrenia	158
	4.2	Bipolar disorder	160
	4.3	Personality disorder	162
	4.4	Emotional disturbance in children	163
	4.5	Behavioural disorders in children	165
Section B: Data analysis exercises			166
	4.6	Schizophrenia	166
	4.7	Bipolar disorder	174
	4.8	Personality disorder	179
	4.9	Emotional disturbance in children	181
	4.10	Behavioural disorders in children	183
Suggestions for further reading			184

5 Pragmatics and discourse in other disorders and populations — **186**

Data analysis exercises			187
	5.1	Early corrective heart surgery	187
	5.2	Functional illiteracy	189
	5.3	Hearing loss	191
	5.4	Augmentative and alternative communication	192
	5.5	Aging and the elderly	196
Suggestions for further reading			197

Answers to questions and exercises	198
Glossary	242
References	252
Index	257

Preface

The need for a workbook on pragmatic and discourse disorders has been apparent to me for some time. Like many other instructors, I have been frustrated at the lack of available resources in this area of communication disorders. While published texts and data in clinical phonetics and phonology are commonplace, lecturers on speech–language pathology (SLP) courses have always had to do extra work to secure similar material on pragmatic and discourse disorders for use with their students. This lack of resources can be explained in part by the fact that pragmatics and discourse are still relative newcomers to linguistics in general and to the study of language pathology in particular. These important linguistic disciplines have not had as much time as phonology and syntax to become embedded in SLP curricula. Certainly, pragmatics and discourse do not command the same emphasis within the clinical education of SLP students as structural aspects of language (e.g. syntax and semantics). An essential first step in giving pragmatic and discourse disorders the prominence they deserve is the availability of accessible material that can be readily employed with SLP students in the clinic and in the classroom. This workbook is intended to be just such a resource.

In devising this workbook, my overriding aim has been to give its readers maximum exposure to data obtained from children and adults with impaired pragmatic and discourse skills. These data take a number of forms. There are transcriptions of conversational exchanges between clinicians, clients and family members. Non-dialogical forms of discourse are also used throughout the volume. These include the production of narratives which are either generated spontaneously or are elicited through specific discourse tasks (e.g. storytelling based on the events depicted in a wordless picture book or in a sequence of pictures). The use of procedural discourse to give directions to an individual or to explain the rules of a game to a listener will be examined on occasion. Referential communication tasks which involve naïve listeners are the source of some of the data which will be featured in the following pages. Alongside the production of discourse there will be consideration of a range of data relating to the comprehension of discourse and pragmatic aspects of language. This includes the ability to draw causal and temporal inferences during story listening and to respond to pragmatically demanding questions. In short, no aspect of the pragmatic and discourse performance of clients is omitted from consideration in this workbook.

The workbook also acknowledges that the successful analysis of clinical data is only possible under certain conditions. These conditions include a sound understanding of the types of clients who are likely to experience pragmatic and discourse disorders. Among these clients are children and adults with autism spectrum disorder, intellectual disability and traumatic brain injury. Alongside these well-known conditions there are a number of other client groups in which pragmatic and discourse disorders are only just beginning to be captured (e.g. adults with non-Alzheimer dementias). It is vitally important for SLP students to have knowledge of all aspects of these conditions and of their likely impact on language and communication. To this end, four chapters in the workbook contain a number of short-answer questions which are designed to test students' knowledge of the clinical conditions in which pragmatic and discourse disorders are found. These questions will serve instructors well both as classroom exercises and as assessment tasks. With answers provided to all questions, SLP students can also use them independently of their tutors to test their knowledge of particular topics. Additional features of the volume, which will be equally useful to instructors and students, are a detailed glossary of clinical terms and numerous suggestions for further reading.

Acknowledgements

There are a number of people whose assistance I wish to acknowledge. I particularly want to thank Dr Andrew Winnard, Commissioning Editor in Language and Linguistics at Cambridge University Press, for responding so positively to the proposal of a workbook in the area of pragmatic and discourse disorders. I wish to acknowledge the assistance of Judith Heaney, who prepared the index for the volume. I have also been supported by family members and friends who are too numerous to mention individually. I am grateful to them for their kind words of encouragement during my many months of work on this volume.

List of data analysis exercises

1.4 *Pragmatics and discourse in human communication*   10
Scenarios examining pragmatic processes in human communication
Scenarios examining discourse breakdown in normal language subjects
Scenarios examining the role of inferences in pragmatic and discourse skills

1.5 *Disorders of pragmatics and discourse*   13
Scenarios examining the assessment of pragmatic language skills
Scenario examining the pragmatic language assessment of a boy with
   suspected autism spectrum disorder
Scenario examining the cognitive basis of pragmatic and discourse
   impairments in a man with severe traumatic brain injury

1.6 *Clinical distinctions*   15
Scenarios examining developmental and acquired pragmatic and discourse
   disorders in children and adults
Scenarios examining primary and secondary pragmatic and discourse
   disorders in children and adults
Scenarios examining receptive and expressive pragmatic and discourse
   disorders in children and adults

2.7 *Pragmatic language impairment*   33
Conversational and discourse data from a 10-year-old boy with pragmatic
   disability
Expressive pragmatics of two Swedish girls with semantic–pragmatic
   disorder
Receptive pragmatics of a girl called Sarah between the ages of 9;8 and
   10;3 years
Longitudinal investigation of pragmatic abilities in a boy called Tony
   between 3;4 and 7;0 years
Narrative production in children with language disorder aged 7;6 to
   10;6 years
Comprehension of non-literal language in students with specific
   developmental language disorder
Co-constructed narratives between mothers and children with specific
   language impairment aged 50 to 68 months
Conversations between mothers and their preschool, language-delayed
   children
Communicative skills of a child with SLI and his MLU-matched younger
   sibling
Narrative production in children with SLI aged 8;6 and 9;0 years

2.8   *Intellectual disability*   59
    Narrative production in children and adolescents with Down's syndrome
    Interviews with adults with mild and moderate intellectual disability

2.9   *Autism spectrum disorder*   64
    Semi-structured conversational data from children with ASD aged 10 to
       16 years
    Narrative introductions in high-functioning children with autism spectrum
       disorder
    Irrelevance in answering questions in children with Asperger's syndrome or
       high-functioning autism
    Spoken and written narrative production in children with ASD and SLI
    Conversational exchanges between a researcher and a woman with autism:
       part 1
    Conversational exchanges between a researcher and a woman with autism:
       part 2

2.10 *Childhood traumatic brain injury*   81
    Narrative discourse production in a girl of 7;4 years with traumatic brain
       injury
    Discourse summarisation ability of children with mild and severe TBI

2.11 *Epileptic syndromes*   85
    Narrative discourse production of three hemidecorticate adolescents: part 1
    Narrative discourse production of three hemidecorticate adolescents: part 2
    Inference generation from connected discourse in clients with
       childhood-onset temporal lobe epilepsy

2.12 *Childhood cancer*   91
    Case study of a 39-year-old woman who underwent intracranial surgery at
       16 years of age for removal of a posterior fossa tumour

3.7   *Acquired aphasia*   108
    Fable retell and explanation of proverb meaning by an adult with fluent
       aphasia
    Use of reported speech in two adults with aphasia caused by a
       left-hemisphere CVA
    Spontaneous speech in adult 15 months post-onset left-hemisphere CVA
    Discourse production in an adult with severe and chronic agrammatic
       aphasia
    Conversational turn-taking in three adults with stroke-induced aphasia
    Conversational strategies during word searches in aphasia
    Repair of trouble sources in conversations between adults with aphasia and
       carers
    Discourse production pre- and post-therapy in a 41-year-old man with
       Broca's aphasia

3.8   *Right-hemisphere language disorder*   126
    First-encounter conversations with adults with right-hemisphere damage:
       part 1

First-encounter conversations with adults with right-hemisphere damage: part 2

3.9 *Traumatic brain injury*   131
Conversation in a 24-year-old man with closed head injury
Pragmatic skills in French-speaking adults with frontal lesions following TBI
Narrative discourse production in adults with severe penetrating head injuries
Discourse production in adults with TBI across three contexts

3.10 *Dementias*   139
Fable retell and explanation of proverb meaning by an adult with Alzheimer's disease
Conversation in a 36-year-old man with AIDS dementia complex
Conversation in adults with senile dementia of the Alzheimer's type
Conversation and picture description in adults with semantic dementia and adults with early- or middle-stage dementia of Alzheimer's type
Conversation in a 71-year-old man with semantic dementia

3.11 *Neurodegenerative disorders*   150
Storytelling in two adults with Parkinson's disease
Discourse production in Huntington's disease and corticobasal syndrome

3.12 *Central nervous system infections*   153
Spontaneous speech and picture description in an adult with seizures following encephalitis

4.6 *Schizophrenia*   166
Comprehension and production of linguistic and extra-linguistic pragmatic phenomena in adults with schizophrenia
Discourse topics of three adult speakers with schizophrenia
Clinical interviews with a 26-year-old man with thought-disordered schizophrenia

4.7 *Bipolar disorder*   174
Narratives of an adult with bipolar disorder: part 1
Narratives of an adult with bipolar disorder: part 2

4.8 *Personality disorder*   179
Life story interviews with adults with features of borderline personality disorder

4.9 *Emotional disturbance in children*   181
Case study of a 9-year-old girl called Mimi with selective mutism

4.10 *Behavioural disorders in children*   183
Conversations between a teacher and two children with ADHD

5.1 *Early corrective heart surgery*   187
Narrative discourse in 4-year-old children at risk for brain injury following early corrective heart surgery

5.2 *Functional illiteracy*   189
      Narrative discourse production in French-speaking adults with functional
          illiteracy

5.3 *Hearing loss*   191
      Conversation in a woman with congenital hearing loss and no language
          exposure until adulthood

5.4 *Augmentative and alternative communication*   192
      Narrative discourse in children who are users of augmentative and
          alternative communication

5.5 *Aging and the elderly*   196
      Narrative production in normal, elderly speakers

Chapter 1

Introduction to pragmatic and discourse disorders

For a significant number of children and adults, difficulties with communication are linked to problems with pragmatics and discourse. These aspects of language have been variously defined within linguistics and a range of other disciplines. Pragmatics is often defined as the study of the use of language or of language meaning in context (Cummings, 2005). The emphasis is on speaker meaning rather than sentence meaning (the latter is studied by semantics), and on how hearers draw on features of context to derive meaning beyond that which is expressed by the proposition of a sentence. (Of course, even this definition of pragmatics is somewhat simplistic, as it is now widely recognised that pragmatic factors are very much involved in determining propositional meaning.) The standard definition of discourse in textbooks on linguistics talks of discourse as being 'language above the sentence'. In much the same way that sentences have an internal structure, extended extracts of spoken, written or signed language (discourse) are believed to observe certain structural patterns. Revealing these patterns across all forms of language use, from spoken narratives to conversations and written texts, is the focus of the study of discourse analysis.

As these definitions demonstrate, there is much that unites the study of pragmatics and discourse. Both areas are concerned to look beyond individual sentences to understand how speakers and hearers (readers and writers) construct and interpret language meaning. While language is abstracted from the contexts (including its users) in which it is found in linguistic disciplines such as syntax and semantics, pragmatists and discourse analysts seek to understand the complex interrelationships that exist between language, its users and the wider context. Given the shared concerns and goals of these disciplines, it should not be surprising to discover that neat boundaries cannot be drawn around pragmatics and discourse. By the same token, the reader should not be surprised to learn that many of the same children and adults who experience breakdown in the pragmatics of language also encounter a range of discourse difficulties. The co-occurring deficits in pragmatics and discourse, which are found in children and adults with autism spectrum disorder or traumatic brain injury, attest to the considerable overlap that exists between these linguistic domains. It is the interconnectedness of pragmatics and discourse that is the basis of their joint examination in this volume.

So what exactly is a pragmatic or discourse disorder? One of the clearest ways of explaining these disorders is to describe how language and communication are compromised in individuals who have them; see Cummings (2009, 2012a, 2014a) for detailed discussion. A child or an adult with a pragmatic or discourse disorder may misinterpret non-literal language in such a way that a sarcastic utterance – 'What a delightful child!' spoken in the presence of a boisterous 5-year-old boy, for example – may be understood in a literal way. Children and adults with these disorders may fail to recover the implicature of an utterance, may be unable to represent shared knowledge as a presupposition of an utterance, and may misunderstand the illocutionary force of a speech act (e.g. 'I will leave early' is understood as a threat rather than as a promise). Individuals with pragmatic and discourse disorders may produce irrelevant responses to questions, may contribute too much or too little information in a conversational exchange, or may be unable to initiate, develop and terminate a topic of conversation. These same children and adults may produce disorganised narratives in which information is presented in a confusing and illogical manner. They may fail to establish cohesive links between utterances in a narrative, so that a listener is unable to follow the events in a story. Children and adults with pragmatic and discourse disorders may use pronouns and other linguistic expressions (e.g. definite noun phrases) in the absence of clear referents. The combination of these various difficulties can lead to marked deficits in communication with attendant problems in other areas of functioning; see Cummings (2011, 2014a, 2015) for discussion of the impact of these disorders.

Each of the above pragmatic and discourse problems may occur in a developmental and an acquired form. The child with autism spectrum disorder, for example, may never have acquired the pragmatic knowledge which is needed to use a range of speech acts appropriately or interpret the non-literal utterances of others. This child exhibits a *developmental pragmatic disorder* because the onset of the disorder occurs in the developmental period. However, the adult who sustains a cerebrovascular accident (or stroke) in the right hemisphere of the brain may be unable to produce coherent narratives, interpret metaphorical language or use linguistic expressions to achieve reference. This adult's difficulties constitute an *acquired pragmatic disorder* which is related to the disruption of previously intact pragmatic knowledge. It should be emphasised that children can experience an acquired pragmatic disorder and that adults can exhibit a developmental pragmatic disorder. The adult with Down's syndrome who cannot recover the implicature of a speaker's utterance has a developmental pragmatic disorder. This adult's difficulties are the consequence of anomalies in the developmental period, specifically the presence of intellectual disability. The adolescent who sustains a traumatic brain injury and produces disorganised narratives to a wordless picture book has an acquired pragmatic disorder. This teenager's pragmatic difficulties are related to the onset of a brain injury after the point at which narrative competence may be expected to have been acquired.

Alongside the distinction between developmental and acquired pragmatic and discourse disorders rests a further distinction between receptive and expressive disorders. The comprehension or understanding of pragmatic and discourse phenomena (*receptive pragmatics*) covers a wide range of skills from the interpretation of non-literal utterances to the ability to understand the temporal and causal relations between entities and events in a narrative. The production of pragmatic and discourse behaviours (*expressive pragmatics*) involves an equally diverse set of skills including the contribution of relevant, informative utterances to a conversational exchange and the use of a range of speech acts. It is important in the clinical management of clients with pragmatic and discourse disorders for clinicians to recognise a distinction between receptive and expressive aspects of pragmatics and discourse in order that these aspects may be separately assessed and treated. It is possible, for example, for the expressive pragmatic skills of the adult with non-fluent aphasia to be disproportionately impaired relative to receptive pragmatic skills. By the same token, the adult with dementia related to Alzheimer's disease may struggle to comprehend the non-literal language of humour in a conversational exchange while still contributing relevant, meaningful turns to a conversation. Of course, it is also possible – and more probable, in fact – that the child or adult who struggles to comprehend certain speech acts will also fail to use these same speech acts appropriately.

A final clinical distinction should be introduced at this stage. It is the distinction between a primary and a secondary pragmatic or discourse disorder. It is undoubtedly the case that some pragmatic and discourse disorders are unrelated to any deficits in structural language. These so-called *primary pragmatic disorders* include many (most) of the pragmatic problems found in children and adults with autism spectrum disorder as well as pragmatic and discourse impairments found in conditions such as schizophrenia, traumatic brain injury and right-hemisphere damage. While cognitive factors may play a role in the pragmatic and discourse impairments associated with these conditions – and in cognitive–communication disorders found in traumatic brain injury (TBI), for example, they almost certainly do – it is not the case that these impairments are the result of structural language deficits. (Adults who sustain a TBI can often pass standardised language batteries and yet still exhibit significant communication disorder.) A quite different situation obtains in the case of a child with specific language impairment (SLI) or an adult with aphasia. The often severe deficits in expressive and receptive structural language in these clients may give rise to pragmatic and discourse disorders. For example, the child with SLI who cannot perform the syntactic operations needed to achieve the inversion of the subject pronoun and auxiliary verb in the question 'Can you open the window?' is unlikely to employ certain indirect speech acts in his or her verbal output. In such cases, the child with SLI and the adult with aphasia have *secondary pragmatic disorders*. This workbook will examine both types of pragmatic and discourse disorders.

Section A: Short-answer questions

1.1 Pragmatics and discourse in human communication

(1) The following statements describe linguistic behaviours that are commonly found in human communication. For each statement, indicate if it captures pragmatic or discourse features of language.

(a) A speaker uses the utterance 'It's cold in here' to get his hearer to close the window.

(b) A speaker makes extensive use of temporal expressions such as *last week*, *later* and *shortly afterwards* to relate events in a story.

(c) John infers from the utterance 'I have an essay to complete for tomorrow' that Mary does not want to go to the cinema.

(d) On listening to a story which contains the utterances 'Sally unpacked the picnic supplies. The beer was warm', a hearer infers that the picnic supplies contained beer.

(e) In describing a picture of a family meal, a speaker gives prominence to the people present and the food they are eating over the cuckoo clock on the wall and the vase of flowers in the corner.

(2) Fill in the blank spaces in these paragraphs using the words in the box below.

Linguistic utterances can be used to perform a range of functions beyond simply conveying information or describing _____ in the world. For example, the utterance 'Big Jim will be at the party' can be used to _____ or warn someone beyond its use as an informative utterance. Similarly, the utterance 'I will be at Sally's lecture this evening' can be used to _____ a friend's invitation to dinner or to make a promise to a colleague beyond simply serving as a description of one's future whereabouts. Language users must be adept at using features of _____ to determine which of these functions of utterances holds in a particular case. Let us imagine that Big Jim has a reputation for violent behaviour and other misdemeanours and that the speaker of the utterance 'Big Jim will be at the party' is a trusted friend of the hearer. This background _____ might be used by the hearer to conclude that the speaker intends his utterance to function as a _____. If, however, the speaker is a notorious gang member, a prudent hearer would do well to conclude that a threat is the intended function of the utterance.

The context sensitivity which has been demonstrated by the above examples is a feature of the interpretation and use of all utterances. It is a feature of _____ context, namely, shared knowledge between speakers and hearers, which allows the speaker of the utterance 'It was the teenager who stole the car' to represent certain information – someone stole the car – as a _____ of that utterance. The speaker who utters 'Fred wants to live here' is using an aspect of physical context – a particular location (building, town, etc.) – as the intended _____ of the indexical expression 'here'. The author who writes 'An opposing viewpoint will be presented in the next chapter' is pointing to an upcoming extract of written text (i.e. _____ context) as the referent of the indexical noun phrase 'the next chapter'. The grandmother who utters to her grandson 'Tommy must be well behaved for granny' is reflecting a feature of _____ context – her more powerful role in the situation as an adult and a caregiver of the child – in her selection of the nouns *Tommy* and *granny* over the personal pronouns *you* and *me*, respectively.

social	implicature	context	referent
knowledge	deixis	speech act	promise
states of affairs	warning	request	discourse
entailment	threaten	decline	cooperative principle
presupposition	maxim	epistemic	felicity condition

(3) *True* or *False*: The speaker who utters 'I would' in response to the question 'Would anyone like a drink?' is making use of ellipsis.

(4) *True* or *False*: The words *I* and *tomorrow* in the utterance 'I'm flying to Paris tomorrow' are examples of social and temporal deixis, respectively.

(5) *True* or *False*: Conjunctions such as *and* and *because* have a cohesive function in narrative discourse.

(6) Select a word from the box below that best characterises the pragmatic or discourse behaviours described in each of the following statements.

   (a) The speaker who utters 'I have read some of the books for the module' is communicating to a hearer that he or she has not read all of the books for the module.

   (b) The speaker who utters 'The doctor managed to save the baby's life' is intending to communicate that the doctor tried to save the baby's life.

   (c) The utterances 'Mary was exhausted. She had been caring for the children all day' are linked by means of the referring function of the pronoun *she*.

   (d) Sentences can be linked by the use of words which are synonyms or near-synonyms, e.g. 'Sally battled her illness over many months. The disease took her life in the end.'

   (e) The lexical item *even* in the utterance 'Even Bill passed the grammar exam' communicates the speaker's belief that the grammar exam was easy.

deixis	anaphoric reference	entailment	collocation
scalar implicature	cataphoric reference	speech act	
presupposition	conventional implicature	substitution	

(7) Which of the Gricean maxims is exploited by Sally in the following conversational exchange?

BILLY: Where are you going?
SALLY: I'm heading to the V-E-T (uttered in the presence of the family dog)

(a) relation
(b) quality
(c) manner
(d) quantity
(e) relation and manner

(8) Which of the following lexical items and constructions in the utterance 'The old house on the hill is haunted' triggers a presupposition to the effect that there exists an old house on the hill?
(a) adjectives *old* and *haunted*
(b) nouns *house* and *hill*
(c) lexical verb *is*
(d) noun phrase *the old house on the hill*
(e) locative preposition *on*

(9) Which of the following cohesive relations is exemplified by the underlined words in the sentences 'Fran spotted a dress with polka dots. It was the only one in the shop'?
(a) collocation
(b) substitution
(c) lexical reiteration
(d) reference
(e) conjunction

(10) Underline the deictic expressions in each of the following utterances. Also, label each expression as a form of personal, social, temporal, discourse or spatial deixis.
(a) She had always wanted to live in Berlin.
(b) I visited the dentist last week.
(c) That paragraph is particularly weak.
(d) Sally walks to work this way.
(e) Well behaved pupils get gold stars from teacher.

1.2 Disorders of pragmatics and discourse

(1) Identify each of the following statements as describing a breakdown of pragmatics or discourse.
(a) The adult with schizophrenia fails to use cohesive devices to link the utterances in his spoken narratives.
(b) The child with autism spectrum disorder replies 'yes' to the indirect speech act 'Can you take this note to Mrs Black's room?'

(c) The child with a traumatic brain injury produces repetitive language during storytelling to a wordless picture book.

(d) The adult with right-hemisphere damage interprets metaphorical utterances like 'The players were lions on the field' in a concrete, literal way.

(e) The adult with dementia related to Alzheimer's disease cannot convey the rules of a simple card game to a listener.

(2) *True* or *False*: A narrative produced by a child with a discourse disorder may exhibit many cohesive links and yet still be incoherent.

(3) *True* or *False*: The adult with pragmatic disorder who consistently makes explicit in communication knowledge which he shares with his interlocutor is not using presupposition when it is appropriate to do so.

(4) *True* or *False*: The child with pragmatic disorder who fails to understand utterances such as 'Can you sit down?' and 'It's cold in here' has a problem with the interpretation of indirect speech acts.

(5) Fill in the blank spaces in the following paragraphs using the words in the box below.
A pragmatic disorder can compromise all aspects of the use and interpretation of utterances. At the outset of communication a speaker must form an appropriate _____. The formation of these intentions is determined by the speaker's goal in speaking as well as by certain constraints which characterise the communicative context. In this way, we entertain many more thoughts than we can ever, or should ever, communicate. I may believe that your new dress makes you look overweight. However, my concern to maintain our pre-existing _____ prevents me from representing that belief in the form of a communicative intention which I then proceed to transmit to you by means of linguistic utterances. For a child or an adult with pragmatic disorder, the formation of communicative intentions may be disrupted, with the result that _____ or otherwise inappropriate utterances come to be communicated. Even in the case where an appropriate communicative intention is formed, a pragmatic disorder may then compromise the linguistic processes by means of which that intention is _____ within an utterance. For example, a child or an adult with pragmatic disorder may fail to reflect the formality of the communicative context and may make _____ selections and choose grammatical constructions for direct speech acts over indirect speech acts. This pragmatic anomaly may be compounded by other pragmatic difficulties relating to the use of _____ (stress, intonation, etc.) and non-verbal behaviours such as _____ expressions and gestures (smiling, head nods, etc.).

The same pragmatic disorders that impair the use of linguistic utterances can also compromise the _____ of these utterances. On hearing an utterance, the child or adult with pragmatic disorder must employ linguistic decoding processes in order to obtain the _____ meaning of an utterance. These decoding processes involve a series of rules which reveal the syntactic and _____ structures of the utterance. However, these processes are also influenced by pragmatic factors which permit the _____ of utterances, the narrowing of concepts and the assignment of _____ to expressions. The child or adult with pragmatic disorder may struggle to resolve the lexical ambiguity in an utterance such as 'She stood next to the bank' or to assign referents to the indexical expressions in the utterance 'We took that route to Madrid during our holiday last year.' The individual with pragmatic disorder may also be unable to achieve the narrowing of universal quantifiers in utterances such as 'Everyone danced until early morning' (*everyone* = everyone at the party). Even in the case where pragmatic factors do successfully intrude into the _____ form of an utterance, this form is often only the beginning of a process of interpretation which terminates in the communicative intention that motivated the speaker to produce the utterance. It is during this stage in the interpretation of utterances that conversational _____ are recovered, a process that is often compromised in children and adults with pragmatic disorders. Breakdown at this point in the communication cycle may result in the concrete, literal interpretation of utterances.

phonetic	referents	decoded	deixis	syntax
implicatures	comprehension		communicative intention	
phonology	social relationship		propositional	impolite
encoded	speech production	logical	facial	interpretation
prosody	disambiguation	grammatical	semantic	lexical

(6) Which of the following statements is *true* of discourse impairments in children?
   (a) These impairments almost invariably have their origin in structural language deficits.
   (b) These impairments are increasingly being linked to cognitive deficits in executive function and theory of mind.
   (c) These impairments typically occur in the absence of a clear aetiology.
   (d) These impairments have little or no implications for academic achievement.
   (e) These impairments are inadequately assessed using formal language batteries.

(7) Which of the following statements is *false* of pragmatic disorders in adults?
   (a) These disorders are always found alongside aphasia.
   (b) These disorders always have their onset in adulthood.
   (c) These disorders have little or no implications for occupational functioning.
   (d) These disorders can compromise verbal and non-verbal skills.
   (e) These disorders are most often caused by an acquired brain injury.

(8) Which of the following tasks can be used to examine discourse production skills in the clinic?
   (a) The description of events depicted in a series of pictures in front of the speaker.
   (b) The comprehension of events related during storytelling to a wordless picture book.
   (c) The recovery of the implicatures of a speaker's utterance during conversation.
   (d) The production of single words in response to picture stimuli.
   (e) The production of a single sentence to describe the events in a picture.

(9) Which of the following is *not* among the aetiology of pragmatic and discourse disorders?
   (a) cranial nerve damage
   (b) cerebral infection
   (c) cerebral neoplasms
   (d) cerebral infarction
   (e) genetic syndromes

(10) Which of the following statements is *true* of the assessment of pragmatic language skills in the clinic?

(a) These skills are often assessed by means of checklists of verbal and non-verbal behaviours.

(b) These skills are readily assessed in formal language tests.

(c) These skills are often subordinated to structural language skills in clinical assessment.

(d) Conversation analysis may be used to examine pragmatic language skills.

(e) Sentence production tasks are an effective means of testing pragmatic language skills.

1.3   Clinical distinctions

(1) Which of the following statements describes an *acquired* pragmatic disorder?

    (a) A child with an autism spectrum disorder makes irrelevant responses to questions.

    (b) An adult with Down's syndrome makes use of a limited range of speech acts.

    (c) An adult with right-hemisphere damage points to a picture of a man hitting a sack when he hears the utterance 'John decided to hit the sack.'

    (d) An adult with frontotemporal dementia displays problems with topic management during conversation.

    (e) A child with pragmatic language impairment asks inappropriate questions of his teacher.

(2) Which of the following statements describes a *developmental* discourse disorder?

    (a) A teenager with a severe traumatic brain injury produces repetitive language during a personal narrative.

    (b) An adult with AIDS dementia complex fails to understand temporal and causal relations between events in a story.

    (c) An adult with Williams syndrome uses verbose language to explain the steps in making popcorn to a hearer.

    (d) A child with attention deficit hyperactivity disorder omits important information during a picture description task.

    (e) A child with pragmatic language impairment explains the rules of a board game to a hearer in the wrong order.

(3) *True* or *False*: Children with pragmatic language impairment have a secondary pragmatic disorder.

(4) *True* or *False*: The child with Down's syndrome who has a limited repertoire of speech acts on account of expressive language impairment has a primary pragmatic disorder.

(5) *True* or *False*: An adult with agrammatic aphasia who cannot develop a topic of conversation has a secondary pragmatic disorder.

(6) For each of the following statements, indicate if a *receptive* or *expressive* pragmatic disorder is described.

    (a) An adult with schizophrenia makes several impolite remarks during an interview with a psychiatrist.

    (b) A child with epilepsy contributes irrelevant utterances during a play session with a speech and language therapist.

    (c) A child with fragile X syndrome utters 'yes' when asked by his teacher 'Can you collect the books?'

(d) A child with autism spectrum disorder fails to laugh at a joke told by one of his classmates.

(e) An adult with dementia related to Alzheimer's disease fails to respond to a carer who asks 'Do you have the time?'

(7) Fill in the blank spaces in the following paragraphs using the words in the box below. Clinicians use a number of labels to help them characterise pragmatic and discourse disorders in children and adults. The distinction between a developmental and an acquired pragmatic disorder conveys important information about the ———— of a disorder. For some children and adults, pragmatic skills and knowledge are not acquired normally during the ————. This may be on account of an intellectual disability as in the child with a ———— syndrome, or as a result of a more specific cognitive impairment of the type found in autism spectrum disorder. The resulting developmental pragmatic disorder has implications for the ———— skills of these children amongst other areas of functioning. Alternatively, pragmatic skills and knowledge may develop along normal lines in childhood but then be disrupted by the onset of conditions such as ————, schizophrenia and cerebrovascular accidents in adolescence and adulthood. These later-onset conditions can cause an ———— pragmatic disorder which has implications for the social and occupational functioning of affected individuals.

Clinicians also draw a distinction between primary and secondary pragmatic disorders. This distinction reflects the fact that some pragmatic disorders arise in consequence of deficits in structural language (———— pragmatic disorder) while other disorders appear to be unrelated to any structural language impairment. The child with ———— may lack the syntactic and semantic structures that are needed to form certain ———— (e.g. indirect requests) or to achieve pronominal reference. In such cases, a pragmatic disorder is secondary to a primary deficit in structural language. However, there are other cases where a pragmatic disorder appears to be not so readily explained by an impairment of ————. The pragmatic impairments of children and adults with a traumatic brain injury fall within this category of ———— pragmatic disorders. A final clinical distinction concerns that between a receptive and an expressive pragmatic disorder. This distinction reflects the fact that pragmatic disorders can compromise both the ———— of utterances (receptive pragmatic disorder) and the production of utterances (expressive pragmatic disorder). Examples include the misinterpretation of non-literal language such as ———— and the use of irrelevant utterances in conversation, respectively.

embryological development	acquired	traumatic brain injury
intellectual disability	structural language	primary
onset	pervasive developmental disorder	interpretation
pragmatic language impairment	genetic	speech acts
developmental period	deixis	secondary	irony
social communication	gesture	specific language impairment

(8) Which of the following is *not* an expressive discourse disorder?

(a) The adult with right-hemisphere damage produces egocentric discourse during a picture description task.

(b) The adolescent with a closed head injury fails to relate the events in a story in such a way that they can be followed by a listener.

(c) The child with attention deficit hyperactivity disorder interjects on the turns of others during conversation.

(d) The adult with autism spectrum disorder cannot recover the implicatures of his interlocutor's utterances.

(e) The adult with schizophrenia fails to use conjunctions to establish cohesive links between the utterances in his spoken narratives.

(9) Which of the following conditions is *not* within the aetiology of an acquired pragmatic disorder?
(a) genetic syndromes
(b) meningitis
(c) pervasive developmental disorders
(d) brain tumour
(e) vascular dementia

(10) Which of the following conditions is *not* within the aetiology of a developmental pragmatic disorder?
(a) frontotemporal dementia
(b) closed head injury
(c) autism spectrum disorder
(d) epilepsy
(e) Parkinson's disease

Section B: Clinical scenarios

1.4   Pragmatics and discourse in human communication

(1) Pragmatic processes pervade human communication. These processes are variously involved in the following stages of communication: the formation of communicative intentions; the recovery of those intentions during utterance interpretation; and the development of the semantically underspecified logical form of utterances. Below are several scenarios that draw upon pragmatic processes. Relate each of these scenarios to one of these three stages of communication.

(a) John uses his knowledge that coffee can keep a person awake to recover the implicature that Mary wants more coffee in the following exchange:

JOHN: Would you like more coffee?
MARY: I need to be alert when I drive home later.

(b) A hearer uses his or her knowledge of context to disambiguate the words *ball* and *plane* in the utterances:

In Frank's opinion, it was a fantastic ball.
They were standing next to the plane when the accident happened.

(c) A hearer draws upon pragmatic knowledge to arrive at the propositional meaning of B's utterance in the following utterance:

A: How was your cruise in Norway?
B: Everyone was sick [*everyone on the ship* was sick].

(d) Jack, Jack's wife Fran and Jack's colleague Sally meet at a garden party. Jack and Sally last met two days earlier when Sally ran into Jack and his mistress at a performance of *Les Misérables*. Sally commits a *faux pas* when she asks Jack in front of Fran if his mistress enjoyed the performance.

(e) Barry is woken in the middle of the night by a loud knock on his front door. He runs downstairs, opens the door and is greeted by an emergency worker who shouts 'The river has burst its banks.' Barry uses his knowledge of context to establish the illocutionary force of the emergency worker's utterance – he has been given a warning to leave his home. He rushes back upstairs and throws a few essential items into a bag.

(2) Discourse competence in communication involves a wide range of skills and abilities. Communicators must be able to establish relations between spoken and written utterances so that an extract of text is cohesive and can be followed by a hearer or reader. Utterances must also progress or develop a discourse in a particular way so that an utterance in a narrative, for example, can be shown to develop the plot of a story or reveal the intentions of one of its characters. Information management is also an important discourse skill. Speakers and writers must be adept at recognising the information needs of their listeners and readers and tailoring the informational content of their messages accordingly. These discourse skills can occasionally break down even in children and adults with no discourse impairment. Several such scenarios are presented below. Indicate if the discourse difficulty in each case relates to cohesion, narrative development or information management.

(a) Bob and Sue are at the village fête when they run into their neighbour Brian. He has just returned from a walking trip in the French Alps in which one of his fellow walkers broke her leg. Brian attempts to explain how this accident happened. However, he has been drinking free cider at the fête all afternoon and his account is difficult to follow. His utterances are disconnected and do not appear to relate to each other. Bob and Sue leave the interaction with much confusion about the events Brian attempted to relate.

(b) Derek has a reputation as the office bore. If you are unlucky enough to find yourself in his company, he will detain you indefinitely with lengthy personal narratives. These contain excessive detail, much of which is already known to the listener. Barbara is a new employee in the office. While queuing to use the photocopier one day, she decides to engage Derek in conversation. He quickly begins to dominate the conversation with a story about his trip to work that morning. The story conveys all sorts of details that Barbara might be expected to know – Derek starts work at 8 a.m. (all employees do), he eats breakfast before leaving home, etc. After fifteen minutes, Barbara abruptly terminates the conversation and walks away.

(c) It is the first day back at school after the summer holidays. The pupils in Mrs Smith's class have been asked to write a short story about a funny event that happened to them during the break. Poppy proceeds to write a story about a trip to the park in which her brother fell into a pond while he was trying to feed the ducks. However, her written narrative contains many statements which do not develop the theme of her story. For example, she writes that her daddy is a postman and that her mummy works in a supermarket. The teacher points out these problems to Poppy and asks her to write the story again.

(d) Paul is jet-lagged after his return from a three-week business trip to New York. His wife wants to hear all about the trip as she is contemplating going on a shopping break to New York with her friend at Christmas. However, she finds her husband's account of his stay to be unsatisfactory in a number of ways. He tells her nothing about the large department stores and shopping precincts even though he visited many of them. He talks incessantly about a baseball game he watched with his business colleagues. Also, his account is somewhat fragmented with few of his utterances appearing to flow from each other. She decides to ask him again later when he has had a chance to rest.

(e) Alex is a teenage boy who has the very latest in mobile phone technology. He has just been given a new phone by his parents for his birthday. Two days after his birthday, Alex's mother hears about an incident in which Alex was involved in a fight with another teenage boy at his school. As soon as she returns home from work, she asks Alex to explain what happened. His account sets out clearly but soon begins to deteriorate when he starts to receive texts from a friend. His explanation of the events at school is deemed unsatisfactory by his mother who still does not know what triggered the fight, who threw the first blow, and many other important details.

(3) It is becoming increasingly clear to researchers that cognitive factors play an important role in pragmatic and discourse skills. One factor which holds particular relevance for pragmatics and discourse is the ability to draw inferences. Some of these inferences are used to establish the mental states, and especially communicative intentions, of speakers (*mental state inferences*). Other inferences are used to relate utterances and sentences to each other within spoken and written texts (*textual inferences*). Still other inferences allow speakers to leave information implicit in language on the assumption that a hearer can use world knowledge to draw them during constructive comprehension (*elaborative inferences*). For each of the scenarios below, indicate if a language user is employing mental state, textual or elaborative inferences.

(a) Sam and Joe are caught in a heavy downpour of rain on their way to the bus stop. When they eventually get to the stop, Sam turns to Joe and says 'What wonderful weather we're having!' Joe detects the sarcasm in Sam's utterance and replies 'I would say it has never been better!'
What type of inference has Joe drawn?

(b) Alice's mother is reading her a story about a family's preparations for Christmas. The picture Alice is looking at shows a woman unpacking a large box of Christmas decorations which has just come down from the attic. The story continues: 'The woman takes tinsel and baubles out of the box for decorating the tree. The lights are dusty and several are broken.' Even though the picture only shows the woman taking tinsel out of the box, Alice infers that the box also contained lights.
What type of inference has Alice drawn?

(c) Bob has been trying to pluck up the courage to ask Susie out to dinner for several weeks. He meets her one day in the stairwell of the flats where they both live. He says to her 'I've heard the new Italian restaurant in town is excellent. Would you like to join me for dinner there on Saturday evening?' Susie smiles and replies 'My brother is visiting this weekend.' Bob is dejected when he realises his invitation to dinner has been declined.
What type of inference has Bob drawn?

(d) Tom is listening to a bedtime story that is being read by his father. It is about a chemist called Dr Smith who is very clumsy and has many accidents. The story describes how he trips over steps, walks into doors, and stands on the family dog among many other clumsy actions. The story continues: 'One day there was a loud explosion in the garden shed. Dr Smith threw open the door and staggered into the garden in a shocked state.' Tom immediately asks his father what Dr Smith did to cause the explosion.

What type of inference has Tom drawn?

(e) Billy is 13 years old and has an inquisitive mind. He hears his mother tell a friend the following story about his auntie Cynthia: 'Cynthia has been unwell for a number of weeks. After much persuasion from her husband, she eventually decided to make an appointment to see her doctor. The doctor conducted a thorough examination. He took her blood pressure, listened to her heart and tested her reflexes. He also recorded her temperature, which was slightly raised. After a 15-minute consultation, Cynthia left the medical practice with a course of antibiotics in her hand.' On hearing this story, Billy immediately asks his mother 'Why did the doctor prescribe Cynthia antibiotics?' His mother replied 'He thought she had an infection.'

What type of inference has Billy drawn?

1.5   Disorders of pragmatics and discourse

(1) A speech and language therapist wants to assess the pragmatic language skills of a child. The clinic where the therapist works has an extensive array of assessments and equipment which can be used for this purpose. Read each of the following short passages and decide which, if any, of them describes a procedure that could be used to assess this child's pragmatic language skills.

(a) A published assessment contains a booklet of colour drawings. Each set of four drawings relates to a stimulus utterance. For the utterance 'Jack wanted to hit the sack' there is a drawing of a man sleeping in bed, a man hitting a sack with a stick, a man soaking in a bath tub and a man beating a carpet clean.

(b) A published assessment contains a booklet of black and white line drawings. Each drawing depicts an object (e.g. spoon), action (e.g. jumping) or natural phenomenon (e.g. tree) that is within the cultural experience and vocabulary level of the child to be assessed. The child's task is to name as many drawings as possible.

(c) A published assessment contains a booklet of colour drawings. Each set of two drawings depicts a different pair of antonyms. For example, for the gradable antonyms *tall–small*, there is a picture of a tall man next to a picture of a small man. The therapist prompts the child to produce the target antonyms by saying 'This is a picture of a tall man, and this is a picture of a ... [*child completes utterance*].'

(d) The speech and language therapist has an extensive range of colourful toys that are of interest to the child. They include a doll, a teddy bear and a small drum that the child has previously enjoyed manipulating during play sessions. In the presence of the child the therapist takes each toy and places it on top of cupboards in the room. From this position, the toys are within the child's view but beyond his or her grasp. The aim is to encourage the child to request each of the toys of the therapist.

(e) The speech and language therapist sets a series of objects on a table in front of the child. The child is seated and watches the therapist take each object out of a box and place it on the table. As the therapist sets each object on the table, she names it for the child. The objects are a comb, a spoon, a small doll, a bed and a cup. All objects are within the child's receptive vocabulary level. The therapist records the child's actions in response to a series of indirect speech acts such as 'Dolly is tired' (target action: child puts Dolly in bed) and 'Dolly is thirsty' (target action: child puts cup up to Dolly's mouth).

(2) A speech and language therapist is referred a 5-year-old boy by a paediatrician. The boy has a suspected autism spectrum disorder and has developmental delay in a number of areas including language and communication. The referral report describes a range of social interaction problems. The child's verbal and non-verbal communication skills are characterised by the paediatrician as being markedly deviant. After a session in which the child is observed during play with his mother, the therapist decides to undertake a full communication assessment with special emphasis on the boy's pragmatic and discourse skills. Impairment of these skills is believed to be responsible for the child's lack of competence as a communicator. Which of the following behaviours will the therapist need to consider within an assessment of this child's pragmatic and discourse skills?

(a) The therapist will want to assess the child's ability to produce words belonging to semantic fields such as *fruit* and *animals*.

(b) The therapist will want to examine the child's ability to produce simple sentences such as 'The man is running' and 'The book is blue' in description of a series of pictures.

(c) The therapist will want to consider the child's use of story grammar in producing a narrative to a wordless picture book.

(d) The therapist will want to assess the child's ability to use speech acts such as requests and to respond to the speech acts of others.

(e) The therapist will want to establish if the child is sensitive to the turn-taking rules of conversation and can exchange turns with his or her interlocutors.

(f) The therapist will want to establish the child's phonetic inventory by conducting an articulation test.

(g) The therapist will want to consider the child's ability to initiate, develop and terminate topics of conversation.

(h) The therapist will want to assess the child's use of inflectional suffixes through sentence completion tasks such as 'Today, the girl walks home from school; yesterday, the girl ...'

(i) The therapist will want to establish if the child can draw simple inferences about temporal and causal relations between events in a story.

(j) The therapist will want to assess the child's ability to use gestures and facial expressions appropriately during interaction with others.

(3) A speech and language therapist has been treating a 45-year-old man called Paul for a period of two months. Paul sustained a severe traumatic brain injury in a road traffic accident six months earlier. Initially, he was in a coma. When he emerged from his coma, he was mute for several weeks. During this time, he used an alternative means of communication to make his needs known to medical staff and family members. A recent assessment conducted by a neuropsychologist revealed Paul to have significant cognitive deficits in executive functions (e.g. working memory, attention). The speech and language therapist believes Paul's marked pragmatic and discourse impairments are related to these deficits. Which of the following aspects of Paul's communication performance in clinic are suggestive of a significant cognitive basis to his pragmatic and discourse impairments?

(a) During an account of his injury and hospitalisation, Paul repeats information that he has just conveyed to the therapist, with the result that his personal narrative is somewhat uninformative.

(b) Paul's speech intelligibility is best during morning therapy sessions, but can decrease slightly during a late afternoon session.

(c) Paul regularly interjects on the turns of his interlocutors during conversation and appears unable to wait until an appropriate transition relevance place becomes available.

(d) Paul struggles to retain instructions from the therapist, with the result that he appears not to comply with therapy tasks.

(e) Paul displays a moderate anomia which responds well to the therapist's use of semantic cues (e.g. *toothbrush*: you use this object to clean your teeth).

(f) Paul is highly distractible and can allow stimuli in his environment (e.g. a bird on the window sill) to intrude into the topic of conversation.

(g) Paul is unable to suppress some socially inappropriate behaviours, and offensive remarks are frequently expressed in conversation with others.

(h) Paul exhibits some velopharyngeal incompetence which is heard as mild-to-moderate hypernasality during speech production.

(i) Paul can be heard to make syntactic errors in his verbal output, especially when the cognitive demands of a task are great.

(j) Paul can often establish the intended meaning of speakers' utterances, although his processing of non-literal language proceeds at a delayed rate.

1.6 Clinical distinctions

(1) The following scenarios describe a range of pragmatic and discourse disorders in children and adults. For each scenario, indicate if the disorder is developmental or acquired in nature.

(a) Jack is 19 years old. He is six months post-onset a severe traumatic brain injury which was sustained in a motorbike accident. His account of the event contains repetitive language with frequent digressions from the topic of his personal narrative.

(b) David is 15 years old and has autism spectrum disorder. He attends mainstream school where he receives additional support. When describing his day at school to a speech and language therapist, he includes much irrelevant information about his favourite television programmes.

(c) Frank is 65 years old and has chronic schizophrenia. He lives in supported accommodation in the community. He attends regular meetings with his psychiatric nurse. She reports a deterioration in Frank's communication skills since his drug regimen was changed. Where he was previously able to give a reasonably coherent account of his daily activities, he now appears to misrepresent causal and temporal relations between events.

(d) Michael is a sociable 13-year-old boy with Williams syndrome. His non-verbal behaviours during conversation are described as 'intense' by his mother and include excessive eye contact and close physical proximity to his interlocutor. He is also verbose during conversation.

(e) Sally is 5 years old and has sensorineural hearing loss as a result of meningitis which she contracted at 6 months of age. She has a number of developmental difficulties.

Her acquisition of phonology and syntax is delayed. She struggles with turn-taking during conversation, which her speech and language therapist attributes to her difficulty with reading prosodic cues at the end of her interlocutor's turns.

(2) The following scenarios describe a range of pragmatic and discourse disorders in children and adults. For each scenario, indicate if the disorder is primary or secondary in nature.

(a) Florence is a friendly 8-year-old girl with pragmatic language impairment. She attends a special language unit where she is well integrated with her peers. She frequently misses the implication of her teacher's remarks. When asked if she could hang up her coat, she replied 'yes' and continued to play with her classmates.

(b) Bob is a retired miner who has severe non-fluent aphasia following a left-hemisphere stroke. He is eager to communicate and is very frustrated by his expressive difficulties. His use of single-word utterances limits the range of speech acts he can produce to simple requests and refusals. A severe right-sided hemiplegia restricts his use of gesture during communication.

(c) Marjorie is 70 years old and has early-stage dementia related to Alzheimer's disease. Her speech is intelligible and her structural language skills are intact. However, she frequently fails to grasp humour and jokes used by others in conversation. Her comprehension of non-literal language such as idiomatic expressions and sarcasm also appears somewhat compromised.

(d) Billy is 5 years old and has been diagnosed by a speech and language therapist as having specific language impairment. His expressive language skills are very limited. Billy is a sociable child and wants to communicate with his peers. However, his severely impaired expressive language means that he has a limited repertoire with which to initiate verbal exchanges. His attempts to do so are frequently unsuccessful and have led on some occasions to conflict with his peers.

(e) Tom is 30 years old and has been an inpatient in a head trauma unit for six months. For nearly two of those months, he was in a coma following a severe head injury which was sustained while he worked on a construction site. Tom has been receiving speech and language therapy as part of an intensive rehabilitation programme. His therapist has conducted a full communication assessment which revealed no frank aphasia. However, Tom's spoken narratives are repetitive, tangential and under-informative.

(3) The following scenarios describe a range of pragmatic and discourse disorders in children and adults. For each scenario, indicate if the disorder is receptive or expressive in nature.

(a) Oscar is 4 years old and is in the care of foster parents. He had a very low birth weight as he was born prematurely to a mother with a substance use disorder. Oscar is currently on the caseload of a paediatrician for a range of developmental problems. An assessment of his communication skills by a speech and language therapist revealed Oscar to be largely passive in his interactions with others. Certainly, he was not observed to initiate any form of communication during his clinical assessment. The therapist attributes Oscar's difficulties to an inability to generate communicative intentions.

(b) Alan is a 50-year-old financial analyst who has recently suffered a severe right-hemisphere stroke. He has moderately severe dysarthria. An assessment of his language skills by a speech and language therapist revealed no frank aphasia.

However, Alan's communication skills in clinic are still noticeably aberrant. For example, during a number of storytelling tasks he was frequently observed to relate anecdotes to the therapist and to discuss issues within his personal experience. In consequence, his spoken narratives were judged to have a peculiarly egocentric quality.

(c) Miriam is 65 years old and has recently been diagnosed with Parkinson's disease dementia. During a consultation with the neurologist, Miriam's daughter reported that her mother had displayed conversational difficulties for some time. The neurologist reported these concerns in his referral of Miriam to the hospital's speech and language therapy department. On initial assessment, the speech and language therapist observed that Miriam's structural language skills were largely intact. However, her comprehension of higher-level language such as metaphor and sarcasm was judged to be impaired.

(d) Jonathan is a 15-year-old boy with Asperger's syndrome. He attends mainstream school where he receives classroom support. Jonathan's teacher reports that he wants to communicate with his peers, but that many of his communicative efforts fail on account of his difficulties comprehending humour and jokes. Jonathan also responds poorly to banter and playful teasing from the other teenage boys in his class. The school's speech and language therapist observes Jonathan in interaction with his peers, and concludes that his difficulties arise from a specific deficit in the pragmatics of language.

(e) Simon is a 10-year-old boy with fragile X syndrome and intellectual disability. His expressive language skills are limited to single words and some phrase-level productions (e.g. *big doggie*). Notwithstanding his limited expressive language and cognitive difficulties, Simon has a strong social interest and actively seeks out the company of other children and adults. His poor expressive language skills restrict the range of speech acts which he can perform. However, Simon is able to use gestures very effectively to help compensate for his expressive language impairments.

SUGGESTIONS FOR FURTHER READING

Asp, E. D. and de Villiers, J. 2010. *When language breaks down: analysing discourse in clinical contexts*, New York: Cambridge University Press.

Cummings, L. 2009. *Clinical pragmatics*, Cambridge: Cambridge University Press.

Cummings, L. 2014. *Pragmatic disorders*, Dordrecht: Springer.

Müller, N., Guendouzi, J. A. and Wilson, B. 2008. 'Discourse analysis and communication impairment', in M. J. Ball, M. R. Perkins, N. Müller and S. Howard (eds), *The handbook of clinical linguistics*, Malden, Oxford, Victoria: Blackwell Publishing, 3–31.

Perkins, M. 2007. *Pragmatic impairment*, Cambridge: Cambridge University Press.

Chapter 2

Developmental pragmatic and discourse disorders

For many individuals, pragmatic and discourse skills do not develop along normal lines. For these children and adults with *developmental* pragmatic and discourse disorders, a large range of conditions, illnesses and events in the period from conception through birth to the first months and years of life can compromise the acquisition of these skills. Genetic syndromes such as Down's syndrome, Williams syndrome and fragile X syndrome can cause intellectual disability of varying severity. In cases of severe or profound intellectual disability, language may fail to develop altogether. Even mild to moderate intellectual disability can have adverse implications for the development of language in general, and pragmatic and discourse skills in particular. Exposure to teratogens such as alcohol, illicit substances (e.g. cocaine) and lead during the embryological period can compromise neurodevelopment and can cause long-term language impairment (Cummings, 2008). Pragmatic and discourse disorders may be found alongside structural language deficits in children who have experienced prenatal exposure to these noxious substances. Prenatal infections such as rubella, cytomegalovirus, toxoplasmosis and human immunodeficiency virus (HIV), pose a risk to neurodevelopment and may be possible factors in the aetiology of pragmatic and discourse disorders.

Even if prenatal neurodevelopment has not been compromised by any of these challenges, events in the postnatal period can pose a risk to the development of pragmatic and discourse skills. These events include infections such as meningitis, and traumatic brain injuries which are most often sustained through falls, road traffic accidents or child abuse. It is also in the postnatal period that the first signs of autism spectrum disorder begin to emerge. Children and adults with these neurodevelopmental disorders often experience severe impairments of pragmatics and discourse, and have been the focus of considerable research. Two clinical populations which have been less extensively studied, but in which there is evidence of pragmatic and discourse disorder, are children with epilepsy and children with cerebral and other neoplasms. One epileptic syndrome in particular, Landau–Kleffner syndrome, has implications for pragmatic and discourse skills. In childhood cancer, postnatal neurodevelopment can be compromised by cranial irradiation and by the neurotoxic effects of chemotherapy drugs. Finally, there is a significant group of children for whom pragmatic and discourse skills are compromised in the absence of any clear aetiology. These children with so-called pragmatic language impairment form a distinct subgroup within the specific language impairment (SLI) population.

The pragmatic and discourse disorders of these different clinical populations are very wide-ranging in nature. These disorders may include problems with topic management in conversation, difficulty processing non-literal language such as irony and indirect speech acts, and a failure to consider the perspective and knowledge of others in the construction of linguistic utterances. Other pragmatic and discourse disorders may manifest as problems with the use of story grammar during narrative production, difficulty undertaking repair work during conversation and a failure to produce relevant responses to questions.

Many of these pragmatic and discourse impairments occur alongside structural language deficits. In some cases, they arise in consequence of those deficits. For example, the child with expressive SLI may lack the structural language skills that are needed to form indirect speech acts or to represent shared knowledge in the presuppositions of an utterance. In other cases, significant pragmatic and discourse problems exist in the absence of structural language deficits or they appear to be not so readily explained by those deficits. Children with pragmatic language impairment (PLI), for example, may have relatively intact phonology and syntax (unlike most other children with developmental language disorder). Yet, children with PLI often exhibit a severe impairment of pragmatics.

Aside from structural language, there is growing awareness of the role of cognitive factors in pragmatic and discourse disorders. Investigators are increasingly finding evidence of a relationship between theory of mind (ToM) impairments and executive function deficits and developmental pragmatic and discourse disorders in children and adults; see chapter 4 in Cummings (2009) and chapter 3 in Cummings (2014a) for discussion. Theory of mind describes the ability to attribute mental states such as beliefs, knowledge and communicative intentions both to one's own mind and to the minds of others. A ToM impairment has consistently been identified in children and adults with autism spectrum disorder (ASD), and is believed to play a causal or other role in the pragmatic and discourse impairments of this clinical population. ToM impairments are increasingly being identified in a range of other populations (e.g. schizophrenia) in which there are pragmatic and discourse impairments; see Cummings (2013, 2014b) for discussion. Executive functions are cognitive processes which are involved in the planning, execution and regulation of goal-directed behaviour. These processes include deployment of attention, impulse control and mental flexibility. Executive dysfunction will be addressed alongside several of the disorders examined in this chapter (e.g. traumatic brain injury).

An eclectic range of procedures exists for the assessment of developmental pragmatic and discourse disorders. Pragmatic profiles and checklists are a popular means of establishing an overview of a client's pragmatic language skills. Three assessments of this type are the Pragmatics Protocol (Prutting and Kirchner, 1987), the Pragmatics Profile (Dewart and Summers, 1988) and a widely used checklist called the Children's Communication Checklist-2 (CCC-2; Bishop, 2003). Similar profiles and checklists can also be found as part of larger language batteries. For example, the fourth edition of the *Clinical Evaluation of Language Fundamentals* (Semel et al., 2003) also includes a Pragmatics Profile. The target age range, structure and administration of these profiles and checklists vary considerably. For example, the CCC-2 may be administered by a caregiver to children between the ages of 4 and 16 years, while the Pragmatics Profile can be administered to school-age children up to 10 years of age by a range of professionals (e.g. speech and language therapists, clinical and educational psychologists). There are also commercially available tests of pragmatics. For example, the Test of Pragmatic Language-2 (Phelps-Terasaki and Phelps-Gunn, 2007) is a standardised, norm-referenced test of pragmatic language which is administered by speech–language pathologists to children aged 6 years to 18 years 11 months.

There are also commercially available instruments for the assessment of discourse skills in children. One such instrument is the Strong Narrative Assessment Procedure (SNAP; Strong, 1998). The SNAP is designed for use with children between 7 and 12 years of age. Four wordless picture books of similar narrative and syntactic complexity are used to elicit stories from children. After listening to a narration provided on an audio cassette, subjects are encouraged to retell the story and answer comprehension questions. Measures such as C-units (communication units) are then used to analyse the length of narratives (number of C-units) as well as their syntactic complexity (average number of words and clauses per C-unit). Outside of published assessments, clinicians often use a range of informal techniques to assess the pragmatic and discourse skills of children. These include clinical observation of communicative behaviour during play and other activities, and video- and audio-recordings (the latter transcribed) of children's verbal and non-verbal communication skills in conversational exchanges and other forms of discourse (e.g. relating personal narratives). These analyses may reflect a certain analytical approach (e.g. conversation analysis) or theoretical perspective (e.g. systemic functional linguistics). Alternatively, they may be conducted in the absence of a specific approach, framework or methodology.

The treatment of pragmatic and discourse disorders draws upon an equally eclectic range of approaches and techniques. Some approaches directly teach conversation skills to children. This may include instruction in the use of turn-taking in conversation or how to achieve the opening and closing stages of a conversation. These skills may be rehearsed in role-play situations with therapists and peers. Video-recordings of these exercises can provide useful feedback to children, and can help them develop a better metalinguistic awareness of their language and communication skills. There is increasing recognition that pragmatics is a key competence in social communication. Many pragmatic language interventions are now targeting social communication skills as a more ecologically valid way of treating pragmatics. In a social communication intervention undertaken by Adams (2005), therapy targeted 'formal aspects of pragmatics' such as topic management, speech acts and linguistic cohesion; see chapter 7 in Cummings (2014a) for further discussion of social communication. An ability to attribute mental states to others (theory of mind) is a key cognitive skill in utterance interpretation. Pragmatic interventions are increasingly including training of ToM skills as a means of securing gains in pragmatics. Pragmatic assessment and treatment approaches are examined further in chapter 6 of Cummings (2009).

Section A: Short-answer questions

2.1 Pragmatic language impairment

(1) Which of the following statements are *false* of children who are diagnosed with pragmatic language impairment (PLI)?
   (a) Children with PLI have pragmatic impairments in the presence of an intellectual disability.
   (b) Children with PLI have deficits in other domains (e.g. motor development) as well as language.
   (c) Children with PLI have a non-verbal IQ in the normal range.
   (d) Children with PLI display deficits of imagination.
   (e) Children with PLI have a clear organic basis to their disorder.

(2) *True* or *False*: The expressive language of children with PLI contains many errors of morphosyntax.

(3) *True* or *False*: Receptive and expressive aspects of pragmatics are disrupted in children with PLI.

(4) Fill in the blank spaces in the following paragraphs using the words in the box below.

The diagnostic label 'pragmatic language impairment' was first introduced into the clinical literature on _____ language disorder by Dorothy Bishop as a successor to the earlier terms of 'semantic–pragmatic syndrome' and 'semantic–pragmatic disorder'. These earlier labels were employed by Rapin and Allen (1983) and Bishop and Rosenbloom (1987), respectively, to capture a group of children that had previously evaded clinical description. As Rapin and Allen characterised these children, they spoke aloud to no one in particular, displayed inadequate _____ skills, exhibited poor maintenance of _____ and verbosity, and produced _____ responses to questions. They also displayed comprehension deficits for connected speech, made _____ word choices and had _____ deficits. However, unlike most children with developmental language disorder, these children's deficits in semantics and pragmatics occurred in the presence of unimpaired _____ and syntax. Rapin and Allen applied their new label to children with known _____ aetiologies (primarily hydrocephalus), to children with no brain damage and to children with and without _____.

When Bishop and Rosenbloom introduced the term 'semantic–pragmatic disorder' (SPD) some four years later, it was intended to apply to a group of specific developmental language disorders of _____ origin. Children with SPD displayed aberrant language skills in the presence of normal _____ and _____ intelligence. There was no sign of physical, genetic or _____ abnormality and the family home was conducive to normal language acquisition. Today, Bishop takes the view that SPD does not form a distinct syndrome. Rather, it is possible to find pragmatic difficulties in children with _____ problems and in fluent children who have good structural language skills. Also, pragmatic difficulties do not co-occur with _____ problems, as the term 'semantic–pragmatic disorder' suggests, but can also be found in children who have no word-finding or _____ problems. Pragmatic difficulties, Bishop argued, are more accurately a 'variable correlate' of specific language impairment. To capture this pattern of pragmatic impairments, Bishop proposed the label 'pragmatic language impairment' as a more satisfactory successor to 'semantic–pragmatic disorder'.

structural language	lexical	psychogenic	non-verbal	phonology
conversational	word-finding	intelligence	irrelevant	topic
acquired	hearing	intellectual disability	genetic	vocabulary
developmental	literacy	psychiatric	semantic	dyslexia
organic	verbal	atypical	delayed	unknown	lexicon

(5) Which of the following is a pragmatic deficit of children with pragmatic language impairment?
  (a) Children with PLI have marked deficits in executive functions such as attention.
  (b) Children with PLI display verb errors such as 'He fall off his bike' and 'She climbing the tree.'
  (c) Children with PLI misinterpret indirect speech acts such as 'Can you open the window?'
  (d) Children with PLI exhibit frequent word-finding problems.
  (e) Children with PLI display phonological processes such as fronting and stopping.

(6) In which of the following scenarios would a diagnosis of pragmatic language impairment be appropriate?

    (a) Jack is 5 years old. He has been diagnosed as having autism spectrum disorder and intellectual disability. His acquisition of language is delayed and he has use of a limited repertoire of speech acts.

    (b) Sally is 9 years old. She suffered a traumatic brain injury following a fall in the playground at school. Her academic performance is compromised by an inability to comprehend and construct short stories.

    (c) Penny is a shy 7-year-old girl. She has had bilateral, sensorineural hearing loss following meningitis contracted at 6 months of age. Her expressive language is markedly delayed and she struggles with turn-taking in conversation.

    (d) Nigel is 15 years old and has attention deficit hyperactivity disorder. He frequently interrupts during conversation, fails to listen to instructions in class and produces confusing personal narratives.

    (e) Melanie is a sociable 10-year-old who has a range of interests including baking cakes and playing computer games. Her speech is clearly articulated and her production of sentences is intact. She misinterprets non-literal utterances and does not grasp the verbal humour of her peers.

(7) *True or False*: The child who is diagnosed with pragmatic language impairment also has impairments of socialisation and imagination.

(8) *True or False*: A social communication intervention is appropriate for children with pragmatic language impairment.

(9) Which of the following statements are *true* of the assessment of children with PLI?

    (a) Assessment should prioritise the use of pragmatic checklists over informal techniques.

    (b) Assessment should examine the structural language skills of a child with suspected PLI.

    (c) Assessment must be informed by a detailed case history that considers the child's hearing status and intellectual level.

    (d) Assessment should only consider verbal communicative skills.

    (e) Assessment should seek to exclude a psychiatric condition as the cause of the child's language disorder.

(10) Which of the following statements are *true* of the treatment of children with PLI?

    (a) Treatment should remediate verbal and non-verbal communicative skills.

    (b) Treatment should include the use of extensive articulatory drills.

    (c) Treatment should include the use of sentence-level production tasks.

    (d) Treatment should remediate receptive and expressive pragmatic deficits.

    (e) Treatment should address cognitive deficits if they exist.

2.2   Intellectual disability

(1) Which of the following is *not* a cause of intellectual disability in children and adults?

    (a) genetic syndromes

    (b) prenatal alcohol exposure

    (c) birth anoxia

(d) cerebral palsy

(e) maternal rubella

(2) Which of the following genetic syndromes is the most common inherited form of intellectual disability?

(a) Williams syndrome

(b) Down's syndrome

(c) cri du chat syndrome

(d) fragile X syndrome

(e) Prader–Willi syndrome

(3) *True* or *False*: Intellectual disability causes greater impairment of structural language skills over pragmatic language skills.

(4) *True* or *False*: Language skills are always commensurate with non-verbal cognitive performance in children with intellectual disability.

(5) *True* or *False*: Pragmatic language skills are largely intact in children and adults with Williams syndrome.

(6) Fill in the blank spaces in the following paragraphs using the words in the box below. Pragmatic language skills have been extensively investigated in children and adults with intellectual disability. Some of these skills have been characterised as follows. Conversational _____ is an area of relative strength, although it is uncertain if individuals with intellectual disability can deal with _____ variations in turn-taking rules. Individuals with intellectual disability have particular difficulty formulating their utterances in such a way as to make clear their intended _____. The expression and understanding of _____ such as questions and requests are also delayed. When expressing speech acts, individuals with intellectual disability have difficulty with linguistic _____. For example, they may use a direct, _____ form such as 'Close the door!' over an _____, polite form such as 'Can you close the door?' Individuals with intellectual disability are also delayed in learning how to signal when an utterance has not been _____ and in learning how to respond to these signals in others. Although the quality of their contributions to a _____ may be problematic, they are able to produce utterances that are on topic.

Aside from these general features, investigators have attempted to characterise the pragmatic language skills of children and adults with specific _____ syndromes. Laws and Bishop (2004) examined pragmatic skills and _____ relationships in individuals with Williams syndrome, Down's syndrome, specific language impairment and in typically developing children. The Children's Communication Checklist was administered to these subjects by parents, _____ or speech and language therapists. Only children and adults with Williams syndrome achieved a pragmatic composite score which was below the 132 cut-off indicative of impairment. On all five subscales of the composite – inappropriate initiation, coherence, stereotyped conversation, use of _____ and rapport – individuals with Williams syndrome obtained significantly lower scores than controls. In two of these subscales – inappropriate initiation and stereotyped conversation – individuals with Williams syndrome achieved a significantly poorer score than subjects with Down's syndrome and SLI. Even though all three clinical groups produced less _____ narratives and conversations than normal controls, it was only in the subjects with Down's syndrome and SLI that depressed performance was related to poor _____ skills.

genetic	presupposition	syntactic	deixis	direct
phonological	speech acts	turn-taking	theory of mind	
referents	implicature	politeness	topic	intention
social	context	relevant	understood	intelligible
contextual	indirect	teachers	semantic	coherent	impolite

(7) For each of the following scenarios, indicate what aspect of pragmatics the child with intellectual disability succeeds in performing. Describe how verbal and non-verbal communication skills contribute to the performance of each pragmatic aspect of language.

   (a) Alice is a 10-year-old girl with Down's syndrome. Her expressive language consists largely of two-word utterances. She makes extensive use of gesture alongside utterances such as 'Daddy car' when she wants to be taken for a drive.

   (b) Michael was born prematurely with foetal alcohol syndrome. He uses 'empty', stereotyped utterances regularly in conversation as a means of discharging his conversational turn.

   (c) Patrick is 8 years old. He has intellectual disability as a result of meningitis contracted at 3 months of age. His comprehension of language is impaired. When asked by his teacher 'Can you close the door?', he continued to sit at his desk until the teacher repeated her utterance while simultaneously pointing at the door.

   (d) Rosie is a 5-year-old girl with Prader–Willi syndrome. She has expressive language delay and reduced speech intelligibility. She signals a desire to talk about her doll Becky to her school teacher by repetition of the doll's name and putting Becky in her teacher's hand.

   (e) John is 10 years old. He has autism spectrum disorder and intellectual disability. He makes extensive use of an utterance he heard in a TV advertisement. When his mother asks him if he wants juice for lunch, he replies 'The price must be right.'

(8) Which of the following statements is *true* of pragmatic and discourse disorders in intellectual disability?

   (a) Pragmatic and discourse impairments in intellectual disability are often over-looked during clinical assessment.

   (b) There is no evidence of a specific role for ToM impairments in the pragmatic and discourse deficits of clients with intellectual disability.

   (c) Pragmatic and discourse disorders do not require direct remediation but improve with gains in structural language skills.

   (d) There is evidence of a role for executive function deficits in pragmatic and discourse disorders in clients with intellectual disability.

   (e) The non-verbal child with intellectual disability can perform a number of communicative functions through the use of gesture, facial expressions and body movements.

(9) Each of the following syndromes has intellectual disability as part of their phenotype. Which is caused by prenatal exposure to a teratogen?

   (a) cri du chat syndrome

   (b) fragile X syndrome

   (c) foetal alcohol syndrome

     (d) Angelman's syndrome

     (e) Wolf–Hirschhorn syndrome

(10) *True* or *False*: Intellectual impairment can occur in children who undergo cranial irradiation for the treatment of cerebral neoplasms.

2.3   Autism spectrum disorder

(1) Which of the following is *not* part of the behavioural phenotype of autism spectrum disorder (ASD)?

     (a) restricted interests or activities

     (b) social communication deficits

     (c) social interaction impairments

     (d) repetitive patterns of behaviour

     (e) motor coordination problems

(2) Which of the following is a communication feature of autism spectrum disorder?

     (a) echolalia

     (b) pronoun reversal

     (c) phonemic paraphasia

     (d) glossomania

     (e) theory of mind deficits

(3) Which of the following is a feature of pragmatics and discourse in autism spectrum disorder?

     (a) impaired interpretation of non-literal language

     (b) production of incoherent narratives

     (c) word-finding difficulty

     (d) impaired topic management

     (e) impaired knowledge of semantic fields

(4) *True* or *False*: Theory of mind deficits are believed to play a role in some pragmatic and discourse disorders in autism spectrum disorder.

(5) *True* or *False*: Perspective-taking is an area of relative strength in autism spectrum disorder.

(6) Fill in the blank spaces in these paragraphs using the words in the box below.

Theory of mind (ToM) describes the ability to attribute mental states both to one's own mind and to the minds of others. These mental states include a range of phenomena such as knowledge, beliefs, _____, pretence and _____. One mental state in particular – _____ – has special relevance for pragmatic interpretation. This is because the interpretation of any utterance has really only been achieved when a hearer recovers the particular communicative intention that motivated the utterance in question. For example, the speaker who observes his son's doodles on a sheet of paper and utters 'What a masterpiece!' is clearly intending to be _____. The hearer who treats this utterance as a genuine evaluation of the merits of the drawing is clearly not able to determine the communicative intention – the intention to be ironic – that prompted this utterance. This is exactly the situation that obtains for many children and adults with autism spectrum disorder. Investigators have been able to establish that children with ASD are on average 10 years of age before they can pass _____ tests, a standard test of theory of mind. Most _____ children pass these tests for the first time between 3 and 4 years of age.

A ToM impairment has significant implications for pragmatics and discourse in ASD. In order to recover the _____ of an utterance, establish the illocutionary force of a speech act, or represent knowledge that is shared with one's interlocutors within the _____ of an utterance, one must exercise a ToM capacity. Unsurprisingly, these pragmatic language skills are _____ in children and adults with ASD. But a ToM impairment causes other pragmatic and discourse problems beyond these obvious ones. In order to successfully relate the events in a story to a hearer, a narrator must make an accurate assessment of the listener's _____ state and tailor his or her utterances accordingly. Certain information may be left _____ in the narrative on the assumption that the hearer can use his or her knowledge to fill it in. Other information, which is particularly important to a story and is new to the hearer, may need to be _____ in a developing narrative. A narrator must also be able to establish the knowledge state of his or her hearer in order to make good use of reference in narrative discourse. A hearer who lacks a _____ for *she* in the utterance 'She bought a new dress' will not be able to integrate the information in this utterance within his or her _____ of a story.

normally developing	backgrounded	implicit	referent
false belief	intact	sarcastic	explicit	deixis
ignorance	impliciture	mental representation	emotions
disrupted	communicative intentions	anaphoric reference	
presuppositions	foregrounded	implicature	knowledge

(7) For each of the following scenarios, indicate if the child or adult with autism spectrum disorder has a receptive or an expressive pragmatic disorder.
   (a) Billy is 7 years old and was diagnosed with ASD by the school psychologist. He frequently misunderstands the teacher in class especially when she uses utterances such as 'Can you put the paints away?'
   (b) Sally is a teenager who has Asperger's syndrome. She frequently fails to grasp the verbal humour used by her peers, and is often upset by the playful teasing of her classmates.
   (c) Mark has high-functioning autism. He is an administrator in a busy office. He tends to dominate office conversations with topics that are of little interest to his fellow workers.
   (d) Jack is 30 years old. He has ASD and lives in supported accommodation. During meetings with his support worker, he often contributes irrelevant utterances in response to questions.
   (e) Rosemary is 45 years old and works in a local shop. Despite having ASD, she has a good level of functioning. However, she sometimes misunderstands what customers are saying to her, especially when it involves non-literal or figurative language.

(8) *True or False*: Children and adults with autism spectrum disorder typically display intact use and understanding of gesture.

(9) *True or False*: Augmentative and alternative communication is an appropriate intervention for the non-verbal child or adult with ASD.

(10) Which of the following communicative behaviours in autism spectrum disorder can be explained by the presence of ToM impairment?
(a) use of echolalia
(b) use of verbal perseveration
(c) use of neologisms
(d) impaired understanding of complex syntax
(e) impaired understanding of indirect speech acts

2.4 Childhood traumatic brain injury

(1) Which of the following is *not* a cerebral pathology associated with traumatic brain injury in childhood?
(a) diffuse microvascular damage
(b) contusion
(c) deposits of amyloid plaques
(d) diffuse axonal injury
(e) haematoma formation

(2) Which of the following is associated with childhood traumatic brain injury?
(a) dysarthria
(b) dysphagia
(c) executive function deficits
(d) psychosis
(e) personality change

(3) Which of the following is among the neuropsychological sequelae of traumatic brain injury in children?
(a) reduced processing speed
(b) hemiplegia
(c) impaired working memory
(d) ataxia
(e) impaired visuospatial function

(4) Fill in the blank spaces in the following paragraph using the words in the box below. While significant _____ impairments are often found in paediatric clients with TBI, by far the most pronounced deficits occur in pragmatic and discourse skills. In terms of pragmatic deficits, children with TBI have been found to have difficulty understanding _____ language such as _____ and irony and problems comprehending inferences. Inferential comprehension problems are greatest when demands on _____ are high. Children who sustain a TBI can have difficulty understanding the mental states and _____ that are the basis of pragmatic processes such as the appreciation of _____. Studies of narrative discourse have revealed high-level difficulties with the _____ organisation, event sequencing and informational content of narratives produced by children with TBI. Many of these narrative discourse problems are related to _____ deficits in these children. For example, the ability to summarise information presented in narratives has been found to be related to working memory and _____ skills in children with TBI. The same discourse problems which are evident in the spoken narratives of children with TBI have also been found to occur in other forms of discourse (e.g. _____ discourse) and in _____ discourse.

theory of mind	intentions	literal	structural language
working memory	set shifting	written	verbal fluency
executive function	non-literal	metaphor	inference
thematic	problem solving	topic irony	expository

(5) *True* or *False*: Pragmatic and discourse problems in children with TBI are secondary to structural language deficits.

(6) *True* or *False*: Brain damage in childhood traumatic brain injury is multi-focal in nature.

(7) Which of the following is a feature of discourse production in childhood TBI?
(a) echolalia
(b) glossomania
(c) reduced content and information
(d) impaired cohesion
(e) flight of ideas

(8) Which of the following skills would *not* be tested as part of a pragmatic language assessment of children with TBI?
(a) set-shifting abilities
(b) comprehension of embedded clauses
(c) recognition of maxim violations
(d) picture-naming skills
(e) use and understanding of speech acts

(9) *True* or *False*: Pragmatic and discourse disorders in childhood TBI always improve with gains in structural language skills.

(10) *True* or *False*: An alternative communication system may be instituted when a child is mute in the period following a TBI.

2.5   Epileptic syndromes

(1) Which of the following is *not* associated with Landau–Kleffner syndrome?
(a) auditory agnosia
(b) intact receptive language
(c) language regression
(d) impaired expressive language
(e) epileptiform discharges during electroencephalography (EEG)

(2) Which of the following is *not* true of language and discourse in temporal lobe epilepsy (TLE)?
(a) There is impaired confrontation naming in left TLE.
(b) There is evidence of lexical retrieval deficits in right TLE.
(c) Speakers with left TLE produce increasingly verbose narratives with repetition.
(d) Speakers with TLE do not differ from neurologically normal controls in terms of lexical and syntactic aspects of discourse production.
(e) Discourse impairments in TLE are unrelated to attention and memory.

(3) Fill in the blank spaces in the following paragraph using the words in the box below.

Most research on the effects of epilepsy on language has employed tests and measurements from _____, with the result that little attention has been given to the quality of discourse. From the small number of studies which have examined discourse _____ in children with epilepsy, clear discourse anomalies have emerged. There is decreased use of the _____ which link sentences and utterances together and enable a hearer to follow the events in a story or other form of discourse. For example, there is evidence that children with epilepsy use fewer coordinating and subordinating _____ such as *and* and *because* to tie clauses and sentences together. There is also evidence of _____ disturbances during discourse production. Children with epilepsy tend to use fewer _____, demonstratives and comparatives to refer to people or objects in _____ spoken discourse. In the absence of these referential links between different parts of discourse, hearers typically struggle to follow a speaker's _____. Investigators have also examined the relationship between discourse anomalies and a number of variables. They have found, for example, that the severity of discourse impairment is related to poorer _____ control, earlier age at epilepsy _____ and global cognitive dysfunction, but is not related to the laterality of _____ abnormalities.

referential	lexical verbs	narrative	comprehension
cohesive devices	cataphoric reference		preceding
aphasiology	lexical reiteration	coherence	seizure
production	onset	conjunctions	relative clauses
anaphoric reference	pronouns	EEG	auditory agnosia

(4) *True* or *False*: Discourse dysfunction in temporal lobe epilepsy is not related to language measures.

(5) *True* or *False*: Episodic memory is intact in children with temporal lobe epilepsy.

(6) *True* or *False*: Executive deficits in planning, self-control and problem solving have been reported in children with frontal lobe epilepsy.

(7) Fill in the blank spaces in the following paragraph using the words in the box below. Complex partial seizures (CPS) are frequent in children with seizures. A CPS can arise from a focus in any region of _____ although the temporal and frontal lobes are most common. This type of seizure results in impairment of _____. Primary generalised epilepsy (PGE) with absence is an epilepsy syndrome of idiopathic or _____ cause. Absence seizures are one of three types of seizure that can occur in PGE. These seizures, which last just a few seconds, involve brief staring spells with arrest of activity, often with eye fluttering. CPS and PGE have their _____ in middle childhood. This is a stage in children's neurodevelopment when the frontal lobes are undergoing continued _____ with an increase in white matter and volume. Certain communication behaviours depend on _____ skills which are mediated by the brain's frontal lobes. One such behaviour is the use of self-initiated _____ during conversation. To the extent that the onset of seizure activity can compromise frontal lobe cognitive skills, one may reasonably expect the development of repair skills in affected children to be _____. This appears to be the case. Investigators have found evidence that children with CPS, particularly those with a temporal lobe focus, use significantly more revision of _____ and syntax than normal children. However, children with CPS and PGE who have _____ lobe involvement have been found to use significantly fewer fillers during repair compared to normal subjects.

intact	myelination	parietal	consciousness	onset
degeneration	reference	cognitive	brain stem	
unknown	repair	cortex	conversational breakdown	
frontal	metalinguistic	impaired	Landau–Kleffner syndrome	

(8) Studies of pragmatic language skills in children with epilepsy have produced inconsistent results. This has been explained in terms of a number of methodological limitations of these studies. Which of the following statements describes a limitation of these studies?
   (a) Studies have investigated children with epilepsy who are comorbid for autism.
   (b) Studies have only investigated receptive pragmatic language skills.
   (c) Studies have failed to control for the effects of intellectual functioning on pragmatic language skills.
   (d) Studies have only investigated expressive pragmatic language skills.
   (e) Studies have adopted research tools which do not measure pragmatic language skills.

(9) Which of the following statements is *true* of the prognosis of pragmatic and discourse skills in children with epilepsy?
   (a) These skills improve as soon as seizure activity has been brought under control through the use of medication.
   (b) These skills remain disproportionately impaired relative to structural language skills.
   (c) There is no empirical evidence relating to the long-term course of these skills in children with epilepsy.
   (d) These skills improve following neurosurgical interventions such as multiple subpial transection.
   (e) These skills display the best recovery in children with Rolandic epilepsy.

(10) *True* or *False*: Pragmatics is the first language subsystem to deteriorate in children with Landau–Kleffner syndrome.

2.6 Childhood cancer

(1) Which of the following is *not* a brain tumour?
   (a) malignant glioma
   (b) acoustic neuroma
   (c) basal cell carcinoma
   (d) astrocytoma
   (e) medulloblastoma

(2) Which of the following is a sequela of brain tumour in children and adolescents?
   (a) dysarthria
   (b) mutism
   (c) reduced intellectual functioning
   (d) psychosis
   (e) aphasia

(3) Fill in the blank spaces in the following paragraphs using the words in the box below.

The five-year survival rates of many childhood cancers such as _____ and posterior fossa tumours have increased in recent years. This has led to an increase in the number of children who require rehabilitation services such as _____ for the treatment of the adverse effects of medical interventions. CNS-directed chemotherapy and _____ for childhood acute lymphoblastic leukaemia or lymphoma have various neurotoxic effects. For example, survivors of cranial radiotherapy show decreased _____ integrity. Younger age at cranial irradiation and higher dose are associated with _____ outcome of white matter integrity. These _____ effects of treatment have adverse implications for children's cognitive functioning. In this way, children with primary brain tumours have been found to have significantly reduced performance compared to controls in tests of performance IQ, _____ speed, verbal and visual _____ and selective attention. Variables such as tumour site, high tumour grade, hydrocephalus, radiotherapy and _____ are associated with poorer _____ functioning.

There is a high incidence of speech, language and _____ problems in children with brain tumours. Some of these problems are present prior to surgery while others arise as a result of medical interventions. _____ and dysphagia are common sequelae of surgery in children with posterior fossa tumours. A range of language deficits have been reported in children following _____ tumour resection. These deficits include agrammatism, _____, impaired verbal _____ and comprehension problems. There has been little research into the pragmatic and discourse skills of children with brain tumours. However, studies which have been conducted indicate that there is significant disruption of these skills in the context of intact _____. Reported pragmatic problems include difficulty resolving _____ and impaired understanding of inferential, _____ and figurative language. It may be reasonably predicted that the significant, long-term _____ deficits of children with brain tumours may contribute to the pragmatic difficulties of this population. Certainly, such a link should be explored in future research into the pragmatic and discourse skills of these children.

neurotoxic	better	grey matter	cognitive	fluency
speech–language pathology		semantic	structural language	
planning	white matter	acute lymphoblastic leukaemia		anomia
medulla	dysarthria	cranial radiotherapy		radionecrosis
posterior fossa	ambiguity	sensation	reasoning	worse
metaphoric	chemotherapy	hearing	sarcastic	neurocognitive
processing	communicative intention	memory		organisation

(4) *True or False*: Pragmatic and discourse impairments in children with brain tumours are secondary to structural language deficits.

(5) *True or False*: Pragmatic and discourse deficits in children with posterior fossa tumours resolve following surgical intervention.

(6) *True or False*: The neurocognitive status of a child following surgery for a brain tumour should be considered within a clinical assessment of pragmatic language skills.

(7) For each of the following scenarios, indicate if the child with a brain tumour or other cancer exhibits a receptive or expressive pragmatic or discourse disorder.

    (a) Marcus is 10 years old. When he was 8, he received cranial radiation therapy for a medulloblastoma. His teacher reports a number of academic difficulties. For example, when asked to write on topics like his best summer holiday in class, he produces repetitive, uninformative accounts which omit much of relevance.

    (b) Penelope is 13 years old. She is receiving an assessment of her language skills at the neurosurgical unit where she underwent surgery, radiotherapy and chemotherapy six months earlier for a brainstem glioma. The speech–language pathologist observes that Penelope has particular difficulty with a task in which she must point to pictures that correspond to utterances such as 'Mary jumped the gun' and 'Fred has a chip on his shoulder.'

    (c) Timothy is 9 years old. He is still in recovery from neurosurgery conducted ten months earlier to remove an ependymoma from the left cerebellar hemisphere. A clinical assessment of Timothy's language skills confirmed the impression that he is a verbose but somewhat uninformative speaker. Specifically, during storytelling he produced a large number of words and a sub-average number of information units.

    (d) Sally is 15 years old. Six months ago she completed radiotherapy and chemotherapy for the treatment of a juvenile pilocytic astrocytoma of the right cerebellar hemisphere. A neuropsychological assessment revealed reduced processing speed and a number of other cognitive difficulties. Sally's mother reports that she frequently does not grasp humour and joking during family meals and can make impolite remarks to others.

    (e) Jonathan is 8 years old. Twelve months ago, he received CNS-directed chemotherapy and cranial radiotherapy for the treatment of acute lymphoblastic leukaemia. Prior to his treatment, Jonathan enjoyed listening to bedtime stories which were read to him by his father. His father reports that since receiving treatment, he cannot follow the plot in these stories. Jonathan also frequently asks questions which indicate that he has not understood the causal and temporal relations between events.

(8) *True* or *False*: Language intervention in children with brain tumours does not target pragmatic and discourse skills directly but does so indirectly through the remediation of structural language.

(9) Pragmatic language skills have a much longer developmental course than structural language skills. The development of certain aspects of pragmatics can extend throughout the adolescent years and even into adulthood. In view of this, which of the following statements best characterises the pragmatic language impairment of a 14-year-old girl with a brain tumour?

    (a) This girl has a developmental pragmatic disorder.
    (b) This girl has an acquired pragmatic disorder.
    (c) This girl's pragmatic disorder has developmental and acquired components.
    (d) This girl's pragmatic disorder has cognitive components.
    (e) This girl's pragmatic disorder has structural language components.

(10) *True* or *False*: Pragmatic and discourse deficits in children with posterior fossa tumours resolve following cranial radiotherapy.

Section B: Data analysis exercises

2.7   Pragmatic language impairment 1

Background

The following data are taken from a study of a 10-year-old boy by McTear (1985). This child had such marked conversation and interaction difficulties that he attended a special language unit (i.e. he was not in mainstream education). Some data are from spontaneous conversational exchanges between the boy and the investigator of the study. Other data arose in response to specific discourse tasks such as telling a story based on a sequence of pictures. Examine each data set and then answer the following questions.

Key

A	adult
C	child
(1.0)	timed pause (in seconds)
=	no perceptible gap between turns
(.)	micropause

Data set 1

A: can you tell me about it ('it' refers to a TV programme)
C: yes
    (1.0)
A: well tell me about it
    what's it like?
C: the man always fights the bad men . . .

Data set 2

The adult is introducing one of the communication tasks.

A: now do you want to see if you can play some games with me?
C: yes
A: they're very easy games um (1.0)
C: they are indeed
A: well we'll see

Data set 3

A: are they friends of yours?
C: they are friends of mine

Data set 4

C: it's got twenty windows in it
A: um
C: it has rooms (.) it has (.) it has a lift

A: um
C: in it
   (2.0)
   has a lift in it
   (1.5)
   lift in it
A: how long did you stay there for?

Data set 5

The boy is concluding a story about all the things that he does during a day.

C: then I go to bed at nine and sleep
   is that the end of the story?
A: yes I think it is
   yes
   well, I mean, I don't know
   is that everything you do in the day?
C: yes

Data set 6

A: do you play with P?
C: yes I do =
A: = umhmm =
C: = play with him
A: after school?
C: yes
A: umhmm
C: I play with him after school

Data set 7

The child is talking about his favourite television programmes.

A: what do you watch now?
C: I watch (.) I watch 'The Two Ronnies' now
A: ah yes
C: the Two Ronnies
A: do you like them?
C: yes
   Mummy doesn't let me watch them at seven-fifteen, because she watches 'Coronation Street' at
   half seven
A: so can you watch them then?
C: no, I can't watch them
A: oh what a pity
C: she watches 'Coronation Street' all the time

Data set 8

The boy is asked to explain the events in a picture. The picture shows a young boy standing outside the door of his house with the contents of his pockets emptied onto the ground.

A: this is a picture about a little boy, see?
C: yes
A: and you see he's standing outside the house
C: he's dropped something
A: yes
C: he's dropped something
A: well, what, he's dropped it all out of his pockets, hasn't he?
C: yes
A: do you know why?
C: yes
   outside on the step is a pencil
A: mm
C: and his . . . his money fell out of his pocket
A: why did he drop it do you think?
C: because he didn't know
A: mm
C: he didn't know
A: do you think he's maybe looking for something?
C: yes, I think he is looking for something, I think he is looking for money

Data set 9

The boy is talking to a speech therapist about a forthcoming sports day at his school.

A: which race would you like to be in?
C: I like to be in X [name of town several miles from school] at the Sports Day
A: in X?
C: yes
A: what do you mean?
C: I mean something
A: is there a Sports Day in X?
C: there is not, there is a Sports Day in Y [name of child's school]
A: then what's X got to do with it?
C: nothing
A: then why did you mention it?
C: indeed I did mention it
A: why did you mention it?
C: I don't know

Data set 10

The boy is describing a series of pictures which shows a child (a boy) getting up in the morning, getting dressed, eating breakfast, and so on.

C: the boy is getting out of the bed and his mummy is opening the curtains
A: mm
C: now she is drying herself and she's got the soap
A: ah, now you said 'she', but it's a boy, isn't it?
C: yes
A: ah ha, so what do we say here?
   not she is drying herself but . . .
C: that's a boy

A: yes, but you said 'she'
C: here's a boy drying himself and he has soap in his hand

Question 1 This child displays particular difficulties in the use of ellipsis. Your task is to (a) give one example of where the child's failure to use ellipsis leads to a repetitive, redundant response and (b) give one instance of where the child fails to use ellipsis even when he is prompted to do so by an interjection from the adult.

Question 2 This child displays a number of receptive pragmatic difficulties. You should (a) indicate one instance where the child fails to comprehend an indirect speech act and (b) give one example where he fails to derive an inference which provides a causal explanation of events.

Question 3 This child also displays a number of expressive pragmatic difficulties. Among these difficulties are (a) the contribution of turns which convey no new information and (b) the provision of false, misleading or contradictory information. Give one example of each of these difficulties.

Question 4 Other pragmatic impairments evident in this child include an inappropriate use of presupposition. This may be related to a wider difficulty on the part of this child in recognising when his state of knowledge differs from that of the adult. You should (a) give one example of the inappropriate use of presupposition in the data and (b) indicate one instance where the child appears unable to distinguish the adult's knowledge state from his own.

Question 5 The child also displays (a) referential anomalies in the use of pronouns and (b) limited metalinguistic awareness in relation to utterance meaning. Give one example of each of these pragmatic impairments.

2.7   Pragmatic language impairment 2

Background

The following data were obtained from two Swedish girls, Lena and Märta, who were studied by Sahlén and Nettelbladt (1993). Both girls attended a language unit for children with severe and specific developmental language disorders in Lund. They were studied longitudinally at 5;6 and 6;6 years and at 8;0 and 9;0 years, respectively. Their language problems were suggestive of semantic–pragmatic disorder.

History

The pre-, peri- and postnatal period was unremarkable for Lena. Although Märta's mother had congenital rubella at the beginning of the fourth gestational month, there was no evidence of congenital infection. Lena had a positive family history for developmental language disorders, with both her older and younger brothers receiving language intervention for severe developmental language disorders. Also, Lena's mother had a hearing impairment of unknown aetiology. Early motor milestones were normal for both girls. At

7;4 years, Märta underwent a neurological examination, a CT scan and an EEG examination, all of which were normal. Both girls had experienced recurrent bouts of otitis media with effusion. With the exception of slightly reduced speech discrimination scores (78–86% for Lena at 5;10 years, and 88–96% for Märta at 6;6 years; > 90% is normal), the results of an audiological examination were otherwise normal. Psychological examination revealed better performance scores than verbal scores for both girls.

Data set 1

Lena (L) is 8 years old in the following extract. She is responding to questions from an examiner (E) on general knowledge.

E: What do you usually see on the ground when it is autumn?
L: Mosquitoes and birds and crows
E: What season comes after autumn?
L: Winter and then spring then autumn and then spring . . . usually many days are passing
E: What is it like in the winter?
L: (pause) You just build a snow man
E: Mm . . . and in the spring?
L: At day nursery when was winter then everybody went out and played and she throw snowballs on the wall and it was red
E: But look, if I tell you that right now there are already some flowers outside and small, small buds on the trees and so on . . .
L: Flowers . . . on the apple trees I think are beautiful to see
E: So what season is it when it is like this outside?
L: (pause) Mm . . .
E: Is it winter then?
L: No . . . spring! This is probably not spring (picks up a pen on the table). What sort of pen is this?

Data set 2

Lena is 5;6 years in the following dialogue with the examiner.

E: And afterwards when the cat was about to climb down the tree, what happened?
L: What happened?
E: Yes, what happened when she was about to climb down the tree?
L: That's the tree!

Data set 3

Lena (5;6 years) is asked to produce the names of clothes in the following exchange.

L: clothes for my pony, pony has a rainbow, pony lives in a house [Lena's toy pony is on the table]
E: What kind of clothes are you wearing now?
L: shirt, braids, black and black [points to her trousers and shoes] and pink [points to a pink ribbon in her hair]

Data set 4

Märta (M) is 5;6 years in this exchange with the examiner.

E: What would you do if you cut your finger?
M: Take it down! [Looks at her hand on the table and takes it down]

Data set 5

This exchange follows a task in which Märta was asked to describe a picture of a fire. In the picture, a woman was screaming for help from a window in the middle of the flames.

E: Why do you need windows in houses?
M: Burns down like this

Data set 6

Märta (9;0 years) is responding to general knowledge questions.

E: Why shouldn't you play in the middle of the street?
M: You shouldn't throw balls – the ball broken.
E: Yes, can you think of any other reason?
M: If you play 'daddy and kid' – can drive into children
E: Why do you need lamps?
M: It is so dark – can you have lamps – bikes. [Interpretation: If it is dark you need a lamp on your bicycle]
E: Why do you have doors on houses?
M: Not thieves in.

Data set 7

Märta (9;0 years) is attempting to repeat sentences produced by the examiner.

E: The dog sees a cat in the street
M: The dog . . . no!
E: [repeats target sentence]
M: The dog sees a the cat in the street
E: Olle saw a blue bird on the stone
M: The dog the bird sat – no!
E: [repeats target sentence]
M: The dog saw a bird that sat on blue stone
E: The sleeping girl woke up when mummy washed the dishes
M: The girl was sleeping when mummy washed the dishes
M: The happy dog was chased by all the children
M: The girl . . . the dog is chasing lots cat . . . cats

Question 1 Data set 1 exemplifies many of the difficulties that are experienced by children with semantic–pragmatic disorder. Give <u>one</u> example of each of the following difficulties:

(a) tangential response to a question
(b) bizarre lexical choice
(c) intrusion of irrelevant utterance
(d) topic perseveration
(e) lack of world knowledge or semantic paraphasias

Question 2 Lena has particular difficulty understanding wh-questions. In data set 2, how does she respond to that difficulty? What aspect of conversational performance do these responses serve to maintain?

Question 3 As part of the disruption of Lena's semantic knowledge, she is unable to give many examples of words belonging to particular semantic categories. Name <u>three</u> features of her responses in data set 3 which would indicate that this is the case.

Question 4 Using data sets 4 to 6 inclusive, give <u>one</u> example of each of the following pragmatic deficits: (a) an egocentric response, (b) a tangential response and (c) topic perseveration.

Question 5 Märta has considerable difficulty with the repetition of sentences in data set 7. Which of the following verbal behaviours is particularly evident in this set? Give <u>two</u> examples of this behaviour:

(a) echolalia
(b) circumlocution
(c) verbal perseveration
(d) neologisms
(e) semantic paraphasia

2.7 Pragmatic language impairment 3

Background

Sarah was studied by Leinonen and Letts (1997) for an eight-month period between 9;8 and 10;3 years of age. Her teacher and speech and language therapist reported a number of behaviours which suggested that Sarah had pragmatic impairment. These behaviours included relatively good expressive language skills in the presence of comprehension problems in conversation. Sarah was also noted to make irrelevant contributions in conversations, to have problems with time and space concepts and to have difficulties with extended discourse including narrative construction. Notwithstanding these difficulties, Sarah was very eager to communicate.

Language assessment

Two pragmatic profiles revealed that Sarah had a number of pragmatic strengths alongside these difficulties. She was able to produce minimal and extended turns in conversation. Sarah was able to use statements to initiate conversations, to make use of cohesive devices (conjunctions, pronouns, ellipsis), and to respond to requests for confirmation and specification. She was also able to make requests for clarification. Sarah was able to read well, although she tended not to read for meaning. Her expressive syntax was also good. However, she exhibited some formulation difficulties, evidenced by pauses, repetitions and false starts followed by self-correction, in certain places (e.g. at the start of an unfamiliar task). Receptive syntax was poor, with Sarah achieving a score on a test of receptive grammar equivalent to age 5;3 years when she was 8;10 years. Narrative construction was also poor. When Sarah was 8;10 years, she received a score on a narrative assessment that had an age equivalent of 4;0 years. Vocabulary comprehension was also an area of weakness. At

10;2 years, Sarah achieved a receptive vocabulary score which was equivalent to 6;11 years. These various language deficits occurred alongside normal non-verbal intelligence.

Tasks

Sarah undertook four tasks in total, two of which are relevant to the data presented below. She was shown two composite pictures which she examined for a period of time. She was then asked a number of questions. Some questions were descriptive in nature and could be answered on the basis of information explicitly represented in the pictures. Other questions were inferential and could only be answered by Sarah combining information in the pictures with her world knowledge. In the first picture, *The Park*, two men are shown sitting on a park bench in overalls. One of the men is eating sandwiches while the other one reads a newspaper. A hole has been dug in the ground. Next to it are garden tools such as a fork and a spade. There are three trees in the picture. Two of these trees have been planted and a third one remains to be planted. In the second picture, *The Flood*, household items, a cow, trees and people are seen to be swept away by a flooded river. People are pictured standing on the roofs of their cars and clinging onto pieces of wood. It looks as if they were caught unawares and had little chance to get out of harm's way.

Data set 1

Sarah is responding to questions about *The Park*. In response to the inferential question 'Are the men going to do any more work?', she replies as follows.

Q: Are the men going to do any more work?
A: No.
Q: Why is that?
A: Because they (mumbled syllables) have the rest.
Q: What is the hole for?
A: I think it is to put a treasure in it.
Q: Why do you say that?
A: (no response)

Data set 2

Sarah is responding to questions about *The Flood*. Two expected inferences based on this picture are that the flood must have happened during the day as people have been caught unawares (people are standing on the roofs of their cars, etc.), and that the telephone system cannot be working as telephone lines have fallen down. In response to the inferential question 'Did the flood happen during the night?', Sarah replies as follows.

Q: Did the flood happen during the night?
A: No.
Q: Why is that?
A: Because it's I can see a sunny day.

In response to the inferential question 'Is the telephone system working?', Sarah replies as follows.

Q: Is the telephone system working?
A: Umm No.

Q: Why is that?
A: Because I can see one there. I think it's a basket actually. That's a basket.

Question 1 Which feature(s) of Sarah's profile indicate that her pragmatic difficulties have not arisen as a consequence of (a) autism spectrum disorder and (b) intellectual disability?

Question 2 Which feature(s) of Sarah's profile indicate that her pragmatic difficulties might arise in part as a result of problems in obtaining the logical form of an utterance?

Question 3 When asked if the telephone system is working, Sarah correctly replies that it is not. However, she then produces a response which indicates that she has not drawn a certain inference between the fallen telephone lines in the picture and the lack of a working telephone system. Which of the following labels best characterises that inference?

(a) bridging inference
(b) deductive inference
(c) causal inference
(d) inductive inference
(e) conversational inference

Question 4 When asked to justify her responses to inferential questions, Sarah produces a range of inappropriate replies. One reply in particular suggests that she has drawn a somewhat 'fanciful' inference. Which reply is it?

Question 5 In data set 2, Sarah correctly infers that the flood did not happen during the night. However, her justification of this inference reveals a neglect of the most salient features of the scene which would have warranted this particular inference – the fact that people have been caught unawares going about their *daytime* activities. Which of the following statements best characterises Sarah's inferential difficulty in this case?

(a) Sarah produces an inference which is consistent with depicted events but is not consistent with world knowledge.
(b) Sarah produces an inference which is consistent with world knowledge but is not consistent with depicted events.
(c) Sarah produces an inference which is consistent with depicted events and is consistent with world knowledge.
(d) Sarah produces an inference which is not consistent with depicted events and is not consistent with world knowledge.
(e) Sarah produces an inference which cannot be characterised by any of the above statements.

2.7 Pragmatic language impairment 4

Background

Tony was 3;4 years at the time of his referral to a Regional Child Development Centre. He was studied from the time of referral by Conti-Ramsden and Gunn (1986). Tony is the son of Ghanaian parents who were born in the UK. Although his parents are native speakers of Twi, they are fluent English speakers and have always spoken English to Tony. Tony has also attended an English-speaking playgroup. He has two female siblings, neither of whom has communication difficulties. His general development was normal. Tony's father is an insurance clerk and his mother is a staff nurse.

Language profile

Tony's parents reported that his early communicative development appeared to be normal. However, during his second year he stopped communicating and seemed not to respond to language. Tony's verbal comprehension is very poor. At 4;0 years, he scored below three standard deviations from the mean on a standardised test of verbal comprehension. At 6;11 years, he was still below one standard deviation from the mean. Concepts such as 'before' and 'after' were difficult for Tony, as were words relating to feelings (e.g. happy, sad). Tony's expressive syntax and phonology were relatively intact. One exception was his use of pronoun reversals (e.g. *your* used for *my*) and the use of his proper name to refer to himself. Tense marking and maintenance from one utterance to the next was also difficult for Tony. Tony can read fluently and write well above his age level.

Non-verbal abilities

Although Tony's non-verbal profile was unremarkable, and he consistently scored above average in a test of non-verbal intellectual functioning, it was felt that he had significant non-verbal deficits. The drawing of both verbal and non-verbal inferences was considered to be an area of difficulty. He also appeared to have problems distinguishing between essential and accidental aspects of situations and information, and developing generalised, flexible schemes or scripts which indicate what to do, when and how.

The following conversational exchanges between Tony (TO) and his teacher (TE) were recorded over a three-year period between 3;9 and 6;9 years. Examine each exchange and then answer the questions below.

Data set 1

Tony is 3;9 years of age.

TE: Hello everyone
 Hi Ken (greeting taxi driver who had brought Tony)
TO: Hi Ken

Data set 2

Tony is 4;5 years of age.

TE: Who cut your hair? (Tony has a new hair cut)
TO: Daddy cut your hair
TE: What are they? (points to picture of eggs)
TO: Eggs
TE: How many eggs?
TO: Two eggs.
TE: What does the cow say? (points to next picture)

TO: Cow says moo and all farm animals.
TE: Whose turn is it?
TO: Tony's

Data set 3

Tony is 5;1 years of age. The teacher has brought a fresh bunch of flowers and put them in a vase.

TO: (points to vase) Flowers

Tony is playing with water and a toy frog.

TO: (talking to himself) Wind it up (winds it up). Jump inside (throws it in).

Data set 4

Tony is 5;4 years of age.

TO: Alex has new socks.
TE: What is Alex doing?
TO: Playing with a bus.
TE: Whose is it?
TO: Mine.

Data set 5

Tony is 6;2 years of age. Tony feels sick and wants the teacher to ring home.

TO: Judy talk mummy.
TE: How?
TO: Orange (referring to orange drink that may have made him feel sick)
    Tony is sick
    Can I talk to mummy?
TE: What do I do to talk to mummy?
    What shall I do to talk to mummy?
TO: Because I am sick.

The teacher and Tony are playing with a doll called Carl. The doll has fallen.

TE: Is Carl frightened?
TO: Yes.
TE: Why is he frightened?
TO: He is falling down, he cried, he is sore mouth.
TE: What happened?
TO: Carl is crying.
TE: Why?
TO: Because he is frightened.
TE: Why has he got a sore mouth?
TO: Because you are falling (to doll). Why are you getting on the floor?

Data set 6

Tony is between 6;6 and 6;9 years of age. Specific questions are being asked to illustrate Tony's difficulties working things out.

TE: Why do you have to be quiet when there's a baby in the room?
TO: 'Cos she's crying.
TE: What would happen to a flower if it didn't get any water?
TO: 'Cos it spilt.
TE: What might happen to your teeth if you were always eating lots of sweets?
TO: 'Cos I go to the dentist.

Question 1 Tony can use ellipsis on some occasions, but fails to use it on other occasions. Give one example of the successful and unsuccessful use of ellipsis in the data.

Question 2 There is evidence of echolalia, the use of a proper name for self-reference and pronoun reversal in Tony's verbal output. Give one example of each of these verbal behaviours in the data. In which other clinical condition are echolalia, use of a proper name for self-reference and pronoun reversal linguistic features?

Question 3 At least some of Tony's comprehension problems stem from a difficulty understanding question words like *how* and *what*. Give three examples of where Tony misunderstands utterances which are introduced by these words. What appears to be Tony's default interpretation of these question words?

Question 4 Although Tony's pragmatic language skills are delayed, he is able to perform a number of functions through his use of language. Give one example of each of the following uses of language in the data.

(a) Language is used to perform a labelling function.
(b) Language is used to initiate a conversational exchange.
(c) Language is used to describe actions as they happen.
(d) Language is used to make a request.
(e) Language is used to ask a question.

Question 5 In data set 6, Tony displays problems with the understanding of the concepts of consequence and causation. For each of Tony's responses in this data set, characterise his comprehension difficulty.

2.7 Pragmatic language impairment 5

Background

Narrative production of 20 children with language disorder was examined by Liles (1987). These children were aged between 7;6 and 10;6 years at the time of the study. A group of 20 age- and sex-matched children with no language disorder or other impairment served as control subjects. Children with language disorder were all enrolled in a management programme and met the following criteria for inclusion in the study: an early history of and continuous diagnosis of language disorder; normal vision, hearing, and articulation ability; problems mild enough so that they could produce grammatically adequate sentences and could generate a sufficient number of sentences to produce a usable sample of a narrative; no less than 7 years of age; not primarily identified as learning disabled as indicated by their attendance at classes at their grade level; within normal range of intelligence; and no history or evidence of organic disorders. By fulfilling these criteria, the children in this study warrant a present-day diagnosis of specific language impairment.

Narrative production task

All subjects watched a 45-minute children's film along with an examiner. After the viewing, each subject had to retell the story to two adult listeners. One listener had watched the movie with the child, while the other one had not. Following the verbal narrative recall about the film, the examiner posed two sets of questions to the child. One set examined factual information about the characters and sequential events of the movie. The other set of questions examined relationships between the characters and events, their consequences and resolutions. A short synopsis of the movie follows.

The movie is about two boys, one of whom believes that a comic strip hero named Super Duper is a real life superman. The second boy believes that Super Duper's adventures are confined to comic strips and movies. The boys meet Super Duper at the movie theatre one day where he is promoting a Super Duper movie. After their personal encounter with Super Duper, they view the movie, which depicts Super Duper as a Hero overcoming an evil scientist's efforts to destroy the world. On their way home from the movie, the boys see Super Duper drive off the road; they see him stuck in a ditch as well as become caught in a barbed wire fence. He is unable to 'lift the car up with one hand' as one of the boys expects and instead accepts the boys' help in towing and repairing his damaged car. The boy who believed in Super Duper as more than a comic strip hero loses some of his hero worship and is willing to trade his extensive Super Duper comic book collection for a broken baseball bat. (Liles, 1987: 194)

Three narratives from the study are presented below. Two are from children with language disorder. A narrative from a child with no language disorder is included for comparison. Examine each narrative and then answer the questions that follow.

Data set 1

Child aged 10;2 years with language disorder and good comprehension.

Episode 1

1 It was about the kids who liked Homer.
2 I mean who liked Super Duper man except for one.
3 And he liked reading them from the comic books.
4 And he has a lot of comics.
5 And then he uh, he brought him over to his house.
6 And they read it.
7 But he keeps on saying, 'It's all the same thing.'
8 He's always smashing spaceships, picking them up and all that.

Episode 2

9 So that kid called him up.
10 And he said, 'There's going to be a movie on Super Duper man,
11 Would you like to come and see it?'
12 And he goes, 'Sure, sure thing.'

13 He goes, uh, and they picked him up.
14 And they met him then.
15 They shook hands.
16 Then they went and saw the movie.

Episode 3

17 No . . . and then they saw him coming down the road.
18 And he went off the edge.
19 And they spied on him for a few minutes.

Episode 4

20 And he asked if there was any, uh, station around, a gas station.
21 And they said we got a horse.
22 They said, 'Yeah, we got a horse up there.'
23 'So we'll help you pull him out of the ditch.'

Episode 5

24 And they brought him to his house right where there was a gas station.
25 Then the mother fixed up his cuts.
26 And he went off.
27 And he went home.

Data set 2

Child aged 10;1 years with language disorder and poor comprehension.

Episode 1

1 Well, there was these magazines from somebody.
2 And a kid named Homer and Lou Lou and some other kid like, named Hoe or something, looked at them outside.

Episode 2

3 Then they wondered if the movie was playing of the Super Duper at a theatre where Super Duper was being nice to the kids.
4 And then they watched the movie.

Episode 3

5 Then this Doctor X destroyed a missile.
6 And he was in the street.
7 Then the Super Duper came in the sky flying like a bird.
8 And Doctor X tried to destroy him two times.
9 And he couldn't destroy him.
10 So he landed and punched this wall and used his body to break through it.

11 Then he destroyed Doctor X's machine by a box, rectangle box.
12 Then he got out a secret passageway.

Episode 4

13 Then they went home.
14 Then they saw Super Duper in his fast car.
15 He went in the ditch.
16 And he, but before he ran into the ditch he saw the skunk.
17 He didn't want to run over it and get smelled, that skunk smell.
18 So the kids came down and saw Super Duper, who got caught.
19 He was sitting there by his car.
20 Then he got caught by the barbed wire.

Episode 5

21 And the kids said, 'We'll tow your car down to a garage.'
22 And after that they repaired his fender that got kind of bent.

Incomplete information

23 Then after that he just reached in the box for one drink for one kid and another drink for the other kid.

Data set 3

Child aged 10 years with no language disorder.

Episode 1

 1 Well, from the beginning, there's this person called Homer.
 2 There were three people in the movie.
 3 The main people are Homer, Louie, and Freddie.
 4 And Louie and Freddie were over at Homer's house.
 5 And they were watching a football game.
 6 And they got bored and went downstairs to get something to eat.
 7 And Freddie wanted to read the comics called Super Duper.
 8 So they all read it.
 9 And they got into a conversation about it.
10 But then Louie and Freddie had to go home.

Episode 2

11 After a while, Freddie called up Homer and told him that there was a movie Saturday about Super Duper.
12 And he was gonna be there.
13 So that Saturday they went to the movie.
14 Then they met Super Duper.
15 And they saw the movie.

Episode 3

16 And after, then after they were going home they saw Super Duper coming, coming fast, going fast down the road in his car.
17 And they heard a crash right around the corner.
18 And they thought that Super Duper was hurt.
19 So they went to see what happened.
20 And then they saw his car was in a ditch.
21 And Freddie was all excited because he thought Super Duper was gonna lift the car with one hand.
22 But he got caught in some barbed wire.
23 And they went.
24 And they helped him out.
25 And they were all wondering.
26 They didn't ask him, but they were wondering why he didn't lift it with one hand.

Episode 4

27 So they brought him home.
28 And they fixed his car.

Incomplete information

29 But he left and gave them some comic books.
30 But Freddie traded his for a broken baseball bat.

Question 1 Give <u>one</u> example of each of the following discourse features in the narrative produced by the child with language disorder and good comprehension in data set 1:

(a) use of self-initiated repair of utterance
(b) use of direct reported speech
(c) use of object pronoun with no preceding referent
(d) use of subject pronoun with unclear preceding referent
(e) use of a cohesive conjunction that expresses a temporal relationship between sentences

Question 2 Give <u>one</u> example of each of the following discourse features in the narrative produced by the child with language disorder and poor comprehension in data set 2:

(a) use of vague or non-specific vocabulary
(b) use of utterances in incorrect temporal order
(c) use of a cohesive conjunction that expresses a causal relationship between sentences
(d) use of definite over indefinite noun phrase to introduce new entity into narrative
(e) use of a cohesive conjunction that expresses a temporal relationship between sentences

Question 3 There are significant differences in how these three children open their narratives in episode 1. Describe <u>three</u> ways in which the child with no language disorder does this more effectively than the two children with language disorder.

Question 4 The purpose of this story is to relate to the listener that one of the children in the movie, Freddie, eventually becomes disillusioned with Super Duper when the car accident exposes him as having no superhuman powers after all. The child with no language disorder conveys this key information quite skilfully to the listener. Is this also the case for the children with language disorder?

Question 5 The transitions between episodes in this narrative also set the children with language disorder apart from the child with no language disorder. Describe how these transitions are achieved by both types of children.

2.7 Pragmatic language impairment 6

Background

The interpretation of non-literal language can be problematic for children with specific developmental language disorder (SDLD). This aspect of pragmatics was examined by Rinaldi (2000) in a study of 64 students with SDLD who were aged 11;11 to 14;10 years. These students undertook two procedures which assessed the comprehension of different types of ambiguity. Only one of these procedures, a test of the comprehension of multiple meanings in context (MMC), is discussed here. Two control groups were also included in the study. One group was matched to the subjects with SDLD on chronological age, while the other group was matched to these subjects on language age. Data from subjects with SDLD and the language-matched control group will be examined below.

Task

The MMC procedure took the following form. Students were shown a set of four pictures at the same time as they heard a contextualised stimulus item on an audiotape. Each stimulus item was a word or phrase which was ambiguous in some respect. For example, the stimulus item 'jam' (*fruit preserve* vs. *traffic congestion*) was presented within the sentence 'The road was jammed solid this morning.' Two of the pictures represented a pragmatic interpretation of the item, that is, an interpretation that was plausible given the context. For the stimulus item 'jam', the correct pragmatic interpretation of the utterance was depicted by a picture showing traffic congestion, while the incorrect pragmatic interpretation showed a car driving along a road. The other two pictures depicted a literal, non-pragmatic interpretation of the stimulus item which was implausible in the given context. For the stimulus item 'jam', these pictures showed a road covered in jam (literal interpretation) and a van laden with jam travelling along a road (interpretation related to literal meaning). The data presented below are some of the verbal comments made by subjects with SDLD and by language-matched control subjects as they completed this task. The chronological age (CA) and language age (LA) of subjects with SDLD are shown in brackets.

Data set 1

STIMULUS ITEM: JAM
CONTEXT: Mrs Blue was late for school. She said, 'I'm sorry I'm late, the road was jammed solid this morning.'
COMMENT: A truck must have jam on it and it fell out (control subject, 8;9 years)
COMMENT: She couldn't get through that strawberry jam (SDLD subject, CA = 12;4 years, LA = 8;4 years)

Data set 2

STIMULUS ITEM: PULL YOUR SOCKS UP

CONTEXT: Mrs Blue said, 'Well Sam, if you want to pass your test, you'll have to pull your socks up.'

COMMENT: She doesn't mean-actually mean – your socks up – that's got nothing to do with passing a test has it? (control subject, 8;7 years)

COMMENT: He's got to pull his socks up (miming the literal action) (SDLD subject, CA = 12;4 years, LA = 8;4 years)

Data set 3

STIMULUS ITEM: CAUGHT RED-HANDED

CONTEXT: There was a robbery yesterday, but luckily the man was caught red-handed.

COMMENT: He's wearing gloves (control subject, 8;7 years)

COMMENT: He cut his hands (control subject, 7;10 years)

COMMENT: It means caught in the act, doesn't it? (control subject, 12;0 years)

COMMENT: 'cause that one hasn't got red hands (SDLD subject, CA = 14;4 years, LA = 8;4 years)

Data set 4

STIMULUS ITEM: BESIDE HIMSELF

CONTEXT: Mrs Blue said, 'Peter was completely beside himself this morning.'

COMMENT: Peter's standing next to a Peter that looks like him (control subject, 7;2 years)

COMMENT: There's a reflection (control subject, 10;2 years)

COMMENT: They're brothers (SDLD subject, CA = 12;3 years, LA = 11.5 years)

Data set 5

STIMULUS ITEM: WRONG SIDE OF THE BED

CONTEXT: Mrs Blue said, 'I think Joanna got out of the wrong side of the bed this morning.'

COMMENT: Most children get out on that side of the bed (SDLD subject, CA = 14;2 years, LA = 7;2 years)

Data set 6

STIMULUS ITEM: THREW

CONTEXT: Mrs Blue said, 'I think I really threw Emma with that spelling test.'

COMMENT: She's jumping in the air – she's really happy (control subject, 10;2 years)

COMMENT: Through means passed (selected picture of girl looking pleased) (SDLD subject, CA = 13;7 years, LA = 7;0 years)

Question 1 Many words in language have multiple, unrelated senses which are a potential source of ambiguity. The relationship between these senses is one of *homonymy*. Other words can have a literal meaning in one context. However, when these words come together to form *idiomatic expressions*, they assume a non-literal meaning which is often unrelated to the literal meanings of the words in these expressions. Which of the stimulus items used in this study are examples of homonymy and which are examples of idioms?

Question 2 Do any of the comments of the children with SDLD suggest that they have grasped a non-literal interpretation of the stimulus item? Support your answer with evidence from the above data sets.

Question 3 Which of the following statements best characterises the comprehension of children with SDLD?

(a) Comprehension is consistent with these children's chronological age.
(b) Comprehension is consistent with these children's language age.
(c) Comprehension at a language age of 8;4 years is beginning to reveal the emergence of non-literal interpretation.
(d) Comprehension of homonyms is superior to comprehension of idioms.
(e) Comprehension at a language age of 11;5 years is consistently in favour of a non-literal interpretation.

Question 4 The comprehension of non-literal language has a long developmental window even in typical children. On the basis of the data presented above, which of these statements best characterises this aspect of pragmatic development?

(a) This aspect of pragmatic development is complete by 10 years of age.
(b) Comprehension of idioms precedes the comprehension of other non-literal language.
(c) Literal interpretation persists beyond 10 years of age.
(d) Comprehension of homonyms precedes the comprehension of other non-literal language.
(e) Comprehension of non-literal language is a later developmental achievement than comprehension of structural language.

Question 5 Is there an example of the use of an idiom to explain the meaning of a stimulus item in the above data?

2.7 Pragmatic language impairment 7

Background

The following data were taken from a study of narrative production in mother–child dyads by Tompkins and Farrar (2011). The children in these dyads were aged between 50 and 68 months. Children were classified as having specific language impairment on the basis of their medical history and language assessments. In this way, all children passed hearing screenings, had a history of language delay, had no previous medical conditions that could cause language delay, scored within normal limits on a non-verbal measure of intellectual ability, and had impaired expressive morphosyntax (each child scored below the age of 4 years on a measure of expressive morphosyntax). All child participants were from an English-speaking home.

Procedure

Two types of narrative – autobiographical memory and storybook narratives – were examined in the study. Mother–child dyads were audio-recorded and video-recorded as they engaged in production of these narratives. In order to produce autobiographical narratives, mothers were asked to think of unique events and to discuss them with their children as they would normally do. Memories of birthdays or holidays were not included as it was thought that children would already have a schema for these activities. Storybook narratives were obtained through the use of two wordless picture books. These books were *Frog, where are you?* (Mayer, 1969) and *Frog goes to dinner* (Mayer, 1974). The first of these books concerns a boy who has lost his frog and his subsequent quest to find him. In the second book, the same boy who searched for his frog in the first book goes to dinner in a restaurant with his family. The mischievous frog tags along with them. Mothers were asked to co-construct a narrative with their children based on these books.

Analysis

The resulting narratives were analysed to investigate the type of narrative style on the part of the mothers which was most effective in eliciting new information from the children. To this end, four types of maternal utterance were recognised: (1) *elaborative wh-questions*, a wh-question that requested new information from the child; (2) *elaborative yes–no questions*, questions that required a child to confirm or deny a new piece of information; (3) *elaborative statements*, statements that provided a child with new information but did not require a response; and (4) *repetitions*, any type of utterance that replicated the content of a previous utterance.

The following data sets are taken from recordings of autobiographical memory and storybook narratives between mothers (M) and their children (C). Examine each data set and then answer the questions below.

Data set 1

Autobiographical memory narrative: female child with SLI aged 53 months.

M: What were those big animals that we saw?
M: What were they?
M: Remember we went up that big tram and we saw? In the cage?
M: And they would bite you if you got too close.
M: Remember what they were?
C: Lions.
M: No, they weren't the lions.
C: Baby lions.
M: Were they bears?

Data set 2

Storybook narrative: female child with SLI aged 50 months.

M: They were getting ready to go to dinner.
M: And the driver dropped them off.
M: And they're at the restaurant.
M: And they waited in line.
M: And now they're sitting at the table.

Data set 3

Autobiographical memory narrative: male child with SLI aged 56 months.

M: Remember we went camping in the big tent?
M: Or the little, the pop up.
M: Remember our camper we went in?
C: No.
M: Remember we made fires?
C: No.
M: You don't remember the fires?
M: And you got to carry a walkie-talkie.
C: Yeah.
M: Yeah?
C: I get to hold the black walkie-talkie.
M: And you got to hold the black walkie-talkie.

Data set 4

Storybook narrative: male child with SLI aged 56 months.

M: Uh oh, look at that.
C: Frog!
C: He going to jump into that.
M: Yeah, that's not going to be good, is it?
C: No.
M: Not uh.
C: I know that the frog would do it.
M: Yeah, what's he looking for?
C: A frog.
M: He's looking for a frog?
M: Do you think the frog is going to jump on his face?
M: Oh!
C: I know the frog going to jump on his face too.

Question 1 Using the above data sets, give <u>one</u> example of each of the following maternal utterances:

(a) elaborative wh-question
(b) repetition
(c) elaborative statement
(d) statement of denial
(e) elaborative yes–no question

Question 2 The repetition of what type of maternal utterance is eventually successful in eliciting participation from the child in data set 1?

Question 3 In data set 2, the mother fails to secure any conversational participation from her child. Explain this failure in terms of the type of utterance used by the mother.

Question 4 Data sets 3 and 4 are from the same mother–child dyad. However, there is much greater conversational participation from the child in this dyad during the storybook narrative than during the autobiographical memory narrative. How would you explain this difference?

Question 5 In data set 3, the child produces no topic-controlling utterances. However, in data set 4 the control of topic is much more balanced between this same child and his mother. Explain how the child achieves greater control of topic in data set 4.

2.7 Pragmatic language impairment 8

Background

Eight mother–child dyads were videotaped in a 15-minute free-play situation by Moseley (1990). Four of the eight children in the study had normal language development. They ranged in age from 1;10 to 2;0 years. The other four children were diagnosed by speech–language pathologists as having language delay. These children had inadequate vocabulary and sentence structure in the absence of known anatomical or physiological problems. The ages of these children ranged from 2;10 to 3;11 years. Recordings took place through a one-way mirror in a speech–language clinic. Mothers were requested to play as naturally as possible with the children using toys in the clinic as well as books, favourite toys and games that they brought from home.

   In the following data sets, transcribed extracts from conversational exchanges between two mothers and their normal language children and two mothers and their children with language delay are presented. Examine these extracts and then answer the questions below.

Data set 1

Exchange between a mother (M) and her normally developing child (C). The child is pulling pieces of toy out of a box.

C: There some red ones. There some red ones.
M: The red ones.
C: Those are the red ones (child points to pieces in the box)
M: Those are the red ones.
   That's right.
   What else is in there?

Data set 2

Exchange between a mother and her child with language delay. The child is pointing to the blocks on top of a pile of blocks.

M: You're putting 'em on the bridge pretty good, huh?
C: Yeah (child continues to stack the blocks side by side)
M: Gonna line 'em up like cars?
C: Yeah, mom (child puts the blocks on the pile until there is no room left for another)
   N' more (child shakes head left to right)
M: Can't fit no more?
C: Uh-uh (child shakes his head left to right)

M: You can put some on top.
C: Yeah.

Data set 3

Exchanges between a mother and her normally developing child. The mother and child are looking at pictures in a book. The mother points to a picture in the book.

C: Happy birthday.
M: Happy birthday?
    How do you sing it?
    Sing it.
C: Happy birthday to Carl.
M: To Carl?
M: What's this? (mother points to a picture in the book)
C: Sucker.
M: A sucker?
    Purple sucker, hmmmm (mother turns the page)
C: Oh, popsicle (child turns the page back and touches the same picture he called a 'sucker')
M: Popsicle?
C: Under there (child points to the same picture)
    Boy ha a popsicle.
M: The boy has a popsicle.

Data set 4

Exchange between a mother and her child with language delay. The child and mother are putting together a cootie bug toy. The legs fall off the bug in the child's hand.

M: Uh-oh his legs are fallin' out (mother reaches for a leg)
C: Me tell that.
    Me tell that girl that (child points toward the door)
M: You're gonna tell her what?
C: Help me.
    Help me do that.
M: To help you do that?
C: Yeah.
    And mommy, no (child takes the piece apart and puts it in the box)
M: And I'm not going to?
C: Don't make it.
    Mommy, no.
M: You don't like me to help you?
C: (shakes head no)

Question 1 Despite the expressive language problems of the children with language delay, they are still able to perform a range of speech acts. Give <u>one</u> example of each of the following speech acts in the data:

(a) command
(b) confirmation
(c) statement

(d) refusal

(e) request

Question 2 The mothers of the children with language delay use two types of utterance in conversation. State what these types are and suggest why they are used so extensively in these mothers' conversations with their children.

Question 3 Topic exchange is only possible to the extent that speakers are able to contribute content to a conversation which can then be sustained over several turns. Topic exchange occurs in data set 1 but is limited in data set 2. Explain this difference in terms of the type of contribution made by the child in each case.

Question 4 In data sets 3 and 4, the mothers are making a number of clarification requests of their children. However, the clarification requests made of the normally developing child in data set 3 are qualitatively different from those directed to the child with language delay in data set 4. What is this difference and why does it occur?

Question 5 The normally developing children and the children with language delay make use of gesture and body movements. However, there are important differences in how gesture and body movements are used by these children. State what these differences are, and explain why they occur.

2.7   Pragmatic language impairment 9

Background

The communicative skills of five children with SLI and their normally developing younger siblings were examined by Rollins et al. (1994). The chronological ages of the children with SLI ranged from 4;9 to 6;9 years. The children with SLI had severe expressive language deficits. This was reflected in their mean length of utterance (MLU) which fell well below age expectancies. Because normally developing siblings were matched to children with SLI on their MLU, the chronological ages of these children (1;11 to 3;2 years) were considerably lower than the ages of the children with SLI. All children had normal non-verbal intellectual functioning. They also had normal bilateral hearing and there was no history of chronic otitis media. There was also no history of neurological or emotional problems in any of the children. All children were monolingual speakers of British English. Children with SLI were found to have moderate-to-severe delays on a test of receptive vocabulary and normal-to-moderate delays on a test of the comprehension of grammatical structures.

Procedure

All children were video-recorded at home during interaction with either their mother or father. A free play situation was used in order to impose as little structure as possible on the interaction. Families selected the toys they played with and were instructed to play as they would do so normally. A recording of 15 minutes' duration was made, with the first 10 minutes being used for the analysis. Two native speakers of British English transcribed the recordings.

The following data are from an interaction between Sid, a child with SLI, and his father. Sid has a chronological age of 4;9 years and a mental age of 5;10 years. Sid's younger sibling Sue is in interaction with her mother in the second exchange. Sue has a chronological age of 2;5 years and a mental age of 2;3 years. Examine both data sets and then answer the questions below.

Data set 1

Exchange between Sid (S), a child with SLI, and his father (F).

S: mom. that right (points to structure)
S: that right.
S: dada (motions towards Dad)
S: that right.
S: dada.
S: that right. that right (shakes his head no)
F: no that's not right is it?
S: no.

Data set 2

Exchange between Sue (S), a normally developing child, and her mother (M).

S: car (moves a car up the toy slide)
S: car fall down (walks the car down the other side of the slide)
S: car.
S: fall down.
M: (mother reaches in front of Sue, takes the car and places it on top of the slide)
S: no (whines and takes the car from mother and puts it on the slide)
M: no.
S: all fall down (accidentally knocks over the slide)

Question 1 In data set 1, Sid's expressive language limitations are very much in evidence during his interaction with his father. Using data to support your claims, describe Sid's expressive language output.

Question 2 Notwithstanding Sid's expressive language problems, he is able to use language to perform a number of communicative functions. Name three such functions. Provide data to support your answer.

Question 3 Although Sue's MLU is comparable to that of her brother Sid (1.25 and 1.50, respectively), she has a more limited communicative repertoire than him. Describe that repertoire using data to support your answer.

Question 4 There are significant differences in the use of non-verbal behaviour by Sid and Sue in these exchanges. State what these differences are and explain why they occur.

Question 5 Sid displays considerable pragmatic competence alongside his very limited expressive language skills. An aspect of pragmatic competence which has received increasing attention in recent years is the ability to attribute mental states to the minds of one's interlocutors. This ability is described as theory of mind (ToM). Describe three features of Sid's interaction with his father which suggest that he has an intact ToM capacity.

2.7 Pragmatic language impairment 10

Background

The following narratives were produced by children with specific language impairment (SLI) who were investigated as part of a study of narrative form and content by Colozzo et al. (2011). In a single picture production task, the children were asked to invent a story about an alien spaceship landing in a park. They were encouraged to produce a story that was as long and as complete as possible. The investigator administered additional probes only if the children did not initiate a narrative, if they appeared to lose attention during the task, or if they did not signal the end of their narrative. Otherwise, the investigator delivered neutral but enthusiastic responses (e.g. 'great') and occasionally repeated the child's previous utterance by way of verification. Stories were audio-recorded and transcribed.

Examine each narrative and then answer the questions below. Parentheses in the narratives contain repeated words and phrases, word elements, fillers and corrected errors.

Data set 1

Child with SLI aged 8;6 years.

> One (s*) Saturday (um Daniel no) Mark and Daniel went for a walk.
> And (they) there was a spaceship (on) on the ground.
> And (then here they're th* they) then (they went) they came and saw the (s* um) aliens.
> And they had six legs.
> And the dog was alien.
> And there [sic] were pretty funny.

Data set 2

Child with SLI aged 9;0 years.

> Once upon a time (there is) there is a brother and sister.
> The brother's name was (um) John.
> (And the other) and the sister was named Mary.
> (And) and (when they) when they want to go to the park, they saw an alien (um) ship.
> (They try) they hide.
> (Then) (hhmm) and Mary didn't want to hide.
> He wanted to look at the aliens.
> (And) and (this) this little girl (um) had an alien dog.
> (And and the family) one day (the f* the f* hhmm which um um) Mary wanted to go near them.
> (And and) and John tries to stop her.
> (But) but she couldn't.

(And and) and when she was there, the aliens (skir* s* um) scared her.
And (she) she hided right under the bushes.
And then the aliens said 'Where did she go?'
'Where (d*) did she go?'
And then (one day) one day the brother stand up called John.
(he) he ran up (to) to the alien and then said 'Go back to the ship.'
And then they did and forgot (the) the alien dog.
And the alien dog ran as fast as (I) he can right in his ship.
And then the aliens (righ*) go right out of the planet.
(And then) and then (they) they have fun again.

Question 1 There are a number of linguistic errors in the narrative output of these children. Give two examples of (a) the incorrect use of past tense verb forms and (b) the incorrect use of pronouns. Which of these linguistic errors has an adverse impact on the ability of a listener to follow a narrative?

Question 2 There are also several instances of quite sophisticated language use in these narratives. Give two examples of (a) the use of direct reported speech and (b) the use of self-initiated repair. Which of these aspects of language use achieves listener engagement in an unfolding narrative?

Question 3 One cohesive device dominates the narratives of these children. What is this device? What meaning relation is expressed through its use?

Question 4 Clearly, the child with SLI in data set 2 is a more skilled narrator than the child with SLI in data set 1. Name five narrative features which are mastered by the former child, but which are lacking in the latter child's narrative.

Question 5 The aim of this study was to demonstrate that some narratives which are grammatically quite accurate can have poor content while other narratives are less grammatical but have an elaborated content. Indicate which of the above narratives fits these different descriptions.

2.8 Intellectual disability 1

Background

Narrative production was examined by Boudreau and Chapman (2000) in a group of 31 children and adolescents with Down's syndrome. These subjects ranged in chronological age from 12;2 to 26;10 years and had a mental age in the range 2;5 to 10;0 years. They were matched to three typically developing control groups on mental age, syntactic comprehension, and mean length of utterance (MLU) based on morphemes. Typically developing subjects ranged in chronological age from 2;3 to 8;5 years. Children were excluded from the study if they had a hearing loss of greater than 40 dB in the better ear, if they had severe visual impairment, or if they had a history of illness which was associated with cognitive or language loss.

Procedure

All participants completed a narrative task which consisted of watching a brief, silent video called *The Pear Film* (Chafe, 1980) with an examiner. The film was viewed in black and white and lasted approximately 6.5 minutes. After the film ended, a second examiner entered the room. The subject was asked to tell this examiner about the film. Participants were not aware that this examiner was familiar with the film. Open-ended prompts such as 'What else happened in the movie?' were used by this examiner if the subject hesitated during story retelling. A summary of the story is presented below.

A rooster is heard crowing twice before a man on a ladder comes into view. The man is picking pears which he places in the large pocket of his apron. When the pocket is full, he climbs down the ladder and puts the pears into one of three baskets at the bottom of the tree. One of the pears falls. The man picks it up and cleans it with his bandana before putting it in the basket. A second man with a goat comes into view. The goat is bleating. They walk past the baskets of pears but not without the goat trying to eat a pear. The pear picker climbs back up the ladder and continues his work. Next, a boy on a bicycle comes into view. He gets off his bike next to the baskets of pears, takes a pear and then loads a full basket of pears onto the front of his cycle. He has not been seen by the fruit picker. The boy cycles off but is soon distracted by a girl who is cycling in the opposite direction. He drives into a large stone. This causes him to lose his balance and he falls off his bike. The basket of pears spills onto the ground. The boy gets up and is brushing himself down when three other boys come along and help him put the pears back in the basket. After helping, the boys continue walking along the road. They find a hat which fell off the 'thief' boy moments earlier. One of the boys returns the hat to the 'thief' boy and is given three pears in return. The three pears are shared among the boys who immediately begin eating them. Meanwhile, the fruit picker has realised that one of his baskets of pears is missing. He appears puzzled, but is then seen watching the three boys pass by him while they are eating pears.

The following data sets contain the narratives that were produced by three subjects with Down's syndrome and two mental age-matched control subjects. Unintelligible speech is indicated by the use of 'X'. Parentheses contain fillers, repeated words and phrases and word elements. Examine each narrative and then answer the questions below.

Data set 1

Subject with Down's syndrome (MLU: 4.25).

> That boy steal apples.
> Yeah, and the boys help him put those apples in.
> He gives him three apples.
> And that's all.
> It's a short one.

Data set 2

Subject with Down's syndrome (MLU: 6.5).

> One kid stole the basket of pears.
> A kid (uh) stole the basket (away from hi*) away from him.
> So he will shared a pears with the (B*)>
> He shared the pears with the boys.

A girl got (a) pears too.
She take the pears away.
That's it.

Data set 3

Subject with Down's syndrome (MLU: 6.57).

(W*) A (b* l*) little XX start watching.
A man was (do uh) picking pears on the tree.
Yeah, four of them.
(N* an* so* uh some some boy um) some boy taked (it) all of the pears.
He steal the whole basket.
(And he goes) and (he, he) he went in on the bike.
And he put it in the basket and then he put it on the bike to hear why the XX way in the walk.
He started to ran over the walk and kicked her.
XXX (she's she's) she's X boys XX picked the pears.
They picked them up.
And they put them back in the basket again.
(N* a* A* Th* Th*) This was a real funny part.
(Um) and (it uh uh the bas*) the basket is going to be but (that) right back to the ground.
And the boys are all gone.
And the man was looking for all the pears XX.

Data set 4

Mental age-matched subject (MLU: 5.80).

First this guy (uh) was picking (uh) some fruit from the tree.
(Um) then a kid stealed it.
They steal but just three.
They just steal three and (uh)>
(That) and then he was looking and (then was um) then he was looking at them.
And then it was done.
Some fruit.
He stole one big pail of it.
They stole three of it.
(Then they looked) then the man who was picking looked at the X and XX.
And (the) the man (uh) was looking for all the paper on XX.

Data set 5

Mental age-matched subject (MLU: 12.09).

Well, (it w*) it was about a boy and (um) his dad was picking pears off the pear tree.
And (um he um he) he put them in a bucket and (he wanted he wanted to s*) he wanted to go down to the ocean so well he fell on his bike.
And (um) these kids came along and they picked up all the pears that fell out.
(And um) and he was so grateful that he gave them three pears.
Because there were three people then he gave them three pears.

(And and then um) and then he gave them his hat.
And he said 'thanks.'
(he he) he rode along again.
And then when his dad (when they) saw that they had pears, he got really mad.
(And) and then that was the end.

Question 1 Give <u>one</u> example of each of the following linguistic errors in the narratives of the subjects with Down's syndrome. Which of these errors is most likely to compromise a listener's ability to follow a narrative?

(a) non-finite verb used in place of finite verb
(b) finite verb used in place of non-finite verb
(c) use of incomplete prepositional phrase
(d) use of demonstrative noun phrase with no referent
(e) use of object pronoun with no referent

Question 2 Describe the use of inter-sentential cohesion by both groups of subjects. Include examples from the above data sets in your answer.

Question 3 One of the subjects in the above data sets has drawn an erroneous inference about the relationships between the individuals in this story. Which subject is it? Describe the mistaken inference which has been drawn by this subject.

Question 4 Using examples from the above data sets, describe how these different subjects conclude their narratives.

Question 5 There are interesting differences in how these subjects introduce the 'thief' boy into their narratives. Describe how this introduction is achieved in each case.

2.8 Intellectual disability 2

Background

The ability of adults with mild and moderate intellectual disability to respond to questions was examined by Brinton and Fujiki (1994). Forty adults were included in the study. Twenty lived in an institutional setting, and twenty lived in the community. Simple and complex questions were posed by an investigator within the context of a job interview. The 30-minute language samples, which were collected from these interviews, were analysed for the informativeness and truthfulness of the responses to questions. Extracts from the interviews between the investigator (I) and subjects (S) are presented below. Examine each interview and then answer the questions which follow.

Data set 1

I: What happens if you make a mistake at work?
S: You're supposed to, to correct it.
I: Uh-huh.

S: And if you do you're supposed to go up and say, 'I'm going to do it over.' And if they tell you to do it over, then do it over. It's called follow instructions.

I: Oh, uh-huh.

Data set 2

I: How do you spend your free time?

S: On the cottage?

I: Uh-huh.

S: Are you married?

Data set 3

I: What are some chores you have to do where you live?

S: Well, uhm, at Ellenbrook we clean up the cottage.

I: Uh-huh.

S: Clean it nice and clean. Not the whole mess, clean up again. We take shower over there every night.

I: Uh-huh.

S: So I take a shower and clean myself up. Get my deodorant on every morning. So I don't smell bad.

I: Uh-huh. Oh, put your deodorant on every morning?

S: Every night I do.

I: Oh, every night.

S: I don't wanna get smelly like god bad. You know Frances don't like me smelling. So I just clean up.

Data set 4

I: What would you do if you found out someone else was stealing?

S: He'd probably be in deep trouble.

I: Uh-huh.

S: I don't steal nothing at work.

I: Uh-huh.

S: I used to steal. But not no more. But I know, I, I ask Jackie. I got in trouble working at the canteen.

I: Yeah.

S: Got fired.

I: Oh yeah.

S: They don't, we did, they don't like sticky fingers over there.

Data set 5

I: How can you tell if you have done a good job at work?

S: My supervisor tells me that I did okay. He says you did it just right.

Data set 6

I: What do you do at work?

S: Work.

Data set 7

I: How do you spend your free time?

S: I like to go fishing. I like to catch lot of fish and take them back to the cottage. I scare all the girls. I put fish in their shoes. Mary really hates it when I do that to her.

Question 1 Give one example of each of the following grammatical features in the utterances of subjects in the above data sets. Which of these features is likely to be attributable to the dialect of the speaker?

(a) use of incorrect preposition
(b) use of double negative construction
(c) omission of indefinite article
(d) use of singular over plural noun
(e) use of subordinate clause

Question 2 There is evidence of considerable pragmatic competence in the utterances of the subjects in this study. Give one example of each of the following pragmatic features in the contributions of these subjects:

(a) use of direct and indirect reported speech
(b) use of idiomatic expression
(c) use of request for clarification
(d) use of spatial deixis
(e) use of ellipsis

Question 3 Several subjects in this study display difficulties in the use of Gricean maxims. One such maxim is quantity. Give two examples in the data sets where subjects exhibit difficulty in the use of the quantity maxim.

Question 4 These subjects with intellectual disability also have difficulty observing the maxims of relation and quality. Give one example in the above data sets where each of these maxims is not correctly observed.

Question 5 Several subjects in this study made contributions to their interviews which were likely to be damaging to their prospects of securing a job. Indicate two instances where this occurs in the data sets.

2.9 Autism spectrum disorder 1

Background

It is now well established that children and adults with autism spectrum disorder (ASD) have difficulty with pragmatic processes that contribute to the non-literal contents of utterances. In this way, these individuals have difficulty recovering the implicatures of utterances, understanding metaphor and irony, and so on. Much less investigation has been undertaken into the pragmatic determinants of the literal contents of utterances in individuals with ASD. These latter pragmatic processes allow hearers to establish the referents of indexical expressions (e.g. 'I would love to live here') and to restrict the domain of quantifiers (e.g. 'Everyone [on the ship] was ill'), among other aspects of literal content. These pragmatic processes were the focus of a study by De Villiers et al. (2012).

Procedure

These investigators collected semi-structured conversational data from 12 youths with ASD who were aged 10 to 16 years. All subjects were verbal communicators who could speak in sentences. A psychometric test was used to ensure that they had sufficient expressive language skills to participate in conversation. The 12 subjects underwent audio-recordings in their own homes. Topics of discussion included school and family life. Conversations were transcribed. Transcripts were then annotated for several kinds of pragmatic determinants of literal content.

Several extracts from these conversations appear below. Examine each exchange between the researcher (R) and the participant (P). Then answer the questions that follow.

Transcription notation

-:	syllable lengthened
#	pause
[?]	uncertain
[<]	overlaps with preceding text
[>]	overlaps with following text
XXX	indecipherable

Data set 1

The topic of conversation is staying in a hotel.

R: so you're staying with some friends here while you're in Toronto eh?
P: yes
R: mmhm?
R: that must be nice not to have to stay in a hotel.
P: I I I want to.
P: but it seems that they did they didn't agree.
R: who didn't agree?
P: mom and dad.

Data set 2

The topic of conversation is the movie star Kevin Costner.

R: what's your favourite one you've seen with him?
P: no.
P: I haven't really seen much o(f) him in it.

Data set 3

R: who's in your family?
P: hm I don't know.
R: are there five of you?

P: yes.
P: my cat.

Data set 4

R: Do you have a sister?
P: Yes and she won!
R: What did she win?

Data set 5

R: you were showing me your iguanas.
R: c what can you tell me about them?
P: one escaped for two day -:.
P: and one # and uh he started <not to he ate> [?].
P: but he n not very much.
R: where did you find him?
P: behind the piano.
R: and was he difficult to catch again?
P: mmhm.
P: but uh I wasn't.
P: and uh my mom she hired somebody to help her do some stuff around the house.
P: and uh they had to do it.
P: and one was holdin(g) it like like this.
P: and uh the person that was holdin(g) it was terrified of them.

Data set 6

R: do you get an allowance?
P: not really.
R: not really?
R: just some money <XXX> [>]?
P: <maybe> [<] at the end of the month.
R: yeah.
P: I'm starting.
R: oh yeah.
R: sounds good.
R: are there any subjects that you really don't like?
P: well -: there's one subject I had I did bad on.
P: that was health.
R: health?
P: I got a C.

Question 1 There are some aspects of pragmatics which appear to be intact in these subjects with ASD. Give one example of each of the following pragmatic behaviours in the above conversational data:

(a) subject can use ellipsis
(b) subject can use a demonstrative pronoun to achieve reference

  (c) subject can respond to a request for clarification

  (d) subject can engage in self-initiated repair

  (e) subject can use substitution to achieve cohesion

Question 2 Indexical pronouns are not always used by the subjects with ASD in a way that allows the hearer to establish the literal content of the utterances that contain them. Give two examples in the data where this occurs. What behaviour on the part of the researcher indicates that he has not succeeded in establishing the referent of an indexical pronoun?

Question 3 On occasion, the subjects with ASD in this study produced utterances in which a phrase lacked a complement. This was despite the fact that the head of the phrase semantically required one. This can be seen in data set 4 where the participant utters 'Yes and she won!' (*won what?*). Give two further examples of this type of error in the data.

Question 4 On one occasion in the above data a subject with ASD produces a sub-sentence error. That is, he uses a phrase instead of a complete sentence to convey a thought, with the result that the hearer struggles to establish the literal content of the utterance. (This should not be confused with syntactic ellipsis where the hearer can readily establish the literal content of an utterance.) Indicate where this sub-sentence error occurs in the data, and indicate the two literal contents which are consistent with it.

Question 5 Towards the end of data set 5, the participant describes how his iguana was captured. This description is not particularly easy to follow. Explain why this is the case.

2.9 Autism spectrum disorder 2

Background

A shortcoming of much research into pragmatics and discourse in autism spectrum disorder is the emphasis on impairment and deviance to the almost complete exclusion of any discussion of strengths in these areas. A study of narrative introductions by Solomon (2004) revealed that high-functioning children with autism spectrum disorder (ASD) have considerable competence in this aspect of narrative production. Moreover, their skills in crafting narrative introductions are not always mirrored in other aspects of narrative production which can exhibit many of the anomalies that are typical of communication in ASD (e.g. preoccupation with unusual details).

  The following narrative introductions are taken from video- and audio-recordings of 14 children with high-functioning autism or Asperger's syndrome. The recordings were made during breakfast, dinner and transit interactions. Three of these subjects are girls and 11 are boys. Their chronological ages ranged from 8;1 to 13;0 years. The full-scale IQ of these children ranged from 73 to 139. In total, 67 narratives were recorded. Extracts of some of these narratives are presented below.

Transcription notation

<u>yes</u> YES	underlining is louder and capitals are louder still
° Weird °	material between 'degree signs' is quiet
(0.5)	timed pause (in seconds)
(*takes a deep breath*)	something hard, or impossible, to write phonetically
ou:t	prolonged sound
(.)	micropause
( )	unclear talk
↑	sharp rise in pitch
[	start of overlapping talk
]	end of overlapping talk
>What did I do?<	faster speech

Data set 1

Exchange between mother (M) and Adam (A), a boy of 11;1 years with Asperger's syndrome. Adam is telling his mother about his school day. The exchange begins with Adam telling his mother the exact moment in time when fall begins.

M: Yeah, of course, but it still makes more sense to have it tomorrow
A: It still <u>does</u>, but everyone tries to celebrate it <u>today.</u>
M: ° Weird °
A: So, I have a <u>story</u> to tell you about – (0.5)
　　that Mister- Mister Gregory told us today
M: Yeah.
A: Have you ever- you know-
　　you've heard of- uh- Clara Schumann, right?
M: Who?
A: Clara Schumann.
M: Uh-
A: Wait a second. Clara Schumann, you know –
M: You mean, Schumann the composer?
A: Yeah, you know Robert Schumann?
M: Mmm hmm.
A: It's his wife. Clara Schumann.
　　And there's a <u>big</u> background behind Clara Schumann.
　　(*takes a deep breath*)
　　And Mister Gregory told us a <u>wonderful</u> story about it.
　　He said, 'In eighteen-twenty, there- the- there was a – . . . '
　　((*narrative continues*))

Data set 2

Exchange between mother (MO), father (FA) and Mark (MA), a boy of 8;11 years with Asperger's syndrome. Mark is introducing a narrative about a movie during family dinner.

MO: ((*to Mark*)) Want some more rice?
MA: Hey Dad. I'll tell you about this movie called 'Napoleon'.
MO: ((*gesturing for him to sit*)) Mark, sit down.
MA: ((*sits down*))

It's about this little puppy.
And he goes into a- ((*takes a bite of food*))
and he accidentally gets carried away in a balloon.
FA: I don't know this story.
((*narrative continues*))

Data set 3

Exchange between mother (M) and Karl (K), a boy of 9;8 years with high-functioning autism. Karl is telling his mother over breakfast a story that originates in a computer game.

K: Just- just wait- I just have to get that Rice Krispie out. (.)
  Because you gotta crun:ch it ou:t. And mush it.
M: Go sit down.
K: I wanna tell you about the kitchen. Princess Camista.
M: Alright. Tell me about the kitchen. Sit down.
K: Uhh- In 'Mordack's Castle',
  there's a princess scrubbin' the floo::r.
  Because she tells her to get to work.
M: Yeah.
K: And she has a lot of work
  until she's done scrubbing the floo:r.
M: Just like mom. Princess Camista.

Data set 4

Exchange between father (F) and Anthony (A), a boy of 9;2 years with Asperger's syndrome. They are talking about an upcoming fieldtrip during a drive home from school and how it would be 'selfish' for Anthony's class to go without the other class in his grade.

F: Right
  (1.0)
  It's not nice to be selfish either (   )
A: Yeah
F: I mean (.) I don't like it when people are selfish to me:
  Do you?
A: No!
  (2.0 sec)
  ((*sniffs his nose*))
  I saw like that girl that always-
  third grade girl that always bugs me again!
  (1.5 sec)
F: (   )
  What do you mean she always bugs you?
A: YES she always BUGS me when she sees me!
F: What- what does she do?
A: ((*sounds upset*)) She's calls me a retarded kid.
  (*narrative continues*)

Data set 5

Adam is telling his mother about his first day in middle school.

A: Anyway, so that was Mrs. Coo:lidge
    and she was nice.
    So the: ↑ n we went to <u>lunch</u>.
    And uh- (.) oh and I uh-
    By the way
    I ate only about <u>half</u> of my lunch.
    I didn't eat mo:st of it.
    I ate one half of a sandwich.
    I didn't eat the other ha:lf and stuff.
    That sandwich was so <u>me:ssy</u> and [stuff.
M: [That's what Katie said!
    It was like <u>wet</u> [or something!
A: ((*laughing*))   [Yep! It was like- <u>wet</u>!

Data set 6

Exchange between mother (M) and Sylvester (S), a boy of 8;1 years with high-functioning autism.

S: ((*with his arms behind him, stands over the pot of macaroni*
    bends forward and blows on the boiling water))
    [Can I blow on the bubbles?
M: [Remember when you did that once
    ((*looks at Sylvester*)) when you were a <u>ba:by</u>?
S: Uhu?
M: ((*Stirring the pot of macaroni*))
    When you saw those <u>bubbles</u>?
S: >What did I do?<
M: You put your hand in it.
S: ((*shocked, looks up at the mother*)) OH-OHOH!
    ((*narrative continues*))

Data set 7

Anthony is talking to his father in the car on the way home from school. The topic of conversation is sibling relationships and loss.

A: Because <u>Daniel</u>! always (.) <u>bugs</u>! Me
    (2.5) ((*sound of cars*))
F: I- get a funny feeling
    that if <u>Daniel</u> was no longer <u>arou:nd</u>
    that you'd be <u>very</u> very very very sad (0.5)
    I mean after all (.)
    when you go to bed at night
    you like him to come (.) to bed with you
A: 'cause I want some <u>company</u>
F: Imagine if he wasn't <u>around</u> at all.
A: Mm-hmm

F: So I would think that Burton would feel the same way
about his sister (.)
if you asked him now
he'd probably say my sister drives me <u>nuts</u> from time to time
but- if she wasn't around he'd really be sad

A: Maybe- maybe- when um Burton C. is watching something?
Maybe his s- sister comes in an' interrupts him (.)
and she's like (.) she's like 'what are you watching?'
an' he said '<u>shh!</u>'

F: well that happens to everybody (.) right?

A: mm-hmm

F: Not just <u>them</u>!
(16.0)

A: Did you feel sad when your brother died?
(1.5 sec pause)

F: Very.
((*narrative continues*))

Question 1 Adam displays a number of linguistic and cognitive skills which mark him out as competent in introducing narratives to his interlocutor. Some of these skills are indicated below. Give <u>one</u> example of each skill in the above data sets.

(a) Adam uses theory of mind skills to establish his interlocutor's state of knowledge.
(b) Adam uses discourse and disjunct markers to signal a break in prior discourse.
(c) Adam uses repetition to indicate thematic continuity with prior discourse.
(d) Adam displays cognitive flexibility when he shifts between different meanings of words.
(e) Adam uses linguistic and prosodic devices to amplify the 'tellability' of the story.

Question 2 In data set 2, Mark uses three linguistic features to introduce his narrative. Identify these features and describe their contribution to the introduction of Mark's narrative.

Question 3 The narrative introductions in data sets 1 to 3 inclusive include constructions which contain the preposition *about*. These constructions are performing an important procedural function in these introductions. What is this function and how does it go slightly awry in Karl's narrative introduction in data set 3? What other discourse problem is evident in Karl's narrative introduction?

Question 4 In data set 4, Anthony introduces a story about being bullied by a third grade girl at school. On first sight, this appears to be unrelated to the prior discourse in which Anthony and his father are talking about an upcoming fieldtrip. However, there is some thematic continuity between Anthony's narrative introduction and this prior discourse beyond simply the connection of both events to school. What is this continuity? Also, what evidence is there in this exchange that Anthony can engage in the type of mental state attribution typical of theory of mind?

Question 5 In data sets 6 and 7 narratives are introduced, respectively, about Sylvester burning himself as a baby and about how Anthony's father felt when his brother died. What triggers or prompts the telling of the narratives in these data sets?

Describe Sylvester's role in the construction of the narrative introduction in data set 6. Anthony is making use of considerable theory of mind (ToM) skills when he introduces his narrative in data set 7. Describe the role of ToM skills in this case.

2.9 Autism spectrum disorder 3

Background

Among the many pragmatic deficits found in children and adults with ASD is a tendency to contribute irrelevant utterances to conversation and to produce irrelevant responses to questions. However, judgements of relevance are relative rather than absolute so that even irrelevant utterances can display different gradations or degrees of irrelevance. Loukusa et al. (2007) examined the responses to questions of 39 children with Asperger's syndrome or high-functioning autism (AS/HFA). These children were 7 to 9 years of age and 10 to 12 years of age and all were native Finnish speakers. All children with AS/HFA had normal intelligence and language development. The language test results of the younger AS/HFA subjects were equivalent to a group of control children of the same age who were also included in the study. Children were asked a total of 31 questions which related to pictures, verbal scenarios and/or a story which was presented in short chunks. The researcher read aloud a short verbal scenario and then posed a question.

The responses to several of these questions are presented in the following data sets. Examine each of these responses and then answer the questions below.

Data set 1

Boy aged 10 years with Asperger's syndrome. The researcher tells part of the story:

The woman runs over and calls the dog to come to her. However, the dog doesn't obey the woman. Two boys are standing near the dog watching them. The woman shouts 'Help!' to the boys and 'Here!' to the dog. What does the woman mean when she shouts 'Here!' to the dog?

Boy's RESPONSE: 'The woman has problems with the dog.'

Data set 2

Boy aged 7 years with Asperger's syndrome. The researcher shows a picture of a girl and a boy playing in the garden. There are a lot of children's toys lying on the ground. Their mother is calling them from the window. The researcher reads the following verbal scenario aloud and then asks a question:

The children are playing in the garden. The boy has a ball in his hand. The mother shouts to the children: 'Dinner will be ready soon.' What does the mother mean?

Boy's RESPONSE: After initially answering correctly, the researcher asks the child to explain his answer. At this point, he responds: 'Because there is that door' (he refers to the door of the picture).

Data set 3

Boy aged 9 years with Asperger's syndrome. The researcher shows a picture of a man mowing grass with a lawn mower. The grass in front of the lawn mower is longer than the grass behind it. A woman is standing on the lawn holding a rake. There is a flowerbed in the middle of the grass. The researcher reads the following verbal scenario aloud and then asks a question:

The man is mowing the grass with a lawn mower. The woman says to the man: 'There are flowers growing in the middle of the grass so remember to be careful.' Why does the woman say this?

BOY'S RESPONSE: The boy sets out with a correct answer and then responds to a follow-up question: 'Because women usually like flowers and they don't want to destroy them. Does he destroy his feelings though he is mowing the lawn? He runs over every dandelion there is.'

Question 1 In data set 1, the woman who shouts 'Here!' to the dog is clearly intending to get the dog to come to her. In order for the boy with Asperger's syndrome to establish this meaning of the woman's utterance, he must undertake a particular pragmatic process. Is that process related to (a) the pragmatic enrichment of the logical form of the utterance or (b) the recovery of an implicature of the fully specified logical form of the utterance?

Question 2 The boys' responses in the above data sets are actually explicable even as they are judged to be irrelevant by the investigators in this study. How might one explain the boy's response in data set 1?

Question 3 In data set 2, the mother who shouts to her children 'Dinner will be ready soon' is clearly implicating to her children that she wants them to come indoors in order to eat their meal. Given this interpretation of the mother's utterance, how might one proceed to explain the response of the boy with Asperger's syndrome in this case?

Question 4 In data set 3, mowing the lawn comes to signify one's mental states and emotions for the boy with Asperger's syndrome. Which of the following concepts best captures the relationship between these domains?

(a) entailment
(b) metonymy
(c) metaphor
(d) presupposition
(e) implicature

Question 5 Which three words in the response of the boy in data set 3 suggest that he possesses some theory of mind skills?

2.9 Autism spectrum disorder 4

Background

Narrative retelling is an area of considerable difficulty for individuals with autism spectrum disorder (ASD). To investigate the nature of the impairments in this area, Stirling et al.

(2009) and Prud'hommeaux and Rouhizadeh (2012) conducted a narrative retelling task in 20 children with ASD aged 6 to 13 years and 42 children with ASD aged 4 to 8 years, respectively. All children had an IQ above 70 indicating no intellectual disability. The children examined by Stirling et al. were enrolled in mainstream primary schools and demonstrated evidence of productive language and competence in English. The children investigated by Prud'hommeaux and Rouhizadeh had an MLU of at least 3, indicating an adequate level of verbal fluency. Typically developing children were included in both studies. Additionally, Prud'hommeaux and Rouhizadeh included a group of 17 children with specific language impairment who did not meet criteria for autism.

Procedure

Different narrative retelling procedures were used in these studies. A researcher read the story *The three little wolves and the big bad pig* on two consecutive days to the children with ASD in Stirling et al.'s study. The children then wrote their stories in a book format using the StoryLincs programme, an internet-based story elicitation environment. On the first day, the children completed a narrative composition task in order to familiarise themselves with this programme. They wrote their narratives on the second day. They were given up to 40 minutes to complete the task. In the study conducted by Prud'hommeaux and Rouhizadeh, the narrative retelling task took the form of the narrative memory task from the NEPSY (Korkman et al., 1998). The text of this narrative is presented below.

Jim was a boy whose best friend was Pepper. Pepper was a big black dog. Jim liked to walk in the woods and climb the trees. Near Jim's house was a very tall oak tree with branches so high that he couldn't reach them. Jim always wanted to climb that tree, so one day he took a ladder from home and carried it to the oak tree. He climbed up, sat on a branch, and looked out over his neighbourhood. When he started to get down, his foot slipped, his shoe fell off, and the ladder fell to the ground. Jim held onto a branch so he didn't fall, but he couldn't get down. Pepper sat below the tree and barked. Suddenly Pepper took Jim's shoe in his mouth and ran away. Jim felt sad. Didn't his friend want to stay with him when he was in trouble? Pepper took the shoe to Anna, Jim's sister. He barked and barked. Finally, Anna understood that Jim was in trouble. She followed Pepper to the tree where Jim was stuck. Anna put the ladder up and rescued Jim. Wasn't Pepper a smart dog?

Three narratives from these studies are presented in the following data sets. Examine each narrative and then answer the questions below.

Data set 1

Child with specific language impairment (SLI): narrative task from NEPSY.

He had a friend named Pepper. Pepper was a black dog. Pepper. I forgot. Pepper got his shoe. I don't know. Jim was a little boy. Pepper was his friend. Pepper was a black dog, and Pepper rescued his shoe when he brought it to Anna. That's all I know. And then they, then Anna rescued him.

Data set 2

Child with ASD and language impairment: narrative task from NEPSY.

The way he go down and hurt himself. His shoe fell off. And the ladder go down to the ground. The boy took a picture of the girl. And he stopped taking a picture. And he was about to walk to the best thing. He went off to the zoo, and the girl went on with us, too because she went to the zoo. She sold lots of animals, and the boy sells lots of animals, too.

Data set 3

Child with ASD: narrative task *The three little wolves and the big bad pig.*

One day, the big bad pig came prowling down the road. When he saw the house that the three little wolves had built, he said 'Little wolves, little wolves, let me come in, or I'll huff and I'll puff and I'll blow your house down!' So he huffed and he puffed and he puffed and he huffed, but the house would not come down.

Question 1 In data set 2, the child with ASD and language impairment displays significant difficulty retelling the narrative. Give at least one example of each of the following narrative difficulties. Which of these difficulties poses the greatest compromise to this child's narrative?

(a) intrusion of irrelevant information
(b) use of pronouns with no referents
(c) use of definite noun phrases for first mention of characters
(d) lack of proper names for protagonists
(e) limited range of inter-sentential cohesion

Question 2 The narrative of the child with SLI in data set 1 also exhibits significant shortcomings. Using examples, describe <u>five</u> problems with this narrative. What feature(s) of this narrative suggest that cognitive difficulties may contribute to this child's narrative problems?

Question 3 The narrative extract produced by the child in data set 3 is easier to follow than the narratives in data sets 1 and 2. List <u>three</u> features of this narrative which help the reader to follow it.

Question 4 Give <u>one</u> feature of (a) the narrative retelling task, (b) the retold narrative and (c) the narrator which might account for the superior quality of the narrative extract presented in data set 3.

Question 5 Unlike the narrators in data sets 1 and 2, the narrator in data set 3 includes a type of language use which is likely to increase reader engagement in the unfolding narrative. State what this type of language use is and give an example of it.

2.9   Autism spectrum disorder 5

Background

Mary is a 28-year-old woman with autism who was studied by Dobbinson et al. (1998). She is a resident in a community in Yorkshire, England for people who have autism. Mary's caretakers describe her as being a talkative individual. However, much of her talk involves lengthy monologues on her favourite topics. Two of these topics are the British royal family and the dates of birthdays of her acquaintances. Mary has a full-scale IQ of 66, with her verbal score (70) slightly higher than her performance score (65).

The conversational exchanges between Mary and a researcher which are presented below (and in the next data analysis exercise) were recorded in the residential centre where Mary had been living for eight years. Sessions were audio-recorded with some also video-recorded. Conversations were transcribed on the basis of the notation shown below. Examine these conversational exchanges and then answer the questions which follow.

Transcription notation

<u>kind</u>	emphasis
ca::ke	prolongation of sounds
da-	cut off sounds
(1.3)	timed pause (in seconds)
(.)	micropause
[]	overlapped speech
=	no interval between speakers
?	rising intonation
.	falling intonation
↑up↑	marked rising tone
↓down↓	marked falling tone
YES	loud volume
°yes°	softness
hhh	out breath
.hhh	in breath
(hhh)	laughter or crying

Data set 1

Conversation opens with Mary (M) and the researcher (R) discussing Mary's participation in the Mini Olympics.

```
 1   R:  what happens at ↑tho::se↑ then.
 2        what will happen at them? (.)
 3   M:  we- well (.) you choose the:: errr (3.66)
 4        you choose the:: errr (.) the event that you want to go in (1.87)
 5        the eve- it depe- pending on what you're good enough (.)
 6        but I want t- to learn how .hhh to get better at badminton so I can play with Amy (.)
 7   R:  ↑aaa::h↑ does Amy play badminton. =
 8   M:  = yes she does (1.23)
 9   R:  is she good at it. (.)
10   M:  .hh yes but I've got to get a lot a got to (.) get a lot better (.) a lot better .hhh
11        and last night they went to the er speak up advocacy group .hhh
12        and err (3.28) we signed (.) a birthday card f for Amy from the speak up .hhh
13        advocacy speak up grou::p. .hh and e- (.) and e- (.) Amy was (2.9) cutting her cake
14        cutting her birthday cake .hh and we sang (.) and we all sang happy birthday to
15        Amy (.)
```

16 R: ↑o:::h↑ that's lovely. (.)
17   how ↑old↑ was she. (.)
18 M: she was twenty ni:ne. (.)
19   she'll be thirty next year (.)
20 R: she wi::ll. (.)
21   is she ↑old↑er than you. (.)
22 M: yes she is (.)
23 R: how [old are] you.
24 M: [two year]
25   two years old (.) she's two years older than me (.)
26   I'm twenty six (.)
27   I'll be twenty seven in er (.) September.
28 R: aa:::h ri::ght (1.12)
29   so- (.) you had a ↑birthday↑ party then. (1.26)
30 M: .hh we sa- (.) we sang (.) Amy took her birthday cake to the sp- (.) advocacy speak up
31   group for everybody to have. (1.24)
32 R: w- who made her ↑birthday↑ cake for her.

Data set 2

Mary and the researcher are continuing their conversation from above.

1   M: errrr (.) Juliette went down to the (1.05) cake shop to order it for her
2   and Patty (.) brought it up to the erm (.) the day center for her. (1.69)
3   R: that's lovely
4   that was kind of them. wasn't it. (.)
5   M: yes (.)
6   R: and was it a sur↑prise↑. (.)
7   M: it was a surprise yes .hhhh
8   it was a (.) it was a very nice birthday ca:ke. (.)
9   R: what was it li:ke. (1.27)
10 M: I had a look at it (.) and it was pink and it was very nice (.)
11   and Gloria (1.19) wh gl- gl- Gloria came down .hhhh to the day centre she says to me
12   what's that (.)
13   she says to Amy wh- what's that is that- is that a- (1.01) is that a cake
14   or- (.) is that a pi- (.) is
15   that (.) cake or piece of or or is it a rabbit. (1.03)
16 R: (hhhhhhhhh) .hhh
17   why was it- why did she say that. (.)
18 M: just a joke. (.)
19 R: why- (.) what was (.) why =
20 M: = when I was walking up with Katy Post. (2.09)
21 R: aa:::h right
22   why did she make a joke like that
23   why [was that]
24 M: [she was just] saying it (1.72)
25 R: what did the cake look like. (.)
26 M: it looked very ni::ce. (1.10)
27 R: wh- what shape was it. (1.13)
28 M: it's like a hea:rt shape. (.) but she still got some left for toni::ght. (.)
29 R: ↑aa↑:::::h. (1.37)

30   what [color]
31 M: [en we-] en we had that (.)
32   its pink (.)
33   en we had that errr- (.) chocolate gateau for- (1.08) that we we
34   bought with Kirsty (1.07) .hhh
35   l- (.) last ni::ght (.) with Katy Post that we bought with Kirsty Barker
36   the day .hh from the
37   Lo-Cost. (.) the errr the night before .hhh for Amy's birthday. (1.39)
38   that we had it after tea last ni::ght (.)
39 R: chocolate ↑gat↑eau. (.)
40 M: ye:s (.)
41 R: was it ni::ce.

Data set 3

Mary is discussing the topic of housework.

M: .hh I'd made ss- (1.64) ev yesterday::y (.) I made some errrr (4.71) apple (.) fr- fruit crumble with
    er- Anita (.) then err (.) Matt Lewis hoovered the the the landing downstairs .hhh I hoovered
    the hallway (1.26) downstairs (.) I hoovered the stairs and hoovered the landing upstairs. .hhh
    and then errr (.) then I hoovered (.) the the lounge room and I dusted and polished (.) the
    lounge room. (.) then I hoovered th (.) the dining room then er (.) then helped Anita Sales to err
    (.) to mow the back (.) back lawn with a lawnmower (.) at Bankfield yesterda::y (1.27)

Question 1 In data set 1, several topics feature in the exchange between Mary and the researcher. The conversation begins with a discussion of the Mini Olympics, moves onto Amy playing badminton, then addresses Amy's birthday, then moves to Amy's and Mary's respective ages before returning to the topic of Amy's birthday. How are these topics introduced and managed by Mary and the researcher?

Question 2 In lines 21 to 27 of data set 1, Mary displays considerable skill in her handling of the researcher's questions. What conversational knowledge on Mary's part does this sequence reveal and what cognitive skill makes this sequence possible?

Question 3 In lines 17 to 24 of data set 2, Mary displays considerable difficulty explaining Gloria's remark about Amy's birthday cake to the researcher. How can Mary's difficulty be accounted for in terms of the cognitive deficits of autism?

Question 4 In data set 2, Mary is able to contribute to the topic of the birthday cake at the outset of the exchange. However, between lines 17 and 32 there is a noticeable decrease in Mary's ability to contribute to the topic. How is this manifested by Mary and how does the researcher maintain the conversational exchange in the face of it?

Question 5 In data set 3, Mary is discussing the topic of housework. How does she manage to maintain this topic over a single, extended turn?

2.9   Autism spectrum disorder 6

Background

The data sets presented below were also collected from the 28-year-old woman with autism who was studied by Dobbinson et al. (1998) and discussed in the last exercise. They are intended to demonstrate additional strengths and weaknesses on Mary's part in managing conversational exchanges. Examine each data set in detail and then answer the questions below.

Data set 1

Exchange A

```
1  M:  it's like a hea:rt shape. (.) but she still got some left for toni::ght. (.)
2  R:  ↑aa↑:::::h. (1.37)
3      what [colour]
4  M:       [en we-] en we had that (.)
```

Exchange B

```
1  R:  ↑mmm↑hm. (2.09)
2      why –why do you fee::l like you don't want to go ↑swim↑ming sometimes. (.)
3  M:  I just ↑do↑ someti:mes (.)
4  R:  don't you want to get wet. (2.97)
5      does it- does it not [feel]
6  M:                       [because] I want to do the same things as what
7      Matt Lewis and Peter Smith do. (.)
```

Exchange C

```
1  R:  ↑aa↑ah::. (.)
2      is that (.) one of those pools that's got (.) slides [and] things.
3  M:                                                        [yes] (.)
4      slides and things (.)
```

Exchange D

```
1  R:  but Ella and Haley didn't. (.)
2  M:  no she just saw Elly and she (.) [told (1.00) told] Ella (.)
3  R:                                   [oh she told Ella]
4      yeah (1.34)
5      that's ↑bril↑liant
```

Data set 2

Exchange A

```
1  R:  ↑ye↑a::h. (2.45)
2      what does everybody else do at the swimming pool (.)
3      do they a:ll =
```

4 M: = just have a swim abo- (.) bou::t (.)
5   Elly Grey (2.15) guess what (.) Elly Grey came came back to Bankfield once. and she told
6   (1.14) whoever was on that she she'd done (1.05) <u>thirty</u> lengths (.) across the swimming
7   pool

Exchange B

1 M: and I'm thinking of training for badminton as well, and table-tennis. (1.5)
2 R: whi- which (.) of <u>tho:se</u> do you like =
3 M: = I'm getting a progressing at badminton. an (.) s-so I can play with Elly Elly <u>Grey</u> .hhh in
4   the errr (.) mini- mini <u>lym</u>pics. (.)

Exchange C

1 M: I liked (.) dressage doing the dress- I did the <u>dressage</u> last time .hhh and I came <u>third</u>
2   with the bronze medal. (.) and Donald H[owe (.)] came er (1.05) ca- came <u>first</u> with a
3   <u>gold</u> cup
4 R: [wow]
5 M: gold cup .hhh cos <u>Donald's</u> dad (.) <u>Donald Howe's</u> dad came to (.) watch Donald Donald
6   Howe (1.00) <u>ride</u> in the dressage. (1.05) and err (.) m- my mum and dad came to watch
7   <u>me</u> (.) r- ride in the dressage .hh and they thought I was very <u>good</u> (.)
8 R: I bet that was =
9 M: = I got an awkward horse called <u>Lo::fty</u> (.) who wouldn't trot (.) so I had to have a .hh
10   have a <u>stick</u> to make it trot (.) and I came thi:rd (.)

Data set 3

Mary is responding to questions in the information subtest of the Wechsler Adult Intelligence Scale–Revised (WAIS–R; Wechsler, 1981).

1   R: ↑right↑ (.) shall we start (.) with some <u>questions</u> then
2   M: yes
3   R: ok. (.) what are the <u>colors</u> of the British flag.
4   (4.4) do you know [what they are]
5   M: ∗   [red blue] and whi::te
6   R: tha::ts ri::ght (.) very good
7   (4.5) what is the shape of a <u>ba::ll.</u>
8   M: (1.3) a <u>round</u> shape.
9   R: °tha::t's ri:ght (2.8) very good° (2.7) how many <u>months</u> are there in a year.
10 M: (0.9) there are twelve months in a year
11 R: (2.3) I've got to write down what you say y'see. (3.6) a:::n ↑what's↑ a <u>thermo</u>meter.
12 M: (2.1) dunno
13 R: (1.9) °↑okay↑° (1.6) how many <u>weeks</u> are there in a year.
14 M: (3.5) are there one undred and eighty.
15 R: (4.1) °↑okay↑° (2.3) let's put this up so I've got (.) some more <u>roo::m</u> (1.4) °no::w°
16   (1.7) can you <u>na:me</u> a prime minister of <u>great</u> Britain during the second world war.
17 M: (7.0) was it John Astley.
18 R: (3.4) °that's a good answer° (2.4) right (0.7) okay (.) who wrote <u>Hamlet.</u>
19 M: (2.8) I don't know
20 R: °ri::ght° (2.1) a:::nd (.) <u>what's</u> the capital of Italy.

21 M: (2.1) ROME
22 R: <u>very</u> good. (3.1) °excellent° (1.5) .h.h.h do you know who was L-<u>Louis</u> A::rmstrong.
23 M: (1.1) he was a singer
24 R: (1.9) <u>very</u> good. (.) °excellent° (1.6) errr d'you know who was Amy <u>John</u>son.
25 M: (1.0) no
26 R: (4.4) <u>where</u> does the sun rise.
27 M: (1.0) in the morning

Question 1 Most conversational overlaps arise because an interlocutor wishes to take over the turn of the current speaker. Does that appear to be the reason for the overlaps that occur in data set 1? Support your answer with evidence from this data set.

Question 2 The exchanges in data set 2 contain a number of latched utterances indicated by '='. Describe <u>three</u> features of these latched utterances.

Question 3 The latched utterances in data set 2 are similar to certain of the overlaps in data set 1. What is that similarity?

Question 4 Mary makes extensive use of pauses in her verbal output. Describe the types of pauses which occur in data sets 1 and 2. What function or purpose is served by these pauses? Alternatively, what difficulty is revealed by them?

Question 5 Pauses are also evident in Mary's verbal output in data set 3. However, their function in this data set differs from that in sets 1 and 2. Describe the function of pauses in data set 3.

2.10 Childhood traumatic brain injury 1

Background

Narrative production can be particularly challenging for children who sustain a traumatic brain injury (TBI). Often, narrative difficulties are related to cognitive deficits in this clinical population. Biddle et al. (1996) examined narrative production in ten children with TBI (age range = 7;4 to 16;2 years) and ten children with no history of head injury (age range = 7;1 to 16;2 years). These children were matched on the basis of age, gender, ethnicity, educational level and US geographical region. None of the children with TBI had a premorbid history of learning or emotional difficulties. Time post-injury ranged from 22 to 46 months. An assessment of TBI severity was available for nine of the ten children, with seven classified as having a mild to moderate injury and two a severe TBI. Only one child had any obvious physical disability. Five children received resource room support services, and three of these children also received speech–language services. All children in the comparison group were of average intellectual ability and none received special educational services.

Narratives were collected in the children's homes. The interviewer first related a personal experience and then asked the child if he or she had had a similar experience. Four narrative prompts were administered to each child: a pet does something funny; a trip to an amusement park; getting lost; and being stung by a bee. The narratives of two children (one with and one without TBI) on the last of these themes are presented below. Examine these narratives in detail and then answer the following questions.

Data set 1

Girl aged 7;4 years with traumatic brain injury.

Ummm, I, once, there was a, we went. There was a for. There was this umm fort. A tree fell down. And there was dirt, all kinds of stuff there. It was our fort. And one day, I have a friend named Jude. She's umm grown up. She has a kid. She has a cat named Gus, a kitten. It's so cute. But once, when she didn't have that kitten, one day, me, my brother, my cousin Matt, and her, and my dad, and one of his friends, went into the woods to see the fort, to show her. And we went up there. I stepped on a bee's nest. And they chased us all the way back. And I got stung and my cousin Matt got stung in one of the private parts. And umm I had a bite right here (points), right here (points), right there (points), and umm one on my cheek. And right here. And when I umm went over, when we got back to my friend Jude's house, in her bathroom she had this clean kind of stuff. And I put it on me. She put it on me right here (points). But umm, I had to go to the bathroom to put it on, you know. It hurt! And my brother Jason he got stung once. He got stung I think three right here (points). I remember where I got stung, but I don't remember where Jason got stung. My friend Jude didn't even get stung. She ran so fast that she didn't even get stung. The bees chased us and I looked back. And there was one right in front of my face. That's when I got stung here (points). There was like two hanging around my legs. I was running and trying to get them off me. They both went, 'Bzzzzz.' It hurt! I was crying my head off.

Data set 2

Girl aged 7;1 years with no neurological injury.

I got stung on the same place twice. One time I was running home because I was playing with my neighbour. Her name is Holly. I was in my bare feet. And I got my foot stung. The next time, I got my toe stung. We had like cement steps that were going up to where we park. There was a bee hive. I was stepping on a step. And it stung me again.

Question 1 Give one example of each of the following discourse problems in the narrative of the child with TBI:

(a) multiple restarts of an utterance
(b) use of incongruent temporal expression
(c) use of pronoun instead of proper noun
(d) provision of misleading or contradictory information
(e) use of repetitive language

Question 2 The narrative in data set 1 is inefficient in comparison to the narrative in data set 2. Describe three features of the former narrative which contribute to this impression of inefficiency. Use examples from this narrative to support your answer.

Question 3 Which of the following cognitive impairments might explain the discourse difficulties of the child with TBI in data set 1?

(a) memory deficits
(b) theory of mind deficits
(c) planning deficits
(d) slowed information processing
(e) impaired reasoning

Question 4 The type of inter-sentential cohesion used by the child with TBI in data set 1 is quite basic in nature. Identify the type of inter-sentential cohesion used by this child. What complex conceptual relations which would facilitate this child's narrative are not expressed by this type of inter-sentential cohesion?

Question 5 Is there any evidence that lexical retrieval problems may be contributing to the discourse difficulties of the child with TBI? Support your answer with evidence from data set 1.

2.10   Childhood traumatic brain injury 2

Background

The ability of children with mild or severe traumatic brain injury (TBI) to summarise narratives was examined by Chapman et al. (2006). These investigators examined 38 children with TBI, 25 of whom had a mild injury and 13 had a severe injury. Children were admitted to the study if they suffered a TBI requiring hospitalisation at least two years prior to assessment, if their injury resulted from a non-penetrating head trauma, if there was documentation that their head injury was mild (Glasgow Coma Scale ≥ 13 upon hospital admittance) or severe (Glasgow Coma Scale ≤ 8 upon hospital admittance), if they were aged 8 to 14 years at the time of assessment, and if English was the primary language of at least one of the child's caregivers. Children were excluded from the study if there was a prior history of neurological or psychiatric disorder, if there was grade failure or a previous diagnosis of intellectual disability, if there was evidence of child abuse or if there had been a previous head injury resulting in hospitalisation. A group of 24 typically developing children of similar age was also included in the study.

Procedure

Children received guidance in how to produce a narrative summary using the synopsis on the back of a popular children's video. They were then instructed to listen carefully to a 578-word didactic narrative about a man's life. After hearing the narrative, they were asked to provide a shortened version of the story in their own words. Children were also asked questions regarding the explicit and implicit (i.e. inferential) content of the narrative discourse. Measures of immediate and working memory performance were also undertaken.

   The narrative summaries of three children are presented below. The first summary received the highest ratings for cohesion and coherence and was produced by a typically developing child. The other two summaries were produced by children with TBI. These children exhibited performance within normal limits on the immediate memory and discourse content measures and comparatively decreased performance on working memory measures. Examine all three summaries and then answer the questions below.

Data set 1

Typically developing child.

John Pierpont, I think, was actually really brilliant. I mean, he was able to do many careers. And he started out trying to be a teacher, and he started out trying to be a lawyer, and just going through many different jobs, and then going into politics and going into being a minister and then finally just being a file clerk. And so, very broad span of jobs that he held. But still, he saw himself as a failure because he wasn't able to succeed in any of these. And the way that success appears at that time is, you know, being the best lawyer and bringing in the most money. He wasn't able to do that because of his care for humankind. But in the end of the story, you find this legacy that he's left that lasts so much longer than just the money he would have brought into his office. He showed the world, you know, and just that, having a kind heart and just so many things were reformed because of the way he did them, like education, and slavery was abolished, and major differences like that. And it was all due to him. And maybe his success wasn't short-lived, but rather yet long, long-lived and was so much deeper and able to survive so much longer than just money is. And even his song, Jingle Bells, is sung like around the world, and, to remember him. And I think his legacy still lives on.

Data set 2

Child with mild traumatic brain injury.

It's about, um, this guy who would try to do, he tried to, to succeed at work, but he couldn't. So he tried a lot of different stuff until he was seventy. And then this person, thing, something, found him and sent him to this place where he could find a job, and he, he did that for the last five years of his life, and then he passed away. That's so sad.

Data set 3

Child with severe traumatic brain injury.

John was a failure at everything mostly that he did because he would always, like, in math, um, give, treat the students like easily and make their homework really easy and like make them get good grades when they really shouldn't have gotten that, and the stuff was too easy. And like when he was, um, selling things, he'd sell the things way too low. But the things that he could, he did get in, he quit. And he just quit because he didn't like the things that he got into. And when, when he was older, he um, wrote some poetry and some songs that we still use today.

Question 1 Both children with TBI do not succeed in capturing the abstract or central meaning of the narrative. However, they fail to do so in different ways. Describe the ways in which the abstract meaning of the narrative is not successfully captured by these children.

Question 2 The narrative summary in data set 2 is particularly uninformative. What linguistic feature(s) of this summary contribute to its low informational content?

Question 3 The child with TBI in data set 3 focuses on two jobs of the main character of the story at the same time as he is unable to derive the 'gist' of the narrative. Which of the following cognitive impairments best accounts for this pattern of difficulty?

(a) reduced general intellectual functioning
(b) theory of mind deficits
(c) weak central coherence
(d) planning deficits
(e) slowed information processing

Question 4 Certain features of the narrative summary produced by the typically developing child suggest that this child possesses good theory of mind skills. What are these features, and are they present in the narrative summaries of the children with TBI?

Question 5 The narrative summaries of both children with TBI contain several intact discourse features. Give <u>one</u> example of each of the following features in these summaries:

(a) use of ellipsis
(b) use of pronominal reference
(c) use of inter-sentential cohesion
(d) use of deixis
(e) use of conventional summary statement

2.11 Epileptic syndromes 1

Background

Narrative discourse production in three adolescents (two male, one female) with Sturge–Weber syndrome was examined by Lovett et al. (1986). All three subjects underwent hemispherectomy during infancy for the control of intractable seizures. In two subjects (SM and CA) the left hemisphere was removed. The right hemisphere was removed in the third subject (MW). At the time of the study, MW, SM and CA had a chronological age of 12;09, 12;11 and 13;01 years, respectively. The full-scale IQ of these children was between 90 and 99. All three subjects had been free of seizures during the first five years of life. MW had had a single seizure at 9 years of age.

Procedure

Four narrative texts were used in the study: Little Red Riding Hood, The Frog Prince, The Practical Princess, and Goldilocks. Each text was read to the subjects by the examiner. At the same time, puppets were used to perform the roles of the main protagonists. After hearing each narrative, subjects retold the story to the examiner, using the puppets as and when required. All narratives were audio-recorded.

Data relating to the narratives on Goldilocks and The Practical Princess are discussed in this exercise. Narrative extracts produced by all three children are presented below. The segments of the stories that correspond to these extracts are also displayed. Examine these extracts in detail and then answer the following questions.

Data set 1

Goldilocks

They went into the bedroom. Now Goldilocks had pulled the pillow on Father Bear's bed. He cried out, 'Someone's been sleeping in my bed!' in his big rough voice. And Goldilocks had messed up the sheets in Mother Bear's bed. She said, 'Who's been sleeping in my bed?' And when Baby Bear came to look at his bed, there was a big lump in the bed. He cried out, 'Someone's been sleeping in my bed, and SHE'S STILL THERE!!' Goldilocks woke up suddenly. When she saw the bears she was quite frightened. They said angrily, 'Why do you come into our house and eat our porridge and break our chairs and sleep in our beds?' And they chased Goldilocks out of the house and into the woods. And the three bears never saw anything more of her.

SUBJECT MW: So they went upstairs to see – trying to see who ate the porridge and who sat in their chairs. And Father Bear came up and he said, 'Somebody's been laying in my bed.' And Mother Bear said, 'Look! Somebody's been sleeping in my bed.' And Baby Bear said, 'Look! Somebody's been sleeping in my bed and there's a lump there, too!' So Goldilocks woke up and she saw the three bears and the three bears started accusing her, said, 'Why did you start eating our porridge?' Mother Bear said, 'Why did you start sitting in our chairs?' And Baby Bear said, 'What were you doing in our beds?' And so she was so afraid she ran off and she was never heard of again.

SUBJECT SM: And so they went upstairs and . . . looked in the bedroom. And Father Bear said, 'Someone's been sleeping in my bed.' Mother Bear said, 'Someone's been sleepin' in my bed.' And Baby Bear said, 'Someone's been sleeping in my bed and she's still in it.' And all of a sudden Goldilocks woke up, and she seen the three bears looking at her. And so she was so frightened that she ran downstairs. She ran out of the house and the three bears never seen her again.

SUBJECT CA: And then they went – they went to their beds. And then Father Bear said, 'Who's been sleeping in my bed because my little pillows gone-been-loose?' And Mother Bear says, 'Who's been sleeping in my bed?' because the sheets were all crimpled-like. And then Baby Bear said, 'Who's been sleeping in my bed because she's still here!' And then Gol- then they went to Baby Bear's bed and then they saw Goldilocks. And then Goldilocks woke up and she was surpri- she was astoniged then she ran out the door. They never saw her again.

Data set 2

The Practical Princess

Sadly, King Ludwig called together his councillors and read them the message. 'Perhaps,' said the Prime Minister, 'we had better advertise for a knight to slay the dragon. That is what is generally done in these cases.' 'I'm afraid we haven't time,' answered the King. 'The dragon has only given us until tomorrow morning. There is no help for it. We shall have to send him the princess.' Princess Bedelia had come to the meeting because, as she said, she liked to mind her own business and this was certainly her business. 'Rubbish!' she said, 'Dragons can't tell the difference between princesses and anyone else. Use your common sense. He's just asking for me because he's a snob.' 'That may be so,' said her father, 'but if we don't send you along, he'll destroy the kingdom.' Bedelia said, 'I see I'll have to deal with this myself!'

SUBJECT MW: So the King got together his councillors and he tried . . . to decide wh-what to do. And he said, 'Well, I guess we'll have to give her to the dragon.' And the Princess overheard the meeting and she said 'Rubbish! I'll not have myself given to the dragon.' And so then she said 'Well, I'll nev- why don't you get a knight to slay the dragon?' And she- and he said- the King said, 'There's no time for that in the message he said there was only till tomorrow morning to give you to him.'

SUBJECT SM: One day the King- um- called his councillors for a meeting . . . (oh-uh) . . . yeah . . . So one day the King . . . he called a meeting and . . . he told his Prime Minister that- um- him- he told the Prime Minister the bad news. And um . . . and the Princess- oh- was at the meeting and so they tried to think of something to . . . uh . . . from the- tried to think of something for the Princess.

SUBJECT CA: And then she said- the wolves- I mean the frog- the King said, 'We would have hold the council-s council meeting.' And then they decided that they would have to do it because they only had twenty-four hours. So the Princess was there too because it went- she had to mind her own business and boy! was that it was her own business.

Question 1 Subject MW exhibits intact and impaired discourse skills. Using examples from the above data sets, indicate three intact discourse skills and three impaired discourse skills in this subject.

Question 2 Subject CA exhibits a number of narrative discourse problems. Give one example of each of the following difficulties:

(a) incorrect attribution of mental states to characters
(b) poor temporal ordering of information
(c) intrusion of information from other narratives
(d) lack of pronominal reference
(e) poor comprehension of semantic meaning of conjunctions

Question 3 Notwithstanding CA's discourse difficulties, she is able to represent causal relationships in her narratives which are omitted in the narratives produced by MW. Give two examples of these relationships in the data.

Question 4 SM's second narrative is particularly uninformative. What feature of this narrative is responsible for its uninformative nature?

Question 5 In the original Goldilocks narrative, dramatic tension is created through the use of increased volume on the part of the narrator, the use of adverbs such as 'suddenly' and 'angrily' and the use of menacing language such as 'big rough voice'. Do any of the adolescent subjects in this study succeed in recreating this dramatic tension through the use of these or other linguistic devices?

2.11 Epileptic syndromes 2

Background

This exercise examines further the narrative discourse produced by three adolescents who were studied by Lovett et al. (1986). These subjects had Sturge–Weber syndrome. Each underwent a hemispherectomy in infancy for the treatment of intractable seizures. Further details of these subjects can be found in the preceding exercise. That exercise also describes how the narratives of these adolescents were elicited and recorded. Two narratives – Goldilocks and The Practical Princess – were analysed in this earlier exercise. Here, extracts from two further narratives – Little Red Riding Hood and The Frog Prince – are presented for analysis, alongside the corresponding segment of narrative that was read to the subjects. Examine the extracts of narrative produced by each of these adolescents and then answer the questions below.

Data set 1

Little Red Riding Hood

The wolf got there first. He knocked at the door. 'Who's there?' said Grandmother. 'Little Red Riding Hood,' said the wolf. 'Oh, come in,' said Grandmother. And the wolf came in, locked Grandmother in a cupboard and put on all her clothes. Then Little Red Riding Hood came to the house and knocked on the door. 'Who's there?' said the wolf. Little Red Riding Hood thought her grandmother sounded funny and she wondered if she had a cold. 'It's Little Red Riding Hood,' she said. 'Come in,' said the wolf.

SUBJECT MW: And the wolf, he took a shortcut to Gran- to Grandmother's house and he took-
  so he sai- he knocked on the door and Grandmother said, 'Who is it?' And the wolf said,
  'Little Red Riding Hood.' And Grandmother said, 'Oh, come in.' So she came in- so he came
  in, and he grabbed Grandmother and he locked her in the closet! And he got dressed into
  Grandmother's clothes and he even put her cap on. Then- he lied into- in her bed. And then
  there came a rap on the door and it was Little Red Riding Hood. And the w- the wolf said in a
  rather weird voice, 'Who is it?' 'Little Red Riding Hood,' she said. 'Oh, come in.'

SUBJECT SM: And . . . so the wolf got to the um- Grandmother's house first, and he, the wolf
  knocked on the door and . . . Grandmother said, 'Who's there?' And the wolf- the wolf said,
  'It's Little Red Riding Hood.' And Grandmother said, 'Come in.' And so the wolf- um- came
  in and he gobbled Grandmother up. And so- um- the wolf put on Grandmother's clothes
  on . . . the wolf- um- locked Grandmother in the closet and he put on Grandmother's clothes.
  And later on, Little Red Riding Hood knocked on the door and the wolf answered, 'Who's
  there?' And Little Red Riding Hood said, 'It . . . it's Little Red Riding Hood.' And the wolf
  said, 'Come in.' And so Little Red Riding Hood came in.

SUBJECT CA: And then when the wolf got there she knocked on the door and- um- the
  Grandmother came and she answered the door and she said, 'Um- hello-' No- he said, 'Who's
  there?' And the wolf said, 'Little Red Riding Hood.' So she opened the door. Then- uh- the
  wolf grabbed her and he locked her up into the closet. And then she put on all her clothes and
  everything like that. And then later on Little Red Riding Hood came to the door and then she
  knocked on the door. And then the wolf said, 'Who is it?' And the Little Red Riding Hood
  said, 'It's Little Red Riding Hood.' So she came in. So when she- when she came in.

Data set 2

The Frog Prince

So the frog ate dinner with the princess. After they had eaten, the frog said, 'Carry me upstairs and put me on your bed.' And the princess did what he asked, even though she still thought he was a wet and nasty frog. She secretly hoped that he would be gone when she woke up.

SUBJECT MW: And he started eating off the plate with her. And after dinner, he said, 'Wi you-
  will you please carry me up to your bed?' So she- she did. She laid him on the bed, hoping
  that by the morning he would be gone.

Subject SM: But she kept her promise and she told the frog to come in and eat dinner with her and sleep in her her bed. And that night the princess hoped that the frog wouldn't be in her bed the next morning.

Subject CA: So the- then the princess remembered the promise that what she made to him. So they brought into the house and they started to eat. And- and then after that he was tired. So the princess took the frog up to her room and then- um- they went to sleep. And then the next day- and then she thought the frog would be gone the next day.

Question 1 The discourse difficulties of these adolescents are not caused for the most part by structural language impairments. However, structural language deficits are still present in the narratives of these subjects. Give <u>one</u> example of each of the following problems in the data sets:

(a) omission of direct object noun or pronoun
(b) incorrect past tense verb form
(c) word-finding difficulty
(d) problematic relative clause
(e) omission of clause

Question 2 Subject CA displays a number of difficulties in the use of pronominal reference. Describe these difficulties using evidence from the data sets to support your answer.

Question 3 Subject MW also commits an error of pronominal reference. However, this error is at least explicable. State what this error is and suggest why it occurs.

Question 4 In retelling the Little Red Riding Hood story, two subjects report events that did not take place in this fictional narrative. Identify the subjects in question and describe how they fail to report events accurately. Also, these inaccurately reported events create further difficulties in these subjects' narratives. Characterise what those difficulties are.

Question 5 There is also evidence of considerable discourse competence in the narratives of these children. Give <u>one</u> example of each of the following narrative discourse skills in these data sets:

(a) use of ellipsis
(b) attribution of mental states to protagonists
(c) use of inter-sentential cohesion
(d) indirect reported speech
(e) temporal deixis

2.11   Epileptic syndromes 3

Background

Significant language and cognitive problems have been reported in individuals with childhood-onset temporal lobe epilepsy. Brockway et al. (1998) examined the language skills and memory performance of 19 patients who underwent anterior temporal lobectomy for the treatment of intractable temporal lobe epilepsy. The average age of subjects was 32.37 years. The mean age of onset of seizures was 6.2 years (range 0.5–22 years) and the median age was 4 years. All but two patients were left-hemisphere dominant for language and memory. The memory performance of these subjects was worse than that of normal controls on 16 of 23 memory tests. The most significant area of difficulty for these subjects was in remembering and generating inferences from connected discourse.

Procedure

In one of the memory tests, short paragraphs were (simultaneously) aurally and visually presented to subjects using a computer. After a period of 35 minutes, during which other tasks were undertaken, subjects were asked five questions about each story. Subjects' answers were recorded verbatim and were scored for the presence or absence of a range of inference types. One of the paragraphs presented to subjects is shown below, along with the five questions relating to it. Also shown are eight responses of subjects to these questions. Examine these responses and test stimuli and then answer the questions that follow.

Paragraph

Judy saw flashing lights behind her. After she pulled over, a uniformed man approached her vehicle. He asked her a few questions, then took something from her. When he returned, she was wiping her eyes. He started to speak to her.

Questions

(1) What happened to Judy?
(2) How did Judy feel?
(3) What did the man take from her?
(4) Why did Judy pull over?
(5) What will Judy do now?

Data set

Verbatim responses of subjects to five questions.

(1) Judy has been pulled over by the police.
(2) Judy was caught speeding.
(3) Judy was driving a car or truck or van.
(4) Judy was going too fast.
(5) Judy is embarrassed.
(6) The policeman altered Judy's self-respect and dignity.
(7) Judy pulled over because it is a law.
(8) Judy will go to a magistrate or to jail.

Question 1 One of the five questions posed to subjects was intended to establish if they had drawn an inference about the main character's affective state. Which question is this? Do any of the responses in the data set suggest that subjects were able to establish Judy's affective state? Based on these responses, which cognitive capacity appears to be intact in these subjects with epilepsy?

Question 2 One of the questions is testing the subjects' ability to derive an inference about the gist of the story. Which question is this? Which responses suggest that at least some of the subjects in the study were able to derive a gist-based inference? Which of the following cognitive skills is intact in a subject who can establish the gist of a story?

(a) theory of mind
(b) general intellectual functioning
(c) verbal reasoning
(d) central coherence
(e) spatial reasoning

Question 3 In three responses in the data set, there is evidence that subjects have drawn an inference which is an instantiation of a more general category. Identify the responses in question and explain the instantiations evidenced by these responses. Which of the following types of knowledge are integral to these instantiations?

(a) syntactic knowledge
(b) world knowledge
(c) phonological knowledge
(d) semantic knowledge
(e) morphological knowledge

Question 4 One of the responses in the data set is a reasonable inference about future events for a subject to draw. Which response is it? What type of knowledge shown in (a) to (e) of question 3 is integral to this predictive inference?

Question 5 One of the responses in the data set describes a presupposition of the events related in the passage. Which response is it? Also, a specific linguistic construction used in the passage triggers a presupposition. What is the linguistic construction and what presupposition does it trigger?

2.12 Childhood cancer

Background

Children who receive radiotherapy for the treatment of brain tumours can experience significant cognitive and language problems, often many years after treatment has been completed. This is caused by radiation-related structural brain changes such as necrosis, calcification and atrophy. Pragmatic and discourse skills are also disrupted by these radiation-related changes and may be impaired alongside deficits in structural aspects of language. Murdoch and Chenery (1990) describe the case of a 39-year-old, right-handed woman who underwent intracranial surgery at 16 years of age for the removal of a posterior fossa tumour. Following surgery, a course of radiotherapy was undertaken. This involved the administration of 6000 rads of radiation to the tumour site. Examine this case in detail and then answer the questions that follow.

Recent history

Twenty years after treatment, this woman's family noted deterioration in the intelligibility of her speech which until that time had been normal. Specifically, her speech displayed an increasing degree of hypernasality which was not successfully treated by the use of a palatal lift. Three years after the onset of her speech disorder, the woman was referred to a specialist unit at the University of Queensland for further investigation of her speech problems.

Neurological examination

A neurological examination was conducted two months prior to the woman's referral to the unit. It revealed malfunctioning of the Xth (vagus) cranial nerve bilaterally, and deep tendon reflexes were mildly hyperactive on the right. There was no hemiplegia, hemisensory loss, Babinski sign or visual field defect.

Neuroradiological examination

A CT scan was undertaken prior to the woman's referral to the unit. It revealed the presence of central focal calcification at the pontomesencephalic junction and scattered throughout the medulla oblongata and pons. The anterior limb of the left internal capsule and both thalami were additional foci of calcification. The scan also revealed dilation of both lateral ventricles and the third ventricle.

Speech evaluation

The woman presented with a flaccid dysarthria which was associated with pharyngolaryngeal palsy. During phonation, there was no evidence of elevation of the soft palate with the result that speech exhibited a high degree of hypernasality and nasal emission. The woman also displayed a reduced ability to regulate the volume and pitch of speech.

Language evaluation

An evaluation of the woman's language revealed a severe impairment of word fluency and sentence construction. Visual naming was mildly impaired. There were mild difficulties observed in the auditory comprehension of long and complex sentences. Repetition abilities were remarkably well preserved. Naming errors, mostly semantic paraphasias, were evident. Two naming errors appeared to be related to a visual–perceptual disorder. The woman's naming ability improved with the use of phonemic cues. The absence of phonemic paraphasias combined with the relative preservation of repetition suggested that the phonological level of language was intact. The woman did not exhibit an overt aphasia and her language impairment could not be classified according to a classical aphasia syndrome. An analysis of connected speech revealed reduced efficiency of information transfer as well as a reduction in the amount of information transferred.

Neuropsychological evaluation

The woman exhibited difficulty in learning and utilising novel visual and verbal stimuli or information. She had difficulty abstracting general from specific information in order to obtain the wider meaning of language, pictorial material and cause–effect relationships. Her interpretation of language was literal, and she showed little regard for the wider semantic aspects of language. Her performance and verbal IQ were both in the low average range. Long-term memory and immediate memory were intact. She undertook a figure copy in a relatively unsystematic fashion. There were no obvious difficulties with angles, orientation or neglect, suggesting that parietal lobe function was intact. The woman's recall of a figure revealed a profound retention deficit for complex material.

Question 1 Based on the above evaluations, which of the following statements are likely to be true claims about this woman's management of information during narrative production?

(a) The woman is likely to produce under-informative narratives.
(b) The woman is likely to produce narratives that meet the informational needs of the hearer.
(c) The woman is likely to produce over-informative narratives.
(d) The woman is likely to produce egocentric narratives.
(e) The woman is likely to produce narratives that contain anecdotal information.

Question 2 Is there any evidence to support the claim that this woman would have difficulty establishing the gist of a story? Indicate what that evidence is in your response.

Question 3 We are told that the woman's interpretation of language is literal. Which of the following forms of utterance interpretation are most likely to be compromised in this case?

(a) The interpretation of the utterance 'Jack was hit by a car.'
(b) The interpretation of the utterance 'Mary left the office with a heavy heart.'
(c) The interpretation of the utterance 'The woman who is next to Bill is a neurosurgeon.'
(d) The interpretation of the utterance 'Take the third turn on the left.'
(e) The interpretation of the utterance 'It wasn't long before Bob let the cat out of the bag.'

Question 4 Is there any evidence to support the claim that this woman would have difficulty establishing the causal relationships between events in a story? Indicate what that evidence is in your response.

Question 5 For each of the following linguistic levels, indicate if it is intact or impaired in this woman. Provide a statement in support of each response.

(a) phonetics and phonology
(b) syntax
(c) semantics
(d) pragmatics
(e) discourse

SUGGESTIONS FOR FURTHER READING

Broeders, M., Geurts, H. and Jennekens-Schinkel, A. 2010. 'Pragmatic communication deficits in children with epilepsy', *International Journal of Language & Communication Disorders* **45**:5, 608–16.

Fujiki, M. and Brinton, B. 2009. 'Pragmatics and social communication in child language disorders', in R. G. Schwartz (ed.), *Handbook of child language disorders*, New York and Hove: Psychology Press, 406–23.

Hatton, C. 1998. 'Pragmatic language skills in people with intellectual disabilities: a review', *Journal of Intellectual and Developmental Disability* **23**:1, 79–100.

Murdoch, B. E., Boon, D. L. and Hudson, L. J. 1999. 'Discourse abilities of children treated for neoplastic conditions', in B. E. Murdoch, *Communication disorders in childhood cancer*, London: Whurr, 158–69.

Murdoch, B. E. and Theodoros, D. G. 2001. 'Language disorders following traumatic brain injury in childhood', in B. E. Murdoch and D. G. Theodoros (eds), *Traumatic brain injury: associated speech, language, and swallowing disorders*, San Diego, CA: Singular Thomson Learning, 247–71.

Tager-Flusberg, H. and Caronna, E. 2007. 'Language disorders: autism and other pervasive developmental disorders', *Pediatric Clinics of North America* **54**:3, 469–81.

Chapter 3

Acquired pragmatic and discourse disorders

Pragmatic and discourse skills may be acquired normally during childhood and adolescence only to be disrupted by the onset of disease, injury and illness in adulthood. Many of these events (e.g. traumatic brain injury) are also causes of pragmatic and discourse impairments in children (Cummings, 2014c). Other conditions which give rise to these disorders are more often found in adults (e.g. the dementias). By far the most significant cause of acquired pragmatic and discourse disorders is cerebrovascular accidents (CVAs) or strokes. The brain lesions which are caused by CVAs can have a devastating impact on an individual's language skills in the form of aphasia. As part of a stroke-induced aphasia, pragmatics and discourse may be impaired to the same extent as other aspects of language (e.g. syntax). Alternatively, pragmatics and discourse may be more or less impaired than other language levels. Pragmatic and discourse disorders may be unrelated to structural language deficits in aphasia or may arise in consequence of these deficits (i.e. *primary* versus *secondary* disorder, respectively).

Aphasic language disturbance is most often associated with lesions in the language-dominant left hemisphere of the brain. Pragmatic and discourse disorders are an even more prominent feature of the language disorder which can arise following a CVA in the brain's right hemisphere. Furthermore, right-hemisphere language disorder (RHLD) has a substantial cognitive component. For example, clients with RHLD are frequently reported to have difficulty generating and manipulating a range of inferences during utterance interpretation and the production and comprehension of discourse. These additional cognitive problems are the basis of the term 'cognitive–communication disorder' which has come to be applied of adults with RHLD. There are also substantial cognitive deficits in clients with traumatic brain injury (TBI) and dementia. Many of these deficits are now known to play a significant role in the pragmatic and discourse disorders of these clinical populations. Certainly, cognitive deficits must always be considered by speech and language therapists who assess and treat clients with a cognitive–communication disorder.

Strokes, head injuries and dementias are some of the most common aetiologies of pragmatic and discourse disorders in adults. But they are by no means the only causes of these disorders. Several neurodegenerative conditions including, but not limited to, Parkinson's disease, Huntington's chorea and multiple sclerosis, have implications for pragmatics and discourse, often alongside other language and cognitive skills. Benign and malignant brain tumours, and the therapies which are used to treat these neoplasms, can disrupt the pragmatic and discourse skills of adults. Cerebral infections such as encephalitis and meningitis can cause temporary and permanent disruption of language including pragmatics and discourse. Adult-onset epilepsy poses a risk to language function and must be considered within the aetiology of pragmatic and discourse disorders. The onset of mental illnesses such as schizophrenia can significantly disrupt the pragmatic and discourse skills of affected individuals. (The pragmatic and discourse features of these clinical conditions are examined in detail in chapter 4.) In short, clinicians who assess and treat clients with pragmatic and discourse disorders must consider an extensive range of organic conditions within the aetiology of these disorders.

The assessment and treatment of pragmatic and discourse disorders in adults make use of many of the same techniques and approaches which were examined in chapter 2. However, the management of adult clients also involves a number of distinct considerations which are less relevant or not relevant at all to child clients. The goals of pragmatic language intervention in adults may include gains in vocational functioning or an increase in one's ability to live independently, neither of which is a consideration in the management of children with pragmatic and discourse disorders. Also, adult clients with progressive conditions such as dementia or motor neurone disease will not experience recovery or stabilisation of language function. The aim of assessment and intervention in these clients may be to maximise remaining pragmatic and discourse skills or to use these skills in compensation of other impaired aspects of language. Finally, pragmatic and discourse skills are the very essence of the forms of communication – conversation, storytelling, etc. – which help us achieve social integration with others and psychological adjustment to disability and illness. These skills are, therefore, a priority for intervention in adults who, unlike children, need to re-establish a sense of community involvement and control over life events following injury and illness.

With so many acquired pragmatic and discourse disorders under the influence of cognitive factors, the assessment and treatment of adult clients must be particularly attentive to the cognitive status of these clients. Often, cognitive skills such as executive functions are thoroughly examined as part of a separate, neuropsychological assessment of clients. An assessment of this type in clients with traumatic brain injury, for example, is typically undertaken by neuropsychologists within the rehabilitation team. However, it is the responsibility of the speech and language therapist to interpret the significance of findings such as poor organisation strategies and impaired cognitive set shifting and maintenance for the client's ability to use and interpret language. The effective assessment and remediation of cognitive–communication disorders may find the speech and language therapist working in close partnership with psychologists as part of a multidisciplinary team. Similar considerations apply to clients with dementia or conditions such as Huntington's disease where psychiatric disturbances complicate the language picture and may necessitate the involvement of psychiatrists and psychologists.

Finally, the assessment and treatment of adults with pragmatic and discourse disorders force us to confront issues such as the ecological validity of our techniques. It is doubtful that retelling a story to a wordless picture book or describing the Cookie Theft picture from the Boston Diagnostic Aphasia Examination (Goodglass et al., 2001) can tell us much about the pragmatic and discourse skills that adults use in their everyday communication with others. Certainly, the ability to narrate stories from one's personal experience is a key communication skill. However, this type of story narration is likely to differ in significant respects from the narrative discourse which is elicited from adults with aphasia and dementia through the use of child-oriented stimulus materials such as Mayer's frog stories (Mayer, 1969, 1974). The use of more naturalistic forms of assessment places considerable demands on clinicians, as the recording, transcription and analysis of even small amounts of spoken narrative or conversation is very time-consuming and costly. These practical difficulties have certainly limited the widespread use of discourse analysis and conversation analysis in a clinical setting. Some of these difficulties may be success-fully addressed with the development of reliable discourse measures that can be made online.

Section A: Short-answer questions

3.1 Acquired aphasia

(1) Which of the following statements is *not* true of acquired aphasia?
    (a) Acquired aphasia always results from damage to the left hemisphere of the brain.
    (b) Acquired aphasia is most often caused by cerebrovascular accidents.
    (c) Acquired aphasia is most often caused by head trauma.
    (d) Acquired aphasia adversely affects the comprehension and production of language.
    (e) Acquired aphasia only compromises structural language skills.

(2) *True or False*: Pragmatic language impairments may be secondary to structural language deficits in acquired aphasia.

(3) *True or False*: The client with non-fluent aphasia produces many irrelevant utterances in conversation.

(4) During a story retell task, a client with non-fluent aphasia is noted to produce an uninformative narrative. Which of the following linguistic features may account for this client's narrative difficulty?
    (a) The extensive use of non-specific lexemes such as 'thing' and 'stuff'.
    (b) The extensive use of jargonistic language.
    (c) The contribution of many off-topic utterances.
    (d) The extensive use of echolalia.
    (e) The loss of content words such as nouns and verbs from verbal output.

(5) During a language assessment, a client with fluent aphasia responds to the utterance 'The man is fishing next to the bank' by pointing to a picture in which a man is standing beside a bank in the form of a large grey building. Which of the following pragmatic processes would appear to be compromised in this client?
    (a) pronominal reference
    (b) recovery of implicature of utterance
    (c) disambiguation
    (d) determination of illocutionary force of utterance
    (e) quantifier domain restriction

(6) *True or False*: Pragmatic language impairments are more commonly found in clients with fluent aphasia than in clients with non-fluent aphasia.

(7) Fill in the blank spaces in the following paragraph using the words in the box below. There can be little doubt that _____ language impairments contribute in part to the pragmatic and discourse deficits of clients with aphasia. In English, for example, it is conventional to use the construction 'Can you return this book to the library?' when making an indirect _____ of someone. However, the syntactic _____ of the subject pronoun and _____ verb that is required by this construction is likely

to be problematic for the client with non-fluent aphasia whose expressive _____ is severely limited. The reduced grammatical output of such a client may compromise other pragmatic aspects of language. The _____ expressions *I* and *here* in the utterance 'I hope to live here in the future' may also be difficult for the client with non-fluent aphasia to produce, while certain linguistic constructions which serve as _____ triggers – for example, the _____ construction in the utterance 'It was Sally who lost her purse' – may also be compromised by this client's deficit in expressive syntax. It is worth noting that even aphasic clients with reduced sentence structure can still contribute _____ utterances to conversation or during discourse production tasks such as storytelling. This is on account of the retention of content words such as nouns and _____ even as grammatical _____ words are omitted in most utterances.

prepositions	lexical	syntax	wh-movement	request
pragmatic	adjectives	promise	function	
inversion	structural	referential	deictic	cleft
auxiliary	presupposition	implicature	informative	

(8) A client with agrammatic aphasia is completing a series of receptive language tests with a speech and language therapist. The therapist asks the client to point to the picture that corresponds to the utterance 'The cat was chased by the mouse.' The client points to the picture which shows the cat chasing the mouse. On another occasion, the therapist asks the client to point to the picture that corresponds to the utterance 'The man was bitten by the dog.' The client makes the correct picture selection. What aspect of receptive language is problematic for this client? Which of the following types of knowledge is integral to the decoding strategy used by this client?
(a) lexical knowledge
(b) syntactic knowledge
(c) world knowledge
(d) semantic knowledge
(e) phonological knowledge

(9) A client with aphasia is listening to a story about a family picnic. During the narration of the story, the client is told 'Mary unpacked the picnic supplies from the trunk. The beer was warm.' When later asked if the picnic supplies contained beer, the client replies 'no'. Which of the following inferences appears to be problematic for this client?
(a) deductive inference
(b) bridging inference
(c) inductive inference
(d) analogical inference
(e) *modus ponens* inference

(10) Which of the following conversational problems is a feature of acquired aphasia?
(a) domination of conversation with topics relating to special interests
(b) failure to take turns with other conversational participants
(c) difficulty contributing to topic development

(d) frequent use of impolite and offensive utterances

(e) domination of conversation with directive speech acts

3.2 Right-hemisphere language disorder

(1) Which of the following statements is *not* true of right-hemisphere language disorder (RHLD)?

(a) RHLD occurs alongside one of the aphasia syndromes.

(b) RHLD is most often caused by a cerebrovascular accident.

(c) RHLD is associated with cognitive deficits.

(d) RHLD is associated with significant structural language deficits.

(e) RHLD is most often caused by neurodegenerative disease.

(2) Which of the following statements describes a discourse feature of RHLD?

(a) Clients with RHLD use ellipsis inappropriately.

(b) Clients with RHLD often produce egocentric discourse.

(c) Clients with RHLD make extensive use of neologisms.

(d) Clients with RHLD may be verbose in discourse.

(e) Clients with RHLD may be tangential in discourse.

(3) *True* or *False*: Adults with RHLD have a tendency to concrete interpretation of non-literal language.

(4) *True* or *False*: Prosody is intact in adults with RHLD.

(5) Fill in the blank spaces in the following paragraphs using the words in the box below.

The communication impairment in clients with RHLD has been examined in relation to a number of cognitive deficits. These deficits include inferencing difficulties, theory of mind and ――――― impairments, and problems with ――――― processing. Several studies have reported significant problems with inferences in adults with RHLD. These adults have been found to have difficulty drawing inferences based on text and inferences based on general ――――― during the presentation of a short film. Difficulty with the ――――― of inferences in adults with RHLD has been shown to be related to the ――――― of discourse stimuli that require inference revision. Also, the performance of subjects with RHLD during a picture description task has been found to be ――――― strongly related to the inferential complexity than to the visual complexity of pictured stimuli.

As well as difficulty generating and manipulating inferences, adults with RHLD have been found to have ――――― impairments. These adults have difficulty understanding materials that require the attribution of ――――― particularly when this involves second-order belief attributions (e.g. 'Mary believes that Fred thinks that the show has been cancelled'). Moreover, the ability of subjects with RHLD to distinguish lies from ――――― appears to correlate strongly with measures of second-order belief attributions. Executive function deficits have been reported in adults with RHLD, although their relationship to the ――――― performance of these subjects is unclear. A more clearly established relationship appears to exist between pragmatic and ――――― skills in adults with RHLD and visuospatial function. Visuospatial skills, but not executive functions, have been found to correlate to ――――― discourse measures in RHLD.

generation	less	theory of mind	world knowledge
semantic	visuospatial	more	felicitous utterances
executive function	expository	comprehension	pragmatic
suppression	mental states	implicatures	discourse
jokes	reasoning	inference	narrative

(6) During a language assessment, an adult with RHLD is asked to explain the meaning of the utterance 'My friend's mother-in-law is a witch.' The adult replies: 'It means being tied down to religious sects [...] My friend's mother-in-law practices black magic.' Which of the following statements best characterises the comprehension difficulty of this adult?
   (a) The adult exhibits a concrete interpretation of the idiom in the utterance.
   (b) The adult exhibits an abstract interpretation of the metaphor in the utterance.
   (c) The adult exhibits a concrete interpretation of the proverb in the utterance.
   (d) The adult exhibits a concrete interpretation of the metaphor in the utterance.
   (e) The adult exhibits an abstract interpretation of the proverb in the utterance.

(7) During a language assessment, an adult with RHLD is asked to point to the picture which illustrates the meaning of the utterance 'The man has a heavy heart.' The adult points to a picture which shows a man carrying a large heart. Which of the following statements best characterises the comprehension difficulty of this adult?
   (a) The adult exhibits a concrete interpretation of the idiom in the utterance.
   (b) The adult exhibits an abstract interpretation of the metaphor in the utterance.
   (c) The adult exhibits a concrete interpretation of the proverb in the utterance.
   (d) The adult exhibits a concrete interpretation of the metaphor in the utterance.
   (e) The adult exhibits an abstract interpretation of the proverb in the utterance.

(8) Which of the following aspects of language interpretation is likely to prove difficult for the adult with RHLD who has a theory of mind impairment?
   (a) The interpretation of the utterance 'Close that door!'
   (b) The interpretation of the utterance 'Bill is in London this week.'
   (c) The interpretation of the utterance 'Sally is an angel.'
   (d) The interpretation of the utterance 'What a glorious day!' said during a thunderstorm.
   (e) The interpretation of the utterance 'The lecture starts promptly at 11am.'

(9) An adult with RHLD struggles to integrate the second of these two utterances within his representation of the meaning of a story: 'The truck driver stirred his cup of tea. The spoon was not particularly clean.' Which of the following statements best describes the adult's difficulty in this case?
   (a) The adult is unable to use world knowledge to make an inference about a likely candidate to fill the instrument slot of the verb 'stirred'.
   (b) The adult is unable to draw a text-based inference to the effect that the truck driver likes tea.
   (c) The adult is unable to use world knowledge to make an inference about the cause of the unclean state of the spoon.
   (d) The adult is unable to draw a text-based inference to the effect that the truck driver paid for his tea.

(e) The adult is unable to use world knowledge to make an inference to the effect that the truck driver is sitting in a diner.

(10) On hearing the utterance 'The karate champion hit the cement block', an adult with RHLD fails to infer that the karate *broke* the cement block. Which of the following statements captures the inferential failure in this case?

(a) The adult does not draw an inference about the cause of an action based on world knowledge.

(b) The adult does not draw an inference about the consequence of an action based on world knowledge.

(c) The adult does not draw a text-based inference to the effect that it was easy to break the cement block.

(d) The adult does not draw a text-based inference to the effect that the karate champion tried to break the cement block.

(e) The adult does not draw an inference to the effect that the karate champion is highly successful.

3.3 Traumatic brain injury

(1) Which of the following is *not* associated with traumatic brain injury (TBI) in adults?
(a) raised intracranial pressure
(b) oedema
(c) epilepsy
(d) intracranial infection
(e) demyelination

(2) *True* or *False*: Most traumatic brain injuries are severe in nature.

(3) *True* or *False*: Aphasia is among the sequelae of TBI in adults.

(4) *True* or *False*: Damage to the temporal lobe of the brain is responsible for many of the cognitive deficits which occur in TBI.

(5) Fill in the blank spaces in the following paragraphs using the words in the box below. Adults who sustain a TBI can experience disruption of language and _____ functions, often for many years post-injury. Although _____ language impairments can occur in clients with TBI, by far the most significant deficits are found in pragmatics and discourse. Among the pragmatic deficits of this clinical population are difficulties with _____ management, conversational repair and the use of _____ markers in conversation, and the contribution of _____ and illogical utterances to conversation. For example, adults with TBI often engage in topic _____ and struggle to use hints and other indirect forms to make _____ of others. The effect of these pragmatic deficits is to increase the burden on the interlocutors of the speaker with TBI, as they attempt to _____ for these difficulties by asking more _____ and introducing more topics. The discourse impairments of adults with TBI are also significant and include errors of _____, difficulty establishing local and global _____ and reduced information efficiency. Although discourse impairments in TBI have been reported across a number of forms of discourse, they have most often been studied in relation to _____ discourse.

Increasingly, investigators are linking pragmatic and discourse impairments in adults with TBI to a range of cognitive deficits. Many of these deficits involve _____ which are related to frontal lobe pathology in TBI. Frontal lobe cognitive deficits like rigidity, _____ and poor planning and _____ have been found in adults with TBI who have a range of pragmatic impairments. Cognitive deficits such as perseveration and poor planning need to be fully investigated for their contribution to pragmatic and discourse problems such as topic repetitiveness and aberrant discourse _____, respectively. Aside from executive function deficits, studies have also reported theory of mind (ToM) impairments in adults with TBI. These impairments are detrimental to pragmatic interpretation for the reason that the recognition of one type of mental state – _____ – is the essence of the understanding of utterances. Indeed, studies have shown that _____ ToM judgements – the attribution of beliefs not about the world but about another interlocutor's mental states – are related to the ability to understand _____ inference.

perseveration	procedural	cohesion	information
topic	first-order	comprehension	repetitiveness
inference	problem-solving	compensate	intellectual
communicative intentions		irrelevant	conversational
representation	executive functions	politeness	deixis
second-order	promises	organisation	coherence
receptive	questions	narrative	cognitive	reasoning
aphasic	third-order	affective states	requests

(6) Which of the following aspects of language is likely to be compromised in an adult with TBI and ToM impairment?
   (a) appreciation of social *faux pas* in a cartoon series
   (b) use of embedded clauses in a written narrative
   (c) understanding of ironic utterances during a conversational exchange
   (d) description of motivations of characters during narrative retelling
   (e) comprehension of locative prepositions during language testing

(7) Which of the following aspects of language is likely to be compromised in an adult with TBI and executive dysfunction?
   (a) comprehension of hyponyms of *fruit*
   (b) use of passive voice constructions
   (c) presentation of instructions in procedural discourse
   (d) production of meronyms of *face*
   (e) comprehension of inflectional suffixes such as *-ing*

(8) Which of the following language and cognitive functions is likely to be compromised in an adult with TBI and significant frontal lobe pathology?
   (a) auditory discrimination
   (b) impulse control
   (c) initiation of activity
   (d) language decoding
   (e) mental flexibility

(9) *True* or *False*: Some adults who sustain a TBI are unable to vary politeness markers to reflect the tenor of a social relationship between a speaker and a hearer.

(10) Which of the following statements best characterises the information management of clients with TBI?

    (a) Clients with TBI produce mostly under-informative utterances.

    (b) Clients with TBI often use utterances which do not meet hearers' informational needs.

    (c) Clients with TBI produce mostly over-informative utterances.

    (d) Clients with TBI produce highly redundant utterances.

    (e) Clients with TBI display intact skills of information management.

3.4   Dementias

(1) Which of the following conditions is *not* associated with dementia?

    (a) Creutzfeldt–Jakob disease

    (b) Korsakoff's syndrome

    (c) Parkinson's disease

    (d) myasthenia gravis

    (e) Huntington's disease

(2) Name <u>three</u> infectious diseases which can cause dementia.

(3) Which of the following conditions is *not* a form of frontotemporal dementia?

    (a) Alzheimer's dementia

    (b) semantic dementia

    (c) AIDS dementia complex

    (d) progressive non-fluent aphasia

    (e) acquired epileptic aphasia

(4) *True* or *False*: Referential communication is rarely disrupted in adults with Alzheimer's disease.

(5) *True* or *False*: Patients with behavioural variant frontotemporal dementia can make use of socially inappropriate language, including profanity.

(6) Which of the following is *not* a topic management problem of clients with dementia related to Alzheimer's disease?

    (a) domination of conversation with one or two topics that are of interest only to the client with dementia

    (b) difficulty contributing to the propositional development of a topic

    (c) difficulty initiating or introducing a topic during conversation

    (d) introduction of topics during conversation which address personal, inappropriate issues

    (e) domination of conversation with topics on the themes of illness and dependency

(7) Fill in the blank spaces in the following paragraphs using the words in the box below. Along with other cognitive functions, language deteriorates with the onset and progression of _____. However, there is evidence that this deterioration does not affect all language subsystems to the same extent or at the same time. The decline of language in Alzheimer's disease is hierarchical in nature, with _____ aspects of language deteriorating before aspects of language which are acquired early in _____. Semantic and _____ aspects of language are thus more vulnerable to early deterioration in Alzheimer's disease than phonological and _____ aspects. Even within language subsystems there is an age of acquisition effect. This effect has been demonstrated for

word production and _____, for example. Patients with Alzheimer's disease have been found to produce words which have an _____ age of acquisition during semantic _____ tasks. Patients have also been shown to recognise fewer _____ than early acquired words correctly during word recognition tasks.

Pragmatic and discourse aspects of language are still being acquired long after phonology and syntax are well-established components of a child's linguistic _____. To this extent, one might reasonably expect pragmatic and discourse skills to be particularly _____ to early deterioration in Alzheimer's disease. There is evidence to indicate that this is the case. Significant discourse impairments have been identified in patients with Alzheimer's disease at stages of the disease when _____ skills are still relatively intact. At the stage when patients exhibit the earliest, clear-cut clinical deficits of dementia, their performance on oral reading, _____ identification, auditory comprehension and _____ to dictation is 90% or more of the normal mean, while their performance on discourse tasks involving _____ and object description is only 55% of the normal mean. Patients in the late _____ stage of Alzheimer's disease still approximate normal performance on oral reading, reading _____ and auditory comprehension. However, their performance on picture description is 50% of the normal mean and is even less than that on object description. The performance of patients who have moderately severe _____ decline and exhibit early dementia is still greater than 50% of the normal mean on auditory and reading comprehension. However, their performance on object and picture description is less than _____ of the normal mean.

spelling	cognitive	development	subordinate	late
morphological	fluency	25%	picture	competence
late-acquired	semantic dementia		earlier	syntactic	50%
Alzheimer's disease	confusional	reasoning	vulnerable
superordinate	phonological	recognition	structural language
lexical	comprehension	inference	writing	75%

(8) A 65-year-old woman with non-fluent primary progressive aphasia is observed to produce many turns during conversation that consist only of stereotyped utterances such as 'oh gosh' and 'oh dear'. What function might these utterances perform for this client?
(a) These utterances express a range of affective states on the part of the client.
(b) These utterances help the client discharge her conversational turn.
(c) These utterances encourage the previous speaker to continue his or her turn.
(d) These utterances contribute to the development of the topic of conversation.
(e) These utterances signal that the client wants to change the topic of conversation.

(9) A 65-year-old man with frontal lobe dementia responds to a question about the problems he has been experiencing by describing the tests (MRI and CAT scans) he has been having. Which of the following areas is problematic for this client?
(a) conversational repair
(b) conversational openings and closings
(c) conversational turn-taking
(d) topic termination
(e) topic relevance

(10) A patient with dementia with Lewy bodies relates a story based on a wordless picture book. The story is judged to be uninformative by a speech and language therapist. Which of the following linguistic features may explain its lack of informativeness?
   (a) use of non-specific vocabulary like 'stuff' and 'things'
   (b) use of repetitive language
   (c) presence of morphosyntactic errors
   (d) presence of phonological errors
   (e) use of metaphorical language

3.5   Neurodegenerative disorders

(1) In which of the following neurodegenerative disorders is demyelination the primary pathological process?
   (a) Parkinson's disease
   (b) motor neurone disease
   (c) multiple sclerosis
   (d) Huntington's disease
   (e) myasthenia gravis

(2) Which of the following neurodegenerative disorders is related to reduced production of the neurotransmitter dopamine?
   (a) Parkinson's disease
   (b) motor neurone disease
   (c) multiple sclerosis
   (d) Huntington's disease
   (e) myasthenia gravis

(3) *True* or *False*: Pragmatic deficits in adults with Parkinson's disease are always related to the presence of dementia.

(4) *True* or *False*: Discourse skills are impaired in Huntington's disease in the presence of intact structural language.

(5) Fill in the blank spaces in the following paragraph using the words in the box below.
Pragmatic disorders have been quite extensively investigated in adults with Parkinson's disease. Adults with this neurodegenerative disorder present with marked pragmatic impairments, even in the absence of _____. These impairments include problems with the comprehension of _____, irony and _____. It has been found that patients with Parkinson's disease are less likely than control subjects to automatically activate indirect meanings of _____. They are also overly confident in their interpretations and _____ of errors of interpretation. Significant impairments of pragmatic communication abilities have also been reported in the areas of conversational appropriateness, turn-taking, _____ and proxemics. Less research has been conducted into expressive aspects of pragmatics in adults with Parkinson's disease. One aspect of expressive pragmatics which has been investigated is the use of _____ strategies. Patients with Parkinson's disease have been found to use less polite strategies than control subjects. They also have difficulty varying the politeness of _____ in relation to features of social context such as the _____ of the recipient. Pragmatic impairments have been shown to correlate with the _____ and severity of Parkinson's disease. They also appear to be linked to cognitive deficits (particularly of _____ memory) related to _____ dysfunction.

metonymy	frontostriatal	phonological	implicatures
dopamine	power	substantia nigra	cognitive status
working	speech acts	conversational repair	metaphor
neuropsychiatric	politeness	dementia	duration
unaware	commands	prosodics	inferences	requests

(6) The following language problems have been reported in adults with Huntington's disease. Which of these problems is *not* a pragmatic or discourse deficit?
(a) word retrieval difficulty
(b) impaired metaphor comprehension
(c) echolalic speech
(d) difficulty responding to questions about the implicit content of narrative discourse
(e) difficulty explaining lexical ambiguities

(7) *True* or *False*: Clients with amyotrophic lateral sclerosis can exhibit high-level language problems which are not revealed by standardised language tests.

(8) The following language problems have been reported in adults with multiple sclerosis. Which of these problems is *not* a receptive pragmatic or discourse deficit?
(a) narratives contain incorrect and ambiguous information
(b) poor comprehension of metaphorical expressions
(c) narratives omit essential story information
(d) poor comprehension of ambiguous sentences
(e) poor comprehension of implied relationships in a text

(9) Executive function deficits have been implicated in the language problems of clients with multiple sclerosis. Which of the following is an executive function deficit?
(a) impaired memory
(b) lexical access problems
(c) impaired attention
(d) theory of mind impairments
(e) impaired mental flexibility

(10) *True* or *False*: Discourse production difficulties are found in clients with amyotrophic lateral sclerosis without dementia.

3.6 Central nervous system infections

(1) Which of the following infectious diseases and pathogens can compromise central nervous system (CNS) function?
(a) herpes simplex virus
(b) human immunodeficiency virus
(c) *Helicobacter pylori*
(d) syphilis
(e) human papillomavirus

(2) Name three infectious diseases or pathogens which can cause encephalitis in adults.

(3) *True* or *False*: Aphasia is one of the neurological sequelae of encephalitis in adults.

(4) Which of the following conditions is *not* one of the sequelae of meningitis in adults?

(a) seizures
(b) hydrocephalus
(c) bipolar disorder
(d) deafness
(e) cognitive dysfunction

(5) Fill in the blank spaces in the following paragraphs using the words in the box below.
Transient and persisting language disturbances can be caused by a range of cerebral
infections. They include ———— infections such as *Haemophilus influenzae* meningitis,
viral infections such as ————, fungal infections (e.g. candida meningitis) and parasitic
infections (e.g. toxoplasmosis). Cerebral infections also include a type of infectious
protein, known as a 'prion', which can invade the brain and cause ————. Herpes
simplex encephalitis (HSE) is the brain infection which most frequently produces
————. In adults with HSE, a severe aphasia may be obscured by a generalised
pervasive ———— and by amnesia. However, an anomia may remain as a long-term
consequence of the infection. The ———— in HSE can be highly specific in nature. In
this way, several studies have reported category-specific ———— deficits for living over
non-living things in adults who develop HSE. A ———— aphasia syndrome may arise
from an intra-cerebral abscess. Although such abscesses are quite rare nowadays, in
a pre-antibiotic age temporal lobe abscesses secondary to ———— were a significant
cause of aphasia.

Aside from aphasic language disturbances, pragmatic and discourse impairments
have also been reported in adults with cerebral infections. Discourse deficits have
been reported in adults with medial ———— lobe damage following HSE. These
adults present with severe ———— deficits in the form of hippocampal amnesia. However, they exhibit generally preserved ———— (e.g. language, attention, reasoning) and
———— functioning. The ability of these subjects to produce cohesive and ————
discourse is impaired both in story generation and retelling tasks and across narrative and ———— discourse samples. Specifically, these subjects with amnesia tend to
produce fewer ———— ties per T-unit than comparison adults. (A T-unit is defined as
an independent clause and any subordinate clauses associated with it.) The adequacy
of their ties is more often judged to be incomplete. Also, the ———— coherence of
their discourse is rated to be lower than that of discourse produced by comparison
adults. Moreover, these discourse deficits occur alongside language abilities which are
within normal limits on ———— measures such as the Boston Diagnostic Aphasia
Examination.

parietal	expository	declarative memory	bacterial
Creutzfeldt–Jakob disease		social	dementia	syntactic
working memory	procedural	temporal	otitis media
ataxia	herpes simplex encephalitis	global	executive function
intellectual	anomia	standardised	apraxia	semantic
cognition	theory of mind	aphasia	focal	cohesive
otosclerosis	local	relevance	coherent	inference

(6) *True* or *False*: Discourse impairments in adults with cerebral infections are secondary
to structural language impairments.

(7) *True* or *False*: Discourse impairments in adults with cerebral infections are related to reduced intellectual functioning.

(8) Dementia is a feature of many cerebral infections. Name <u>three</u> such infections.

(9) Which of the following conditions is an infectious cause of seizure disorder and language impairment?
   (a) Landau–Kleffner syndrome
   (b) Rolandic epilepsy
   (c) encephalitis
   (d) vascular dementia
   (e) tuberculosis

(10) Cohesive ties in discourse may be classified as *complete* (the referent is located in the preceding text), *incomplete* (the referent is not evident from the context or supplied in the discourse) or *erroneous* (there is more than one possible referent in the discourse). An adult with HSE produces many incomplete cohesive ties during discourse production tasks. Which of the following examples is likely to occur in this adult's expressive discourse?
   (a) 'Sally adored the dress with a velvet bow. It was what she had always wanted.'
   (b) 'Marcus bought the antique vase and Italian painting at the auction. It was his most expensive purchase to date.'
   (c) 'The policeman detained the suspect outside the shop. They strongly resisted arrest.'
   (d) 'Mabel hid the decorated cake in the larder. It was the only way to prevent her husband from eating it.'
   (e) 'A few old photos were all Bill had left from his time in Paris. But their memories of this period were still very strong.'

Section B: Data analysis exercises

3.7 Acquired aphasia 1

Background

The following extracts of data were produced by adults with fluent aphasia who were studied by Chapman et al. (1998). The data were collected during a range of discourse production tasks. The tasks involved (1) retelling fables, (2) capturing the gist of fables, (3) conveying the lesson of fables, (4) story generation based on a single frame picture, and (5) verbal explanations of the meaning of proverbs. Each of these tasks places different demands on a speaker's cognitive, linguistic and pragmatic skills. The responses of these adults to (1), (3) and (5) are presented below. Contributions by the examiner ('E') are indicated in parentheses. Examine these extracts and then answer the questions that follow.

Fable

A hungry raven saw that pigeons in the pigeon coop had a lot of food. He painted his feathers white to look like them. But when he started to crow, they realised that he was a raven and chased him away. So he returned to his own kind. But the other ravens did not recognise him because he had his feathers painted white, so they also chased him away.

Data set 1

Subjects read and heard the fable above, which they were then asked to retell.

This was a story of the raven that . . . painted his feathers white. And got over, to get over the pigeons and they caught him and made him get away. But he left, let me see, some of them was still there but the pigeons got them all out of the way. *(E: Some of who were still there?)* The pigeons- the ravens, the ravens was there. But they finally got them all out. They all uh had uh yellow-yellow-no white, the was painted white. *(E: And how did the pigeons know . . . that this was a raven and not a pigeon?)* Because they s-I don't know, it's, they sounded different (laughs).

Data set 2

Subjects were asked to convey a lesson which could be learned from the fable.

Uh don't, don't, don't let the ravens get in the chicken coop.

Data set 3

Subjects were asked to explain the meaning of the proverb 'One swallow doesn't make a summer.'

I don't know if that's talking about a bird or (laughs) if-if I got hot. Uh, that-that means that uh, they was a lot more birds. Or there's more of anything. Let's see, a swallow, one swallow does not make a summer. Uh-uh (5 sec). Sw-uh . . . uh . . . b-uh. *(E: One swallow doesn't make a summer.)* (10 sec) See (6 sec) swallow . . . .*(E: Can you think of an example of when you might use a saying like that?)* Uh . . . there's not a uh, let's see, there's not a uh-uh drop of rain, there's not a, there's not any r-uh-rain-uh . . . let's see. Swallow (5 sec) a . . . I don't know***.

Question 1 The fable retell in data set 1 contains discourse strengths as well as weaknesses. Give *one* example of each of the following discourse features in this extract:

(a) use of self-initiated repair
(b) use of spatial deixis in the absence of a referent
(c) use of plural pronoun for a singular referent
(d) use of plural pronoun with more than one possible referent
(e) use of statement to introduce main character

Question 2 When asked to convey the lesson of the fable, the adult with fluent aphasia replies 'don't let the ravens get in the chicken coop'. This response is clearly inadequate. Give an account of its inadequacy.

Question 3 The speaker's attempt to convey the meaning of the proverb in data set 3 is unsuccessful. Which three expressions indicate that the speaker with fluent aphasia has interpreted this proverb in a rather literal, concrete way?

Question 4 The explanation of proverb meaning in data set 3 is compromised by a number of linguistic anomalies. Identify five such anomalies.

Question 5 The proverb 'one swallow doesn't make a summer' means that we shouldn't use a single event to indicate a general trend. In effect, a trend is only supported by the occurrence of *more* than one event. Which <u>two</u> expressions in data set 3 suggest that the speaker with fluent aphasia has some appreciation of this meaning, even as he or she is unable to give a complete account of it?

3.7 Acquired aphasia 2

Background

Reported speech has only rarely been a focus of clinical studies. Yet, this important aspect of communication is integral to storytelling and other forms of discourse. Hengst et al. (2005) examined the use of reported speech by seven adults with mild to moderately severe aphasia during conversation with their routine communicative partners. Data from two of these adults, Mary and Ethel, is presented below. Mary is 47 years old. She suffered an embolic CVA in the posterior left hemisphere six months prior to the study. Ethel is 21 years old. She experienced a haemorrhagic CVA in the anterior left hemisphere 14 months prior to the study. Mary has a college degree and Ethel has a high school equivalency degree. Examine the data sets in detail and then answer the questions below.

Data set 1

Mary (M) is talking to her son Rob (R) and a researcher called Julie (J) about how she successfully rescheduled the bus that took her to her therapy appointment. Reported speech episodes are indicated in bold.

M: Linda called me and **she said she's sick** and **she says**
R:
 J: Okay so it was Linda that called?   Okay
M: **can you come early** and **I said no I can't call you early.**
R:
 J: Sure you can't change the bus.
M: **I says my bus is coming at three.**   And you know she's gonna and I'll be back
R:
 J: Right.
M: for 3:30 and **she says . . . well then I better keep that up to that. I says no I**
R:
 J: m hm
M: **think I can I said I think she can go me to try it again.** And **she says well . . .**
R:
 J: m hm
M: **you give your y-you give your answer over it again with me** . . . and **she says**
R:
 J:
M: **get your things s-see if you can say what your gonna say right.** And I
R:
 J: yeah   uh huh
M: actually I accidentally let her down [laughing].
R:
 J: You hung up on her? [laughing]

Data set 2

Ethel (E) is talking to her husband Barnie (B) about an earlier conversation she had with the researcher. The researcher is present during the exchange and is sitting in an adjacent room. The researcher had asked Ethel why they were having bratwurst for dinner. Ethel had replied by saying it was Barnie's favourite food. Reported speech episodes are indicated in bold.

B: m:::: bra::::twurst.
E: [laugh] *(throws head back)* See. [laugh] (1 sec)
B: What? (2 sec)
E: Um. *(looks towards other room and the researcher)* (4 sec) Um. (2 sec) **Bratwurst?**
B: M hm.
E: No. *(fork down)* ... Um. *(points towards the researcher)* ... (Woman) ... What's her ...
B: *(points to Ethel's plate)*
E: name? (1 sec)
B: Potatoes?
E: No. *(points to the researcher)*
B: ...m...m...m *(shrugs and shakes head)*
E: (2 sec) **Bratwurst? ... Yeah.** ... *(points to Barnie)* **I love, ... um,** *(points to food)*
B: Bratwurst?
E: [laugh] No *(slaps Barnie's arm and points to him)* ...
B: /m/ ... I love bratwurst?
E: Yeah. *(takes her fork and continues eating)*
B: M hm....
E: **I told you.** [laugh]

Question 1 Mary makes skilled use of reported speech in the conversational exchange in data set 1. Give <u>one</u> example of each of the following reported speech behaviours in this data set:

(a) Mary is able to use direct reported speech.
(b) Mary is able to use indirect reported speech.
(c) Mary is able to report her own speech.
(d) Mary is able to report affirmative and negative utterances.
(e) Mary is able to report questions and statements.

Question 2 Mary has better expressive language skills than Ethel. What linguistic device is Mary able to use in order to signal her use of reported speech? Is Ethel able to use this same linguistic device?

Question 3 Ethel's reported speech is frequently misunderstood by Barnie. One instance where this occurs is in the utterance 'Bratwurst? ... Yeah.... *(points to Barnie)* I love, ... um *(points to food)*' which is taken by Barnie to mean that Ethel loves bratwurst. This misunderstanding appears to be related to the omission of a particular linguistic feature of reported speech. What is this feature, and how does Ethel attempt to compensate for its omission?

Question 4 Ethel uses ellipsis in the final reported speech episode in data set 2. If ellipsis had not been used, what form would this utterance take? To whom is this reported speech episode directed?

Question 5 Respond with *true* or *false* to each of the following statements.

(a) Ethel uses reported speech to display her identity as a knowing wife by confirming her claim that bratwurst is Barnie's favourite food.

(b) Mary uses reported speech to avoid relinquishing her conversational turn to Rob and Julie.

(c) Mary uses reported speech to animate the voices of the two participants in the conversational exchange that she is relating to Rob and Julie.

(d) Ethel uses reported speech to compensate for her poor expressive language skills.

(e) Mary uses reported speech to compensate for Rob's lack of conversational participation.

3.7   Acquired aphasia 3

Background

The study of spontaneous speech samples can reveal information about a client's pragmatic and discourse functioning which is not always readily discerned from formal assessments alone. The following samples are taken from recordings of conversations between an interviewer and a woman (HW) with Broca's aphasia who was studied by Bastiaanse (1995). HW, who is a native Dutch speaker, became aphasic at 41 years of age. She is the mother of two children called Reinier and Renate. A CT scan was performed two weeks post-onset of aphasia. It revealed an ischaemic infarct in parts of the temporal and frontal lobes with extension to the parietal lobe in the left hemisphere. A linguistic assessment was conducted 15 months post-onset while HW was an outpatient. The following extracts are taken from spontaneous speech recordings which were conducted during that assessment.

Data set 1

The interviewer (INT) and HW are discussing HW's language problems.

INT: Can you tell me what are your problems?
HW: Er talking problem yes but forming difficult sentences easy when no easy when first not er difficult words er to think yes doesn't soon occur to me
INT: You have problems finding the words?
HW: Yes yes
INT: But, as I understand, you also encounter problems when making a sentence?
HW: Yes it doesn't come at moment when I write er goes that er slow er no
INT: When you are writing?
HW: Yes before the time I did know writing down er I write down nothing remembers me
INT: Yes, but when you really want to, can you speak in correct sentences?
HW: Yes
INT: Why don't you do that?
HW: Er too fast to talk
INT: What do you mean, too fast?
HW: Er I too fast to talk er I cannot er search for words
INT: Yes, when you talk in sentences, you can't look for words?

HW: No
INT: And looking for words, is that difficult too?
HW: Yes
INT: That's why you talk in short sentences?
HW: Yes the a and I leave out I just leave er
HW: Do you do that on purpose?
HW: No on God no
INT: That happens automatically?
HW: Yes I hear always what I says sentences quick I hear er and the I hear er always er what I says wrongly
INT: You do hear that
HW: Yes yes

Data set 2

The interviewer and HW are discussing Christmas and HW's new house.

INT: Okay, something else, it will soon be Sinterklaas and Christmas
HW: Yes yes
INT: Do you have any plans?
HW: Yes no plans not not Sinterklaas shopsbusiness me purse always empty future no past er
INT: Won't you celebrate Sinterklaas?
HW: No absolutely
INT: Don't you do anything?
HW: In the pan tasty things snacks tasty
INT: But no presents?
HW: No no
INT: And at Christmas and New Year's Eve, are you going to do something?
HW: Er eat tasty things presents Christmas draw numbers all er get presents ten guilders ten guilders each
INT: You are not going out?
HW: I don't know
INT: You don't know
HW: No we sold house our house new about March er er we saving pennies
INT: Yes, I can imagine. Where did you buy a house?
HW: In G. M-straat centre of G. the middle in G. ah beautiful place puh
INT: Where do you live now?
HW: G.
INT: You live in G. already?
HW: Yes outskirts of G. near D.
INT: The house you bought, what does it look like?
HW: New building subsidized beautiful house oh dear
INT: Tell me
HW: Yes beautiful house magnificent from the outside windows extremely beautiful house
INT: And what size is it?
HW: Er room er ninety meters no
INT: No, that seems very large
HW: No nine meters all thresholds gone oh nice
INT: And how many floors does it have?
HW: Er three ground floor first bed-rooms two shower
INT: Three floors, upstairs two bedrooms

HW: Yes and an attic a bed-room Reinier row about I want in the attic Renate no I want in the attic
INT: And who is going to the attic?
HW: Reinier
INT: That is the oldest one, isn't it?
HW: Yes yes
INT: Do you have a bedroom downstairs yourself?
HW: No upstairs I can walk on the stairs
INT: Is there also a garden?
HW: Ah big one big one behind the house fifteen meters width seventeen no seven meters
INT: That's nice
HW: Yes nice
INT: Is it brand new?
HW: Yes built now
INT: So there is nothing in the garden yet?
HW: No now tiles on roof
INT: So you will have a bare garden
HW: Yes er ah future eh trees apple-trees ah delicious pear-trees pears
INT: Yes, you want to plant trees
HW: Yes blossoms beautifully oh magnificent new trees small trees
INT: You are going to move in May?
HW: No er about March new house delivered extremely beautiful
INT: You are glad with it, aren't you?
HW: Oh beautiful
INT: Were you eager to move?
HW: Yes
INT: What kind of house did you have?
HW: Old house about after the no war built block

Question 1 The interviewer in data set 1 adopts a conversational style which is intended to reduce the burden on HW's impaired expressive language skills. Describe this conversational style using examples from the data set to support your answer.

Question 2 Notwithstanding her limited expressive language skills, HW is an effective communicator in pragmatic terms. Give one example from data set 1 of each of the following behaviours in HW's pragmatic repertoire.

(a) HW displays metalinguistic knowledge by explaining the meaning of a prior utterance.
(b) HW can establish the referents of demonstrative pronouns within utterances.
(c) HW can establish the referents of demonstrative pronouns across utterances.
(d) HW can use utterances with novel content which contribute to topic development.
(e) HW can understand indirect speech acts.

Question 3 Several pragmatic and discourse skills are also evident in HW's conversational exchange with the interviewer in data set 2. Some of these skills are listed below. Give one example of each skill from this data set.

(a) HW makes use of direct reported speech.
(b) HW makes use of self-initiated repair.
(c) HW can use and understand lexical substitution.

(d) HW responds to other-initiated repair.

(e) HW can comprehend sub-sentences (i.e. utterances which have a reduced form but express the content of a full sentence).

Question 4 There is considerable evidence in these data sets that HW can comprehend mental state language. Give five examples of HW's intact comprehension of this language in the above conversational exchanges. What cognitive capacity appears to be intact in HW?

Question 5 Notwithstanding the above pragmatic and discourse strengths, there are parts of these exchanges where HW contributes contradictory information. Identify two instances where this occurs. What linguistic error found in aphasia accounts for this feature of HW's utterances?

3.7 Acquired aphasia 4

Background

The communicative partners of adults with aphasia can adapt their own conversational style to accommodate the needs of the aphasic individual. These adaptations are often successful in allowing the adult with aphasia to make most effective use of their residual language and communication skills. Some of these adaptations were investigated by Beeke et al. (2007) in a study of a man called Roy who has severe and chronic agrammatism. At the time of study, Roy was in his mid-to-late 40s (his exact age was not known to investigators). Roy sustained a left-hemisphere cerebrovascular accident seven years earlier while he was waterskiing. He has a dense hemiplegia which affects his right arm. Recordings of Roy were made across a number of formal language tests and discourse production tasks. The latter tasks, which included picture description, cartoon strip description, storytelling and conversation, are of particular relevance in the current context. Transcribed extracts from these recordings are shown below. Level and falling intonation are indicated by a comma and full stop, respectively.

Data set 1

Roy (R) is telling the story of Cinderella to the tester (T).

R: (0.6) so, (0.2) then, (.) all of a sudden, (1.3) uh (2.9) spell.
T: mhm
R: (1.7) and (0.4) ur (1.4) ah (0.7) twenty or something, (.) hh and (0.2) uh uh (0.5) suddenly, (1.5) uh (0.4) rich.
T: mhm

Data set 2

Roy is talking to his adult daughter Di (D) about racing.

R: u- ur (0.1) you know, (0.1) u- uh- ur racing,
D: mm
R: (0.2) ur- (0.3) Newmarket, (0.2) Epsom,
D: yeah

R: anywhere, (0.2) but (0.5) me, (0.5) u- ur (0.2) Ascot, no.
D: you've never been have you
R: no no
D: perhaps you can go next year dad

Data set 3

Roy is talking to Di about her job as a nursery nurse.

R: uh- u e interesting actually, (0.3) uh- bu- bi- because- (2.4) er now, (2.1) me,
D: m
R: (0.3) I (0.9) think no, (0.5) er er- (0.7) u- special. (0.3) honestly.
D: what working with children
R: yeah, definitely.
D: yeah not everyone can do it can they

Data set 4

Roy is describing the Cookie Theft picture from the Boston Diagnostic Aphasia Exami-nation.

R: um (2.8) wu- (0.5) er (1.0) tuh ach! (3.8) plate, (2.2) [sits upright, gazes to middle distance, enacts the woman wiping a plate]
T: [nods]

Data set 5

Roy and Di are talking about Di's upcoming 21st birthday party.

D: it'll be a good night though
R: oh uh- uh- tu- i- really.
   (0.3)
R: yeah
D: mmm
R: u- u- and now, (0.6) o- two weeks innit
D: (1.3) not this weekend (0.4) not the weekend after, the weekend after
R: eh- yeah
D: two weeks this Saturday
R: yeah (0.7) I know and suddenly [clicks fingers]
D: I know.

Data set 6

Roy is describing the end of the Dinner Party cartoon strip where it is revealed that the pet cat has eaten the fish which was intended for the meal.

R: (0.2) uh uhu- ur (0.4) cat. (1.6) yeah. (0.2) actually I thought, (0.3) dog, but no, um yeah exactly yeah
T: mm

Data set 7

Roy is responding to a question from Di about how his friends manage to pay their large mortgage.

D: how do they afford it
R: well yeah eh- because um (0.4) working.

Data set 8

Roy is describing the Dinner Party cartoon strip. The picture relating to this extract shows the host running out of the house (he is going to buy fish and chips), the hostess crying over the stolen fish and the female guest attempting to comfort her.

R: um (1.3) tuh (0.9) ar (0.7) quick, I know. (2.0) and (1.8) oooooh, (0.6) eh (0.4) crying, and, (0.5) er (3.7) never mind. ehh heh heh
T: hm hehm

Question 1 In data sets 2 and 3, Di is adopting a particular conversational strategy in her interaction with Roy. Describe this strategy and indicate if it is effective in facilitating Di's conversational exchange with Roy.

Question 2 Notwithstanding Roy's severe expressive language problems, he is able to undertake a diverse range of communicative functions. Give one example of each of the following functions in the above data sets.

(a) Roy can ask questions.
(b) Roy can produce comments.
(c) Roy can respond to questions.
(d) Roy can report factual information.
(e) Roy can express an evaluative judgement.

Question 3 There are multiple pauses in each of Roy's conversational turns. Clearly, the tester and Di are sympathetic interlocutors who do not take advantage of these pauses in order to initiate their own turn. However, Roy is also making use of linguistic devices to indicate to his interlocutors that he wishes to retain his turn. What are these devices?

Question 4 Roy uses non-verbal communication on only two occasions in the above data sets – he mimes in data set 4 and clicks his fingers in data set 5. Given his expressive language difficulties, it could be expected that he would make more extensive use of non-verbal communication. What three factors might account for Roy's rather limited use of non-verbal communication?

Question 5 Roy makes effective use of a number of discourse features. Several of these features are given below. Give *one* example of each of these features in the above data sets.

(a) Roy can use fixed storytelling phrases.
(b) Roy can use direct reported speech.
(c) Roy can interrelate utterances by means of causal relations.

(d) Roy can use discourse markers to initiate a narrative episode.

(e) Roy can use symbolic noise to animate picture description.

3.7 Acquired aphasia 5

Background

Turn-taking is a complex process which is essential to the management of conversation. This process is not always negotiated successfully by adults with aphasia. Not all turn-taking problems in these adults are attributable to their linguistic impairments, however. The behaviour of conversational partners often directly determines the type of turn-taking that is available to adults with aphasia. Perkins (1995) investigated turn-taking in three adults with stroke-induced aphasia. These adults – two women and a man – were between eight and nine months post-onset. The most significant linguistic impairment of all three subjects was a lexical retrieval deficit. The adults were recorded in conversation with a relative and a researcher. Extracts from these transcribed recordings are presented below.

Transcription notation

[the start of an overlap

*   the end of an overlap

(0.0) pauses in tenths of seconds

()   uncertain passages of transcription

Data set 1

Conversation between a 42-year-old woman with aphasia, known as 'JJ', and her husband (HB).

HB: is there anything you f- you fancy having in in for your (1.0) meals for next week (6.0)

JJ: [wə] well when especially when especially when you're off erm (6.0) we can [aʔ] well (2.5) have something (3.2) a little bits little bits of (2.3) nice things

Data set 2

Conversation between a 65-year-old woman with aphasia, known as 'EN', and a male cousin (MC).

MC: Letts Way but I don't know what er three weeks since I was talking to her and she said well [wə] I'll be away shortly

EN: aha =

MC: = but I don't know whether she was with her
                                         [
EN: no (2 syllables just)* she was er (1.2)
           daughter was waiting for some [t]

MC: 'cause she's got a house

EN: o:h

MC: down there 'cause he's in the police thing down there now in the* in the gaol
           [
EN: aah

MC: he's got his job er er he's off the buses now he's in
    the* on the gaols thing now you see and I thought the way she was
    [
EN: ah
MC: talking I thought she might have been away about a fortnight
EN: no she was [wə] she was supposed to er (0.6) I've forgotten but she was but she was
    (1.6)
MC: I was talking to her at the butchers down down the bottom and* she
                                  [
EN: mm
MC: was telling us she says oh I'll not be long before I'm going
    (1.2)
EN: mm
    [
MC: I says you ganning for good or what she says I'm not sure it's it's a big house she's I'm
    going to live with them
EN: aye but er but she (1.8) ee: I don't know what she said
MC: that's what she said to me anyway hinny and I thought maybe you'd
    heard it whether she'd moved or not you see*
                          [
EN: no

Data set 3

Conversation between EN and a researcher (RE).

EN: yeah and there's this sort of (1.4) [ɛʔ] everything in its er look at this hhh oh it's
RE: you feel as if you can't tidy up either and * that's getting you down* as well
                        [[
EN: yeah yeah
EN: mhm mhm
EN: mhm
    (1.0)
RE: everywhere looks very nice

Data set 4

Conversation between a 68-year-old man with aphasia, known as 'AD', and a researcher (RE).

AD: I did it myself in my in the London (1.0) hhh London (1.4) hhh dear dear London (3.4)
RE: was this a London University
              [
AD: London ['junɪti 'junəf 'junə]
                           [
RE: Uni*versity
AD: that's right yes

Question 1 In data set 1, JJ's husband permits a silence of 6 seconds' duration to develop at the end of his conversational turn before JJ begins speaking. Under most circumstances, how would speakers respond to such a silence? How might the response of JJ's husband to this silence be explained?

Question 2 In data set 2, EN appears to be adopting a particularly passive role in conversation. How may EN's apparent passivity be explained in terms of the behaviour of her male cousin in the exchange?

Question 3 The researcher in data set 3 adopts a more facilitative style of interaction than EN's cousin in data set 2. Describe the quite different responses of the researcher and cousin to EN's conversational turns in these data sets.

Question 4 In data set 4, the conversational turns of the researcher are directed towards achieving a particular goal. State what that goal is and describe the role of the researcher's turns in achieving it.

Question 5 Respond with *true* or *false* to each of the following statements about overlapping turns in data sets 2, 3 and 4.

(a) EN's overlaps occur at grammatical boundaries in the current speaker's turn.
(b) AD uses overlaps to initiate a topic change.
(c) EN uses overlaps to signal agreement with the current speaker.
(d) MC uses overlaps to correct EN's linguistic impairments.
(e) The researcher uses overlaps to produce a target word.

3.7 Acquired aphasia 6

Background

Participatory word searches, in which an adult with aphasia and his or her conversational partners embark on a search for a word, are jointly produced, collaborative phenomena. These searches are complex conversational behaviours which involve a range of language and cognitive skills. Oelschlaeger and Damico (2000) examined these searches between a couple, Ed and M, who had been married for 28 years. Both adults were in their early 50s. Ed sustained a single left CVA six years earlier. This had caused a moderately severe aphasia and right hemiplegia. Ed's understanding of language tended to break down when the utterances of others were too long and linguistically complex, or when comprehension rested on a single word. His expressive language skills were such that he could convey main ideas, although he frequently engaged in lengthy word searches. Examine the data sets below, which contain several of Ed's word searches, and then answer the questions that follow.

Data set 1

Ed is telling M's mother MG about the distance he travelled between home and his work when he was in the military.

ED: Yeah. From here to one there, one mile, one (2.3) no (2.1) can't think of name of it
 M: Hour?
ED: Hour.

Data set 2

Ed is telling MG about the frequency of video-recordings when he received speech and language therapy.

ED: I'd say ten (2.3) uh (1.5) uh (1.8) uhm I can't think of the name of it
 M: Times?
ED: Times.

Data set 3

Ed, M and MG are discussing some of the medical investigations which were undertaken when Ed had his CVA.

MG: Then they realized, then they put you in the hospital.
 M: Uh huh.
ED: Yeah but then they did uh (1.2) the uh (1.9) uh what do you call it (2.1) the uh-
 M: MRI?
ED: No.
 M: Angioplasty?
ED: No.
MG: EEG?
ED: No (1.5) The irr, no (tsk, tsk) srays, what do you call it?
      (1.0)
 M: An x-ray?
ED: X-ray. And he says, 'oh look, he's got a
MG: // Look there!!

Data set 4

Ed, M and MG are talking about gardening and planting.

ED: And there's one more. There's a:::
 M: Okra.
ED: Okra, that's it.

Data set 5

Ed is describing how he needs the authorisation of someone senior in his company in order to undertake an upcoming business trip.

 M: Oh::: it's not Foster.
ED: No no.
 M: Traholi?
      (1.6)
ED: No.
 M: Tom Traholi? No?
ED: It, it uh:::
 M: The president or whatever it's called
ED: Well it, well he's a pres
 M: //He's the local leader there.
ED: Yeah

Question 1 In data sets 1 to 3 inclusive, it is clear from Ed's repeated use of fillers such as 'uh' and multiple pauses that he is experiencing difficulty in finding a particular word. Even though M probably appreciates the significance of these fillers and pauses for Ed's ability to find a word, she does not join him on his word search until later. What additional conversational feature occurs in these data sets before M begins to participate in the word search?

Question 2 In data sets 1 and 2, M successfully guesses the word which Ed is trying to find. Why is this same strategy not successful in data set 3? It is not until three successive guesses by M in data set 3 have failed that Ed offers some additional information which help her identify the target word. What is this additional information?

Question 3 In data set 4, M attempts a different strategy from that used in sets 1 to 3 to assist Ed in searching for a word. Describe that strategy with particular emphasis on how it differs from the plausible guesses of data sets 1 to 3.

Question 4 A different word search strategy again is used by M in data set 5. Unlike the strategies employed in sets 1 to 4, it does not succeed in identifying the particular word Ed had in mind. Nevertheless, M is still making an important contribution to the overall development of the conversation through the use of this strategy. Describe that contribution as part of a wider characterisation of the word search strategy that is employed in this case.

Question 5 In data set 5, M repeats an earlier guess in the form of the utterance 'Tom Traholi? No?' Repetition is not a feature of any of M's other guesses in these data sets. Why do you think M feels compelled to repeat this particular guess?

3.7 Acquired aphasia 7

Background

Any type of conversational repair work suggests that a trouble source has arisen and needs to be addressed in order for a conversation to proceed. Trouble sources occur quite commonly in conversations with aphasic adults on account of the linguistic impairments of these individuals. The way in which trouble sources are repaired can lead to both positive and negative experiences of conversation on the part of adults with aphasia. Booth and Swabey (1999) examined collaborative repair as part of a wider study of communication skills training for carers of adults with aphasia. The four adults with aphasia in this study were at least six months post-onset a single CVA in the left hemisphere. The four carers, who also participated in the study, had a familial relationship to the person with aphasia. Repair sequences from two of these four conversational dyads are presented below. Examine these sequences in detail and then answer the questions that follow.

Data set 1

A 45-year-old man with aphasia (NS) is talking to his wife (LS) about buying a new home.

NS: /juzɛt geɪ gɪt/ ((coughs)) (1.3) /zuzuət/ got two (1.6) /dɛsiməs/ two (1.4) / dəsim/ (1.4) two

LS: is that destinations you're trying to =
NS: = yes yes /tɛ/
LS: yeah
 we've now got two destinations (1.7) ah know we're just making life complicated for ourselves aren't we?

Data set 2

A 62-year-old man with aphasia (JB) is talking to his brother (RB) about what they did the previous day.

JB: well that's her its /ɪtn/ eh/ səwəz/ therapy or somethin' /em/
RB: no what- eh what therapy? /f:/ (1.8)
JB: /wɜ sɜlɜ/ (2.0) /krɪʃ/ therapy/ əu/ therapy (2.3) /a nos us/ therapy is it? naw?
RB: it's no speech no
JB: no
RB: no
JB: /əu/ therapy [no it's not that is it?
RB: [/əu/ eh- no it's not/ əu/
JB: aw ah'm tryin' to understand that, but ah know (1.9) /awawawɪn/ (2.4) /pes zus/ /s/ erapy ah (3.4) ah don't know what it/ mɪn du rɛbəbət rɛn/ no remember it now (1.3) /a əa bə a ra əebəro/

Question 1 Which of the following linguistic impairments give rise to trouble sources which become the focus of repair sequences?

(a) circumlocution
(b) echolalia
(c) neologisms
(d) word-finding difficulty
(e) glossomania

Question 2 Describe the quite different responses on the part of the conversational partners to the emergence of a trouble source. Your answer should focus on the first turn only of each of these partners.

Question 3 LS is clearly determined that the trouble source should not detract from her conversation with NS by ensuring that it is addressed as swiftly and effortlessly as possible. Describe three ways in which LS sets about achieving this outcome.

Question 4 After providing JB with a phonemic cue for the target word in data set 2, RB engages in a series of turns with JB which serve only to reinforce his status as the less powerful conversational participant in the exchange. Describe this series of turns and indicate how they relegate JB to a less powerful role in the exchange.

Question 5 In his last turn in data set 2, JB produces three expressions which could be interpreted as a direct appeal to RB to say the word that is the source of the trouble in the exchange. What are these expressions?

3.7 Acquired aphasia 8

Background

Few studies have undertaken a longitudinal examination of discourse production in adults with aphasia. Although such studies are both time-consuming and expensive to conduct, they provide an invaluable insight into the recovery of language and discourse skills in clients, and into the effectiveness of therapeutic interventions. Jones (1986) undertook a longitudinal investigation of a 41-year-old man with aphasia known as 'BB'. This client's single-word output had remained unchanged since he suffered a left cerebral embolus some six years earlier. As well as causing Broca's aphasia, this CVA had resulted in a right hemiplegia. BB received intensive speech and language therapy, particularly in the first three years post-onset, for his sentence construction problems. This therapy was terminated when it was judged that he had reached maximum potential in individual therapy. A new language therapy which focused on mapping meaning relations between semantics and syntax was subsequently instituted.

The following data are recordings of the Cookie Theft picture from the Boston Diagnostic Aphasia Examination, and an account of BB's previous work. The recordings were made at three points in time: (1) six years after the onset of BB's stroke, but before the commencement of the new language therapy; (2) three months after the commencement of the new language therapy; and (3) nine months after the commencement of the new language therapy. Examine the data sets in detail, and answer the questions that follow.

Data set 1

Before the start of a new language therapy.

Cookie Theft picture description

Girl, boy .... eh .... don't know .... um .... water .... don't know *(Can you tell me anything else – what about this? – pointing to mother)* ....um.................. man .... no .... woman .... window.............. oh .... eh .... /k/............. /k/ .... tea .... eh .... don't know.

Account of previous work

eh .... eh .... oh .... no .... um .... eh .... don't know .... no .... eh .... potatoes .... um .... no.

Data set 2

Three months after the start of a new language therapy.

Cookie Theft picture description

Girl and boy and woman .... and .... /kikiz/ .... /kikiz/ .... and near the .... /a/ .... no .... near the .... don't know ...... no .... and .... eh .... woman .... drying the washing up. Filled the water .... /s/ .... falling to the floor. The window is open and flowers and trees and .... footpath .... the .... no .... oh .... no .... yes alright. Girl wants one.

Account of previous work

eh .... eh .... sold .... potatoes ...... um .... drive van .... to Cambridge .... restaurant .... chips .... no .... um .... don't know .... sorry .... pack the van .... and .... no .... um ...... don't know.

Data set 3

Nine months after the start of a new language therapy.

Cookie Theft picture description

The woman is washing up .... and water is flowing over the bowl .... on concrete floor and the boy is reaching for cookies and the stool falling down. And the girl is reaching up for the cookies. The window is opened and through the window .... see trees and the grass .... and trees and the pebbles. And the two cups on top of the .... table and the .... one bowl is .... there.

Account of previous work

I have a van and drove to the .... Cambridge and ....chips in the restaurant .... shop .... sold chips. I was a vegetable salesman *(The patient then volunteered the following information about his CVA)* I was in bed in October 1978. Well......I don't know! ...... woke up and I was lifeless. I was in bed at home. Drove to Cambridge .... sold chips .... then we went through to the hospital. *(What happened there?)* Don't know .... upstairs .... lie down on the bed .... arm, leg and couldn't talk!

Question 1 BB displays a number of linguistic impairments in his verbal output. Give *one* example of each of the following impairments in the above data sets:

(a) phonemic paraphasia
(b) circumlocution
(c) word-finding difficulty
(d) incorrect noun phrase as object of verb
(e) omission of auxiliary verb

Question 2 At each point in time, BB's description of the Cookie Theft picture is superior to the account he gives of his previous work. Why do you think this is the case?

Question 3 In the post-therapy recordings, BB's structural language skills have undoubtedly shown significant improvement. However, a number of discourse deficits are still in evidence. Give one example of each of the following deficits in data sets 2 and 3:

(a) poor use of lexical substitution as a type of cohesive relation
(b) use of personal pronoun in the absence of a preceding referent
(c) reporting of actions in incorrect temporal order
(d) presence of topic digression
(e) conjunctive cohesion markers express only additive and temporal meanings

Question 4 Notwithstanding discourse deficits such as those identified in question 3, BB displays a number of intact pragmatic and discourse skills. Several of these skills are listed below. Give *one* example of each in the above data sets.

(a) BB can engage in self-initiated repair.
(b) BB can foreground the central elements of a scene during picture description.
(c) BB can use spatial deixis.
(d) BB can comprehend indirect speech acts.
(e) BB can use direct reported speech.

Question 5 On the basis of these data sets, how would you characterise the relationship between structural language and pragmatic–discourse skills? For example, is the relationship a causal one, with improvements in structural language skills directly bringing about improvements in pragmatic–discourse skills? Or is this relationship best characterised in a different (non-causal) way?

3.8 Right-hemisphere language disorder 1

Background

First-encounter conversations are seldom studied in a clinical context where typically the focus is on exchanges between clients and their spouses, carers and other familiar partners. Yet, there are reasons why these conversations should be investigated as a distinct conversational phenomenon. The lack of shared knowledge with an unfamiliar conversational partner alters the ratio of explicit to implicit information which is communicated in these conversations, with exchanges making greater use of explicit utterances. The presence of an unfamiliar partner also influences the politeness of an exchange, the permissible topics of conversation and the type of speech acts employed. The management of these pragmatic and discourse skills is particularly challenging for clients with language and cognitive impairments following right-hemisphere damage (RHD).

Kennedy (2000) examined first-encounter conversations in eight adults with RHD. These adults had sustained a single CVA in the right hemisphere and were 3 to 12 weeks post-onset. All had left hemiplegia or hemiparesis and were inpatients in an acute rehabilitation facility. The average age of these clients was 50.3 years. The control subjects were seven adult volunteers with no neurological impairment who were matched on age, gender and years of education to the adults with RHD. There was no history of psychiatric disturbances, alcohol or drug abuse, seizures or episodes of unconsciousness in any of the subjects in the study. All subjects were instructed to converse as they would when meeting someone for the first time. Conversations of between 12 and 20 minutes' duration were audio-recorded and transcribed. Some extracts from these conversations are presented below.

Data set 1

A 57-year-old woman (JB) with RHD is talking to a 48-year-old woman (DT) with no neurological impairment. The conversation is in its maintenance phase.

JB: But each day's getting better. *(participant begins to leave without warning)*
DT: Can you stay just a little bit longer, Joan?
JB: Yeah, I got to go rinse my mouth.
DT: Okay I'll just wait here for you. Okay I'll just wait here for a few minutes then.
JB: I don't have to be in no hurry, in a hurry for.
DT: You mean you can wait on that for a little bit and we can keep talking? Oh, okay.
JB: Yeah.
DT: Yeah, OK.
JB: Yeah, don't . . . yeah, I can wait, I should have did it when I came from the bathroom.
DT: Oh, you just had lunch, huh?
JB: Uh, huh, I had rice, white rice. Kinda sticks in one spot, know I have this little pocket over here since my stroke. I have to keep, uh, the food out, you know.
DT: Uh huh. So does your family live close by?

Data set 2

A 42-year-old woman (SV) with RHD is talking to a 36-year-old man (ST) with no neurological impairment. The conversation is in its maintenance phase.

ST: Just off the 35?
SV: Yeah, get off on Bloomington Blvd. *(starts to cry)*
ST: Are you okay? You gonna be all right?
SV: Yup. *(pause)*
ST: Would you rather not do this now? Or it's up to you.
SV: I don't care.

Data set 3

A 42-year-old woman (SV) with RHD is talking to a 36-year-old man (ST) with no neurological impairment. The conversation is in its maintenance phase.

SV: I have friends that, they tried to come see me on Saturday but their car broke down.
ST: Oh. *(pause)*
SV: So they're gonna try to come up next Thursday. *(pause)* Ask me something.
ST: Well, you can ask me things, too. This is just a time for us to talk. *(pause)* So, did you say you live in West LaFayette?

Data set 4

A 45-year-old woman (WM) with RHD is talking to a 36-year-old man (ST) with no neurological impairment. The conversation is in its termination phase.

ST: Yeah . . . Well, that's about it.
WM: What were you looking for? How I speak my vocabulary or what?
ST: How you and I talk, back and forth. More just how we converse. We're looking more at the whole participant, not just how you do but how you do when you talk to me and how I respond to you, more the dialogue.
WM: So did I pass muster?
ST: It wasn't a test!

Data set 5

A 45-year-old woman (WM) with RHD is talking to a 36-year-old man (ST) with no neurological impairment. The conversation is in its termination phase.

WM: Really! Cause I have a tendency to let my vocabulary get little graphic . . . depending on who I'm around.
ST: Yeah. Yeah . . . probably depending on the subject, too.
WM: Mmhmm. If I'm being tape-recorded, I'm as good as gold. *(both laugh)*
ST: Yeah. Well, that's probably true for everybody, though.
WM: Yeah, I never know if the FBI is going to tap the lines! *(laughing)*
ST: No, no, this is just a plain old tape recorder. So, thank you!

Question 1 Emotional and behavioural disturbances can attend damage to the brain's right hemisphere. Give <u>three</u> examples of these disturbances in the above data sets.

Question 2 One of the adults with RHD makes appropriate use of non-literal language. Which adult is it? Give <u>two</u> examples of the use of non-literal language by this client.

Question 3 Is there any evidence of inappropriate topic use by these adults? When answering this question, bear in mind that these are extracts from first-encounter conversations.

Question 4 The use and appreciation of humour is often compromised in adults with RHD. However, one of the adults in the above data sets uses humour to good effect in these conversations. Which adult is it? Describe this adult's use of humour.

Question 5 One of the adults with RHD uses a direct speech act when an indirect speech act would be more appropriate in the context of a first-encounter conversation. Identify the adult and the speech act in question.

3.8   Right-hemisphere language disorder 2

Background

The data sets presented below were also collected from the adults with RHD who were studied by Kennedy (2000) and discussed in the last exercise. They are intended to demonstrate additional pragmatic and discourse strengths and weaknesses on the part of these clients in managing first-encounter conversations. Examine each data set in detail and then answer the questions below.

Data set 1

A 63-year-old man (PT) with RHD is talking to a 48-year-old woman (DT) with no neurological impairment. The conversation is in its termination phase.

DT: We'll, I wish we had more time, I'd love to hear more about your travels.

PT: Yeah, I'd like to have a drink. *(alcohol had been brought up previously)*

DT: But I think ———— is expecting us and I think she has something that she wants you to work on – so, it's been nice chatting with you, we will have to talk again.

PT: It's been nice talking with you, ————, very nice. *(pause)* Outside of Yugoslavia, there is a place I'd like to go to and that is Australia.

DT: Really, they are supposed to be beautiful – lots to see.

PT: But, we only have one lifetime.

DT: Yeah, but, it seems like you've made a good whack at it.

PT: Yes, I have.

DT: Well, I hope that you are not going to stay at ———— too much longer and you can get back . . .

PT: I hope not, within a month, I'm supposed to go with Jim to Jamaica.

DT: Oh.

PT: Looking for a lady or whatever . . .

DT: *(laughs)* Good luck.

Data set 2

A 51-year-old woman (GH) with RHD is talking to a 36-year-old man (ST) with no neurological impairment. The conversation is in its maintenance phase.

ST: So you've got friends that'll stop by periodically that'll see you?

GH: Yeah, yeah.

ST: 'Cause you don't want to be there all by yourself, either. At least I wouldn't want to be by myself.

GH: *(screams)* God, what's this!? Take somebody and beat they head in. Never seen anything like this. Look at this *(pointing to shoe)*. They say they got this kind for people who got diabetes.

ST: Uh-huh.

GH: You know, but why they put it on me?

ST: Well, you'll have to ask your physical therapist that, I guess.

GH: Well you know, he look at it, he say he didn't like it either.

ST: Oh.

GH: He did. When I came back, he say 'Why they get you this kind of shoe?' And I say, 'Don't ask me nothing.' He said they usually get this kind for people who've you know . . . got diabetes.

Data set 3

A 46-year-old man (CD) with RHD is talking to a 36-year-old man (ST) with no neurological impairment. The conversation is in its maintenance phase.

CD: I just got a cold.

ST: Oh.

CD: What is this class about? What are we doing? I mean, you say that we just talk here, are you a psychiatrist?

ST: No!

Data set 4

A 46-year-old man (CD) with RHD is talking to a 36-year-old man (ST) with no neuro-logical impairment. The conversation is in its maintenance phase.

CD: I don't like dentists too much either.

ST: No. Well, not too many people do. Except my daughter. She actually likes going to the dentist.

CD: Yeah.

ST: I don't think she's had a cavity yet, so maybe after the first time she has a cavity she won't like it as much.

CD: Yeah.

ST: Yeah, huh.

CD: How long we got to go this session?

ST: Well, we're just talking. We're going to talk for 10 minutes, that's all.

CD: Okay.

Question 1 The adults with RHD display a number of intact aspects of pragmatics and discourse in the above data sets. Some of these are listed below. Give <u>one</u> example of each aspect.

(a) use of direct reported speech
(b) use of ellipsis
(c) use of demonstrative pronoun to achieve reference
(d) use of pronominal reference
(e) use of indirect reported speech

Question 2 These adults with RHD make abrupt topic changes in the above data sets. Identify <u>two</u> instances where this occurs and describe the topic changes that are made.

Question 3 One of the adults with RHD engages in socially inappropriate verbal *and* non-verbal behaviours. Identify the subject who is responsible for these behaviours. Also, what deficits associated with right-hemisphere damage might account for these behaviours?

Question 4 Do the adults with RHD display sensitivity to the phase of conversation in which they are engaged? Support your answer with evidence from the above data sets.

Question 5 One of the adults with RHD appears to misjudge his or her social relationship to the conversational partner in the exchange. Which adult is this? Which particular utterance used by this adult suggests over-familiarity with the partner, particularly in the context of a first-encounter conversation?

3.9 Traumatic brain injury 1

Background

Discourse production has been extensively studied in adults with traumatic brain injury (TBI). Investigations of conversation and other forms of discourse have revealed problems with topic management and the informativeness of discourse, amongst other difficulties. Mentis and Prutting (1991) examined conversation and monologue discourse samples produced by a 24-year-old man who sustained a closed head injury (CHI) in an accident. This subject was 4 years 10 months post-injury at the time of the study. He was also unemployed and living alone. Although he received speech, physical and occupational therapy after his accident, he was not in a rehabilitation programme at the time of the study.

Extracts from two conversations between this man with CHI and a 20-year-old man with no history of neurological disorder are presented below. For the purpose of this exercise, these participants are labelled as 'NB' and 'SM', respectively. Examine these extracts in detail and then answer the questions that follow.

Transcription notation

...   pause of less than 2 seconds
(2.0) pause of 2 seconds' duration
.   falling intonation
?   rising intonation
,   continuing intonation

Each line is a separate intonation unit.

Data set 1

SM: ... have you ever been to a Halloween party, um where there were like really outrageous
     costumes?
NB: ... uh,
SM: ... you know.. when people just went.. all out, and rented costumes, and stuff like that.
NB: ... no.
     ... no I haven't.
     ... I've seen-
     ... no ... I've seen people,
     ... who things,
     ... like go somewhere and,
     you go and coming through and keep going.
     ... oh well that's ... good looking costume.
SM: uh huh.

Data set 2

SM: ... so.. what is this thing,
     that you've been.. kinda working on.
NB: ... well it's like.. art.
     ... you know,

SM: . . . art?
NB: . . . yeah.
SM: . . . uh huh,
NB: . . . you jus' sit down.
　　　. . . and you really concentrate.
SM: . . . um hm,
NB: . . . and it.. seems.. like.. that's-
　　　. . . a big circle,
　　　. . . gets down to a,
　　　.. little circle,
　　　. . . and that's what you're doing.. you know,
SM: . . . um hm,
NB: . . . and.. it seemed to ah,
　　　(2.0) over,
　　　. . . kind go over.. to I do other things,
SM: .. um hm,
NB: . . . you know I really get into it.
SM: . . . so are you talking about trying to focus your attention,
　　　. . . toward doing a.. really.. superior job on one thing,
　　　. . . but not being.. kind scattered,
　　　. . . is that what you're saying?
NB: . . . yeah.

Question 1 NB's contribution to the exchange in data set 1 is particularly unclear and uninformative. This is on account of a number of linguistic features, several of which are listed below. Give one example of each feature in this data set.

(a) use of a personal pronoun in the absence of a referent
(b) use of an incomplete prepositional phrase
(c) use of non-specific lexemes
(d) use of an incomplete relative clause
(e) use of repetitive language

Question 2 Notwithstanding the linguistic problems listed above, NB is able to use other aspects of language appropriately in data set 1. For example, he can use (a) ellipsis and (b) self-initiated repair. Give one example of each of these linguistic behaviours in this data set.

Question 3 What two communicative functions are served by SM's final conversational turn in data set 2?

Question 4 Topic development is not successfully achieved in either of these data sets. Explain why this is the case.

Question 5 NB's utterances in these exchanges exhibit multiple pauses. Which of the following factors may explain the frequency of pauses in NB's conversational turns? What prosodic feature does NB use to good effect to prevent SM from taking over the conversational floor when these pauses occur?

(a) anomic aphasia
(b) impaired episodic memory
(c) reduced attention span
(d) slowed information processing
(e) perseveration

3.9   Traumatic brain injury 2

Background

The brain's frontal lobes mediate a range of cognitive functions which are involved in the regulation of goal-directed behaviour. These so-called executive functions are often disrupted in clients who sustain frontal lobe damage in a traumatic brain injury. Increasingly, investigators are looking to frontal lobe cognitive deficits to understand the pragmatic and discourse impairments of clients with TBI. The expressive and receptive pragmatic skills of 11 French-speaking adults with severe TBI were studied by Dardier et al. (2011). These subjects were aged between 18 and 49 years. All were at least two years post-injury at the time of the study. None of the subjects was aphasic. There was a variable pattern of impaired and intact skills across subjects on the following executive functions: mental flexibility; self-regulation; inhibition ability; conceptual capacity; the ability to keep to a rule. Eleven participants with no known history of psychiatric or neurological disorders were matched to the subjects with TBI on age, gender, handedness and education level.

All subjects completed a number of tasks: (1) an interview in which they were asked to talk about their favourite animals and favourite singers; (2) comprehension of requests in stories based on three photographs; and (3) an explanation of responses to the comprehension task in (2). These tasks assessed, respectively, the production of pragmatics, the comprehension of pragmatics and metapragmatic knowledge. Data from some of the adults with TBI is presented below. Examine this data in detail and then answer the following questions.

Data set 1

An adult with TBI is asked what s/he likes about the singer Janis Joplin.

I remember how I had made some drawings when I was in art school – while listening to the music I had made some drawings while listening to the music – I had made some drawings you know some little sketches as I listened – you listen to music and you draw at the same time about Janis Joplin – I had made a – I had made a stain – I had made the drawings while sketching very fast like crazy and all along you reduce it to a plane – you condense a little piece of time you know into a two-dimensional picture – it's about how to transfer a universe of time onto a two-dimensional plane.

Data set 2

An adult with TBI is asked a question based on a series of three photographs. After responding correctly to the question, s/he produces a follow-up explanation.

FIRST PHOTOGRAPH: A couple in a living room. The woman says, 'Can you pass me the remote control?'
SECOND PHOTOGRAPH: The man gives her the remote control.
THIRD PHOTOGRAPH: The woman is not happy.

QUESTION: Does the ending of the story go with the beginning?
CORRECT ANSWER: No.
EXPLANATION: That's not logical, it's no good. And it's just like they say about couples watching television, it can cause a problem in any couple . . .

Data set 3

An adult with TBI is asked a question based on a series of three photographs. After responding correctly to the question, s/he produces a follow-up explanation.

FIRST PHOTOGRAPH: A couple is seated at a table and the woman says, 'Wear your glasses when you read.'
SECOND PHOTOGRAPH: The man is reading without his glasses.
THIRD PHOTOGRAPH: The woman is not happy.

QUESTION: Does the ending of the story go with the beginning?
CORRECT ANSWER: Yes.
EXPLANATION: Well yes. He's not listening! And he spent a fortune on his glasses and he doesn't even wear them! It's unthinkable! 'Besides, can you believe it, Marcel, they're not even covered by our health insurance!'

Data set 4

An adult with TBI is asked a question based on a series of three photographs. After responding correctly to the question, s/he produces a follow-up explanation.

FIRST PHOTOGRAPH: A couple in a living room. The man is playing the drums. The woman says, 'I have a terrible migraine.'
SECOND PHOTOGRAPH: The man is playing the drums.
THIRD PHOTOGRAPH: The woman is happy.

QUESTION: Does the ending of the story go with the beginning?
CORRECT ANSWER: No.
EXPLANATION: Because he obviously didn't take her situation into account, it's true, and so she should express her discontent, her headache that's gotten much worse.

Question 1 In data set 1, the response of the adult with TBI to the question about Janis Joplin is clearly a digression from the topic of 'favourite singers'. However, even within this digression, there is a difference between the early and later parts of this speaker's response. Describe what that difference is.

Question 2 Which of the following speech acts is examined by the series of three photographs in data set 2? Describe the post-response explanation that is offered by the adult with TBI in this case.

(a) direct request
(b) unconventional indirect promise
(c) conventional indirect request
(d) conventional indirect promise
(e) unconventional indirect request

Question 3 The speaker with TBI in data set 3 produces an interesting post-response explanation. Describe that response.

Question 4 Which of the following speech acts is examined by the series of three photographs in data set 4? The post-response explanation in this case suggests that the speaker with TBI has an intact theory of mind. What aspects of this explanation indicate this?

(a) direct request
(b) unconventional indirect promise
(c) conventional indirect request
(d) conventional indirect promise
(e) unconventional indirect request

Question 5 Which of the subjects with TBI in the above data sets displays evidence of perseveration? Which of the following cognitive impairments is associated with perseveration?

(a) impaired mental flexibility
(b) impaired working memory
(c) impaired inhibitory control
(d) impaired theory of mind
(e) impaired planning

3.9 Traumatic brain injury 3

Background

Investigators use a range of measures to assess narratives produced by clients with TBI. These measures include the number of propositions and content units (micro-linguistic level), the number and type of cohesive devices (micro-structural level), local and global coherence (macro-structural level), and the presence of episodes in a story grammar analysis (super-structural level). Lê et al. (2011) conducted an analysis of story retellings by 24 adults with TBI based on episode structure (story grammar) and story completeness. The three story grammar elements used in the analysis were initiating event (an event that prompts a character to act), attempt (actions related to the initiating event) and direct consequence (the consequence of those actions). Story completeness was scored by awarding one point for the presence of each of the following story components in the 16-frame picture story *Old McDonald had an apartment house* (Barrett, 1998):

(1) The couple/farmer moving to city and/or finding an apartment and/or having an apartment building (i.e. statement regarding urban living)
(2) The farmer having a garden/farm indoors.
(3) Tenants/neighbours becoming upset and/or moving out due to the farmer's indoor activities.
(4) The owner/inspector arriving and attempting to resolve the situation (e.g. couple is evicted and/or the owner has a brainstorm).
(5) Construction/buying of vegetable stand/greenhouse/market, business partnership between the farmer/owner.

The adults with TBI sustained severe penetrating head wounds, were aged between 54 and 62 years and were 34 to 37 years post-injury. The narratives produced by these adults were compared with those produced by 46 individuals with no history of neurological disease or injury. Narratives with high scores on both story grammar and story completeness were produced by 83% of subjects with no neurological impairment and 38% of individuals with brain injury. Narratives with a relatively high score on story grammar and a low score on story completeness were produced by only one participant with no brain injury and 33% of individuals with TBI. An example of each of these types of narrative is shown in data sets 1 and 2, respectively. Examine the narratives in these sets and then answer the questions that follow.

Data set 1

High scores on story grammar and story completeness.

1 Mr McDonald and his wife had this apartment building which had several ten- you know uh tenants
2 and as time went by he turned it into a vegetable farm
3 had vegetables here there each and everywhere
4 uh then later on he brought in some animals
5 and his world like turned into old McDonald's farm instead of old McDonald's apartment house
6 um he had vegetables and animals all over all over the floor
7 uh eventually the people tenants started moving out because of all the vegetables and the animals
8 and eventually uh old McDonald and his wife uh lost the apartment building it looked like according to the pictures
9 and but the landlord or who he owned owed owed the house to or the apartments to found him a diced vegetable stand to sell his produce and stuff out of
10 and all his uh tenants became his customers

Data set 2

High score on story grammar and low score on story completeness.

1 uh, they had uh a man and a woman and a borough
2 and then they had uh uh uh they had a tomato plant
3 and, oh god and everybody got out of the building
4 and they grew all the tomato plants and everything out out there in the building
5 and the owner come along uh hm and said, 'Get out' and then I don't even know what
6 and then he built him a ho-, or a fruits and vegetables or something that's it

Question 1 The lexical choices of the narrators in the above data sets contribute significantly to the informational content of these narratives. Describe these choices and explain how they contribute to an informative narrative in data set 1 and a somewhat uninformative narrative in data set 2.

Question 2 In data set 2, the narrator displays awareness of the need to establish referents for pronouns and other expressions in the narrative. Identify and describe two instances where this occurs.

Question 3 These two narrators use quite different devices to relate events in temporal terms. Explain the different ways in which the temporal relationships between events are expressed by these narrators.

Question 4 As well as failing to express temporal relationships between events, there is evidence that the narrator in data set 2 is relating events in the wrong order of occurrence. Give one example of this error in data set 2. In view of this error, what conceptual relationship appears to be disrupted in this narrator?

Question 5 Story components are variously included and omitted by these narrators. Respond with *true* or *false* to each of the following statements about the story components in these narratives.

(a) Neither narrator mentions that the characters in the story moved to the city.
(b) Only the narrator in data set 2 describes the eviction of McDonald and his wife.
(c) Both narrators describe how the landlord resolved the situation.
(d) Only the narrator in data set 1 describes the farmer's actions that prompted the tenants to move out.
(e) Neither narrator describes the distress of the tenants in the building.

3.9 Traumatic brain injury 4

Background

Different contexts pose unique challenges to the discourse skills of adults with TBI. Demands on these skills vary with the type and number of participants, the setting in which discourse is produced, and the mode of communication (face-to-face interaction or telephone conversation, for example). Some discourse contexts can facilitate communication on the part of adults with TBI, while other contexts may present barriers to communication for these individuals. Increasingly, studies are revealing that participants can both create and limit conversational opportunities for adults with TBI, the latter in ways that may bring about significant disempowerment of these individuals.

Togher and colleagues (Togher, 2001; Jorgensen and Togher, 2009) examined the discourse skills of adults with TBI in monologic and jointly produced narratives and in telephone conversation with an authority figure (a police officer). Extracts from the resulting narrative and conversational discourses are displayed in data sets 1, 2 and 3. Examine these extracts in detail and then answer the questions that follow.

Data set 1

Monologic narrative discourse produced by a 38-year-old man with TBI (time post TBI = 16 years).

Narrative task

Participants were requested to produce a narrative based on a comic strip known as *The Flowerpot Incident*. In this story, a man is walking his dog along the street when he is struck on the head by a flowerpot that has fallen from the balcony of a house occupied by an old woman. The man is angry and enters the building to remonstrate with the woman. However, she placates him by giving his dog a bone and they part on good terms.

Narrative produced by adult with TBI

Seems apparent that there is a person, upstairs obviously, and they have the they want to walk down the stairs. They start walking down the staircase and as they get near the bottom of the staircase they might notice someone else, and I'm unaware that they have a conversation, it doesn't look like they have as past, and the person that's walking down the stairs keeps walking down the stairs, and the other person is on is doing what they're doing, don't know just they just pass staircase, they're walking down the stairs.

Data set 2

Extract from a jointly produced narrative between a 38-year-old man ('PF') with TBI and a friend ('EK') with no neurological impairment. Subjects were asked to retell a segment from a holidays or home improvement video.

EK: Well, what sort of things did they use?
PF: They use –
EK: The sandstone, you said that.

Data set 3

A 30-year-old man ('MB') with a severe TBI is having a telephone conversation with a police officer ('JS') about having his driving licence reinstated after his motor vehicle accident.

MB: Actually I've had a bad car accident
JS: Yeah
MB: I need to get my licence back *(unintelligible)*
JS: Right yeah. What's your name?
MB: R.C.
JS: R.C. is it?
MB: Yeah
JS: Right
MB: And if you could tell me if there are any other requirements I've gotta pass in order to get my licence back
JS: Right
MB: What I've gotta go through to get it back in other words
JS: Yep. Yep. Do you know what the Roads and Traffic Authority is? The R.T.A. where you go to get your licence from
MB: Yeah down at Kogarah
JS: Yeah right
MB: Sure
JS: Um what what what you have to do is you can um if you have to go to the R.T.A. they'll put your application in to get a licence

MB: Sure
JS: Right? If you can understand that
MB: Yeah
JS: but prior to that, um what you have you have to go ah you know a driving school?
MB: Yeah
JS: Right and they um have rehabilitation people that ah can ah put you through oh like your driving lessons
MB: Sure
JS: and they can decide whether you know
MB: Whether you're capable
JS: Yeah whether you're then capable to go and get you licence
MB: Sure
JS: Right?
MB: Ok then

Question 1 The monologic narrative in data set 1 is particularly uninformative. What three linguistic features of this narrative contribute to its lack of informational content?

Question 2 In the jointly produced narrative in data set 2, friend EK uses a conversational strategy which places him in the role of the more powerful participant in the exchange. Describe this strategy and explain how it contrives to place PF in the role of the less powerful participant in the exchange.

Question 3 In data set 3, the police officer, JS, does not ask MB questions to which he already knows the answer. However, he does employ other conversational strategies which also function to place MB in the role of the less powerful individual in the exchange. One of these strategies involves JS's use of questions to force MB to establish his credibility as a reliable *epistemic* agent in the exchange. Identify two instances in data set 3 where this type of questioning occurs.

Question 4 As well as performing checks of MB's knowledge, JS also uses questions and other utterances throughout the exchange to establish if MB has understood the infor-mation which he has been given. Identify two instances where this occurs in data set 3. What effect does this type of strategy have on the exchange between JS and MB?

Question 5 As well as using questions to check MB's understanding of language, JS also uses questions to check MB's expressive language skills. Identify one instance where this occurs in data set 3.

3.10 Dementias 1

Background

The following extracts of data were produced by adults with Alzheimer's disease who were studied by Chapman et al. (1998). The data were collected during a range of discourse production tasks. The tasks involved (1) retelling fables, (2) capturing the gist of fables, (3) conveying the lesson of fables, (4) story generation based on a single frame picture, and (5) verbal explanations of the meaning of proverbs. Each of these tasks places different demands on a speaker's cognitive, linguistic and pragmatic skills. The responses of adults to (1), (3) and (5) are presented below. Contributions by the examiner ('E') are indicated in parentheses. Examine these extracts and then answer the questions that follow.

Fable

A hungry raven saw that pigeons in the pigeon coop had a lot of food. He painted his feathers white to look like them. But when he started to crow, they realised that he was a raven and chased him away. So he returned to his own kind. But the other ravens did not recognise him because he had his feathers painted white, so they also chased him away.

Data set 1

Subjects read and heard the fable above, which they were then asked to retell.

Well, you had now- it was a bird, it was uh, raven uh, who was uh, is a raven and uh I believe he noticed that uh uh the crows uh was a getting something to eat. Uh, so he uh, got uh painted or they painted him, figured he could get more, a better deal on that, that's right – I believe that the uh crows that's what it was, kinda knocked him out of that game. (E: And what happened?) So he went back to his uh (4 seconds), he went back to his own business. (7 seconds) Took care of him it, got his own food.

Data set 2

Subjects were asked to convey a lesson which could be learned from the fable.

There's no- there's no uh uh, it's no one, you can't get it for nothing, you can't get anything for nothing.

Data set 3

Subjects were asked to explain the meaning of the proverb 'Too many cooks spoil the broth.'

Too many cooks spoil the broth . . . too many cooks spoil the broth . . . (E: Got a guess on it?) Well, there's bound to be something there. I know it happens (laughs). I know that's happened. Uh . . . (E: What does it mean in general?) Yeah, well uh . . . you can't get a whole lot of things done with a whole lot of people. You've got to come up with some kind of a thing that's 'doable' and that some people may not be involved with it. Uh . . . you don't want to have uh- you just can't ex- take 'em all. (E: How come?) Well, they got too many eyes- eyes or too- gonna uh, the cooks too as well- too many people get involved in something *** that way responsibility had to be uh and uh . . . you can't have twelve people getting involved with something and somebody's got to do it.

Question 1 The fable retell of the adult with Alzheimer's disease in data set 1 is compromised by expressive language problems. Several of these problems are listed below. Give <u>one</u> example of each of these difficulties in the data set:

(a) semantic paraphasia
(b) omission of pronouns
(c) word-finding difficulty
(d) utterance revision
(e) incomplete relative clause

Question 2   Notwithstanding significant expressive language problems, the adult in data set 1 manages to convey several of the components of the fable. Describe the story components which this speaker succeeds in conveying as well as those which he omits from his retelling.

Question 3   In data set 1, are the story components communicated in an order which reflects the causal relationships between events in the fable? Also, are any story components misrepresented by the adult with Alzheimer's disease?

Question 4   In data set 2, the adult with Alzheimer's disease partially captures the lesson of the fable. Describe the way in which this adult only partially captures the lesson of the fable.

Question 5   In data set 3, the adult with Alzheimer's disease succeeds in conveying the essence of the proverb's meaning. Describe how this adult constructs this meaning across a series of utterances.

3.10   Dementias 2

Background

Few investigations have examined the pragmatic and discourse skills of adults with AIDS dementia complex. Part of the reason for this neglect is that clients with AIDS dementia complex often have pragmatic language deficits which are not detected on standardised language tests. McCabe et al. (2008) reported the case of a 36-year-old man called Warren who had only mild language impairments as measured on standardised tests. However, Warren's pragmatic language skills were severely impaired. This was particularly evident during conversation. McCabe et al. concluded that Warren's poor pragmatic skills in the absence of a frank aphasia and dysarthria may be related to a non-linguistic, cognitive impairment.

Warren underwent a battery of psycholinguistic and observational measures on three occasions during a 13-month period. A semi-structured interview was conducted on the first of these occasions by a researcher who was a speech–language pathologist. This interview was essentially conversational in nature. It addressed Warren's AIDS as well as life in general. In the following conversational extract, Warren (W) is talking to this researcher (R). Examine the exchange in detail and then answer the questions that follow.

Data set

R: So you'd be 34 then?
W: I've been 34 for the last 3 years
R: ah, OK so you're actually?
W: Oh what happened was I added a year and a year at my birthday, didn't celebrate it so therefore I forgot about it. In September as a halfway between two ages I start saying what the next one is
R: Uh huh?
W: So I've added there as well and the years come along and I didn't remember doing either of the first two so I did it again when I was 32
R: Oh dear

W: Someone pointed out that I was 34 last year and 33 last year and I went 'no, I'm not I'm 34', I'm gonna get me a calculator and a new set of batteries that were still in the package so that guaranteed the calculator was working properly 'cause it kept telling me I was 33 and I could'a swore it was lying to me.

R: What year were you born in?

W: '64

R: '64

W: The odd thing was, was I was filling out doctors' forms and hospital forms and all sort of things, putting down the date of birth as xxth of xxxx of '64 and my age was 34 but a diversional therapist in a nursing home was the only person who actually noticed that there was something wrong with this picture. I thought 'well, it's fairly obvious I'm in it' so there's your problem.

Question 1 The speech–language pathologist's clinical impressions of Warren were that he was verbose, unable to maintain a topic and unaware of the needs of his listener. What evidence is there in the above exchange to confirm this clinical impression?

Question 2 Notwithstanding Warren's significant pragmatic difficulties, some aspects of pragmatics and discourse are intact on occasion in the above exchange. Several are listed below. Give one example of each of these aspects:

(a) use of pronominal reference
(b) use of lexical substitution
(c) use of direct reported speech
(d) use of presupposition
(e) use of causal connectives to link actions

Question 3 Some of Warren's utterances are false or contradictory in nature. Give two examples of these utterances. Which Gricean maxim does Warren fail to observe in these utterances?

Question 4 The investigators attribute Warren's pragmatic difficulties to cognitive deficits in executive functioning. However, there is evidence in Warren's use of mental state language that another cognitive capacity may be reasonably intact. You should (a) give three examples of Warren's use of mental state language in the exchange and (b) indicate what cognitive capacity Warren must possess in order to use this language.

Question 5 There may appear to be some inconsistency between the cognitive capacity identified in response to question 4 and the observation in question 1 that Warren is unaware of the needs of his listener. Explain how this is an inconsistency in appearance only.

3.10 Dementias 3

Background

Topic management is a complex cognitive–linguistic process which is often disrupted in clients with dementia. Mentis et al. (1995) examined the topic management skills of

12 individuals with senile dementia of the Alzheimer's type (SDAT). These subjects had a mean age of 78.59 years. They were matched to 12 normal elderly subjects on age, sex and education. The subjects with SDAT fell within the moderate-to-severe dementia range based on an assessment of their mental functioning. The language skills of these subjects were also assessed in the areas of spontaneous speech, comprehension, repetition and naming using the Western Aphasia Battery (Kertesz, 1979). Subjects achieved a mean aphasia quotient on this battery of 74.2 out of a possible maximum score of 100. Topic management skills were assessed during a 20-minute casual conversational interaction with a speech–language pathologist. These interactions were video-recorded and transcribed orthographically. Several extracts from them are presented below. Examine these extracts in detail and then answer the questions that follow.

Data set 1

An adult with SDAT ('HP') is talking to a speech–language pathologist ('SP') about the topic of cooking.

HP: ... and I I can't explain it/ it's just-/ it's just I don't cook/
    I used to when I raised my family/
 SP: now who else is in your family?/

Data set 2

An adult with SDAT ('CD') is talking to a speech–language pathologist ('SP') about the topic of HP's husbands.

 SP: ... were they both American?/
CD: I don't know/ I don't know/
    kinda think that he wasn't/ belonged to other countries/
 SP: hm/
CD: no/ (3 seconds)
 SP: so what are you going to do when you go back today?/

Data set 3

An adult with SDAT ('WP') is talking to a speech–language pathologist ('SP') about the topic of restaurants.

 SP: what's your favourite type of meal to have when
    you go ... when you go out to eat?/
WP: well uh uh we we had uh/ Sally was not was my daughter uh/
    but but uh she she uh uh/ Sally Smith was was was my daughter/

Data set 4

An adult with SDAT ('PS') is talking to a speech–language pathologist ('SP') about her husband and son.

PS: my son is in the army/ and then/ and and and my hu- husband/
    he's-/ he's sick/
SP: um hm
PS: he he gets around/ but he-/ you know/ he can't he can't walk/

Data set 5

An adult with SDAT ('AF') is talking to a speech–language pathologist ('SP') about her hobbies.

SP: do you have any hobbies?/ or little projects that you do?/
AF: ah/ walking/ and ah/ sometimes um/ it's a bit/ you know/
    it can be boring/ because ah/ there are no . . . challenges/

Data set 6

An adult with SDAT ('JK') is talking to a speech–language pathologist ('SP') about his job in the marines.

SP: what did you do in the marines?/ what was your job there?/
JK: well I ah-/ I ah-/ I held it and/ I went from um-/ I sometimes forget/
    I get out and I-/ didn't take me long to change my mind/
    I majored first in landing and/ and ah/ our company of marines/ and ah/
    I majored first in landing/ of ah-/ of ah-/ a lot of us get out/ get off the ships and-/
    didn't take me long to get out/ and I/ I got out and then they got me in again/

Question 1 On the basis of data sets 1 and 2, it is clear that subjects with SDAT can retain considerable language, cognitive and discourse skills even at the stage of moderate-to-severe dementia. Give one example of (a) the retention of long-term memory, (b) the understanding of abstract concepts and (c) the use of ellipsis by the subjects with SDAT in these data sets.

Question 2 One of the adults with SDAT displays a lack of topic relevance. Which subject is it? As well as contributing irrelevant information to the exchange, this subject contributes inconsistent information. Give an example of where this occurs in the appropriate data set.

Question 3 The contributions of the adults with SDAT display evidence of both structural language problems and discourse deficits. Give two examples of each type of impairment in the above data sets.

Question 4 In data set 6, the adult with SDAT is particularly difficult to follow during his extended turn. Describe three features of this turn which make it difficult to follow.

Question 5 In data sets 4 and 5, the speakers with SDAT use a number of cohesive devices to link the various utterances within their turns. Identify five such devices.

3.10 Dementias 4

Background

The management of deixis is a complex pragmatic–discourse skill which is disrupted by the onset of dementias. This can lead to significant conversational difficulties as clients with dementia are often unable to establish the referents of personal and demonstrative pronouns (e.g. you, that), adverbs (e.g. here) and many other linguistic expressions. An awareness of these conversational difficulties, and the ability to repair them, may also be compromised by dementias. These abilities are essentially metalinguistic in nature as they require speakers to take a step back and interrogate the use of language in a particular exchange. This may involve asking what a speaker means by an utterance. It may also involve conducting 'lexical checks' of one's own use of words and the use of words by other speakers, not all of whom are present in an exchange.

The following data sets contain a short picture description by a patient with semantic dementia who was studied by Ogar et al. (2011). There are also short conversational exchanges between clients with early- or middle-stage dementia of the Alzheimer's type and family members who acted as conversational partners. These subjects participated in a study of conversational repair conducted by Orange et al. (1996). The extracts exemplify the pragmatic and discourse behaviours described above including the use (and misuse) of deixis and a range of metalinguistic skills. Examine each data set in detail and then answer the questions that follow.

Data set 1

Description of the picnic scene from the Western Aphasia Battery (Kertesz, 1982) by a patient with semantic dementia. In this scene, a man and a woman are having a picnic. The man is reading a book, and the woman is pouring a drink into a glass. There is a second man in the scene and he is flying a kite. A dog is standing next to him.

Looks like there's a husband and wife. She's reading and she's drinking and then there's another young man who has a . . . I want to say 'flag', but it's not a flag, but he's holding something up in the air . . .

Data set 2

Conversational exchanges between subjects (SUBJ) with early-stage dementia of the Alzheimer's type and their conversational partners (PART).

Exchange 1

PART: So I think I'll go and *(pause)* and watch the golf okay?
SUBJ: Where on *(pause)* on the T.V.?

Exchange 2

PART: The dollar's 86 ½ cents now.
SUBJ: You mean the purchasing power of the Canadian dollar is better than the American?
PART: No not better but but it's up to 86 ½ instead of 70 on the American dollar.

Data set 3

Conversational exchanges between subjects (SUBJ) with middle-stage dementia of the Alzheimer's type and their conversational partners (PART).

Exchange 1

PART: Maybe you can have a ride down to your brother's house and then you can walk from there.

SUBJ: From where?
PART: From Nick's house.

Exchange 2

PART: Do you want to have a drink now or wait until after?
SUBJ: Who me?
PART: Yeah.

Data set 4

Conversational exchanges between subjects (SUBJ) with middle-stage dementia of the Alzheimer's type and their conversational partners (PART).

Exchange 1

PART: What did Paul call it the flea bag or something like that?
SUBJ: Something like that.

Exchange 2

SUBJ: I was gonna say to *(pause)* to um *(long pause)* Isabel *(pause)* about um *(long pause)* what's her name *(pause)* from?
PART: Georgina and Ken?
SUBJ: Yeah.

Question 1 There is evidence in the above data sets of impairment in the use and understanding of deictic expressions including pronouns and adverbs. Give <u>three</u> examples of impaired deixis in these sets.

Question 2 The ability to check one's understanding of others' utterances is an important metalinguistic skill. Identify <u>two</u> instances in the above data sets where this skill is being exercised by a client with dementia to check utterance interpretation.

Question 3 On the basis of your answers to questions 1 and 2, summarise the impact of early and middle-stage Alzheimer's dementia on pragmatic and discourse skills. Your answer should include discussion of cognitive processes such as theory of mind.

Question 4 The subjects with dementia in the above data sets participate in lexical checks of various types. Some of these checks are initiated by the clients with dementia while others are initiated by their partners. Identify <u>three</u> instances where these lexical checks occur in the data sets.

Question 5 Certain of the lexical checks identified in response to question 4 are related to a specific linguistic deficit. What is that deficit? What does the presence of this deficit alongside an intact ability to perform lexical checks suggest about the effect of dementia on linguistic and metalinguistic skills?

3.10 Dementias 5

Background

Semantic dementia is a type of frontotemporal dementia in which there is a marked deterioration in semantic memory. The impairment of semantic memory can affect all modalities and leads to difficulty in recognising and understanding words, objects, faces, sounds, smells, touch and tastes. Expressive language is fluent with vague terms and expressions increasingly replacing content words in speech. Semantic deterioration occurs alongside well-preserved visuospatial skills, and personality and behaviour changes are also common.

Kindell et al. (2013) studied the everyday conversation of a retired engineering lecturer called Doug who received a diagnosis of semantic dementia in 2006. Since his diagnosis, Doug had been known to mental health services and had been in regular contact with the local speech and language therapist. At diagnosis, Doug presented with severe word-finding difficulties, semantic loss on verbal and conceptual tasks, surface dyslexia, preserved repetition, and day-to-day memory and spatial skills. In the data sets below, Doug (D) is in conversation with his wife Karina (K) of 45 years and a researcher called Jacqueline (J). The topics of conversation include everyday activities, such as going to the shops, shopping for shirts, how Doug initiates and sustains a conversation and how he spent his weekend. Examine each of the extracts in detail and then answer the questions that follow.

Transcription notation

<u>need</u>	emphasis
[ ]	overlapping utterances
° °	quieter talk
↑	rising shifts in intonation
↓	falling shifts in intonation

Data set 1

Doug and Karina are talking about going to the shops.

K: So <u>tomorrow</u> then after <u>Susannah</u>'s been I think we should (1.1) go shop↑ping (2.2)
D: ye I [ne-   ]
K: [d' you]
D: <u>yeah</u> I do need some sho- we <u>need</u> some shopping we're [other]wise we'll be running
K: [mmm]
D: around saying [where's where's this and where's the other and <u>blimey</u> no we'll
          [*((hands and eyes side to side . . . tapping on the table . . .*
   we'll go out] out and and get what we <u>can</u>
   points 'out']
K: so is there <u>anything</u> in particular you can think of that we might need or: (2.2)
D: <u>really</u> (at) at that at thats: (1.7) /s:/ you cou- as y you think about (.) what have we got
   we got to <u>take</u> when we get there ans so we can (2.1) an an say oh yeah we
   [need to get those and] then we've got to go and [get the other ones and we got to go
   [*((2 hands holding))*   ]   [*((L hand one side . . .   . . . R hand to*
   on that ways] and and (1.2) you just you walking around and making con conversations
   other side))]
   on in relation to the the actual (2.4) ° items that are ° (0.6) you're looking for

[and that's] that's the

K: [Mmhm]

D: thing is sometimes you you go: and you think [oh blimey forgot that one and you turn
                                              [((hand forward acting out turning
round and walk back to get it and carry on] the next bit
right   hand back & right . . . body forward))]

K: Mmhm↑ ok did ya and you've tried your (0.8) new jumper thing on haven't you that you
bought

Data set 2

Doug and Karina are talking about shopping for new shirts.

K: is there anything else↑ now that we could have a look in the sales do you think
or you think (1.4)

D: er: [mmm]

K: [Have] you got everything↑ (.) couple of sh- new shirts possibly

D: Well I've got some sh ye:s (0.5) erm (1.3) I'm mine- I'm I'm quite happy with em
but er hh (0.7) its just one of those things I quite enjoy [going to this part and w what
                                                          [((2 hands 'going' ....
I've got (0.8) and then I can look down and say oh yes and going for a walk and
           .... *hand across and eye point*   ....
I'll I'll take this one]
.... *2 hand grasp))]*

K: I think we could (0.6) throw a couple of your old shirts out really (1.5) cos the colours
are a bit worn (1.1)

D: [Well we could] have we c- we can de- yeah

K: [aren't they   ]

D: it's worth going and and [looking very closely] saying [I I really want that] or no
                          [*2 hands and tap   *]   [((2 hand point))   ]
[I don't want those] and that that [will be]
[((*2 hand brush aside))*]

K: [mm you] can choose can't you [you can choose]

D: [that that will make]
some sense yeah

Data set 3

Doug and Jacqueline are talking about what Doug did at the weekend.

J: So what did you do at the weekend then anything (.) nice?

D: When it wasn't raining
((Some comments omitted here about the rain and Doug talking about going to the shop))

D: I know most of the people there you see I-

J: Is that at the Spar shop

D: Yes sorry I don't say do I I keep forgetting at the Spar shop

J: yeah

D: Because it's got everything that er an I I go up and say [hello   ] and there's this one
                                                          [((point))]
one wo- woman I say how's ↑ things and and they they just go [(0.8)] I said and I
                                                            [((face))]

[(0.6)] for you as well hhhhhh

[((*face*))]

J: hh mmm

D: hhh its er

J: that's ↑nice

D: oh yeah ° yeah yeah °

J: pass the time of ↑day

D: we don't le- forget that n- [she- she's doin what she's doin and then she goes right

                           [((*2 hands ...... busy hand movements .....*

I said fine and I just walk to the next bit

Data set 4

Doug and Jacqueline are talking about Doug's speech difficulties.

J: cos for a few years now its affected (2.0) your speech hasn't it its

D: erm (0.9) y- I suppose it has in a way but its never (1.1) never been a problem

J: right ok

D: to me if someone said you're a fool I would say [oh thank god for that]

                                      [((*hands open .... *))]

J: hhhh

D: n- that and an another thing another thing you say [oh (1.2) where are we going and

                                         [((*L hand up gaining attention,*

some would say de de de say oh right thanks]

left hand   point beats ...... R hand up))]

J: mmmm

D: er and thats but [it's usually it's not   ] it's just you talk (to people) and you just say

                    [((*hands neg shake*))]

[yeah it's I've had a brilliant day did you ↑have a good night yeah that was brilliant

[*hand and eye points to left .... points to front..................... points to right*

what de de] and [it's most of the time]

   & front))]   [((*2 hands up by face*))]

J: yeah

D: it really really is

J: mmm yeah yeah

D: erm

J: so it sounds li- (checked camera) sounds like you keep carrying on regardless then (1.1)

you just carry on

D: oh yeah

J: don't let it stop you doing things

D: oh no

Question 1 In an effort to compensate for the effects of his degraded semantic system, Doug makes extensive use of an adaptive strategy in which he is seen to act out events during conversation. This strategy, known as 'enactment', employs the following verbal and non-verbal behaviours. Give <u>one</u> example of each of these behaviours across the four data sets:

(a) direct reported speech

(b) prosody

(c) facial expressions

(d) body movements

(e) eye gaze

Question 2 Even aside from the use of enactment, Doug is able to function as a reasonably effective communicator. Several pragmatic and discourse skills enable Doug to operate effectively in conversation with others. Five of these skills are listed below. Give one example of each skill in the above data sets.

(a) Doug is able to respond to requests for clarification.

(b) Doug is able to make referential use of demonstrative pronouns.

(c) Doug is able to use a form of grammatical cohesion called substitution.

(d) Doug is able to make use of anaphoric reference.

(e) Doug is able to use a form of grammatical cohesion called ellipsis.

Question 3 Doug's use of mental state language suggests that theory of mind, or ToM, skills are relatively well preserved in semantic dementia. Give five examples of Doug's use of mental state language in the data. For each example you give, indicate if it is an instance of cognitive ToM or affective ToM.

Question 4 As well as being able to produce direct reported speech, Doug is able to use direct reported thought. Give one example of the latter type of language use in the data.

Question 5 Consistent with the preservation of visuospatial skills in semantic dementia, Doug makes extensive use of spatial and directional language. Give five examples of this use of language in the data.

3.11   Neurodegenerative disorders 1

Background

Pragmatic and discourse skills are often impaired in clients with Parkinson's disease (PD) even in the absence of dementia. These skills were examined by Duncan (2008) in a study of storytelling in two adults with moderately severe PD. These adults watched a 6.5-minute cartoon about a bird (Tweety) and a cat (Sylvester). The cat repeatedly attempts to catch the bird using various disguises and strategies, but fails to do so on each occasion. In the cartoon, the cat is typically located on the right side of the viewing screen and the bird is on the left side, with the cat moving from right to left in pursuit of the bird. In separate viewings, the adults with PD watched the cartoon and retold its story to listener participants. These participants were encouraged to be active and engaged in order that they would be able to retell the story to another listener. Extracts from these adults' narratives are shown below. Examine these extracts in detail and then answer the questions that follow.

Data set 1

This adult with PD is at the point in the development of the disease where she is experiencing the onset of balance problems. She has received Levodopa therapy for several years which has improved many symptoms, including hand tremor. She is describing scenes in the cartoon where Granny, the owner of the bird, is looking out of the window to see who has knocked on the door. Down below, Sylvester is dressed in a bellman's costume. He asks Granny for her bags.

> so he goes up to the room and knocks on the door
> in a- in a bell-/ bell cost-/ costume- bellman's costume
> and knocks on the door and says-/
> granny looks out the top of the/ window *(left hand moves above head and holds)*
> and says/ could I help you *(left hand held)*
> and she said *(left hand held)*
> I'm here to pick the luggage up *(left hand held)*
> okay my bird and the/ luggage is in the door here *(left hand held)*
> I'll be-/ I'll meet you downstairs *(left hand held)*
> so he goes in/ picks the bird up/ takes the bird down/

Data set 2

This adult also has moderately severe PD. The scene being described is one in which the cat climbs up inside a drainpipe that ends near the bird's window. However, the cat fails to reach the window when the bird knocks the cat back down by throwing a bowling ball into the pipe.

> and he/ climbed up the/ drainpipe
> and he dropped a/ bowling ball down the drainpipe/
> and somehow it got inside him
> I didn't understand that/
> and he went rolling over
> to the bowling alley
> and you could hear him hit a strike/

Question 1 These narrative extracts reveal the use of several intact discourse features on the part of these adults with PD. Several of these features are listed below. Give <u>one</u> example of each feature in the above data sets:

(a) direct reported speech
(b) demonstrative reference
(c) self-initiated repair
(d) cohesive conjunction
(e) anaphoric reference

Question 2 The speakers in these data sets commit errors of pronominal reference. Identify <u>one</u> error committed by each speaker.

Question 3 These speakers are producing narratives around an action-based cartoon. A large proportion of action-based language is, therefore, to be expected. Is there any evidence that these speakers are also able to use mental state language? What cognitive skill would appear to be intact in the speaker with PD who uses this language?

Question 4 Describe the use of gesture by the speaker in data set 1. What function is it performing in this discourse context?

Question 5 One of the above speakers appears to abandon her communicative intention in speaking. Identify the speaker in question and the point in the narrative extract at which this abandonment occurs.

3.11   Neurodegenerative disorders 2

Background

Many other neurodegenerative conditions which are less common than Parkinson's disease can also cause pragmatic and discourse impairments. Two such conditions are Huntington's disease and corticobasal syndrome. In Huntington's disease, there is a degeneration of neurones in the basal ganglia which are responsible for movement and coordination. Chorea, cognitive decline (leading to dementia) and psychiatric impairment are features of the disease. Corticobasal syndrome is a clinical syndrome presenting with progressive asymmetric bradykinesia, rigidity, and dystonia accompanied by cortical signs such as apraxia, alien limb phenomenon and cortical sensory loss.

Illes (1989) examined spontaneous language production in patients with Huntington's disease and observed temporal interruptions, reduced syntactic complexity and verbal paraphasias (the latter in moderately advanced patients). Gross et al. (2010) studied the discourse skills of 20 patients with corticobasal syndrome. These patients narrated a picture story which was then analysed for maintenance of the narrative theme, identification of the overall point of the story (global connectedness) and connectedness between consecutive events (local connectedness). Data from both of these studies is presented below. Examine each data set in detail and then answer the questions that follow.

Data set 1

The spontaneous language of an adult with Huntington's disease who is talking about the topic of travel and holidays.

Okay I I had a nice one, my wife and I. Years ago we went down to the Caribbean. And so I saw I had never seen the ocean before. It was really beautiful. I don't know. Have you travelled much? Maybe you've seen the Caribbean. It's just outstanding to see the beauty of the water. Just such a beautiful thing. You know, the the water . . .

Data set 2

An adult with corticobasal syndrome is describing a scene from the wordless picture book, *Frog, where are you?* (Mayer, 1969).

. . . there's a frog . . . in a jar – and there's slippers there and there's uh a shirt and a sock and boots and a stool and a window and a bed and a lamp . . .

Question 1 The speaker with Huntington's disease in data set 1 is using a range of discourse skills to good effect. Several of these skills are listed below. Give <u>one</u> example of each of these skills.

(a) The speaker is able to use a form of grammatical cohesion called substitution.
(b) The speaker is able to use anaphoric reference.
(c) The speaker is able to use self-initiated repair.
(d) The speaker is able to use temporal expressions appropriately.
(e) The speaker is able to use cohesive conjunctions.

Question 2 The speaker in data set 1 is also able to use different types of language. Give <u>one</u> example of each of the following uses of language in the above data sets:

(a) mental state language
(b) evaluative language
(c) descriptive language

Question 3 The speaker in data set 1 is somewhat repetitive in his use of language. Describe the repetitiveness in this speaker's language.

Question 4 Explain why the account of the scene provided by the adult in data set 2 is not particularly satisfactory to a hearer even though it is informative.

Question 5 The following cognitive and language skills were also examined in the study by Gross et al. (2010). Which of them may account for the discourse impairment described in response to question 4?

(a) episodic memory
(b) visual confrontation naming
(c) higher-order integration of visual material
(d) visuospatial ability
(e) visuoperceptual ability

3.12 Central nervous system infections

Background

Infections of the central nervous system (CNS) can disrupt a range of language skills including pragmatic and discourse abilities. One such infection is encephalitis. Smith Doody et al. (1992) studied a 47-year-old Hispanic man, known as D.L., who had seizures following encephalitis. D.L. was admitted to hospital after experiencing the sudden onset of altered mental status. On examination, he was alert but disoriented to person, place, time and situation. His answers to questions were confounded by receptive aphasia. An MRI scan showed that there had been no change since a postcraniotomy study which was conducted 16 months earlier during a hospital admission for the sudden onset of confusion. An EEG was conducted the morning after admission. It showed normal background activity and, every 1–3 seconds, recurrent moderate-to-high voltage spike and slow and sharp and slow wave activity in the left temporal region. D.L. had two episodes of staring with unresponsiveness on the second day after admission. This correlated with continuous spike and wave discharges in the left temporo-occipital region on EEG.

On the fifth day after admission, D.L. underwent neuropsychological and language testing. His attention–concentration performance was variable. When questioned in writing, he was fully oriented. However, he could not understand the orientation questions when he was orally questioned. Comprehension difficulties meant that visual and verbal memory could not be tested. D.L. had moderate auditory comprehension problems. His speech was fluent and paraphasic with discernable phrases. Confrontation naming was moderately defective and his ability to read aloud was only mildly impaired. There was mild to moderate impairment of reading comprehension. D.L. could verbalise his difficulty understanding others, but did not appear to realise when he failed to make sense.

The following data were collected from D.L. during the session in which language testing was conducted. It includes two spontaneous speech samples as well as D.L.'s expressive language during a picture description task. Examine each data set in detail and then answer the questions that follow.

Data set 1

Spontaneous speech (rapidly spoken) during the testing session.

I lost my language – I'm just kind of waking up – I lost my concen – I'm just now concentrating – Everybody that's talking to me I don't understand them.

Data set 2

Spontaneous speech during the taking of D.L.'s history.

I've been disabled all this *(incomprehensible neologisms)*, last week I lost a lot of *(incomprehensible neologisms)*, I lost my concern I'm just now concentrated went to the hospital about an hour on my brain.

Data set 3

Description of the Cookie Theft picture from the Boston Diagnostic Aphasia Examination. In the picture, a woman is standing at the kitchen sink drying a plate, while the sink is overflowing with water. Meanwhile, a boy (presumably the woman's son) has climbed a stool which is rocking precariously and is taking cookies from a jar in the cupboard. A girl (presumably the boy's sister) has her hand raised upwards to receive the cookies that her brother is taking.

O.K. cookie jar, cookin-fallin' water trees. To interpret what he's doing? He's falling . . . to get the cookies I don't know if he's trying to say and ofring? The water the sink. I told you about the she's claimin? the glass. I don't know if he's asking him to drink or what the girl I don't know if I can figure out if he's a girl I mean a boy that's about all the wh . . .

Question 1 There is an overriding theme to D.L.'s spontaneous speech in data sets 1 and 2. What is this theme? How does D.L. use this theme to organise his personal narrative?

Question 2 Although D.L.'s expressive language is often incoherent and incomprehensible, he is partially successful in constructing a meaningful personal narrative around the repetition of two linguistic constructions. What are these constructions? Describe their function in D.L.'s account of what has happened to him.

Question 3 D.L. produces a number of utterances which suggest that he retains some metalinguistic and metacognitive awareness. Give three examples of these utterances.

Question 4 The final utterance in D.L.'s picture description is particularly difficult to follow. Explain why this is the case.

Question 5 Notwithstanding D.L.'s considerable language and cognitive problems he is still able to use certain discourse skills during the picture description task. Some of these skills are listed below. Give one example of each discourse skill.

(a) D.L. is able to use self-initiated repair.
(b) D.L. is able to describe prominent objects in the scene.
(c) D.L. is able to describe the goals of the characters.
(d) D.L. is able to describe prominent actions in the scene.
(e) D.L. is able to interpret actions in intentional terms.

SUGGESTIONS FOR FURTHER READING

Armstrong, E., Ferguson, A. and Simmons-Mackie, N. 2013. 'Discourse and functional approaches to aphasia', in I. Papathanasiou, P. Coppens and C. Potagas (eds), *Aphasia and related neurogenic communication disorders*, Burlington, MA: Jones & Bartlett Learning.

Bayles, K. and Tomoeda, C. 2007. *Cognitive–communication disorders of dementia: definition, diagnosis, and treatment*, San Diego, CA: Plural Publishing.

Holtgraves, T. and McNamara, P. 2010. 'Pragmatic comprehension deficit in Parkinson's disease', *Journal of Clinical and Experimental Neuropsychology* **32**:4, 388–97.

Murdoch, B. E. 2010. *Acquired speech and language disorders: a neuroanatomical and functional neurological approach*, second edition, Chichester, West Sussex: Wiley-Blackwell. (Chapter 5: Language disorders subsequent to right-hemisphere lesions.)

Saldert, C., Fors, A., Ströberg, S. and Hartelius, L. 2010. 'Comprehension of complex discourse in different stages of Huntington's disease', *International Journal of Language & Communication Disorders* **45**:6, 656–69.

Togher, L., McDonald, S., Coelho, C. A. and Byom, L. 2014. 'Cognitive communication disability following TBI: examining discourse, pragmatics, behaviour and executive functioning', in S. McDonald, L. Togher and C. Code (eds), *Social and communication disorders following traumatic brain injury*, Hove and New York: Psychology Press.

Chapter 4

Mental health and pragmatic and discourse disorders

There is increasing awareness among clinicians of the adverse impact of mental health problems on the language and communication skills of children and adults with these problems. Psychiatric disorders such as schizophrenia have significant implications for the pragmatic and discourse skills of clients and have been studied, assessed and treated by speech and language therapists (SLTs) for many years. Other psychiatric conditions such as bipolar disorder and personality disorder have attracted less attention from speech and language therapists, but are nonetheless noteworthy for their capacity to disrupt language and communication. In adulthood, addiction to alcohol and substances such as cocaine, cannabis and heroin can have damaging, long-term consequences for cerebral function. (Of course, these same substances can have even more damaging effects on foetal neurodevelopment during the pre-natal period.) The neurochemical and neurodegenerative changes that are caused by these addictions may lead to dementia, executive function deficits and reduced intellectual functioning, all of which have adverse implications for pragmatic and discourse skills (see chapter 3 for discussion of alcohol-related dementia or Korsakoff's syndrome). Conditions such as attention deficit hyperactivity disorder (ADHD), selective mutism and conduct disorder are increasingly finding their way into the clinical caseloads of speech and language therapists. These emotional and behavioural disturbances can disrupt structural language skills in children. However, they often have an equally detrimental impact on pragmatic and discourse skills.

The psychiatric disorders addressed in this chapter are typically diagnosed by psychiatrists and psychologists. These diagnoses are made on the basis of criteria which are contained in the fifth edition of the *Diagnostic and Statistical Manual of Mental Disorders* (DSM-5; American Psychiatric Association, 2013). Many of the diagnostic criteria in this volume describe communicative anomalies. These anomalies include poverty of speech (alogia) in schizophrenia and the initiation of conversations at inappropriate times in ADHD. It has been argued in Cummings (2012b) that many of these diagnostic criteria capture pragmatic and discourse features of language. Indeed, it is at the level of pragmatics and discourse that individuals with psychiatric conditions often experience their most significant communicative deficits. An increased emphasis on the study of impairments at these language levels would, thus, appear to be warranted.

The clinical management of children and adults with these psychiatric conditions is complex and challenging. The expertise and knowledge of speech–language pathology and psychiatry must come together in order for the assessment and treatment of these clients to be maximally effective. Psychiatric treatment of clients with schizophrenia, for example, cannot achieve a successful outcome in the absence of social communication interventions of the type that speech and language therapy can provide. Similarly, speech and language therapy which is ill-informed about the neurocognitive bases of ADHD or substance-use disorders is destined to achieve limited results. The clinical management of clients with psychiatric disorders is challenging in a further respect. Psychiatric disorders such as schizophrenia and ADHD often co-exist with other conditions which also have implications for language (and, by implication, pragmatics and discourse). These conditions include depression (in the case of schizophrenia) and intellectual disability and autism spectrum disorder (in the case of ADHD). The respective contributions of these conditions to a pragmatic or discourse disorder are difficult to establish and yet are important to decisions regarding assessment and intervention. In this way, the child with ADHD and autism spectrum disorder may exhibit a range of pragmatic and discourse deficits. Some of these deficits may be related to the theory of mind (ToM) impairments which are typical of ASD, while others are a consequence of impulsive behaviour in ADHD. In turn, an intervention which addresses a ToM-based pragmatic impairment is unlikely to be effective in the treatment of a pragmatic impairment that results from impulsive behaviour.

The SLT management of clients with psychiatric disorders is challenging in another, important respect. Many of these clients are beyond the reach of clinical language services. Typically, this is on account of factors such as social isolation, homelessness and incarceration in prisons and other correctional facilities. The provision of clinical language services in forensic settings is highly variable to say the least, with many detainees receiving little or no assessment and treatment of their language and communication problems; see sections 5.7 and 6.3 in Cummings (2014a) for further discussion. Even when clinical language services are available, clients with psychiatric disorders frequently fail to access these services or to derive significant benefit from them. This is related less to the standard of these services than to the inability of clients to comply with their requirements. In the absence of the types of support networks that are normally provided by family members and friends, many clients with psychiatric disorders display poor compliance with language interventions. The adherence of clients to drug regimens may be particularly difficult to achieve in the absence of direct supervision. The resulting relapses in mental functioning which arise when clients are not effectively medicated pose a further, significant obstacle to language interventions. There is also limited opportunity to generalise skills acquired in clinic to everyday communicative settings when clients have restricted social interactions. In short, the population of clients with psychiatric disorders poses unique challenges which are often, but not always, successfully addressed in speech and language therapy.

It is also important to be clear from the outset about the types of problems that this chapter will *not* address. There is now substantial evidence that communication disorders such as aphasia and stuttering can place an individual at risk of developing psychological problems; see section 5.2 in Cummings (2014a) for discussion. These problems include depression, anxiety, low self-esteem and, in severe cases, suicidal feelings. However, this chapter will not address the psychological impact of communication disorders, where problems such as depression are secondary to, or a consequence of, an impairment of communication. Rather, this chapter is interested in those mental health problems where pragmatic and discourse anomalies are among the presenting symptoms of a primary psychiatric disorder. The cohesion problems of the adult with schizophrenia and the turn-taking difficulties of the child with ADHD will be discussed in the exercises to follow. These pragmatic–discourse deficits are a feature of schizophrenia and ADHD in much the same way that hallucinations and impulsive behaviour are, respectively, features of these psychiatric disorders. However, the exercises in the following pages will not consider the adult with right-hemisphere language disorder who has depression. Although this adult, like the adult with schizophrenia, is likely to present with significant pragmatic and discourse deficits, there is no sense in which these deficits are either caused by, or are a consequence of, the client's additional problems with depression.

Section A: Short-answer questions

4.1 Schizophrenia

(1) Which of the following is *not* a positive symptom of schizophrenia?
  (a) auditory hallucinations
  (b) alogia
  (c) delusions
  (d) thought disorder
  (e) affective flattening

(2) *True* or *False*: Pragmatic–discourse disturbances in schizophrenia are only evident during psychotic episodes.

(3) *True* or *False*: Avolition is a negative symptom in schizophrenia.

(4) A doctor is conducting an interview with a client who has chronic schizophrenia. The doctor asks the client a range of questions about his medication, daily activities and interests. These questions almost invariably receive one-word responses such as 'possibly' and 'maybe'. Which of the following terms best describes the linguistic behaviour of this client?
  (a) glossomania
  (b) flight of ideas
  (c) alogia
  (d) semantic paraphasia
  (e) circumlocution

(5) *True* or *False*: Pragmatic–discourse deficits in schizophrenia are secondary to structural language problems.

(6) Fill in the blank spaces in the following paragraphs using the words in the box below.

Pragmatic and discourse deficits pose a significant barrier to _____ communication for adults with schizophrenia. Studies have revealed that speakers with schizophrenia perform poorly on tasks that require skills in discourse planning and comprehension, understanding humour, _____, metaphors and indirect requests, and the generation and comprehension of emotional _____. The comprehension of _____ language is particularly impaired in this clinical population. There is evidence that adults with schizophrenia are poor at recognising when Gricean maxims such as relation are _____ by speakers. Even adults who can appreciate when maxims have been flouted are often unable to use that recognition to establish a speaker's _____. Speakers with schizophrenia also often fail to observe Gricean maxims in their contributions to conversational exchanges and other forms of discourse (e.g. _____). For example, an adult with schizophrenia may contribute irrelevant utterances to a conversation, or produce a personal narrative that contains _____ detail and that fails to report events in the order in which they occurred. These conversational and narrative difficulties suggest an impairment of the use of the maxims of _____, quantity and _____, respectively.

Investigators are increasingly looking to cognitive factors to explain the pragmatic and discourse anomalies of speakers with schizophrenia. There is clear evidence that the _____ of mental states, otherwise known as 'mindreading' or theory of mind (ToM), is impaired in adults with schizophrenia. These mental states include _____, beliefs, desire and, most importantly for utterance _____, communicative intentions. Moreover, this impaired ToM capacity has been found to correlate strongly with the ability to interpret _____ and other non-literal language in schizophrenia. However, studies have also suggested that even a strong correlation between ToM impairments on the one hand and pragmatic deficits on the other hand should not be taken as evidence of a _____ relationship between ToM and pragmatic impairments. Instead, both ToM impairments and pragmatic deficits may be influenced by a third variable – typically, an _____ deficit – which may better explain the nature of the relationship between ToM and pragmatics in schizophrenia. For example, there is some evidence that a context processing impairment which is associated with a lack of mental _____ may explain the co-occurrence of ToM impairments and pragmatic deficits in schizophrenia.

quantity	regulation	narrative	social	flexibility
expressive	communicative intention		proverbs	violated
speech act	interpretation	non-literal		knowledge
prosody	excessive	theory of mind	causal	quality
sarcasm	executive function		flouted	hallucination
reasoning	relation	attribution	maxim	manner

(7) An adult with schizophrenia views a short videotaped scenario in which a husband and wife are sitting in front of the television. The husband gets up to go into the kitchen. His wife asks him 'Can you put the kettle on?' The adult with schizophrenia is asked what the wife means, upon which he replies 'She wants to check if the man can do it.' Which of the following statements best characterises the adult's response?
  (a) The adult with schizophrenia has identified a presupposition of the wife's question.
  (b) The adult with schizophrenia has failed to establish the intended referent of 'you'.
  (c) The adult with schizophrenia has recovered an implicature of the wife's question.
  (d) The adult with schizophrenia has established the illocutionary force of the question.
  (e) The adult with schizophrenia has failed to establish the wife's indirect speech act.

(8) An adult with schizophrenia is describing the Cookie Theft picture from the Boston Diagnostic Aphasia Examination. His description of the scene omits most of the main features – for example, that the boy is attempting to get cookies from the jar – and contains a detailed account of the garden which can be partially viewed through the kitchen window. Which of the following statements best characterises this adult's picture description?
  (a) The adult's picture description contains misleading and inconsistent information.
  (b) The adult's picture description is over-informative about the main characters.
  (c) The adult's picture description is under-informative about background details.
  (d) The adult's picture description omits relevant in favour of less relevant information.
  (e) The adult's picture description contains factually incorrect information.

(9) An adult with schizophrenia is asked 'When is your next appointment with the doctor?' by his speech and language therapist. His response unfolds as follows: 'It's next week, but I don't believe I need one.' Which of the following pragmatic–discourse behaviours is this adult able to use?
(a) spatial deixis
(b) lexical substitution
(c) pronominal reference
(d) presupposition
(e) temporal deixis

(10) An adult with schizophrenia is role-playing a service encounter in which his speech and language therapist is acting the part of a ticket assistant in a train station. The therapist asks 'How can I help you, sir?' to which the adult responds 'You can show me to the toilets and then leave me alone for the rest of time.' Which of the following statements best characterises the adult's utterance?
(a) The utterance is a relevant, but impolite response to the question.
(b) The utterance is an irrelevant, but polite response to the question.
(c) The utterance is an irrelevant and impolite response to the question.
(d) The utterance is an over-informative, but polite response to the question.
(e) The utterance is an under-informative, but polite response to the question.

4.2 Bipolar disorder

(1) Which of the following is *not* associated with bipolar disorder in adults?
(a) mania
(b) grandiosity
(c) depression
(d) affective flattening
(e) euphoria

(2) Which of the following is a communicative feature of bipolar disorder in adults?
(a) flight of ideas
(b) clang associations
(c) semantic paraphasia
(d) pressure to keep talking
(e) impulsivity

(3) There is evidence that the use and understanding of affective prosody is impaired in adults with bipolar disorder. Which of the following pragmatic language skills is this impairment likely to disrupt?
(a) the ability to establish the referents of deictic expressions like 'here' and 'next week'
(b) the ability to convey positive and negative attitudes towards an interlocutor
(c) the ability to establish the presuppositions of an utterance
(d) the ability to use a speaker's emotional states to modulate utterance meaning
(e) the ability to exchange conversational turns with an interlocutor

(4) *True* or *False*: Linguistic deficits do not persist during periods of normal mood (euthymia) in adults with bipolar disorder.

(5) *True* or *False*: Linguistic deficits in bipolar disorder are related to cognitive impairments of executive functions and episodic memory.

(6) *True* or *False*: Adults with bipolar disorder and mania may make tactless remarks in social situations.

(7) Fill in the blank spaces in the following paragraph using the words in the box below. There is now widespread recognition among clinicians and researchers that adults with bipolar disorder experience a range of language deficits. In several studies, adults with bipolar disorder have been found to perform more poorly than healthy controls on tasks that examine affective ⎯⎯⎯, linguistic ⎯⎯⎯ (e.g. following commands and reading comprehension of sentences) and linguistic expression. A question of some interest to investigators is whether these language anomalies are linked to clinical states in bipolar disorder (e.g. ⎯⎯⎯, mania) or whether they are a stable and state-independent trait of the disorder. Perlini et al. (2012) addressed this question in a study of micro-linguistic (lexicon, morphology, ⎯⎯⎯) and macro-linguistic (discourse coherence, ⎯⎯⎯) features in 30 clients with bipolar disorder. The only linguistic variable on which these clients performed more poorly than healthy controls was ⎯⎯⎯. Clients in depressed phases of the illness produced more ⎯⎯⎯ errors than clients in euthymic phases. This finding led these investigators to conclude that linguistic deficits are linked to ⎯⎯⎯ and are not a state-independent trait of the disorder. A quite different finding was obtained by Radanovic et al. (2013) who studied 19 elderly patients with bipolar disorder who were in the euthymic phase. These patients exhibited problems with the comprehension and production of language at the levels of syntactic and ⎯⎯⎯ abilities. The fact that these patients continued to experience significant language disturbance during a non-acute phase of the illness provides support for the claim that language impairment is a state-⎯⎯⎯ trait of bipolar disorder.

mean length of utterance	dependent	mania	phonetics
clinical state	expression	prosody	depression
paragrammatic	phonology	executive function	syntax
perseveration	lexical–semantic	pragmatics	euthymia
comprehension	flight of ideas	independent	episodic memory

(8) Adults with bipolar disorder have been shown to exhibit a context processing deficit. Which of the following aspects of language are most likely to be compromised by this deficit?
   (a) resolution of lexical ambiguity
   (b) temporal ordering of events in a narrative
   (c) syntactic inversion during question formation
   (d) recovery of conversational implicatures
   (e) comprehension of passive sentences

(9) Which of the following statements describes a feature of flight of ideas in a speaker with bipolar disorder?
   (a) The speaker perseverates on a single topic.
   (b) The speaker expresses rapidly shifting thoughts.
   (c) The speaker expresses thoughts in an associative manner.

(d) The speaker produces over-informative discourse.

(e) The speaker defers topic selection to his interlocutor.

(10) Which of the following statements describes a feature of circumstantiality in a speaker with bipolar disorder?

(a) The speaker develops semantic associations between words in utterances.

(b) The speaker produces speech that is delayed in reaching the point.

(c) The speaker perseverates on a single topic.

(d) The speaker produces unnecessary details and parenthetical remarks.

(e) The speaker produces egocentric discourse.

4.3   Personality disorder

(1) Which of the following is *not* associated with personality disorder?

(a) A diagnosis of personality disorder is typically made during adolescence.

(b) Social and occupational functioning is compromised in personality disorder.

(c) Personality disorder may be due to the physiological effects of a substance.

(d) Cognition and affectivity are disrupted in personality disorder.

(e) Patterns of behaviour in personality disorder should be of a long-standing and enduring nature.

(2) *True* or *False*: Antisocial personality disorder is usually preceded by conduct disorder.

(3) *True* or *False*: The individual with schizotypal personality disorder exhibits cognitive or perceptual distortions and eccentricities of behaviour in the context of an intact capacity for close relationships.

(4) Individuals with schizotypal personality disorder can display significant prosodic deficits. Which of the following language and communication skills are likely to be compromised in such individuals?

(a) The production of grammatically well-formed sentences.

(b) The use of declarative utterances to ask questions.

(c) The interpretation of ironic utterances.

(d) The use of cohesive conjunctions in narrative discourse.

(e) The use of mental state language during a conversational exchange.

(5) The narratives of individuals with antisocial personality disorder display a number of features related to impaired processing of emotion. Which of the following statements describes a feature of these narratives?

(a) Narratives contain many negative statements.

(b) Narratives exhibit an increased use of mental state language.

(c) Narratives include emotionally intense vocabulary.

(d) Narratives exhibit a lack of global coherence.

(e) Narratives contain repetitive and irrelevant language.

(6) *True* or *False*: Word categories relating to negative emotion and negation tend to decrease over the course of treatment of individuals with personality disorders.

(7) Narrative coherence has been found to distinguish the life stories of individuals with features of borderline personality disorder (BPD) from the stories of those without features of BPD. Which of the following statements best captures this characteristic of the life stories of individuals with BPD?

   (a) The life stories of individuals with BPD portray the narrator as subject to the whims of external forces.

   (b) The life stories of individuals with BPD display a lack of connection and intimacy on the part of the protagonist.

   (c) The life stories of individuals with BPD display a lack of integration of individual episodes.

   (d) The life stories of individuals with BPD reveal increased use of mental state language.

   (e) The life stories of individuals with BPD display perseveration on certain themes.

(8) Adults with personality disorders present with a range of mentalising deficits. Which of the following aspects of language and communication are likely to be compromised as a result of these deficits?

   (a) decoding of embedded clauses in sentences

   (b) foregrounding of new information in an utterance

   (c) interpretation of an ironic utterance

   (d) knowledge of the semantic fields of words

   (e) use of derivational and inflectional suffixes

(9) The following statements describe aspects of narrative discourse production. Which aspects are most likely to be disrupted in adults with a personality disorder who have mentalising deficits?

   (a) use of cohesive conjunctions to relate events

   (b) description of the motives of the characters in a story

   (c) use of direct reported speech by story characters

   (d) temporal ordering of events in a narrative

   (e) use of evaluative language

(10) Adults with personality disorder can experience impairments of autobiographical memory. Which of the following types of discourse are likely to be compromised in adults with these impairments?

   (a) storytelling based on a wordless picture book

   (b) instructions on how to play a board game

   (c) narrative relating significant events in an individual's life

   (d) storytelling based on a cartoon strip

   (e) conversation on the topic of hobbies and interests

4.4   Emotional disturbance in children

(1) *True or False*: The communicative impairment in children with selective mutism is attributable to expressive language deficits.

(2) *True or False*: In selective mutism there is a consistent failure to speak in all social situations outside of the home.

(3) Hollie is 4 years old and has been diagnosed with selective mutism and social anxiety disorder. At home, she is an articulate, sociable child who has use of age-appropriate vocabulary and grammar. In other contexts, Hollie's attempts to engage her peers in interaction are often rejected because she attempts to achieve this by grabbing their toys or using other non-verbal means. Which of the following language and cognitive skills should be prioritised in a social communication intervention for Hollie?

    (a) the ability to use figurative language
    (b) the ability to produce well-formed utterances
    (c) the ability to initiate a conversational interaction
    (d) the ability to attribute mental states to others
    (e) the ability to engage in topic management

(4) Jack is 11 years old and has been diagnosed with obsessive–compulsive disorder. He has been referred to speech and language therapy following some concern about his social communication skills. The referral from the school psychologist notes that Jack's interactions with his peers fail on account of his limited ability for perspective-taking. Which of the following pragmatic and discourse skills might the speech and language therapist expect to be impaired in Jack?
    (a) description of characters' motives during storytelling
    (b) conversational turn-taking
    (c) use of mental state language in a written narrative
    (d) understanding of non-literal language
    (e) use of facial expressions and gestures

(5) *True or False*: Children with selective mutism may use non-verbal means (e.g. pointing) to communicate even in settings where they do not speak.

(6) *True or False*: Social communication difficulties in children with obsessive–compulsive disorder have few implications for functioning.

(7) Michael is 13 years old and has been diagnosed with depression. His mental health problems have had an adverse impact on his communication skills. He has limited communicative interactions with others. When he does communicate with others, his communicative style is a largely passive one. Which of the following statements are consistent with this account of Michael's communication skills?
    (a) Michael introduces topics into conversation.
    (b) Michael produces minimal responses to open-ended questions.
    (c) Michael does not initiate conversations with others.
    (d) Michael fails to develop topics during conversation.
    (e) Michael asks questions of others in conversation.

(8) Sarah is an 8-year-old girl who was recently involved in a road traffic accident in which she was a passenger in a car. Although she did not sustain serious injury in the accident, she was subsequently diagnosed with post-traumatic stress disorder. Her communicative skills have reflected her level of mental distress. A once sociable, communicative child, Sarah now only speaks in a whispered voice to her closest family members. The family physician has referred Sarah to speech and language therapy. Which of the following aspects of language and communication will be the focus of assessment and treatment conducted by the therapist?
    (a) expressive phonology
    (b) social communication
    (c) receptive syntax
    (d) figurative language
    (e) written language

(9) *True or False*: Children with social anxiety disorder have pragmatic and mentalising deficits which are similar to these same deficits in individuals with autism spectrum disorder.

(10) *True* or *False*: Emotional disturbance can be both a cause and a consequence of pragmatic disorders in children.

4.5   Behavioural disorders in children

(1) Which of the following is *not* associated with attention deficit hyperactivity disorder (ADHD) in children?
    (a) expressive language impairments
    (b) social anxiety
    (c) symptoms of inattention
    (d) poor academic attainment
    (e) reduced intellectual functioning

(2) Each of the following statements describes a communicative feature of ADHD. Indicate if the feature is associated with symptoms of inattention, hyperactivity or impulsivity in ADHD.
    (a) frequent shifts in conversation
    (b) excessive talking
    (c) excessive interruption of others
    (d) conversations initiated at inappropriate times
    (e) failure to listen to others

(3) *True* or *False*: Pragmatic and discourse deficits in ADHD are secondary to structural language impairments.

(4) *True* or *False*: Children with ADHD have similar mentalising deficits to children with autism spectrum disorder.

(5) A child with conduct disorder produces a written narrative on the topic of a recent school trip to the zoo. The narrative displays a diverse range of lexical items particularly in relation to the names of animals. The use of grammatical structures is appropriate for the child's age. However, the following extract from the narrative exemplifies a particular discourse weakness on the part of the child: 'We got off the bus and we watched the lions and we saw camels and we went for lunch.' Which of the following statements best characterises this weakness?
    (a) The child has a limited repertoire of cohesive conjunctions.
    (b) The child does not relate events in the order in which they occurred.
    (c) The child's narrative is under-informative.
    (d) The child's narrative displays a failure of relevance.
    (e) The child's narrative is repetitive.

(6) A child with ADHD is engaging in a task that requires him to tell a story based on a cartoon strip. Although he has a good expressive vocabulary and age-appropriate syntax, his story is nonetheless difficult for a hearer to follow. The teacher who is working with the child notes the following behaviours: the child fails to describe the scenes in the correct order and he overlooks important details in each scene in his rush to progress to the next scene. Which of the following aspects of discourse production are likely to be compromised by this behaviour?
    (a) the expression of temporal and causal relations between events
    (b) the use of evaluative language
    (c) the omission of information that is vital to a hearer's understanding

    (d) the description of the characters' motives and feelings

    (e) the use of cohesive conjunctions

(7) A teenager with conduct disorder is observed by teachers to have difficulty negotiating conflict with his peers. A trigger for this adolescent's aggressive outbursts appears to be the teasing behaviour and jibes of others. Which of the following language and cognitive deficits might contribute to this teenager's difficulty in managing this specific trigger?

    (a) expressive language deficits

    (b) impaired understanding of non-literal language

    (c) executive function deficits

    (d) theory of mind impairments

    (e) visuospatial deficits

(8) A child with ADHD is asked to explain the meaning of the idiomatic expression in the utterance 'Sally decided to let the cat out of the bag.' He responds with 'Mummy lets our cat out of the kitchen.' Which of the following statements best captures this child's response?

    (a) The child has interpreted the idiomatic expression in a concrete, non-literal way.

    (b) The child has responded with a presupposition of the utterance.

    (c) The child has interpreted the idiomatic expression in a concrete, literal way.

    (d) The child has responded with an implicature of the utterance.

    (e) The child has interpreted the idiomatic expression in an abstract, non-literal way.

(9) *True* or *False*: Egocentric discourse is a consistent communicative feature of individuals with ADHD.

(10) *True* or *False*: Children with conduct disorder typically make under-informative contributions to conversational exchanges.

Section B: Data analysis exercises

4.6 Schizophrenia 1

Background

Few clinical studies have examined the comprehension *and* production of pragmatic aspects of language by adults with schizophrenia. An even smaller number have assessed the comprehension and production of gestures by these adults. One study which has considered linguistic and extra-linguistic pragmatic functioning in schizophrenia was conducted by Colle et al. (2013). In a study of 17 adults with schizophrenia, these investigators examined the production and comprehension of a range of pragmatic phenomena including irony, direct and indirect speech acts and the violation of Gricean maxims. These adults were aged 23 to 56 years at the time of the study. The duration of their illness ranged from 2 years to 28 years. Six subjects were taking typical and nine were taking atypical antipsychotic medications. None of the adults was experiencing an acute or florid psychotic state at the time of the study (i.e. all subjects were in the chronic phase of their illness). All subjects achieved normative levels on Raven's Coloured Progressive Matrices (Raven, 1956) and cut-off scores on the Mini-Mental State Examination (Folstein et al., 1975), the Aachen Aphasia Test (Huber et al., 1983) and the Token Test (De Renzi and Vignolo, 1962).

The responses of these adults with schizophrenia on a range of the pragmatic tasks used in this study are presented below. Examine these responses in detail and then answer the questions that follow.

Data set 1

Scenario A

The subject is shown a videotaped scenario in which a girl asks a boy 'Did you go to the gym?' The boy replies 'I haven't felt so tired for so long!'

Test questions and subject's responses
What did the boy say? 'He was tired.'
What did he mean by that? 'He had been working really hard.'
Did the boy go to the gym? 'Yes.'

Scenario B

The subject is shown a videotaped scenario in which a child knocks over a vase. The child's mother asks 'Who knocked the vase over?' The child replies 'It was Bobi [name of dog].'

Test questions and subject's responses
What did the child say? 'The dog had broken the vase.'
What did he mean by that? 'The dog had broken the vase.'
Did the child tell the truth? 'Yes.'

Scenario C

The subject is shown a videotaped scenario in which a girl is wearing a dress that is too tight for her. The girl asks the boy in the scenario 'How does it fit me?' The boy replies 'Your diet is working well.'

Test question and subject's response
What did the boy say? 'He was joking.'

Scenario D

The subject is shown a videotaped scenario in which a husband and wife are sitting on the sofa. The husband is reading the newspaper, while the wife seems annoyed. The wife asks him 'What would you like to do this afternoon?'

Test question and subject's response
What could the husband answer? 'He could tell her what he wants to do in the afternoon, and if he's going to put down that book.'

Scenario E

The subject is shown a videotaped scenario in which a brother and sister are having breakfast. Paying no attention, the brother puts his elbow in a rusk with jam. He then asks 'Can you pass me the jam, please?'

Test questions and subject's responses

What could the girl answer to make fun of the boy? 'I don't know...it's an everyday situation.'

What do you mean by that? 'He is too concentrated on his breakfast.'

Data set 2

Scenario A

The subject is shown a videotaped scenario in which a boy performs a gesture to ask the girl 'Do you want some coffee?' The girl looks at her watch with a gesture meaning 'It's too late.'

Test question and subject's response

What did the girl say? 'She refused the offer.'

Scenario B

The subject is shown a videotaped scenario in which a boy and a girl are eating a disgusting soup. The boy smacks his lips with a gesture meaning 'It's very good!'

Test question and subject's response

What did the boy mean by that? 'He meant to say that she cooked a delicious soup.'

Scenario C

The subject is shown a videotaped scenario in which a boy performs a gesture to ask for some candies. The girl doesn't want to give him any candy. So, she looks at the candies with a disgusted expression that means 'They are awful!'

Test questions and subject's responses

What did the girl say? 'The candies were not good.'

What did she mean by that? 'They tasted awful.'

Did the girl tell the truth? 'No.'

Why did the girl answer like that? 'To make fun of him.'

Data set 3

Scenario A

The subject is shown a videotaped scenario involving two people, Robert and Paola. It's Robert's birthday, and Paola gives him a gift saying 'Happy birthday!' Robert unwraps the gift and discovers an awful tie. With an annoyed expression he says 'Thanks, really, I needed one of those.'

Test questions and subject's responses

What did Robert say? 'He liked the tie.'

In your opinion, did Robert like the tie? 'Kind of.'

Why? 'He made a perplexed expression.'

Scenario B

The subject is shown a videotaped scenario in which a woman is sitting in a waiting room. The waiting room is full, and the woman occupies the chair next to her. Paul comes into the waiting room and says to the woman 'Is this chair occupied?' The woman caddishly replies 'Of course! Don't you see that I put my coat on it?'

Test questions and subject's responses
In that situation, was the woman polite? 'No.'
Why? 'She had an unfriendly expression, she was rude.'

Scenario C

The subject is shown a videotaped scenario in which a husband asks his wife 'Where did John go to live?' The wife replies 'You know, he's gone far away.'

Test questions and subject's responses
In your opinion, is the wife's reply fine? 'Yes.'
Why? 'Because she replied that he's gone far away.'

Question 1 The subjects with schizophrenia in the above data sets exhibit a number of pragmatic deficits. Several of these deficits are listed below. Give <u>one</u> example of each from these sets:

(a) failure to comprehend non-verbal irony
(b) failure to detect violation of the maxim of quantity
(c) failure to use facial expression to determine speaker meaning
(d) failure to establish a speaker's deceitful intent
(e) failure to produce an ironic or other non-literal utterance

Question 2 Alongside the above pragmatic deficits are a number of aspects of intact pragmatic functioning. Several of these aspects are listed below. Give <u>one</u> example of each from these sets:

(a) successful recovery of a non-verbal implicature
(b) successful comprehension of an ironic utterance
(c) successful use of a facial expression to determine speaker meaning
(d) successful detection of an impolite utterance
(e) successful recovery of a verbal implicature

Question 3 Aside from a range of pragmatic inferences (e.g. implicature), the responses of subjects in the above data sets indicate that they are able to draw a number of other inferences. These inferences are described below. Give <u>one</u> example of each inference in these data sets:

(a) an elaborative inference based on world knowledge
(b) an inference that makes a causal link between states
(c) an inference that attributes an action to an agent
(d) an inference that attributes a mental state to an agent
(e) an inference that explains an agent's affective state

Question 4 In responding to these scenarios, the adults with schizophrenia are more or less successfully exercising a range of theory of mind (ToM) skills. Give one example of an affective ToM skill and a cognitive ToM skill on the part of these adults.

Question 5 Some of the responses in the above data sets suggest that semantic processing may also not be completely intact in these adults with schizophrenia. Give two examples of possible semantic impairment in these adults.

4.6 Schizophrenia 2

Background

The discourse of adults with schizophrenia often reflects topics which are part of these individuals' psychotic experiences. An analysis of these topics and how they are developed in monological and dialogical contexts is revealing of a range of pragmatic and discourse skills in clients with schizophrenia. The following data sets contain extracts of spoken language from adults with schizophrenia. The extract in data set 1 is taken from Hella et al. (2013). It is a clinical interview between a doctor and a 26-year-old male with thought-disordered schizophrenia. Yvette in data set 2 has chronic schizophrenia. She is in conversation with her speech and language therapist and is one of three adults with schizophrenia who were studied by Walsh (2008). The final discourse in data set 3 is an extended extract of schizophrenic language reported in Chaika (1982). It is unclear if it is an extended turn in a conversational exchange or is an extract of monological discourse. Examine each data set in turn and then answer the questions that follow.

Data set 1

Clinical interview between a doctor (D) and a man (M) with schizophrenia. Clarifying comments are in brackets and irrelevant hesitation markers and signs of overlapped speech have been deleted.

D: Your mother has told me that you feel that they [referring to the patient's paranoid experiences] don't leave you alone.
M: No, they don't. Well, as J. Karjalainen [a Finnish pop musician] sings in his song: 'Do you remember when we played around with telepathy'. I don't know exactly what telepathy means. But maybe I believe in it a little. But, also my mother has to behave herself, but . . . she is sometimes discourteous in her words and she can be a bit rude. It may be the case that I'm the kind of person that speaks aloud a lot and thinks a lot what to say and so . . .

Data set 2

Conversation between a client with schizophrenia called Yvette (Y) and Irene (I), her speech and language therapist.

I: about YOUR RATE . . . remember?
Y: yeah
I: remember you just said you were going to say something about your rate of speech you'd something to tell me
Y: right

I: about your rate

Y: right

I: you'd been thinking about it $==$

Y: $==$ I found that I say certain things which are out of context and em I find that everything I wanted to say I say it out before anything else could happen I say it out and I find that this is the reason – that this is one of the ways why I say those things I'm thinking too fast

I: yeah and it has to come straight out $==$

Y: $==$ it has to come straight out and this is what makes me say things that are corrupt ( ) and I have no control of

I: yeah and $==$

Y: $==$ some of the things I say I do not have $==$ control of

I: $==$ any control of yeah right and you're sure about that

Y: I'm positive . . . it's not something that I want to say

I: right right – and have you any ideas of how you can help that

Y: ( ) I'd say by speaking slowly

I: yeah do you think you could control it more if you $==$

Y: $==$ well it's not necessarily because I haven't stopped talking but I could I could be in a crowd

I: yeah $==$

Y: $==$ and I mightn't be talking at all and I'd say things . . .

I: oh right so it's not just when you

Y: $==$ it's terrible

I: $==$ already started talking that something like that may come out it could be at any time

Y: yeah

Data set 3

Extended extract of schizophrenic language reported in Chaika (1982).

. . . when I'm not sure if it's possible about the way I think I could read people mind about people's society attitude plot and spirit so I think I could read their mind as they drive by in the car sh – will I see paradise will I not see paradise should I answer should I not answer I not answer w- their thought of how I read think I could read their mind about when they pass by in the car in the house pass by in the car in the house pass by in the car from my house I just correct for them for having me feel better about myself not answer will I should I answer should I not answer will I see paradise will I not see paradise . . .

Question 1 Two topics tend to dominate the discourse of all three of the speakers with schizophrenia. What are those topics? Give examples from the data sets.

Question 2 Of the three speakers, one speaker develops these topics (or at least one of them) reasonably well, while another displays almost no topic development at all. Identify the two speakers in question. What factor may explain this difference in topic development?

Question 3 Certain pragmatic and discourse skills appear to be intact for these speakers with schizophrenia. Give <u>one</u> example of each of the following skills in the above data sets:

(a) ability to use ellipsis

(b) ability to use pronouns and possessives to achieve cohesion

(c) ability to establish referents of demonstrative pronouns
(d) ability to integrate part of prior speaker's turn within current turn
(e) ability to use mental state language

Question 4 The discourse in data set 3 is particularly difficult to follow. Give three reasons why this is the case.

Question 5 In the following conversational turn, Yvette exhibits intact use of both anaphoric reference and cataphoric reference. Identify where each type of reference occurs in this extract:

I found that I say certain things which are out of context and em I find that everything I wanted to say I say it out before anything else could happen I say it out and I find that this is the reason – that this is one of the ways why I say those things I'm thinking too fast

4.6   Schizophrenia 3

Background

The clinical interview between a doctor (typically a psychiatrist) and an adult with schizophrenia is a rich source of data about a client's cognitive and linguistic functioning as well as mental status. It provides clinicians with an opportunity to conduct real-time assessment of a range of skills and provides pointers to specific formal tests which may be performed. A clinical interview also reveals pragmatic and discourse deficits that are largely obscured by other forms of testing and assessment. In the following data sets, a doctor is interviewing a 26-year-old man with thought-disordered schizophrenia. This client was studied by Hella et al. (2013). At the time of interview, he was taking a combination of olanzapine and perphenazine, two antipsychotic medications. He had had hospital treatments several times in the past, the most recent of which was one month prior to the interview. He was living in his own apartment although he had previously been a resident in a rehabilitation unit. He had problems with daily activities. The client had experienced a relapse of psychosis at the time of the interview.

The doctor (D) and client (M) address a range of topics in these data sets. Irrelevant hesitation markers and signs of overlapped speech have been deleted. The authors' clarifying comments are indicated in brackets. Examine both data sets in detail and then answer the questions that follow.

Data set 1

D: Has anybody else ever tried to harm you or tried to lead you to any kind of trouble?
M: Well, I have not thought about that . . . but not [they have not led me] . . . I have seen harm done and stuff, but people, those guys, let me be physically and mentally on my own . . .
D: Have you ever felt you would be especially important or that you would have abilities that no one else has?
M: Well, it's only that my name is John [altered], which happens to be the kind that others are laughing at. They are laughing right to my face, and then . . .
D: Why would they laugh at the name John?
M: Well, in some way that John that you har-har

D: What does John mean?

M: Well I don't know John [aborted utterance] probably . . . it refers to me and that a bit har-har and so on.

D: I can't quite understand. Can you tell what it is . . .

M: Then on the other hand . . .

D: Uh-huh.

M: . . . there are those X-ers [X-er refers to people from area X and is also client's family name] from Y [province capital] but yeah. As a joke, I kind of imagine that it is a kind of sacred relic that I should not be teased for that [laughs].

D: Do you mean that . . .

M: Yeah.

D: . . . that your name is a relic.

M: Or my family name X-er is one, since I am one [i.e. an inhabitant of province X bearing the province name].

D: Yeah, what does it mean . . .

M: Well . . .

D: . . . that it is a relic.

M: Well, it occurs to me all the time that X is the town [literally: municipality] [erroneous statement, confusion of province and hometown names]. It's definitely the town that is called X [erroneous statement repeated with emphasis] which is always seen on the [television] news . . . rolling [makes rolling gestures with arms]

D: Yeah.

M: X, yes. [Yawning] Well, I also do have other names.

D: What names?

M: I'd rather be some Marko, damn it, if I could myself decide upon taking a name.

D: Why would you change your name?

M: Well I don't know. It only occurred to me that it could be cool to be Marko, if not anything else, damn it.

Data set 2

This exchange develops in response to a question from the doctor about the client's future plans.

M: I've been thinking about those that . . . going to work I'm always thinking about. Then some people, well they are stars and the like, they play soccer and we then watch, or they watch it and such like that.

D: Yes, who are watching?

M: Trades/professions I kind of think about.

D: Uh-huh.

M: They are a bit like a group of their own and such. They are jobless.

D: Uh-uh, who are you talking about now?

M: Well, I'm thinking about these kind of things. My father works at the city water works. Workers come to my mind sometimes.

D: Yeah.

M: That's it. Well, that I would want to be a bit better educated, but I am not. Then I am not extremely clever, perhaps. In a way that sometimes, well yes, I do watch something. A group of people can come up with wise things but . . . things are not like that now.

D: Yes. What . . .

M: [yawning] Well, I do have a trade school diploma.

Question 1 In data set 1, the speaker with schizophrenia displays significant problems with topic management. Describe how this speaker manages topics in his exchange with the doctor.

Question 2 Aside from topic management problems, the speaker with schizophrenia in data set 1 displays other pragmatic and discourse competences. Two such competences are the referential use of demonstrative pronouns and the use of lexical substitution as a form of cohesion. Give <u>two</u> examples of each of these aspects of language use in this data set.

Question 3 Although the speaker with schizophrenia makes effective referential use of demonstrative pronouns, his use of other pronouns to achieve reference is problematic. Give <u>three</u> examples of problematic pronominal reference in the above data sets.

Question 4 The contributions of the speaker with schizophrenia in data set 2 are often vague and uninformative. This is related to the use of a large number of non-specific words and phrases. Give <u>five</u> examples of these words and phrases in this data set.

Question 5 The speaker with schizophrenia in data set 2 also makes effective use of anaphoric reference and ellipsis. Identify <u>one</u> example of each of these discourse features in this data set.

4.7 Bipolar disorder 1

Background

Discourse analysis has been employed extensively in the study of individuals with mental health problems in psychiatry and other disciplines. Mancini and Rogers (2007) undertook a discourse analysis of the narratives of two adults with bipolar disorder with a view to determining their experiences of psychiatric illness, the mental health treatment system and recovery from illness. The analysis of these narratives revealed significant themes such as these adults' sense of powerlessness over their condition and its symptoms, the factors to which they attributed their recovery, and so on. However, discourse analysis can also be used to examine features such as cohesion and coherence, narrative structure, topic relevance and a range of other pragmatic and discourse skills.

The narratives of two adults with bipolar disorder, named Kelly and Nancy, were examined by Mancini and Rogers. The first of these adults, Kelly, is a white female in her fifties. She reported that she was diagnosed with 'rapid cycling' bipolar disorder while she was in graduate school for nursing. Following her diagnosis, she was hospitalised at least 4–6 times. The second adult, called Nancy, will be examined in the next data analysis exercise. Examine the narrative extracts below in detail and then answer the questions that follow.

Data set 1

Kelly is describing her various hospitalisations on account of bipolar disorder.

I think it was after my sixth hospitalization, I had a long term stay at Eastern County Medical Center and then they transferred me because I went from the mania and then I went through the profound depression. I went back to the mania, and they felt that I needed a long-term stay so they transferred me to the Barrymore Psychiatric Center, and that was when I felt all hope just [swoosh sound]. So I was at Eastern County Medical Center for about three months, and at that point, I was with, you know, a lot of the staff that I had been hospitalized with before and they had always, they always seemed to sustain hope. You know they would always ask, gee, prior to discharge, if I was feeling well enough, and they were jotting off poetry. 'Oh gee, that's really brave. Will you bring me books?' You know, just encouraging me to go back to school and recognizing my talents.

Data set 2

Kelly is describing a low point in her recovery process.

And then, when I was, you know, once I was there like three or four months, it was almost like you felt this gradual or [swoosh sound] withdraw of energy. They thought, you know, gee, you don't . . . in fact, I even overheard some of the conversations. You know, it was kind of like, you know, 'gee, it's so sad; she has so many talents and she's never really ever going to be able to do anything with them.' 'She's never really going to go anywhere.' 'She's never going to really be able to accomplish anything.' I actually heard a couple of those conversations. At that point then, you know, it was like, you know, just increase the meds. And it was, like, I remember that hospitalization; you just felt the people just withdrawing their energy from you and focusing on people that maybe were admitted for the first or second time and they felt maybe they had a better chance. I felt devastated.

Data set 3

Kelly is describing the paternalistic behaviour of staff.

And then it became kind of like, you know, when I would talk about, you know, when I would feel . . . have a good day and talk about maybe kind of, you know, taking small steps towards claiming those dreams again. It was kind of like, no, Kelly, that would be too stressful. You need to kind of back off. You need to just . . . that was the word I couldn't stand 'maintain.' If you attempted to go back to school, take a course, or attempted to do volunteer work, attempted to work a little bit part time, would just destabilize you even more. You know, and you would end up back in the hospital. So it was kind of like you began to feel like you were this fragile egg thing. You know, you had to be almost like the bubble boy, maintained in a bubble the rest of your life and exposed to no stress. Just kind of, I don't know, you just felt like you were too fragile. And I began to believe that when I had enough people tell me that, I started kind of like that state dependent thing, where you go to self-help.

Data set 4

Kelly is describing how she began to identify with clients who were chronically ill.

I started identifying with the horror stories. Instead of identifying with the people that were making it, I started identifying with the people who were despondent, who were suicidal, who felt there was no meaning to life, you know. So I began to view myself as one of the chronics, not one of the people that were optimistic about, which usually in the past I did, but once the providers, you know, started and then I started seeing myself more, you know. That only lasted for about a year though.

Data set 5

Kelly is describing a turning point in her recovery.

I felt despondent for about two weeks, and I said to myself – and then it was just kind of like there is a fire in me – I said to myself, I can't allow this to happen to me. I mean these are walking dead. You know, it's like, you know, they've given up all hope. I mean most of the people . . . just again, and that was back when, you know, everybody was over drugged. It was this soulless stare look. You couldn't even see a spark of life in a lot of the folks' eyes. They just walked around the deadened state. I just said to myself it was kind of like a kick start. It was a kind of 'get yourself together, Kell.' You know, you've kind of really worked to not end up this way. And I started helping. And I said, 'Oh my God, these poor kids, you know, their hope has got to be kept alive.' So I started hanging out with a lot of the younger kids, you know, when I had privileges and just kind of offering hope to them, you know. You know, kind of nurturing a lot of the young kids that came from catastrophic backgrounds. That just kind of got really ignited, you know, not only terms of myself, but when I saw people's lives around me and knew they were capable of so much more and knew, you know. That's one thing I do have, is passion, and people usually feel my passion, and I thought if I could jumpstart a little bit of spark, you know, like Claire (former psychiatrist) jumpstarted in me.

Question 1 Kelly makes extensive use of reported speech in these narrative extracts. Several different types of this speech are listed below. Give <u>one</u> example of each type of reported speech.

(a) Kelly is directly reporting her own speech.
(b) Kelly is directly reporting someone else's speech.
(c) Kelly is indirectly reporting someone else's speech.
(d) Kelly is directly reporting speech in which she is the addressee.
(e) Kelly is directly reporting speech in which she is described in the third person.

Question 2 Kelly's psychiatric condition appears not to have impaired her capacity to use mental state language. Give <u>three</u> examples each of cognitive and affective states expressed by this language.

Question 3 Kelly's narratives are well oriented to space and time. Give <u>three</u> examples each of spatial and temporal expressions which suggest that this is the case. What do these expressions suggest about Kelly's cognitive skills?

Question 4 In data set 5, Kelly uses a particular metaphor in her account of her recovery from her illness. Identify the metaphor in question and give <u>three</u> examples of its use in this data set.

Question 5 Kelly makes extensive use of discourse particles in her narratives. Give <u>three</u> examples of the use of these particles in the above data sets. Explain the possible functions that are served by these particles.

4.7 Bipolar disorder 2

Background

This exercise examines extracts from narratives produced by the second of the two adults with bipolar disorder who were studied by Mancini and Rogers (2007). The adult in question is called Nancy. She is a white female in her fifties who has had bipolar disorder for several years. She reports having had numerous hospitalisations in that time. Although Nancy acknowledges the importance of psychiatric treatment and attributes her own recovery to finding the right medication, she is a leading activist who is highly critical of the coercive and paternalistic aspects of the mental health treatment system. Examine the narrative extracts below in detail and then answer the questions that follow.

Data set 1

Nancy is describing her experiences prior to recovery.

[It was] 12 or 14 years altogether, where it was, you know, I was a raging lunatic. I can't say that they (family) were exactly part of my recovery and caused some turning point or something. But I just think that it was so crucial and unusual, frankly, from what I've heard, that they . . . it was like they never gave up. For one thing, they never stopped dealing with the messes that I created. I mean each manic episode was a holocaust. There were messes all over the place with employers and friends and acquaintances and landlords and, you know, an entire world of life. My life was blown to pieces, and I was not capable of mending it . . . I would have like two weeks of sanity to deal with things that would take, you know, a lot to deal with. And they always did that. I mean they didn't like it and they became very exhausted and weary of it, but they felt that they couldn't not try to repair some of these things and leave landlords, you know, being owed $400, and leave apartments trashed, and leave people, I don't know, millions of things. So they like handled that kind of stuff, all the messes. And they tried to clean them up over and over and over again . . .

Data set 2

Nancy is describing her life before and after the onset of bipolar disorder.

I was completely functional and thriving until then. Now in retrospect, people close to me think things might have been brewing starting when I was around 30. Nobody questions the fact that there is nothing troublesome going on from birth to age 30 . . . Well, it's oversimplifying but not a great oversimplification to say that my manias, you have to understand, were extremely severe and every once in a great while, psychotic, but always achieving unbelievable delusional state and, you know, dangerous behavior. All the classic symptoms of you know, of incredible grandiosity, all these things.

Data set 3

Nancy is describing her manic states.

But also they were all, every single episode, was what I call a happy manic. These were the greatest trips I have ever taken in my life. I had the greatest time in the world while I was actually going around, you know, wrecking the whole world and all the people important to me, all the situations. But I was basically oblivious to it. I mean, not basically, just completely oblivious to the fact that I was doing any damage, and to the contrary I felt that I was one of the most brilliant, creative, attractive, intelligent people in the world . . . And it was often I traveled around so much in various places, you know, on the street, and in bars, you know, I met a lot of people. And in the earlier phases – I mean I had some, you know, bad hypomanic states, as it was transitioning into this severe mania, and when I was just high I kind of was all those things. I mean I became all those things in a way so that, you know, the people that I met who didn't know me responded. I had a lot of people respond that, you know . . . And not think or show anything about any indication that I thought that they thought that there was something wrong with me. And then within two days when I became crazy, I was pretty much oblivious to peoples' reactions. But clearly they knew I was nuts. So I'm saying all this because the transition from being so called 'normal,' and having this sudden onset, you know, night and day difference. I was mostly oblivious to this and unable to really experience . . .

Data set 4

Nancy is describing how she attributes her recovery to finding the right medication.

My recovery, in a nutshell, to me was, in the dictionary sense, recovering from extremely beyond anything dysfunctional and what I call crazy phase that lasted, that would not respond to any medication. From the beginning, a medical approach was always taken, and one that I accepted. I definitely accepted the chemical imbalance theory without question. At the time, I mean I got my first episode way back in 1975, and for 12 or 13 years it was unremitting, because, as I say, I was what they call a non-responder to everything, starting with lithium and going through everything in the pharmacopoeia. And I had, I think, 14 hospitalizations in 12 years. It was somewhat of a pattern of three months up and to be mania and three months down in bad clinical depressions. I would say the manias were more extreme than the depressions, but the depressions were not pleasant. So very briefly, all recovery means to me is not the kind of journey and, you know, back and forth, one step forward, two steps kind of experience that so many people I know describe and that I know, and that I have seen and that I know very well. And, to me, I have had a little bit of that nonlinear stuff back and forth, forward steps and back steps, definitely, but overall my feeling about my recovery is that it was simply a matter of going from being severely dysfunctional and severely ill and severely crazy and because the proper medication was found after 12 years of searching and experimenting and finally arriving as a research patient at the National Institute of Mental Health, which is the kind of – they don't take anybody. They have like eight or ten people who are patients there, who they accept as patients. And they don't take anybody who isn't at the end of the road, who hasn't been through everything. And my experience there, to make a long story short, I would say due to that experience, that a cocktail finally got developed that worked for the first time in 12 or 13 years.

Data set 5

Nancy is describing her response to medication and her work as a mental health activist.

And I'm very much a part of the political mental patients' rights movement and have been involved with in it in a fairly militant way for many years, so it's [inaudible] I'm sorry, but that's what I think my recovery is simply from. Not a long journey, not being helped by services I received, not being helped by anybody I ever had, you know, any mental health worker from psychiatrists to, you know, a janitor. When I say not helped, I mean not significantly – you know, I certainly met helpful and nice people along the way. I went from crazy to pretty much remission. And due to medication; clearly if I didn't take it I went crazy, if I did take it I was fine. It was that experiment to kind of make sure and that assured me anyway. So to be redundant, unlike a lot of people, especially unlike my colleagues in the movement, as we call it, I feel very strongly that there is a simple answer to my recovery, which I finally found some medication that controls my craziness and that's what I consider it a recovery, qualified by the fact that I believe in never saying never and I always know you know, there can be relapses. But I consider myself definitely in recovery. So that's the ending.

Question 1 Nancy displays referential strengths and anomalies in these narrative extracts. Give one example of each of these aspects of her use of reference.

Question 2 In data set 4, Nancy uses a particular metaphor to characterise her recovery from bipolar disorder. Identify the metaphor in question and give three examples of its use in this narrative extract.

Question 3 Nancy is able to use a number of discourse features in these narrative extracts. Several of these features are listed below. Give one example of each feature.

(a) Nancy is able to use a form of grammatical cohesion called substitution.
(b) Nancy is able to use demonstrative reference.
(c) Nancy is able to use mental state language.
(d) Nancy demonstrates awareness of narrative closure.
(e) Nancy is able to use ellipsis.

Question 4 In data set 4, Nancy produces a number of expressions which indicate that she is at least aware of the need to observe the quantity maxim in her account of her recovery from bipolar disorder. Identify three such expressions in this data set. In your opinion, does Nancy succeed in observing this maxim?

Question 5 Nancy produces a number of metalinguistic utterances during her mental illness narrative. Give three examples of these utterances in the above extracts.

4.8 Personality disorder

Background

The narratives of adults with features of borderline personality disorder (BPD) are distinctive more for what they reveal about these individuals' sense of empowerment and motivations for attachment and friendship than for their use of cohesion and inclusion of narrative episodes. Adler et al. (2012) conducted extensive life story interviews of 20 mid-life adults with features of BPD and compared them to the interviews of 20 adults without features of BPD. These interviews were analysed for their agency, narrative coherence, communion (an individual's motivation for attachment, affiliation, love, friendship and nurturance) and communal fulfilment (the extent to which a protagonist finds their communal needs met). Adler et al. found that with the exception of communion, these features distinguished the stories of adults with and without features of BPD. Several extracts from these stories are presented below. Examine these extracts in detail and then answer the questions that follow.

Data set 1

My life has been a constant pattern of God just putting things in my lap when I need them . . . I mean, I don't even have to ask for it, they just show up.

Everything was going well until one day [my wife] contracted cancer, and about 14–16 months later she eventually died, and it just tore me apart . . . One thing led to another and finally I ended up at the Betty Ford Center and, it took me for a ride . . . I don't know if you know anything about heroin, but it is it is so horribly addictive that I just couldn't do it on my own.

Data set 2

I'm kind of at that place in my life: most of all, I would say, it's time for myself.

We both needed each other and we started seeing each other and he was continually helping me, and not too much later, you know, we ended up getting married . . . When I fell for him, I fell really hard . . . He was just an all around good man, good husband, good grandpa and I liked his family, so when I lost him, I lost everybody . . . I'm still sad that you know, that I didn't get to have my life with him.

Data set 3

These adults were asked to recount a low and a high point in their lives, respectively.

My childhood.

As soon as I quit chanting, this wind came up behind me just as Danny let loose of the ashes, and he said the ashes just swirled; went up . . . it was like his spirit was released.

Data set 4

There's nothing else to do. I mean, my family's starting to die off . . . Since the new millennium I've lost two brothers and a sister, and a couple of brother-in-laws and a sister-in-law. And it's just like my family is just disappearing. And so I figure, maybe it's time to check out before, you know, I see any more die. I don't know. We'll see what happens.

Question 1 The above narratives of adults with BPD do not exhibit many of the discourse problems that are present in other clinical conditions. In fact, on the following discourse features, these narratives appear to be intact. Give <u>one</u> example of each of these features in the above data sets.

(a) use of conjunctive cohesion markers
(b) use of anaphoric reference
(c) use of temporal expressions
(d) temporal ordering of events
(e) use of evaluative language

Question 2 One of the above extracts displays *positive agency* and one displays *negative agency*. Identify the extracts in question and explain how they exemplify these types of agency.

Question 3 The extracts in data set 3 display a lack of narrative coherence. Explain the ways in which these extracts lack this coherence.

Question 4 Two extracts in the above data sets exhibit a lack of communion and a lack of communion fulfilment. Identify the extracts in question and explain the ways in which they reveal a lack of communion and communion fulfilment on the part of their speakers.

Question 5 A particular theme dominates the extract in data set 4. What is that theme and describe how it is manifested in the language used by the speaker?

4.9 Emotional disturbance in children

Background

The lack of normal communicative experiences in children with selective mutism has adverse implications for the development of pragmatic language skills. The mutism of these children means that they are denied opportunities in which to practise the use of a range of speech acts, to contribute topics to a conversational exchange and to develop turn-taking and other skills of conversation. Pragmatic language skills are further compromised when interlocutors modify their communicative behaviour in order to accommodate these children's mutism. In this way, other speakers may only pose questions which can be addressed through non-verbal responses (e.g. the nod of a head) or may assume the role of communicator for these children. These speaker behaviours limit yet further opportunities for the development of important pragmatic language skills on the part of children with selective mutism. This exercise takes the form of a case study of a girl called Mimi who was examined by Giddan et al. (1997). At the time of study, Mimi had been diagnosed with selective mutism for a number of years. Examine Mimi's case in detail and then answer the questions that follow.

Case study

Mimi, a 9-year-old girl with a diagnosis of selective mutism

Communicative history

Mimi was 8 years old when she was referred to a public school special education programme for children with severe behaviour handicaps. By this stage, she had already been silent in regular public school classes for a period of 3 years. Mimi had not spoken to anyone outside her home since she was 3 years old. She used limited gestures and handwritten notes in class to communicate. Although Mimi had never spoken at school or during SLT sessions, she communicated freely and easily at home with certain family members, as evidenced in a videotape recorded by her mother. When asked why she didn't speak, she wrote 'When I was little my mother told me don't talk to strangers.'

Family background

At the time of treatment, Mimi had four older siblings, although she was the only child still living at home. Mimi's biological father spoke Spanish at home. He left when she was young. When Mimi was 4 years old, she moved to another state whereupon her mother remarried. Mimi and her mother were particularly enmeshed in each other. Mimi's mother spoke for her when they were out and described her experiences to others. Dependence was further fostered by Mimi's mother continuing to bathe her, not expecting her to undertake any chores and managing other details of her life.

Medical treatment

Mimi sustained a mouth trauma when she was 2 years old. She fell and cut her mouth on the metal leg of a chair, an injury that required stitches. When she was 3 years old, Mimi was hospitalised for one week on account of a high fever. She experienced a number of needle sticks during this stay. These had frightened her and she did not talk while she was in hospital. After this episode, she did not speak to people outside of her immediate family circle.

Speech and language

Mimi's early communication milestones were reported to be normal. A video-recording of her at 9 years of age revealed significant syntactic and phonological error patterns. The /l/ and /r/ phonemes were distorted. The /s/ phoneme was omitted in plurals, possessives, and present tense verbs. Mimi also made use of immature syntactic structures, e.g. 'This is a boy . . . This one name Andy . . . I'm gonna talk about what family do.' These linguistic problems had not previously been addressed in therapy on account of Mimi's mutism.

Academic performance

When Mimi entered the school programme, she did not speak on the telephone, in public places, to some relatives and even to her best friend. Her limited participation in school combined with her linguistic deficits placed her at great risk academically. When she was 9 years old, Mimi should have been in the fourth grade. However, she was a third-grader who was performing at second-grade level in reading, spelling and mathematics.

Question 1 Explain the effect that Mimi's mutism at school is likely to have on the development of her pragmatic language skills. Make your explanation as specific as possible by including <u>three</u> examples of pragmatic language skills that are likely to be disrupted by mutism.

Question 2 Mimi exhibits a number of linguistic deficits. What role, if any, are these deficits likely to play in Mimi's mutism?

Question 3 Mimi and her mother have developed a particular type of interpersonal relationship. Are there any implications of this type of relationship for the development of Mimi's pragmatic language skills?

Question 4 Children with autism spectrum disorder may also not engage in spoken communication. Yet, Mimi's communication skills still differ in significant ways from those of children with ASD. List <u>three</u> qualitative differences between Mimi's communication skills and those of children with ASD.

Question 5 Does Mimi make use of any other communication skills in the absence of spoken communication in school? How might these skills be harnessed to good effect by both speech and language therapists and teachers?

4.10 Behavioural disorders in children

Background

Attention deficit hyperactivity disorder (ADHD) has significant implications for the pragmatic and discourse skills of affected children. These children tend to interrupt other speakers' turns in conversation, do not listen to and follow instructions, and talk excessively. Alongside the behavioural problems of these children, communication impairments can have an adverse effect on academic performance and other domains.

The following conversations between a teacher and two children with ADHD exemplify some of the communication problems of these children. The two children in question, Abraham and Adam, were popular with teachers and their peer groups. The conversations were recorded in primary school special education classes as part of a study by Peets (2009) of classroom discourse in children with language impairment. Transcription notation has been removed and other modifications have been made.

Data set 1

Conversation between teacher (T) and Abraham (A) in the presence of students (S).

A: Then I throw the ball at my baby brother.
T: Oh why did you do that?
A: So so he can play with it.
T: Did he like you throwing the ball at him?
A: Yeah because I because when I sometimes throw the ball at him he laughs.
T: So you you just threw it gently.
A: Then then he took the pillow.
S: (unspecified turn)
A: Then I said 'look out' then I then he throw the pillow in my face!
    (Students laugh)

Data set 2

Conversation between teacher (T) and Adam (A).

A: I went to my cousin's house and when I went to my cousin's house that was later when I when I we went back home for um from snow tubing.
T: Can you tell us about snow tubing?
A: Snow tubing is is freaky.
T: Freaky. Tell us what it's like. What do you do?

A: They uh they have a machine that will they have a hooks that will pull you back up and then you have eight tickets you give one of them to (th)em then you got hold onto a rope they have like a little round thing and then you go they put the put the hook inside and then and then it pulls you back up and then you slide down they put they maybe the if you want to stay straight you tell my parents from up there if you want a spin they he spins you.

Question 1 Although Abraham's utterances do not overlap with the teacher's turns in data set 1, there are nonetheless features of this exchange which suggest that Abraham is so eager to communicate that he has not always planned adequately what he wants to say. Identify <u>two</u> such features. What behavioural characteristic of ADHD may explain these features?

Question 2 In data set 1, the teacher produces the utterance 'so you just threw it gently'. What type of utterance may the teacher have expected Abraham to contribute in his next turn? How might Abraham's failure to produce this utterance be explained in terms of the behavioural features of ADHD?

Question 3 Adam's first turn in data set 2 violates a Gricean maxim of conversation. Which maxim is violated by this turn?

Question 4 Adam's account of snow tubing is particularly difficult to follow. What <u>three</u> features of this account contribute to its lack of comprehensibility?

Question 5 Notwithstanding the difficulties identified in response to the above questions, there are several instances of pragmatic and discourse skills being used to good effect by both Abraham and Adam. Several of these skills are listed below. Give <u>one</u> example of each skill:

(a) use of direct reported speech
(b) use of anaphoric reference
(c) use of conjunctions that express a causal relationship between events
(d) use of conjunctions that express a temporal order between events
(e) comprehension of indirect speech acts

SUGGESTIONS FOR FURTHER READING

Colle, L., Angeleri, R., Vallana, M., Sacco, K., Bara, B. G. and Bosco, F. M. 2013. 'Understanding the communicative impairments in schizophrenia: a preliminary study', *Journal of Communication Disorders* **46**:3, 294–308.

France, J. 2001. 'Personality disorders', in J. France and S. Kramer (eds), *Communication and mental illness: theoretical and practical approaches*, London and Philadelphia: Jessica Kingsley Publishers, 81–100.

France, J. 2001. 'Depression and other mood disorders', in J. France and S. Kramer (eds), *Communication and mental illness: theoretical and practical approaches*, London and Philadelphia: Jessica Kingsley Publishers, 65–80.

Gilmour, J., Hill, B., Place, M. and Skuse, D. H. 2004. 'Social communication deficits in conduct disorder: a clinical and community survey', *Journal of Child Psychology and Psychiatry* **45**:5, 967–78.

Green, B. C., Johnson, K. A. and Bretherton, L. 2014. 'Pragmatic language difficulties in children with hyperactivity and attention problems: an integrated review', *International Journal of Language & Communication Disorders* **49**:1, 15–29.

Marini, A. and Perlini, C. 2014. 'Narrative language production in schizophrenia', in P. Brambilla and A. Marini (eds), *Brain evolution, language and psychopathology in schizophrenia*, London and New York: Routledge, 181–93.

McInnes, A., Fung, D., Manassis, K., Fiksenbaum, L. and Tannock, R. 2004. 'Narrative skills in children with selective mutism: an exploratory study', *American Journal of Speech–Language Pathology* **13**:4, 304–15.

Chapter 5

Pragmatics and discourse in other disorders and populations

Although the conditions examined in earlier chapters represent the most common pragmatic and discourse disorders, they are by no means exhaustive of the populations in which there are deficits of pragmatics and discourse. As our understanding of these disorders develops, it is becoming increasingly clear to researchers and clinicians that pragmatic and discourse skills are also disrupted in a number of other populations. These populations have been largely overlooked to date by clinical pragmatists. This has occurred for a number of reasons. In some cases, the implications for communication of a particular disorder are believed to involve speech development or aspects of language that are related to academic performance (e.g. writing, reading) and not pragmatic and discourse skills. This is the case in children and adults with congenital hearing loss and illiteracy, respectively.

In other cases, pragmatic and discourse disorders have been overlooked because outcomes have been based on measures that do not address these aspects of language. In children who have undergone early corrective heart surgery, for example, developmental outcomes have been based on standardised tests of intelligence, standardised measures of academic skills and neuropsychological measures. When language skills have been assessed in these children, assessment has typically focused on structural language skills. In still other cases, pragmatic and discourse impairments in certain clients are only just beginning to attract the attention of researchers and clinicians. For example, we currently know very little about age-related changes in the pragmatic abilities of normal, elderly people or the pragmatic and discourse skills of non-verbal communicators who use augmentative and alternative communication systems. In all these disorders and populations, a range of pragmatic and discourse impairments still await detailed examination.

The task of this chapter is to begin this examination through a series of data analysis exercises on just five populations: children who have undergone early corrective heart surgery; individuals with functional illiteracy; children and adults with congenital hearing loss; users of augmentative and alternative communication; and elderly people who are undergoing normal, age-related changes in their pragmatic abilities. These populations are by no means exhaustive of those clients with pragmatic and discourse disorders who have not been extensively examined to date. For example, we could add to this list adolescents and adults in prisons and other correctional facilities and individuals with congenital visual impairment, to name just two further cases. But this list of five populations does at least provide an indication of the types of clients that clinicians of the future will increasingly have on their caseloads, and which the discipline of clinical pragmatics must stand ready to address.

Data analysis exercises

5.1 Early corrective heart surgery

Background

Children with congenital heart disease who undergo early corrective heart surgery (ECHS) are at risk of brain injury. This is often attributable to operative factors such as cardiopulmonary bypass, total circulatory arrest and a range of other procedures that protect vital organs during cardiac repair. These children can experience adverse neurological sequelae including language and learning problems. Hemphill et al. (2002) studied 76 children aged 4 years of age who had histories of early corrective heart surgery. These children were born with d-transposition of the great arteries. They all underwent successful heart surgery for the correction of this birth defect as infants. These children produced narratives of personal experience and performed other spoken discourse tasks as part of developmental assessments which were undertaken at 4 years of age. An interviewer, who was unfamiliar to the children, first engaged them in joint toy play. As play came to an end, the interviewer related three brief narratives about a swimming incident, a bee sting and a spilling accident. The children were then asked 'Did anything like that ever happen to you?' As the children produced their narratives, the interviewer responded only to indicate attention to what was being said (e.g. 'mmhm') and to make non-specific requests for more information (e.g. 'Is that all?').

The data sets below contain extracts of the personal narratives of two children with early corrective heart surgery. An extract from the narrative of a typically developing child is included for comparison. Examine these extracts in detail and then answer the questions that follow.

Data set 1

A child with ECHS called James (J) is relating to the interviewer (I) a time when he went swimming.

I: Did you ever go to the beach and go swimming?
J: *(shakes head no)* When I was three I did.
I: When you were three?
J: *(nods yes)*
I: Tell me about that time.
J: Hmm . . . I went in the water . . .
I: Uh-huh. What else?
J: Then I don't know what happened again.

Data set 2

A child with ECHS called George (G) is relating to the interviewer (I) a time when he was stung by a bee.

G: When I was a little baby and, and I just grow a little bit.
I: Yeah.
G: And I, and I weh weh with a bee and then it caught my ear.
I: Did he sting your ear?
G: *(nods yes)*

> I: Tell me about it. What happened?
> G: Because that's why it did, it did it really hard *(points to ear)*
> I: Uh-huh.
> G: And then . . .
> I: And then what happened?
> G: And then it was it was this and I don't, and I didn't know where it was.
> I: Uh-huh and then what?
> G: Hmm and then that was the end of the bee.

Data set 3

A typically developing child called Darryl (D) is relating to the interviewer (I) a time when he was bitten by a pet dog.

> I: Did you ever get bitten?
> D: He bit me when I was littler.
> I: He did?
> D: Yeah. I went by him and he *(unintelligible material)* and I hit him and he went 'Ahhh.'
> I: He went 'Ahhh'?
> D: Real hard.
> I: Real hard?
> D: Yeah. Real hard.
> I: Real hard?
> D: With his teeth.
> I: Uh huh.
> D: *(demonstrates biting something)*
> I: Oh.
> D: Now he won't bite me 'cause I'm bigger.
> I: Right, right.
> D: Now he knows me and Char-, and Tommy.

Question 1 Even on the basis of the short extract of narrative in data set 1, much can be gleaned about James's pragmatic and discourse skills and impairments. Several of these are listed below. Give <u>one</u> example of each in this extract:

(a) James can make appropriate use of ellipsis.
(b) James's non-verbal communication can contradict utterance meaning.
(c) James contributes uninformative utterances.
(d) James produces a statement of ignorance to foreclose narrative development.
(e) James can provide a temporal context for the events in his narrative.

Question 2 George's narrative in data set 2 is quite difficult to follow in parts. Two pragmatic and discourse anomalies in particular account for this difficulty: (a) a lack of pronominal reference and (b) unclear semantic–logical links between events. Give <u>one</u> example of each anomaly in this data set.

Question 3 Notwithstanding the various weaknesses of George's narrative, he is able to adhere to narrative structure in two essential respects. What are these respects? Support your answer with evidence from data set 2.

Question 4 George and Darryl are both able to express a temporal order on events during their narratives. However, they achieve this in different (but equally successful) ways. Describe how George and Darryl succeed in relating events within a temporal sequence.

Question 5 In data sets 1 and 3, the interviewer repeats part of the child's prior turn in his utterance. However, the children in these data sets respond to this repetition in quite different ways. Describe these children's different responses to this repetition and explain why they occur.

5.2   Functional illiteracy

Background

Functional illiteracy describes impoverished written language skills in adolescents and adults who nevertheless attended school and received formal instruction in these skills. Functionally illiterate individuals may be able to complete their personal details on a form or read listings of TV programmes, but may not be able to write a cheque or read a patient information leaflet. The standard explanation of functional illiteracy has pointed to factors such as sociocultural disadvantage. However, there is now increasing recognition of the role of cognitive abilities in the development of functional illiteracy. One cognitive ability in particular – oral language skills – was investigated in a study of 52 French-speaking functionally illiterate adults by Eme et al. (2010). Along with 20 French-speaking proficient adult readers, these subjects produced an oral narrative in response to a series of eight colour pictures taken from a comic strip ('Wowser' by Dupa). In these pictures, a dog is dreaming about swimming in the water and then being bitten by a fish. After the dog takes its revenge, it sees the approach of a large fish who is about to gobble the dog up. The data sets below contain the oral narratives of five illiterate adults who participated in this study. Examine these narratives in detail, and then answer the questions that follow.

Data set 1

There's a bear having a nice quiet swim, a fish suddenly comes along, he asks himself 'What's that yellow thing?' So Your Lordship, he nibbles him, bites the bear's tail, and then the bear bites the fish's tail, and the fish swims quietly away crying. The bear is VERY pleased, the bear puts a plaster on his tail and the fish the same. They're both swimming along quietly. Suddenly, a big, big fish arrives. The little fish and the bear asked themselves 'What's that?' A big fish that wants to gobble them both up. AND he suddenly woke up with a start. 'What's going on, what's going on? Ah! I know, a bad dream I had!'

Data set 2

Well you've got a dog swimming, then you've got a fish that bites his tail, the dog tries to bite the fish's tail, the fish escapes, the dog thinks, suddenly he realizes he's in for it. There's a big fish that's going to get eaten, he wakes up, it's a nightmare.

Data set 3

So first of all there's a little fish, he's seen a little tail a little bear, and there he's swimming, in the sea. And then suddenly, he hurt because the fish bites the tail of a little bear. And then he hurts, I think, yeah. And then the bear, he bites the tail at the fish, he says 'Ow', and Baby Fish he cries and the bear's cross, yeah, he's cross. And he has a think, Baby Fish, he has a think, thinks. And then the bear here he's seen a big mouth with teeth, then the fish he was pleased, he looked at the bear. And then suddenly a big fish that was coming and the bear he almost ended up in the mouth. And then the fish he smiles, he smiles Baby Fish, and then after a moment he woke up because he's had a nightmare.

Data set 4

There he's swimming the little fish, he's swimming peacefully along, a fish. He sees the tail. He's surprised. He bites the tail. He does the same thing, a little fish, he bites the tail. He does the same thing the dog. The fish he hurts. And the dog says, 'You see who's the boss?' The fish he hurts, he's got a plaster. the dog ..., there's a problem. little fish, over there it's the mummy. He's big, the big fish is going to bite the dog. And it's a dream.

Data set 5

So what would you call it? A bear, a dog or what's that it could be? A bear, a bear having a bad dream. He dreams of swimming in the water. And the dream turns into a nightmare.

Question 1 In data set 1, the adult with functional illiteracy has produced a successful narrative. Using examples, identify five discourse features of this narrative which contribute to its success.

Question 2 The narrative in data set 2 is unlikely to engage a listener. Give three features of this narrative which contribute to its lack of appeal to a listener.

Question 3 The adult in data set 3 displays certain discourse skills while other aspects of discourse are impaired. Several of these discourse strengths and weaknesses are listed below. Give one example of each in this data set:

(a) use of pronouns with unclear referents
(b) use of cataphoric reference
(c) use of poor information ordering
(d) use of temporal conjunctions to relate events
(e) use of anaphoric reference

Question 4 The narrative in data set 4 is unlikely to be judged as satisfactory by a listener. Identify five shortcomings of this narrative that are likely to compromise it for a listener.

Question 5 The narrative in data set 5 is seriously compromised by the omission of most of the key information including the characters (e.g. the fish), what the characters did (e.g. the dog bites the fish's tail) and the results of their actions (e.g. a big fish arrives on the scene). However, there is another feature of this very short narrative which is problematic in terms of narrative development. What is this feature and how does it compromise narrative development?

5.3   Hearing loss

Background

Investigators are increasingly finding evidence of pragmatic impairments in children with hearing loss. Children with hearing loss and who use hearing aids or cochlear implants have been shown to have different or less effective pragmatic abilities than hearing children (Most et al., 2010). Moreover, the pragmatic language skills of deaf and hard-of-hearing students who use spoken language or signed language have been found to have a high, positive correlation with academic outcomes (Thagard et al., 2011). Clearly, there is a need to consider the pragmatic language skills of this clinical population and to intervene as early as possible on any impairment of these skills in order to avoid adverse academic consequences.

Dronkers et al. (1998) describe the somewhat unusual case of a 49-year-old woman called Chelsea who was born with severe-to-profound sensorineural hearing loss. Chelsea was misdiagnosed in childhood as having an intellectual disability. Chelsea's mother believed her to be deaf and refused to have her daughter institutionalised. Instead, Chelsea lived at home with her siblings whom she helped her mother raise. She also learned to do housework and cook. Her admission to local schools and a school for the deaf was denied. At the age of 32 years, a social worker became aware of Chelsea's circumstances and referred her to a neurologist and speech–language pathologist. It was only at this stage that Chelsea was fitted with bilateral hearing aids and was enrolled in an intensive programme of oral and signed language instruction.

A transcribed conversation between Chelsea (C) and an interviewer (I) is shown below. Both participants signed as they spoke. Examine this conversational extract and then answer the questions that follow.

Data set

I: *(addressing second interviewer)* I've told Chelsea for the last two days that I had a gift for her.
C: Gift.
I: From Colorado.
C: Colorado.
I: I remembered! *(presents gift)* Do you want to open it?
C: *(accepts wrapped gift, begins to untie the ribbon.)*
I: Ribbon.
C: Ribbon.
I: What do you think it is?
C: Think? *(shakes head)*
I: A book. Think it's a book?
C: Book? Don't think.
I: Is it a blouse?
C: Blouse? No. You . . . collar.
I: Collar? Oh, a scarf. Yes, for my birthday . . .
C: *(continues unwrapping, still unfolding paper)*
I: There's nothing . . . I tricked you!
C: *(laughs; takes out small box)* Oh! Thank you! *(hugs interviewer)* Jewelry!
I: That is named 'turquoise'. *(finger spells 'turquoise')*
C: Turquoise.

Question 1 Chelsea has very limited expressive language skills. Notwithstanding her linguistic limitations, she is able to use language to perform a number of pragmatic functions. Several of these functions are listed below. Give one example of each in the above conversation.

(a) Chelsea is able to respond to yes–no questions.
(b) Chelsea is able to express gratitude.
(c) Chelsea is able to produce statements.
(d) Chelsea is able to confirm her understanding of her interlocutor's utterance.
(e) Chelsea is able to express mental states.

Question 2 There is a consistent pattern in Chelsea's turns. She uses them to repeat part of the prior speaker's turn and, sometimes, to make an additional verbal or non-verbal contribution. Give three examples of this pattern in the above conversation. Why do you think it occurs?

Question 3 Respond with *true* or *false* to each of the following statements.

(a) Chelsea comprehends metalinguistic utterances.
(b) Chelsea is able to establish the referent of personal pronouns.
(c) Chelsea is not able to establish the referent of demonstrative pronouns.
(d) Chelsea does not appreciate humour introduced by her interlocutor.
(e) Chelsea makes communicative use of body movements.

Question 4 Chelsea uses several non-verbal behaviours in her exchange with the interviewer. However, only some of these behaviours have a communicative function. Identify the behaviours in question. Which of these behaviours supplements a verbal response on Chelsea's part, and which takes the place of a verbal response?

Question 5 Is there any evidence that Chelsea is making a contribution to topic development in the above exchange? Use data from this exchange to support your answer.

5.4   Augmentative and alternative communication

Background

The pragmatic and discourse skills of child and adult users of augmentative and alternative communication (AAC) are frequently overlooked, both in a clinical context and in research studies. An investigation of these skills by Soto and Hartmann (2006) in four child users of AAC revealed that pragmatic and discourse skills are often compromised and in need of direct intervention. The four children in this study had a severe dysarthria which affected the communication of their basic needs, and for which use of an aided augmentative communication system was necessary. Major mobility was also compromised, while the cognitive abilities of these children were within the normal range. Hearing and vision were within normal limits with or without correction.

The four children in this study undertook tasks in the classroom that were designed to elicit the full range of narrative skills involved in literacy and academic growth. The tasks were administered by teachers who were encouraged to interact with the children as they would normally do so. The five narrative tasks were as follows: (1) personal photo description – children were asked to describe a photo of themselves in a favourite situation; (2) familiar book reading and story comprehension – teachers and children engaged in shared reading of a story book, with the children asked a number of questions as the story went along; (3) conversational narrative – teachers engaged children in a conversation about a recent and salient event in their lives; (4) story stem – children were given the beginning of a story and were asked to complete it; and (5) wordless picture book – children were asked to relate the mischievous behaviour of a Rottweiler called Carl, who is asked to look after a baby while her mother goes shopping. Extracts from the narrative discourse produced by these children are shown below. Examine the extracts in detail and then answer the questions that follow.

Data set 1

A is a 9-year-old girl who has a primary diagnosis of arthrogryposis (a congenital, non-progressive condition that causes multiple joint contractures and abnormal muscle development). She also has a surgically repaired cleft palate. A is describing a photograph of clay making at a children's museum. Kevin is A's brother.

A   Teachers: T and G
                                       (T) *How did the clay feel in your hands?*
((looks at photo))
Roll ((makes rolling motion))
                                       (G) *Roll*
                                       (T) *But how did it feel? Go ahead.*
((typing 30 sec))
Not going. Kevin not going.
'Kevin'
                                       (T) *Was Kevin, is Kevin in the picture?*

Data set 2

H is an 8-year-old girl who suffers from muscular dystrophy. She has been asked to complete a fictional story to the following prompt: 'Once upon a time there was a princess who lived in a glass castle. Now tell us what happened . . .'

H   Teacher
                                       Oh, they are outside when they sing?
((head nod yes))
                                       Okay, can I ask you a question, about, hmmm, so they are singing outside?
((init. msg. constr.))
'Song Erica With Outside'
                                       Okay, you were looking and trying to tell me something? You want to go outside?

Data set 3

D is a 5.9-year-old boy who has been diagnosed with choreoathetoid cerebral palsy with hypotonia. D is describing a photograph of plants being watered in his back yard.

D	Teacher
	What did you do?
((points to icon: *in*))	
	In
	((points to board/*in*))
	You are showing me the in. Did you put something in the pot?
((points to photograph))	
	Oh, you ((points to photograph)) *put something in the pot. What'd you put in the pot? What is that sign you used before? What did you and Grandma put in the pot?*
((points to icon: *out*))	
	Oh, you took something out of the pot? What did you take out of that pot?

Data set 4

S is an 11-year-old girl with cerebral palsy. She is telling a story about a hungry princess at the mall.

S	Teacher
'She ate them up'	
	She ate them up. Good sentence. She ate them up. And what do we say when the story is all finalised? How do you . . .
'and'	
	She ate them up and . . .
'Throw up'	
	((laughs))
((prestored msg.)) 'THIS SENTENCE IN MY STORY WILL BE THE END'	

Data set 5

S is engaging in shared storybook reading with the teacher about a bunny getting dressed.

S	Teacher
	And a silly what?
'Cap' 'The bunny has her dress and blouse and a silly cap'	
	Oh *I want to add something*
And	
	Oh you want to add it. Okay

Data set 6

H is narrating a story based on a wordless picture book.

H	Teacher
Aaah ah ah ah	
((msg. constr. cont))	
'Door'	
	The door?
((head nod yes))	
	Oh
	((points to picture))
	They are going in the door?
((head nod no))	
	They are looking in the door?
((head nod yes))	
	Oh they are looking in the door. Oh that's what they are looking at. What do you think is going to be in there?
	((points to picture))
((msg. constr. cont))	
'Door'	
	((init. msg. constr))
	Ahhh
	'Eat'
	'Door eat'

Question 1 In data set 1, child A exhibits impaired and intact pragmatic and discourse behaviours. Several of these are listed below. Give <u>one</u> example of each of these behaviours.

(a) A misunderstands mental state language.
(b) A makes communicative use of body movements.
(c) A has difficulty maintaining topic relevance.
(d) A can engage in self-initiated repair.
(e) A produces under-informative utterances.

Question 2 What type of discourse cohesion is used by these children? What implications does this type of cohesion have for the meaning relations that these children can express?

Question 3 Give <u>one</u> example of each of the following communicative features in the above data sets:

(a) appropriate use of humour
(b) appropriate use of discourse deixis
(c) poor communicative use of pointing
(d) appropriate use of pronominal reference
(e) good communicative use of head nodding

Question 4 The teachers in the above data sets are accommodating to the limited output of the children in these exchanges. Using examples, describe three features of the teachers' utterances which suggest accommodation is taking place.

Question 5 Although many of the teachers' utterances are used to confirm what the children are attempting to communicate, other utterances are used with the aim of expanding the children's output. Give one example of this latter use of utterances in the above data sets.

5.5   Aging and the elderly

Background

Little is known about age-related changes in pragmatic and discourse skills in normal, elderly speakers. Juncos-Rabadán et al. (2005) investigated these skills during a narrative production task in 79 adults aged 40 to 91 years. All participating subjects displayed no history of neurological or psychiatric illness, no history of the use of drugs or other substances that affect the central nervous system and had no sensory or motor impairments that might compromise task performance. These adults were required to produce narratives based on three picture stories. Narratives were analysed for quantity, information content and cohesion.

A transcription of one of these narratives is presented below. The picture story that this narrative was based on is the Nest Story from the Bilingual Aphasia Test (Paradis, 1987). The story contains six panels which depict the following scenario. A woman directs a man's attention to a bird's nest in a tree. The man climbs the tree in order to get to the nest. The branch of the tree breaks and the man falls to the ground. The man is lying on the ground, and an ambulance arrives to take the man away. Finally, the woman is shown visiting the man in hospital. Examine the narrative in detail and then answer the questions that follow.

Data set

Narrative based on the Nest Story from the Bilingual Aphasia Test (Paradis, 1987).

Here they're shaking a plum tree or a woman's pointing to a little bird drinking up there or bringing the little ones something to eat, bringing the chicks something to eat and the lady's looking at the man it must be to, so that ... I don't know what the man wants to do with the birds I don't resolve and here's the woman feeding the little birds and the man, I don't know what he's saying to her I can't hear and this other one does ... they're coming out of this house they're looking at the tree, the tree ... tree it is a vine and the little birds can't find anything to eat, they don't stop still or isn't it like that? There, the gentleman fell down he was in, in the tree and he fell down and the lady ..., they're all standing still looking at him, sleeping I'm not going to be able to figure much out there here go to the police and of course they went to pick up the one that, the one that fell down and as helpers the ones that came out of that house and here he is now in the, in bed of the hospital it must be the nurse around and the little birds, with their father or with their mother I don't know.

Question 1 This narrative is quite difficult to follow on account of a number of referential anomalies. Identify five such anomalies in the above data set.

Question 2 Important information is omitted from this adult's narrative. Identify two such omissions in the above data set.

Question 3 Provide evidence from the above data set in support of each of the following statements.

(a) The speaker reverts to an earlier topic at the end of the narrative.
(b) The speaker uses incorrect lexical items.
(c) The speaker uses mental state language.
(d) The speaker abandons utterances.
(e) The speaker uses anaphoric reference.

Question 4 The narrative is quite repetitive in parts. Give an example of the use of repetitive language by this speaker.

Question 5 Does the speaker succeed in representing temporal and causal relations between events? Provide evidence to support your answer.

SUGGESTIONS FOR FURTHER READING

Bellinger, D. C. 2010. 'Theory of mind deficits in children with congenital heart disease', *Developmental Medicine & Child Neurology* **52**:12, 1079–80.

Freed, J., Adams, C. and Lockton, E. 2011. 'Literacy skills in primary school-aged children with pragmatic language impairment: a comparison with children with specific language impairment', *International Journal of Language & Communication Disorders* **46**:3, 334–47.

Goberis, D., Beams, D., Dalpes, M., Abrisch, A., Baca, R. and Yoshinaga-Itano, C. 2012. 'The missing link in language development of deaf and hard of hearing children: pragmatic language development', *Seminars in Speech and Language* **33**:4, 297–309.

Senner, J. E. 2011. 'Parent perceptions of pragmatic skills in teens and young adults using AAC', *Communication Disorders Quarterly* **32**:2, 103–8.

Surian, L., Tedoldi, M. and Siegal, M. 2010. 'Sensitivity to conversational maxims in deaf and hearing children', *Journal of Child Language* **37**:4, 929–43.

Todman, J. 2010. 'Pragmatics of communication aids', in L. Cummings (ed.), *The Routledge pragmatics encyclopedia*, London and New York: Routledge, 61–3.

Wengryn, M. I. and Hester, E. J. 2011. 'Pragmatic skills used by older adults in social communication and health care contexts: precursors to health literacy', *Contemporary Issues in Communication Science and Disorders* **38**, 41–52.

Answers to questions and exercises

Chapter 1: Introduction to pragmatic and discourse disorders

1.1 Pragmatics and discourse in human communication

(1) (a) Pragmatics; (b) discourse; (c) pragmatics; (d) discourse; (e) discourse. (2) States of affairs; threaten; decline; context; knowledge; warning; epistemic; presupposition; referent; discourse; social. (3) True. (4) False. (5) True. (6) (a) Scalar implicature; (b) presupposition; (c) anaphoric reference; (d) collocation; (e) conventional implicature. (7) (c) Manner. (8) (d) Noun phrase *the old house on the hill*. (9) (b) Substitution. (10) (a) She (personal deixis); (b) I (personal deixis), last week (temporal deixis); (c) that paragraph (discourse deixis); (d) this way (spatial deixis); (e) well behaved pupils . . . teacher (social deixis).

1.2 Disorders of pragmatics and discourse

(1) (a) Discourse; (b) pragmatics; (c) discourse; (d) pragmatics; (e) discourse. (2) True. (3) True. (4) True. (5) Communicative intention; social relationship; impolite; encoded; lexical; prosody; facial; interpretation; propositional; semantic; disambiguation; referents; logical; implicatures. (6) Parts (b) and (e). (7) Parts (a), (b) and (c). (8) Part (a). (9) Part (a). (10) Parts (a), (c) and (d).

1.3 Clinical distinctions

(1) Parts (c) and (d). (2) Parts (c), (d) and (e). (3) False. (4) False. (5) True. (6) (a) Expressive; (b) expressive; (c) receptive; (d) receptive; (e) receptive. (7) Onset; developmental period; genetic; social communication; traumatic brain injury; acquired; secondary; specific language impairment; speech acts; structural language; primary; interpretation; irony. (8) Part (d). (9) Parts (a) and (c). (10) Parts (a) and (e).

1.4 Pragmatics and discourse in human communication

(1) (a) The recovery of communicative intentions during utterance interpretation. (b) The development of the semantically underspecified logical form of utterances. (c) The development of the semantically underspecified logical form of utterances.

(d) The formation of communicative intentions. (e) The recovery of communicative intentions during utterance interpretation. **(2)** (a) Cohesion: Brian's utterances are disconnected and do not relate to each other. (b) Information management: Derek is relating no new information to Barbara. (c) Narrative development: Poppy's written story contains statements which do not contribute to the development of her narrative about her brother. (d) Cohesion and information management: Paul's utterances do not 'flow from each other'; also, he fails to give his wife the information she wants about the shops while giving her information she does not wish to hear about a baseball game. (e) Information management: Alex omits key information from his explanatory discourse; he fails to meet his mother's informational needs. **(3)** (a) Joe has drawn a *mental state inference* to establish the sarcastic intent behind Sam's utterance. (b) Alice has drawn a *textual inference* (a bridging inference) to conclude that the box also contained a set of lights. (c) Bob has drawn a *mental state inference* to establish that Susie is declining his invitation to dinner. (d) Tom has drawn an *elaborative inference* when he concludes that Dr Smith caused the explosion. (e) Billy has drawn an *elaborative inference* when he concludes that the doctor prescribed antibiotics for Cynthia.

1.5 Disorders of pragmatics and discourse

(1) Parts (a), (d) and (e). **(2)** Parts (c), (d), (e), (g), (i) and (j). **(3)** Parts (a), (c), (d), (f), (g) and (j).

1.6 Clinical distinctions

(1) (a) Acquired; (b) developmental; (c) acquired; (d) developmental; (e) developmental. **(2)** (a) Primary; (b) secondary; (c) primary; (d) secondary; (e) primary. **(3)** (a) Expressive; (b) expressive; (c) receptive; (d) receptive; (e) expressive.

Chapter 2: Developmental pragmatic and discourse disorders

Section A: Short-answer questions

2.1 Pragmatic language impairment

(1) Parts (a), (b), (d) and (e). **(2)** False. **(3)** True. **(4)** Developmental; conversational; topic; irrelevant; atypical; word-finding; phonology; organic; intellectual disability; unknown; hearing; non-verbal; psychiatric; structural language; semantic; vocabulary. **(5)** Part (c). **(6)** Part (e). **(7)** False. **(8)** True. **(9)** Parts (b), (c) and (e). **(10)** Parts (a), (d) and (e).

2.2 Intellectual disability

(1) Part (d). **(2)** Part (d). **(3)** False. **(4)** False. **(5)** False. **(6)** Turn-taking; contextual; referents; speech acts; politeness; impolite; indirect; understood; topic; genetic; social; teachers; context; coherent; syntactic. **(7)** (a) Production of requests, which is performed through the use of gesture and two-word utterances. (b) Conversational turn-taking, which is achieved through the use of stereotyped utterances. (c) Interpretation of indirect speech acts, specifically requests, which is facilitated by the comprehension of gestures.

(d) Topic initiation, which is achieved by the repetition of the doll's name and by an action (placing the doll in the teacher's hand). (e) Responding to questions, which is performed through the use of a contextually inappropriate utterance. **(8)** Parts (d) and (e). **(9)** Part (c). **(10)** True.

2.3 Autism spectrum disorder

(1) Part (e). **(2)** Parts (a) and (b). **(3)** Parts (a), (b) and (d). **(4)** True. **(5)** False. **(6)** Ignorance; emotions; communicative intentions; sarcastic; false belief; normally developing; implicature; presuppositions; disrupted; knowledge; implicit; foregrounded; referent; mental representation. **(7)** (a) Receptive; (b) receptive; (c) expressive; (d) expressive; (e) receptive. **(8)** False. **(9)** True. **(10)** Part (e).

2.4 Childhood traumatic brain injury

(1) Part (c). **(2)** Parts (a), (b), (c) and (e). **(3)** Parts (a), (c) and (e). **(4)** Structural language; non-literal; metaphor; working memory; intentions; irony; thematic; executive function; problem solving; expository; written. **(5)** False. **(6)** True. **(7)** Parts (c) and (d). **(8)** Parts (a), (b) and (d). **(9)** False. **(10)** True.

2.5 Epileptic syndromes

(1) Part (b). **(2)** Part (e). **(3)** Aphasiology; production; cohesive devices; conjunctions; referential; pronouns; preceding; narrative; seizure; onset; EEG. **(4)** True. **(5)** False. **(6)** True. **(7)** Cortex; consciousness; unknown; onset; myelination; cognitive; repair; impaired; reference; frontal. **(8)** Parts (a), (c) and (e). **(9)** Part (e). **(10)** False.

2.6 Childhood cancer

(1) Part (c). **(2)** Parts (a), (b), (c) and (e). **(3)** Acute lymphoblastic leukaemia; speech–language pathology; cranial radiotherapy; white matter; worse; neurotoxic; processing; memory; chemotherapy; cognitive; hearing; dysarthria; posterior fossa; anomia; fluency; structural language; ambiguity; metaphoric; neurocognitive. **(4)** False. **(5)** False. **(6)** True. **(7)** (a) Expressive discourse; (b) receptive pragmatics; (c) expressive discourse; (d) receptive and expressive pragmatics; (e) receptive discourse. **(8)** False. **(9)** Part (c). **(10)** False.

Section B: Data analysis exercises

2.7 Pragmatic language impairment 1

Question 1 (a) Child's response in data set 3; (b) child's second turn in data set 6. **Question 2** (a) Child's response to the adult's indirect speech act in data set 1; (b) in data set 8, the child fails to draw the inference that the boy in the picture has emptied his pockets in order to find his key. **Question 3** (a) In data set 4, the child continues to repeat the utterance 'it has a lift in it'; (b) in data set 7, the child conveys contradictory information when he says both that he does and does not watch *The Two Ronnies*.

Question 4 (a) In data set 2, the utterance in the child's second turn presupposes that he is familiar with the games, when in fact he is not; (b) in data set 5, the child assumes that the adult has his (the child's) knowledge of the events in his day. **Question 5** (a) In data set 10, the child uses the pronouns 'she' and 'herself' to refer to a boy; (b) in data set 9, the child is unable to explain what he meant by a particular utterance.

2.7   Pragmatic language impairment 2

Question 1 (a) Lena uses a tangential response when she talks about building a snowman in answer to the question 'What is it like in the winter?' The examiner clearly has in mind a response like 'It's cold.' (b) Lena makes a bizarre lexical choice when she uses 'mosquitoes' alongside 'birds and crows'. Even the latter are somewhat irrelevant, as the examiner was clearly looking for a response like 'leaves'. (c) An irrelevant utterance intrudes into the exchange when Lena remarks that flowers on apple trees are beautiful to see. This breaks up a sequence which is aimed at getting Lena to identify a particular season. (d) Lena engages in topic perseveration when she continues to talk about winter when the examiner has posed a question about spring. (e) When Lena responds to the question 'What season comes after autumn?' with 'Winter and then spring then autumn and then spring', it is not clear if the problem is related to a lack of world knowledge (Lena thinks autumn follows spring) or if a semantic paraphasia has occurred (Lena uses 'autumn' in place of 'summer'). **Question 2** Lena produces an echolalic response ('What happened?') or a tangential response ('That's the tree!'). These responses are serving a conversational obligation to produce an answer to a question and, in so doing, fulfil adjacency pair structure. **Question 3** The three features of Lena's responses which indicate a disruption of semantic field knowledge are (a) her attempt to distract from the task by talking about her pony, (b) the use of colour names rather than clothes names, and (c) the use of 'braid' which refers to Lena's hair rather than her clothes. **Question 4** (a) An example of an egocentric response is Märta's use of 'Take it down!' in reply to a question about what she would do if she cut her finger (data set 4). (b) An example of a tangential response is Märta's use of 'Not thieves in' in reply to a question about why there are doors on houses (data set 6). (c) An example of topic perseveration is Märta's use of 'Burns down like this' in reply to a question about why there are windows in houses (data set 5). **Question 5** The verbal behaviour present in data set 7 is (c) verbal perseveration. The noun phrase 'the dog' is repeated throughout the extract, while 'cat' appears at the beginning of data set 7 and is then used again at the end.

2.7   Pragmatic language impairment 3

Question 1 (a) Sarah is very eager to communicate. (b) Sarah has normal non-verbal intelligence. **Question 2** Sarah has poor receptive syntax and poor vocabulary comprehension. The combination of these linguistic deficits is likely to lead to an impoverished logical form of the utterance. **Question 3** Part (c). **Question 4** In data set 1, Sarah infers that the hole is for the burial of treasure. **Question 5** Part (b).

2.7   Pragmatic language impairment 4

Question 1 Tony makes appropriate use of ellipsis when he utters 'Playing with bus' in data set 4. Tony does not use ellipsis when it is necessary when he utters 'Daddy cut your hair' in data set 2. **Question 2** Tony makes use of echolalia when he utters 'Hi Ken' in data set 1. He uses his proper name for self-reference when he utters 'Tony's' in data set 2. He makes use of pronoun reversal when he utters 'Daddy cut your hair' in data set 2. These linguistic features are also found in autism spectrum disorder. **Question 3** In data set 5, Tony misunderstands the teacher's question 'How?' when he replies 'Orange. Tony is sick.' Also in this data set, Tony misunderstands the teacher's question 'What shall I do to talk to mummy' when he replies 'Because I am sick.' He also misunderstands the teacher's question 'What happened' in data set 5 when he responds 'Carl is crying.' Tony's default interpretation of the question words 'how' and 'what' appears to be 'why'. **Question 4** (a) In data set 3, Tony uses 'Flowers' to perform a labelling function. (b) In data set 4, Tony uses 'Alex has new socks' to initiate a conversational exchange. (c) In data set 3, Tony uses 'Wind it up' to describe an action in progress. (d) In data set 5, Tony uses 'Can I talk to mummy?' to make a request. (e) In data set 5, Tony uses 'Why are you getting on the floor?' to ask a question. **Question 5** When Tony replies ''Cos she's crying', he is using a consequence of not being quiet (the baby is crying) as a reason to be quiet. When he replies ''Cos it spilt', Tony is using an action that would cause a flower not to be watered (the water spilt) to describe a consequence of a flower not being watered. When Tony says ''Cos I go to the dentist', he is using an action that would prevent teeth from rotting (a visit to the dentist) to describe a consequence of eating lots of sweets.

2.7 Pragmatic language impairment 5

Question 1 (a) Utterance 2: 'I mean who liked Super Duper man except for one.' (b) Utterances 10 and 11: 'And he said, "There's going to be a movie on Super Duper man. Would you like to come and see it?"' (c) Utterance 3: 'And he liked reading them from the comic books.' (d) Utterance 4: 'And he has a lot of comics' (does 'he' refer to 'Homer' or 'one'?) (e) Utterances 15 and 16: 'They shook hands. Then they went and saw the movie.' **Question 2** (a) Utterance 1: 'Well, there was these magazines from somebody.' (b) Utterances 15 and 16: 'He went in the ditch. And he, but before he ran into the ditch he saw the skunk.' (c) Utterance 10: 'So he landed and punched this wall and used his body to break through it.' (d) Utterance 3: 'Then they wondered if the movie was playing of the Super Duper at a theatre where Super Duper was being nice to the kids.' (e) Utterances 21 and 22: 'And the kids said, "We'll tow your car down to a garage." And after that they repaired his fender that got kind of bent.' **Question 3** The child with no language disorder achieves a superior narrative opening by (a) explicitly introducing the main characters in the movie ('The main people are Homer, Louie, and Freddie'), (b) describing from the outset how these characters are related ('And Louie and Freddie were over at Homer's house'), and (c) signposting the start of the narrative ('Well, from the beginning, there's this person called Homer'). **Question 4** Neither child with language disorder appears to recognise the purpose of this story. Super Duper's car accident is described as a series of actions: 'And he went off the edge' (utterance 18, data set 1), 'He went in the ditch' (utterance 15, data set 2). There is no sense in which this accident has any significance for what it can tell us about Super Duper's lack of superhuman powers and Freddie's sense of disappointment at making this discovery. It is for this reason that both children with language disorder also neglect to relate to their listeners that Freddie traded in his collection of Super Duper comics for a broken baseball bat. **Question 5** The child with no language disorder uses temporal expressions such as 'after a while' to relate episodes to each other: 'But then Louie and Freddie had to go home. After a while,

Freddie called up Homer and told him that there was a movie Saturday about Super Duper.' Because the content of these conjoined utterances is consistent with the temporal relationship expressed by this sentence connector, the two episodes linked by these sentences cohere well within the wider narrative. This is not the case in the narratives produced by the children with language disorder. These children also make use of temporal conjunctive markers to link episodes within their narratives. But because the content of the sentences which are linked by these markers fits less easily within a temporal relationship, the effect is one in which adjoining episodes cohere less well within the wider narrative: 'Then he got out a secret passageway. Then they went home.'

2.7 Pragmatic language impairment 6

Question 1 *Homonymy*: jam; threw. *Idioms*: pull your socks up; wrong side of the bed. **Question 2** In data set 3, the following comment by the subject with SDLD suggests a non-literal interpretation of the stimulus item: ''cause that one hasn't got red hands'. **Question 3** Parts (b) and (c). **Question 4** Parts (b), (c) and (e). **Question 5** In data set 3, a control subject of 12;0 years utters 'It means caught in the act, doesn't it?' *Caught in the act* is an idiom.

2.7 Pragmatic language impairment 7

Question 1 (a) Elaborative wh-question (data set 1: What were those big animals that we saw?). (b) Repetition (data set 1: Remember what they were?). (c) Elaborative statement (data set 2: And they're at the restaurant). (d) Statement of denial (data set 1: No, they weren't the lions). (e) Elaborative yes–no question (data set 1: Were they bears?). **Question 2** Repetition of elaborative wh-questions. **Question 3** The mother fails to secure conversational participation from the child in data set 2 because she uses elaborative statements exclusively. These statements do not demand a response from the child. **Question 4** The limited conversational participation of the child in data set 3 can be explained in terms of the considerable memory demands of autobiographical memory narratives. The storybook narrative in data set 4 makes fewer memory demands on the child, with the result that his conversational participation increases. **Question 5** In data set 4, the child's utterances contribute much more information than in data set 3. This information is then expanded on by the mother in her next turn. For example, when the child contributes the utterance 'He going to jump into that', the mother is able to take the action of the frog which is reported by the child and make an evaluation of it in her next utterance: 'Yeah, that's not going to be good, is it?' So the child is able to exercise topic control by contributing information which then becomes the basis of the next speaker's turn in the exchange.

2.7 Pragmatic language impairment 8

Question 1 (a) Command: 'Don't make it' (data set 4). (b) Confirmation: 'Yeah, mom' (data set 2). (c) Statement: 'Me tell that girl that' (data set 4). (d) Refusal: 'Mommy, no' (data set 4). (e) Request: 'Help me do that' (data set 4). **Question 2** The mothers of children with language delay use statements ('Uh-oh his legs are fallin' out') and yes–no questions ('You don't like me to help you?') almost to the complete exclusion of other utterance types. The use of these utterances can be explained by the fact that they place minimal demands on the children with language delay to make a response. These children's limited expressive language still permits them to contribute a 'yes–no' response and thus continue to engage in the interaction. **Question 3** In data set 1, the contribution of the utterance 'There some red ones' by the child gives rise to a turn by the mother in which she repeats the content of this utterance. There is then an expansion of the original utterance by the child which is also repeated by the mother. There follows an acknowledgement by the mother and then an invitation from her for the child to contribute further information. The child's original utterance has effectively generated two turns of his own, and a further two turns on the part of the mother. This type of topic exchange is not possible in data set 2 where the child is contributing minimal responses such as 'yeah'. These responses cannot be repeated, evaluated or otherwise developed by the mother, with the result that a topic is not sustained over turns. The effect is that although the mother and child are clearly interacting verbally in data set 2, the conversational exchange has the appearance of a monologue by the mother. **Question 4** In data set 3, the mother makes clarification requests of her child as a means of commenting on his turn and returning the turn to the child for further expansion. This can be seen in the mother's use of 'Happy birthday?' which is subsequently expanded by the child to become 'Happy birthday to Carl.' Another example in the same data set is the mother's use of 'Popsicle?' which is subsequently expanded as 'Boy ha a popsicle' by the child. For the mother of a normally developing child, then, clarification requests are a means of eliciting more language production. However, this is not the case for the mother of the child with language delay in data set 4. This mother is using clarification requests to establish who and what her child is talking about. This can be seen in the utterance 'You're gonna tell her what?' where the mother is attempting to establish what her child wants to tell the girl. This mother's clarification requests are taking on quite a different function – clarifying what the child is attempting to communicate. These requests are not serving to encourage the child with language delay to extend his ideas. **Question 5** When the normally developing children in these data sets use gesture (always pointing), it is to establish the referents of demonstrative pronouns ('<u>Those</u> are the red ones') and adverbs ('Under <u>there</u>'). The children with language delay also use pointing for this purpose ('Me tell <u>that</u> girl that'). However, in addition to pointing, these children use body movements such as head shaking. This movement performs a range of communicative functions such as declining an invitation of help, indicating the end of an activity, and making a 'no' response to a yes–no question. Also, this movement can take the place of a verbal utterance as well as co-occur with these utterances in children with language delay. The greater use and range of non-verbal behaviours in children with language delay reflects an important compensatory function of these behaviours in children with limited expressive language.

2.7   Pragmatic language impairment 9

Question 1 Sid is able to use simple terms of address (e.g. 'dada'), single-word responses ('no') and one two-word utterance ('that right'). **Question 2** Sid is able to use language to perform the following communicative functions: (1) he can solicit the opinion of others (e.g. 'that right' directed towards Dad); (2) he can gain the attention of others (e.g. mom, dada); (3) he can respond to yes–no questions (e.g. 'that's not right is it? No'). **Question 3** Sue is only able to use language to make statements (e.g. 'car fall down') and prevent her mother from performing an action ('no' uttered in response to her mother when she takes the car). **Question 4** Sue performs several non-verbal behaviours during her interaction with her mother. However, with the exception of whining, which serves as a protest, these behaviours do not have a communicative function. Sid also performs a number of non-verbal behaviours. These behaviours include pointing to the toy structure, motioning towards his father and shaking his head 'no'. Unlike Sue, Sid's non-verbal behaviours do perform communicative functions such as directing the attention of an adult and expressing denial or disagreement. These differences in the use of non-verbal behaviours can be explained in terms of Sid's use of these behaviours as a developmental compensation for his very limited expressive language skills. **Question 5** The three features of Sid's interaction with his father which indicate that he possesses an intact ToM capacity are (a) the use of pointing, (b) the attempt to secure the attention of his father, and (c) the attempt to extract an evaluation of the toy structure from his father. All three behaviours indicate that Sid believes that the adults in his environment entertain mental states which he can influence through his verbal and non-verbal interactions with them.

2.7 Pragmatic language impairment 10

Question 1 (a) Incorrect use of past tense verb forms: 'she <u>hided</u> right under the bushes' (data set 2); 'one day the brother <u>stand</u> up called John' (data set 2). (b) Incorrect use of pronouns: '<u>He</u> wanted to look at the aliens' (data set 2); 'but <u>she</u> couldn't' (data set 2). The incorrect use of pronouns has an adverse impact on a listener's ability to follow a narrative. **Question 2** (a) Use of direct reported speech: 'the aliens said "Where did she go?"' (data set 2); 'he ran up to the alien and then said "Go back to the ship"' (data set 2). (b) Use of self-initiated repair: 'One Saturday (um Daniel no) Mark and Daniel went for a walk' (data set 1); 'And (they) there was a spaceship on the ground' (data set 1). The use of direct reported speech achieves listener engagement in an unfolding narrative. **Question 3** The cohesive device which dominates these narratives is 'and then'. This device, which consists of an additive ('and') and temporal ('then') conjunction, expresses a temporal meaning relation between utterances. **Question 4** (a) The child in data set 2 uses the expression 'once upon a time' at the beginning of his narrative. This clearly indicates to the listener that a fictional narrative is to follow. The child in data set 1 uses 'One Saturday' to introduce his narrative. This expression is less effective in indicating to the listener the fictional character of the narrative. (b) The child in data set 2 clearly introduces the main protagonists in the story: 'there is a brother and sister. The brother's name was John . . . and the sister was named Mary.' However, the child in data set 1 moves directly to using the proper names Mark and Daniel without any account of who these individuals are. (c) The child in data set 2 has a good understanding of how to establish the referential links which enable a listener to follow a story. For example, characters are first introduced through the use of indefinite noun phrases with subsequent reference achieved by means of definite noun phrases, e.g. ' . . . there is <u>a</u> brother and sister. <u>The</u> brother's name was . . . ' However, the child in data set 1 uses definite noun phrases on the first mention of characters, e.g. 'And <u>the</u> dog was alien.' The listener will inevitably ask 'What dog?' (d) There is clear plot development within the narrative in data set 2. The child introduces the story, relates a number of interactions between the aliens and the story's protagonists, and finally concludes the narrative by describing the aliens' departure. There is almost no plot development in the narrative in data set 1. (e) A narrative is most compelling for a listener when it addresses the motivations of its characters. Typically, these motivations are represented through mental states such as desires, intentions, and so on. In turn, these mental states are reflected in the use of mental state language such as 'wants' and 'believes'. The narrative in data set 1 contains no mental state language. However, there are a number of mental state terms in the narrative in data set 2. For example, the main verb 'want' in 'they want to go to the park' indicates a mental state of *desire*. The verb 'forgot' in 'And then they did and forgot the alien dog' indicates mental states such as *memories*. And the utterance 'the aliens scared her' suggests a mental state of *fear*. **Question 5** The narrative in data set 1 has reasonably intact grammar but very limited content. The narrative in data set 2 displays grammatical problems but has a well-elaborated content.

2.8 Intellectual disability 1

Question 1 (a) Data set 3: 'He steal the whole basket.' (b) Data set 3: 'He started to ran over the walk and kicked her.' (c) Data set 1: 'Yeah, and the boys help him put those apples in.' (d) Data set 1: 'That boy steal apples.' (e) Data set 3: 'He started to ran over the walk and kicked her.' **Question 2** Subjects with Down's syndrome used the additive conjunction 'and' almost exclusively to link the utterances in their narratives (e.g. '. . . he went in on the bike. And he put it in the basket . . . '). The one exception was the use of 'so' in 'A kid stole the basket away from him. So he will shared a pears . . . ' However, the utterances linked by this conjunction do not cohere particularly well under any of the usual interpretations of 'so'. In addition to the use of 'and', mental age-matched subjects also used the temporal conjunction 'then' to link the utterances in their narratives (e.g. '. . . this guy (uh) was picking (uh) some fruit from the tree. (Um) then a kid stealed it'). The absence of this particular conjunction in the narratives of the subjects with Down's syndrome suggests some conceptual difficulty on the part of these subjects with the temporal relations that it expresses. There is a single use of the causal conjunction 'because' in the narratives of the mental age-matched subjects: '. . . he was so grateful that he gave them three pears. Because there were three people then he gave them three pears.' However, this causal conjunction may not be serving an inter-sentential cohesive function so much as connecting two clauses within a single sentence. **Question 3** The subject in data set 5 has incorrectly inferred that the 'thief' boy and the fruit picker are father and son. This inferential anomaly does not occur in the narratives of subjects with Down's syndrome. Nor is it found in the narratives of subjects with lower MLUs. **Question 4** The subjects in data sets 3 and 4 make no attempt to conclude their narratives. Instead, narratives are left in a state of suspension. The subjects with Down's syndrome in data sets 1 and 2 abruptly conclude their narratives with the utterances 'that's all' and 'That's it'. The most sophisticated conclusion was used by the subject in data set 5. This subject concluded his narrative with the utterance 'and then that was the end'. The superior structural language skills of this subject, indicated by MLU, may account for his use of a more effective conclusion. **Question 5** The 'thief' boy is introduced into the narratives of these subjects as follows. Data set 1: use of 'that boy' in 'That boy steal apples.' Data set 2: use of 'one kid' in 'One kid stole the basket of pears.' Data set 3: use of 'some boy' in 'some boy taked all of the pears.' Data set 4: use of 'a kid' in 'a kid stealed it.' Data set 5: use of 'a boy' in 'it was about a boy and his dad . . . ' Only subjects in data sets 4 and 5 make appropriate use of an indefinite noun phrase for the first mention of the 'thief' boy. The subject in data set 1 uses a demonstrative noun phrase 'that boy' in the absence of a preceding referent. A listener could legitimately ask 'What boy?' The use of 'one kid' and 'some boy' in data sets 2 and 3, respectively, fails to uniquely identify the 'thief' boy from among the other boys in the story.

2.8   Intellectual disability 2

Question 1 (a) Data set 2: 'On the cottage?' (b) Data set 4: 'I don't steal nothing at work.' (c) Data set 3: 'We take (a) shower over there every night.' (d) Data set 7: 'I like to catch lot of fish . . . ' (e) Data set 3: 'You know Frances don't like me smelling.' The use of a double negative construction in (b) is a feature of the speaker's dialect. **Question 2** (a) Data set 5: 'He says you did it just right' (direct); 'My supervisor tells me that I did okay' (indirect). (b) Data set 4: ' . . . they don't like sticky fingers over there.' (c) Data set 2: 'On the cottage?' (d) Data set 4: ' . . . they don't like sticky fingers over there.' (e) Data set 1: 'And if you do (make a mistake at work) you're supposed to go up and say . . . ' **Question 3** The subject's response to the question in data set 6 is under-informative. The subject's response to the question in data set 7 is over-informative. **Question 4** In data set 2, the subject poses an off-topic or irrelevant question (relation maxim) when he asks the investigator 'Are you married?' In data set 3, the subject produces contradictory or misleading information (quality maxim). He first states that he puts deodorant on every morning and then contradicts himself by saying that he puts it on every night. **Question 5** The subject in data set 3 makes an inappropriate disclosure about his or her personal hygiene. The subject in data set 4 makes an inappropriate disclosure about stealing in a previous job.

2.9   Autism spectrum disorder 1

Question 1 (a) Data set 1: 'I want to [stay in a hotel]'. Data set 5: '[I found him] behind the piano'. (b) Data set 6: 'That was health'. (c) Data set 1: 'Who didn't agree? Mom and dad'. (d) Data set 1: 'but it seems that they did they didn't agree'. (e) Data set 5: 'one escaped for two day'. **Question 2** The indexical pronouns in the following utterances are not used in a way that allows the hearer to establish the literal content of the utterances that contain them. Data set 1: 'they didn't agree' (the hearer will conclude that 'they' refers to the friends when it actually refers to the subject's mom and dad). Data set 2: 'I haven't really seen much of him in it'. The researcher's request for clarification in data set 1 ('who didn't agree?') indicates uncertainty on his part about the literal content of the speaker's utterance. **Question 3** Data set 5: 'but uh I wasn't'. Data set 6: 'I'm starting'. **Question 4** Data set 3: 'my cat'. It is unclear if the speaker intends to include the cat within the five members of his family (literal content 1) or if the cat is in addition to the five members (literal content 2). **Question 5** The description of the iguana's capture is not easy to follow because the participant uses no less than four expressions to refer to the person who caught the animal (i.e. somebody – they – one – the person). These different expressions vary in number and specificity, making the description that contains them difficult to follow.

2.9   Autism spectrum disorder 2

Question 1 (a) In data set 1, Adam evidences good theory of mind skills when he checks his mother's state of knowledge about Clara Schumann. He attempts this first by directly asking about her state of knowledge: 'Have you ever- you know- you've heard of- Clara

Schumann, right?' Then, when it becomes clear that his mother is uncertain about who Clara Schumann is, he halts the exchange by saying 'Wait a second' and then attempts to make good his mother's lack of knowledge by 'filling in' missing information: '. . . you know Robert Schumann? . . . It's his wife.' (b) In data set 1, Adam uses the discourse marker 'so' to indicate a break with prior discourse. In data set 5, Adam uses the disjunct marker 'by the way' to signal to his interlocutor that he is moving away from the prior discourse. (c) In data set 1, the repetition of turn-final 'today' indicates that although Adam is breaking with the topic of the exact timing of the start of fall (it is celebrated *today*), he is still continuing his temporal theme by relating to his mother an event that took place *today* at school. In data set 5, the repetition of turn-final 'lunch' indicates that although Adam is digressing from describing the different events during his first day in middle school, one of which is going to lunch, he is continuing this theme to some degree by indicating how much he ate at lunch. (d) Adam displays considerable cognitive flexibility in data set 5 when he is able to shift from the meaning of 'lunch' as an activity during the day to the meaning of 'lunch' as a meal. (e) Adam uses both linguistic and prosodic devices in data set 1 to indicate to his interlocutor that his story is worth the effort of attending to and processing it. He achieves this through the use of adjectives which amplify the significance of the story ('there's a *big* background') and which indicate that Adam has evaluated the story and thinks it is worthy of telling ('Mister Gregory told us a *wonderful* story'). Adam's use of increased loudness during the production of both these adjectives is an important prosodic device for emphasising the worth of the story to his interlocutor. **Question 2** Mark first gains the attention of his father through the use of a vocative 'Hey Dad'. Having gained the attention of his interlocutor, Mark then explicitly indicates his intention to relate a narrative through the use of a verb of telling 'I'll tell you . . . ' He then uses the preposition 'about' on two occasions to signal that his narrative concerns a movie (a type of story) and that its lead character is a little puppy. The first two of these features serves to represent Mark's narrative as a break from prior discourse. The third feature provides his interlocutor with the key information that will be needed to assimilate later narrative details (the actions of the little puppy, etc.) **Question 3** The use of 'about' in the utterances 'I have a story to tell you *about* . . . ' (data set 1), 'I'll tell you *about* . . . ' (data set 2) and 'I wanna tell you *about* . . . ' (data set 3) has an important procedural function in these narrative introductions. That function is to convey to the hearer the 'gist' of the narrative. The use of 'about' in these utterances allows the narrator to enact global, macro-structural organisation at the local level of an individual utterance. Karl's use of 'about' in data set 3 breaks down somewhat. Instead of following 'about' with a key character or protagonist (e.g. 'about this little puppy'), Karl mentions a peripheral detail, a location ('the kitchen'), and only after that states the name of the main character in the story ('Princess Camista'). A further discourse problem in Karl's narrative introduction is his use of the pronouns 'she' and 'her' in the absence of clear referents. **Question 4** When Anthony and his father are talking about the fieldtrip, the theme of this discussion concerns selfish behaviour and how it makes people feel. This theme is continued by Anthony when he introduces a narrative about being bullied at school. The thematic continuity that links Anthony's narrative with prior discourse appears to be one of bad behaviour and how it makes people feel. The very fact that Anthony is able to talk about how he would feel if people were selfish to him shows that he is able to attribute emotional states such as sadness to his mind and to his father's mind. **Question 5** In data set 6, Sylvester's action of attempting to blow bubbles in the boiling water triggers a narrative with his mother about an earlier incident in which

Sylvester was burnt. In data set 7, a narrative about the feelings of Anthony's father when his brother died is prompted by prior discussion of sibling relationships and loss. Sylvester co-constructs the narrative introduction with his mother in data set 6 by providing her with turns in which to develop her story. This can be seen in Sylvester's use of the question 'What did I do?' which hands the turn to his mother to continue developing her story. When Anthony introduces a narrative about his father's feelings upon the death of his brother (i.e. Anthony's uncle), he is able to do so by drawing on ToM skills. These skills enable Anthony to imaginatively project from his own feelings of sadness if Daniel were not around, and his friend Burton's feelings of sadness if Burton's sister were not around, to then ask his father if he also felt sad when Anthony's uncle died.

2.9   Autism spectrum disorder 3

Question 1 (a) Pragmatic enrichment of the logical form of the utterance. **Question 2** The boy in data set 1 states a reason for the woman's utterance: she shouts 'Here!' to the dog because she is having problems with him. **Question 3** In order for the children to go indoors for their dinner, they must pass through the door which is indicated by the boy. **Question 4** (c) Metaphor. **Question 5** The words 'like', 'want' and 'feelings' suggest the possession of theory of mind skills by the boy in data set 3.

2.9   Autism spectrum disorder 4

Question 1 (a) Irrelevant information intrudes into this child's narrative when he talks about taking pictures, going to the zoo and selling animals. (b) The pronouns 'he', 'himself' and 'his' lack referents. (c) The child uses 'the boy' and 'the girl' in place of indefinite noun phrases for the first mention of characters. (d) The child uses 'the boy' and 'the girl' in place of the proper names 'Jim' and 'Anna', respectively. (e) The child only uses the additive conjunction 'and' to link utterances in his narrative. This form of inter-sentential cohesion fails to represent the temporal and causal relations which exist between events in the narrative. The single, biggest compromise to this child's narrative comes in the form of the intrusion of irrelevant information. Of the 12 clauses in this child's narrative, only four are related to the content of the story. **Question 2** Among the narrative difficulties of the child in data set 1 are the following problems. (a) Use of pronouns with no referents, e.g. 'He had a friend named Pepper.' (b) Repetition of information, e.g. 'Pepper was a black dog.' (c) Poor ordering of information, e.g. 'Jim was a little boy' is introduced in the middle of the narrative, rather than at the beginning. (d) Limited inter-sentential cohesion, e.g. only one use of 'and then'. (e) Omission of information, e.g. we are told that Pepper brought the shoe to Anna who then rescued Jim. But key information between these two events (e.g. Pepper alerted Anna to Jim's plight through his barking, Anna realised Jim must be in trouble) is omitted. The expressions 'I forgot', 'I don't know' and 'That's all I know' suggest that memory deficits and limited knowledge may contribute to this child's difficulties in retelling the narrative. **Question 3** (a) The child opens his narrative with 'one day'. This is a rudimentary form of the expression 'once upon a time' which is a conventional opening to a fictional narrative. This opening locates the narrative in time and prepares the reader for what follows. (b) Pronouns have clear referents in prior discourse, e.g. '. . . the big bad pig came prowling down the road. When he saw the house . . . ' These referential links between sentences allow the reader to integrate new information within his mental representation of the story. (c) Events are narrated in the order in which they occur. For example, the pig comes down the road first, then he sees the house and then he issues a threat to the wolves. These events are narrated in this exact order. **Question 4** In data set 3, there are a number of factors which jointly contribute to the superior quality of the narrative. (a) *The narrative retelling task.* This is a written narrative task and, as such, permits considerable editing and reworking on the part of the narrator. This is not possible during the production of a spoken narrative. (b) *The retold narrative.* This is a well-known fictional narrative which can be almost recited automatically by children. This permits a more organised, fluent presentation than is possible in the other fictional narrative. (c) *The narrator.* The child with ASD in data set 3 does not have the additional language impairments of the children in data sets 1 and 2. He will, accordingly, have language structures available to him which are beyond the linguistic repertoire of these other children. **Question 5** The narrator in data set 3 uses direct reported speech: 'Little wolves, little wolves, let me come in, or I'll huff and I'll puff and I'll blow your house down!' Direct reported speech is likely to increase reader involvement in the unfolding narrative.

2.9 Autism spectrum disorder 5

Question 1 The topic of the Mini Olympics is clearly familiar to Mary who is able to discuss it with ease (lines 3 to 6). Moreover, she is given the opportunity to do so by two open-ended questions from the researcher (lines 1 and 2). Mary's extended response to that question mentions badminton with Amy which the researcher then attempts to topicalise through the use of a question in line 7. Mary takes this topic in a different direction in line 11 when she begins to talk about the advocacy group where a card was signed for Amy's birthday. Amy provides thematic continuity with the prior topic of badminton. In line 17, the researcher introduces an ancillary topic by asking about Amy's age. It is only in line 29 that the researcher returns to the topic of Amy's birthday. The re-introduction of this topic is indicated by the researcher's use of the discourse marker 'so' at the beginning of line 29. **Question 2** In line 21, the researcher asks Mary if Amy is older than her. Mary responds in line 22 that she is, and is about to go on to say by how much when the researcher interjects with a follow-up question in line 23. (The grammatical completeness of Mary's utterance in line 22 combined with the presence of a micro-pause clearly indicated to the researcher that Mary had completed her turn.) Mary holds this second question in abeyance while she proceeds to provide a fuller response to the researcher's first question in lines 24 and 25. It is only in line 26 that Mary addresses the researcher's second question. This sequence reveals that Mary has sound knowledge of adjacency pair structure in conversation – that a question demands a response, even if this cannot be addressed immediately in an exchange. This sequence also suggests that Mary has good short-term memory skills as she is able to hold a second question in memory while she deals with a response to a preceding question. **Question 3** Gloria's remark that Amy's birthday cake is a rabbit clearly strikes the researcher as bizarre. It occasions a series of questions from the researcher in which she attempts to establish what Gloria meant by this remark. Mary is clearly unable to describe the communicative intention that motivated Gloria to produce this remark. When pressed for an explanation by the researcher, Mary can do little more than dismiss Gloria's remark as a joke or simply state the fact that it was said ('she was just saying it'). Mary's difficulty in this case can be explained in terms of the autistic inability to attribute mental states to the minds of others (i.e. theory of mind). In this case, Mary is unable to establish what communicative intention prompted Gloria to produce her 'rabbit' remark. **Question 4** In data set 2, Mary's ability to contribute to the topic of discussion between lines 17 and 32 sharply declines. This is manifested in her use of a series of brief, low component turns such as 'just a joke' (line 18) and 'she was just saying it' (line 24). While Mary has difficulty maintaining the topic at this point, the researcher manages to maintain it through the use of four question turns such as 'why did she say that' (line 17) and 'why did she make a joke like that' (line 22). **Question 5** In data set 3, Mary makes extensive use of repetition to maintain the topic of housework. This includes repetition of lexemes such as 'lounge room' and 'downstairs' (and their variants 'dining room' and 'stairs'), as well as repetition of syntactic structures such as 'I hoovered' with a range of direct objects. Repetition is also a feature of the other data sets. For example, in data set 2 there is extensive repetition of relative clauses introduced by 'that' between lines 33 and 38: 'that we bought with Kirsty' (lines 33 to 34); 'that we bought with Kirsty Barker' (line 35); 'that we had it after tea last night' (line 38).

2.9   Autism spectrum disorder 6

Question 1 In exchanges A and B, overlaps seem to arise because Mary is delayed in completing an earlier turn. In both these exchanges, there is a sizeable pause before the researcher pursues a new question. Indeed, the length of these pauses gives the researcher good reason to believe that she can go on to pose a new question. It is during the asking of these questions that Mary proceeds to complete her earlier turn, creating an overlap with the researcher's question. On the basis of these two exchanges it may seem that slowed cognitive processing is responsible for the delay in Mary completing her turn. However, this explanation is not supported by the overlap in exchange C. In this case, Mary's overlap is being used to indicate that she knows what the researcher is going on to say. There is a different function again of overlap in exchange D, where the researcher commits an overlap to indicate that she is using something Mary has just said to revise her understanding of what Ella had been told. So, in short, none of the four exchanges in data set 1 contain overlaps which appear to be motivated by a desire to assume the current speaker's turn. **Question 2** Three features of the latched utterances used in data set 2 are as follows. (a) Latching can occur onto complete turns (exchange B) and onto incomplete turns (exchanges A and C). (b) The latched utterance is always produced by Mary. The researcher is not the latcher in these three exchanges. (c) When Mary produces a latched utterance onto an incomplete turn, the researcher immediately relinquishes her turn. The researcher yields her turn as she understands her role in these conversational exchanges to be one of facilitating Mary. **Question 3** The three latched utterances in data set 2 seem to arise as a result of delays by Mary in completing her prior turn. During these delays, the researcher asks a question or produces a statement which is then latched by Mary as she attempts to complete her turn. This same delay in turn completion appears to be responsible for the overlaps in exchanges A and B in data set 1. **Question 4** Mary makes extensive use of non-grammatical pauses (pauses which fall within a phrase). Examples are 'I liked (.) dressage' (data set 2, exchange C) and 'no she just saw Elly and she (.) told . . . ' (data set 1, exchange D). Mary also makes use of grammatical pauses between phrases and clauses. Examples are 'I just do sometimes (.)' (data set 1, exchange B) and 'I got an awkward horse called Lofty (.) who wouldn't trot (.) so I had . . . ' (data set 2, exchange C). Mary's extensive use of non-grammatical pauses before content words would suggest lexical retrieval difficulties on her part. Mary's use of pauses at grammatical boundaries is likely to reflect the processing that is required to make syntactic choices. **Question 5** In data set 3, the length of pauses reflects the cognitive difficulty that Mary has in responding to a question. When Mary knows a response – such as that a ball is a round shape and that there are 12 months in a year – pauses are relatively short (1.3 and 0.9 seconds, respectively). However, as the difficulty of the WAIS-R questions increases, so too does the duration of Mary's pauses. Her 'dunno' response to the question about the thermometer is preceded by a pause of 2.1 seconds, while her response to the question about British prime ministers is preceded by a long pause of 7 seconds. Prime ministers represent a special interest of Mary's. The long pause time is, thus, likely to reflect a search of her extensive knowledge base in this area.

2.10 Childhood traumatic brain injury 1

Question 1 (a) Multiple restarts of an utterance: 'Ummm, I, once, there was a, we went.' (b) Use of incongruent temporal expression: 'And one day, I have a friend named Jude.' (c) Use of pronoun instead of proper noun: '. . . me, my brother, my cousin Matt, and her . . .' (d) Provision of misleading or contradictory information: We are told Jason was stung once and three times. (e) Use of repetitive language: 'got (get) stung' is used nine times in the narrative. **Question 2** (a) There is intrusion of irrelevant information, e.g. discussion of Jude's cat and mention of her child. (b) There is excessive detail on one aspect of the story, i.e. who was stung, where they were stung and how many times they were stung. (c) The narrative lacks linear progression and unfolds in circles, with the narrator returning to an earlier point in discourse. For example, the child with TBI describes how she and her cousin were stung, then relates how they went to her friend's house and cleaned the stings, and then returns to give a further description of the bee stings. **Question 3** (c) Planning deficits. **Question 4** The child with TBI makes extensive use of the additive conjunction 'and' to achieve inter-sentential cohesion, e.g. 'And we went up there. I stepped on a bee's nest. And they chased us all the way back. And I got stung . . .' This simple form of cohesion precludes the expression of a range of more complex relations through which the events in a story may be interconnected. These include causal relations (e.g. 'The show was very poor. So we left early') and temporal relations (e.g. 'They visited the old chapel. Then they went to a restaurant for lunch'). **Question 5** There is some evidence of lexical retrieval difficulties in the narrative discourse of the child with TBI. This child makes extensive use of filled pauses, often before content words (e.g. 'There was this umm fort'). Also, non-specific expressions and vocabulary are used (e.g. 'she had this clean kind of stuff'). The frequent use of reformulated utterances may suggest some lexical retrieval problems and/or syntactic construction difficulties on the part of this child (e.g. 'And when I umm went over, when we got back . . .').

2.10 Childhood traumatic brain injury 2

Question 1 The child in data set 2 appears to have gleaned no abstract or central meaning from the narrative at all. There is no sense from reading this summary that the main character of the story experienced disillusionment with a range of career paths because he was not motivated by monetary gains or that he made a substantial and enduring contribution to many aspects of life which he could not have recognised while he was alive. These deeper meanings of the story are entirely overlooked. The child in data set 3 appears to have misunderstood the abstract meaning of the narrative. The details of two jobs undertaken by the protagonist dominate the narrative. His failure to succeed at any of the jobs he undertook is mistakenly characterised as 'he didn't like the things that he got into'. The latter may well be true but does not reveal the source of his dislike. An articulation of the latter would have required an appreciation of the deeper meaning of the narrative. **Question 2** The narrative summary in data set 2 is uninformative because it contains an abundance of vague, non-specific vocabulary. The many careers pursued by the protagonist are not described but are simply characterised as 'different stuff'. The characters are described in vague terms such as 'this guy' and 'this person'. Other vague expressions include 'thing', 'something' and 'place'. The combined effect of these lexemes is that little, specific information is conveyed to the hearer. **Question 3** (c) Weak central coherence. **Question 4** The narrative summary of the typically developing child in data set 1 contains the following features which suggest good ToM skills on the part of this child. (a) Use of mental state verbs, e.g. 'I think', 'I mean', 'you know', 'to remember him'. These verbs suggest an ability on the part of the narrator to attribute mental states both to his own mind ('I think') and to the mind of his hearer ('you know'). (b) This child is also able to make an assessment of the emotional state of the main character. We are told, for example, that 'he saw himself as a failure'. These features are generally not present in the narrative summaries of the children with TBI. The one exception is mention of the emotional state of sadness by the child in data set 2 (i.e. 'That's so sad'). **Question 5** (a) Data set 2: '. . . he tried to, to succeed at work, but he couldn't (succeed at work)'. (b) Data set 3: '. . . treat <u>the students</u> like easily and make <u>their</u> homework really easy and like make <u>them</u> get good grades when <u>they</u> really shouldn't have gotten that . . . ' (c) Data set 2: '. . . he tried to, to succeed at work, but he couldn't. <u>So</u> he tried a lot of different stuff . . . ' (d) Data set 3: '. . . wrote some poetry and some songs that we still use <u>today</u>'. (e) Data set 2: 'It's about, um, this guy who would . . . '

2.11 Epileptic syndromes 1

Question 1 *Intact discourse skills.* (a) The narrator uses anaphoric reference to achieve cohesion, e.g. 'And <u>Father Bear</u> came up and <u>he</u> said . . . ' (b) The narrator captures the mental states of main characters, e.g. Goldilocks is described as being afraid. (c) The narrator uses direct reported speech to engage the listener, e.g. '. . . and she said "Rubbish! I'll not have myself given to the dragon."' *Impaired discourse skills.* (a) The narrator omits key information, e.g. there is no mention of the displaced pillow and the ruffled sheets and how these items arouse the bears' suspicion that someone has been in their beds. (b) The narrator does not appreciate causal relations between states, e.g. the lump in Baby Bear's bed is reported as a fact with no connection made between it and Goldilocks' presence in the bed. (c) The narrator attributes some direct reported speech to the wrong character, e.g. it is the Prime Minister, not the Princess, who proposes obtaining the services of a dragon slayer. **Question 2** (a) Subject CA describes Goldilocks as surprised and astonished when she is in fact fearful. (b) Subject CA misrepresents the temporal relationships between checking Baby Bear's bed and discovering Goldilocks in the bed. (c) Subject CA begins his second narrative by talking about wolves and the frog. These utterances are intrusions from the narratives on Little Red Riding Hood and The Frog Prince, respectively. (d) Subject CA uses pronouns in the absence of referents. There are no referents for any of the underlined pronouns in the utterance 'And then <u>they</u> decided that <u>they</u> would have to do <u>it</u> . . . ' (e) Subject CA does not comprehend the meaning of the conjunction in ' . . . Baby Bear said, "Who's been sleeping in my bed <u>because</u> she's still here!"' **Question 3** CA is able to represent causal relationships in her narratives which are lacking in the narratives of MW. Two such relationships are: the Princess was at the meeting because she wanted to mind her own business; the bears asked who had been sleeping in their beds because the pillows and sheets were disturbed. **Question 4** There is extensive repetition in SM's second narrative. The utterances 'one day the King called a meeting', 'he told the Prime Minister' and 'they tried to think of something' are all repeated in this short narrative. **Question 5** With the exception of SM's use of the expression 'all of a sudden', there is no other linguistic expression or device employed by these children which creates dramatic tension in their narratives. The result is that these children's narratives are somewhat dull in comparison to the original Goldilocks narrative.

2.11 Epileptic syndromes 2

Question 1 (a) Omission of direct object noun or pronoun, e.g. 'So they brought . . . into the house . . . ' (data set 2, subject CA). (b) Incorrect past tense verb form, e.g. 'Then- he <u>lied</u> into- in her bed' (data set 1, subject MW). (c) Word-finding difficulty, e.g. use of filler in ' . . . so the wolf got to the <u>um-</u> Grandmother's house . . . ' (data set 1, subject SM). (d) Problematic relative clause, e.g. ' . . . the princess remembered the promise <u>that what</u> <u>she made to him</u>' (data set 2, subject CA). (e) Omission of clause, e.g. 'So when she- when she came in' (data set 1, subject CA). **Question 2** Subject CA makes the following errors of pronominal reference. (a) She selects the wrong pronoun for anaphoric reference, e.g. ' . . . when <u>the wolf</u> got there <u>she</u> knocked on the door . . . ' (data set 1). (b) She selects the correct pronoun for anaphoric reference only to subsequently use an incorrect pronoun, e.g. '<u>the Grandmother</u> came and <u>she</u> answered the door and . . . <u>he</u> said . . . ' (data set 1). (c) She uses pronouns with no clear referents, e.g. 'So <u>they</u> brought into the house and <u>they</u> started to eat' (data set 2); ' . . . and then after that <u>he</u> was tired' (data set 2). **Question 3** Subject MW commits a pronoun error when he remarks of the wolf 'So <u>she</u> came in- so <u>he</u> came in'. However, this error is quite unlike the pronoun errors committed by subject CA. Subject MW is clearly aware of his error as indicated by his self-initiated repair of the utterance. Also, the use of the pronoun 'she' is an understandable error as MW is referring to the wolf who is pretending to be the female protagonist in the story, Little Red Riding Hood. **Question 4** Subject SM states that the wolf gobbled up the grandmother when the original narrative says that he locked the grandmother in a cupboard. Subject CA reports that the grandmother answered the door when the original narrative says that the grandmother shouted to Little Red Riding Hood to come in. These inaccuracies create subsequent difficulties in these subjects' narratives. After saying that the wolf gobbled up the grandmother, subject SM states that the wolf locked her in the closet. However, the former action precludes the latter scenario. When subject CA states that the grandmother answered the door, her subsequent use of 'So she opened the door' appears anomalous. After all, one must open the door in order to answer it. **Question 5** (a) 'So she- she did (carry the frog up to bed)' (data set 2, subject MW). (b) *hopes* (subjects MW and SM), *memories* (subject CA) and *thoughts* (subject CA) are attributed to the princess in data set 2. (c) ' . . . he locked her up into the closet. <u>And then</u>

she put on all her clothes . . . ' (data set 1, subject CA); ' . . . the wolf said, "Come in." <u>And so</u> Little Red Riding Hood came in' (data set 1, subject SM). (d) ' . . . she told the frog to come in . . . ' (data set 2, subject SM); (e) 'next day' (data set 2, subject CA).

2.11   Epileptic syndromes 3

Question 1 Question (2) – How did Judy feel? – requires subjects to draw an inference about Judy's affective state. Responses (5) and (6) suggest that at least some of the subjects with epilepsy are able to establish the protagonist's affective states. These responses suggest an intact theory of mind capacity on the part of these subjects. **Question 2** Question (1) – What happened to Judy? – is testing for the presence of an inference about the gist of the story. Responses (1) and (2) suggest that some subjects were able to derive a gist-based inference. The ability to establish the gist of a story suggests that cognitive skill (d) – central coherence – is intact in at least some of these subjects with epilepsy. **Question 3** Response (3) mentions 'a car or truck or van' which is an instantiation of 'vehicle' used in the passage. Similarly, the use of 'police' and 'policeman' in responses (1) and (6) is an instantiation of 'uniformed man' in the passage. The types of knowledge which are integral to these instantiations are (b) world knowledge and (d) semantic knowledge. **Question 4** The inference in response (8) – Judy will go to a magistrate or to jail – is a reasonable inference about future events. This predictive inference is made on the basis of (b) world knowledge. **Question 5** Response (4) in the data set – Judy was going too fast – is a presupposition of the events in the story. The temporal clause in the utterance '<u>After she pulled over</u>, a uniformed man approached her vehicle' triggers the presupposition that Judy pulled over.

2.12   Childhood cancer

Question 1 Part (a). **Question 2** There is evidence to support the claim that this woman will have difficulty establishing the gist of a story. We are told that she has difficulty abstracting general from specific information, which is the essence of deriving the gist of a story. **Question 3** Parts (b) and (e). **Question 4** There is evidence that this woman would have difficulty establishing causal relationships between events in a story. Her neuropsychological evaluation revealed that she had difficulty abstracting general from specific information in order to establish cause–effect relationships. **Question 5** (a) *Phonetics* (impaired): The woman's production of speech is compromised by a flaccid dysarthria. Her speech production problems include hypernasal speech, nasal emission and an inability to regulate the volume and pitch of speech. *Phonology* (intact): The woman exhibits relative preservation of repetition and an absence of phonemic paraphasias. (b) *Syntax* (impaired): The woman has a severe impairment of sentence construction and mild difficulties in the auditory comprehension of long and complex sentences. (c) *Semantics* (impaired): The woman exhibits naming errors which are predominantly semantic paraphasias. (d) *Pragmatics* (impaired): The woman's interpretation of language is literal in nature and she does not appear to be able to draw on information from different sources to obtain meaning. (e) *Discourse* (impaired): The woman does not display good information management during connected speech, and she has difficulty with high-level meaning relations in discourse such as cause–effect relationships.

Chapter 3: Acquired pragmatic and discourse disorders

3.1 Acquired aphasia

(1) Parts (a), (c) and (e). (2) True. (3) False. (4) Part (a). (5) Part (c). (6) False.
(7) Structural; request; inversion; auxiliary; syntax; deictic; presupposition; cleft;
informative; adjectives; function. (8) The comprehension of passive voice constructions
is problematic for this client. The client's decoding strategy depends on (c) world
knowledge. (9) Part (b). (10) Part (c).

3.2 Right-hemisphere language disorder

(1) Parts (a), (d) and (e). (2) Parts (b), (d) and (e). (3) True. (4) False. (5) Executive
function; visuospatial; world knowledge; suppression; comprehension; more; theory of
mind; mental states; jokes; pragmatic; discourse; narrative. (6) Part (d). (7) Part (a).
(8) Parts (c) and (d). (9) Part (a). (10) Part (b).

3.3 Traumatic brain injury

(1) Part (e). (2) False. (3) True. (4) False. (5) Cognitive; aphasic; topic; politeness;
irrelevant; repetitiveness; requests; compensate; questions; cohesion; coherence;
narrative; executive functions; perseverative; problem-solving; organisation;
communicative intentions; second-order; conversational. (6) Parts (a), (c) and (d).
(7) Part (c). (8) Parts (b), (c) and (e). (9) True. (10) Part (b).

3.4 Dementias

(1) Part (d). (2) Human immunodeficiency virus (HIV); Creutzfeldt–Jakob disease
(CJD); syphilis. (3) Parts (a), (c) and (e). (4) False. (5) True. (6) Parts (a), (d) and (e).
(7) Alzheimer's disease; late-acquired; development; lexical; syntactic; recognition;
earlier; fluency; late; competence; vulnerable; structural language; superordinate; writing;
picture; confusional; comprehension; cognitive; 50%. (8) Part (b). (9) Part (e). (10) Parts
(a) and (b).

3.5 Neurodegenerative disorders

(1) Part (c). (2) Part (a). (3) False. (4) False. (5) Dementia; speech acts; metaphor;
implicatures; unaware; prosodics; politeness; requests; power; duration; working;
frontostriatal. (6) Parts (a) and (c). (7) True. (8) Parts (a) and (c). (9) Parts (a), (c) and (e).
(10) True.

3.6 Central nervous system infections

(1) Parts (a), (b) and (d). (2) Cytomegalovirus (CMV); herpes simplex virus (HSV);
human immunodeficiency virus (HIV). (3) True. (4) Part (c). (5) Bacterial; herpes

simplex encephalitis; Creutzfeldt–Jakob disease; aphasia; dementia; anomia; semantic; focal; otitis media; temporal; declarative memory; cognition; intellectual; coherent; procedural; cohesive; local; standardised. **(6)** False. **(7)** False. **(8)** Human immunodeficiency virus (HIV); Creutzfeldt–Jakob disease (CJD); herpes simplex encephalitis (HSE). **(9)** Part (c). **(10)** Parts (b), (c) and (e).

Section B: Data analysis exercises

3.7 Acquired aphasia 1

Question 1 (a) 'They all uh had uh yellow-yellow-no white . . . '. (b) '. . . the ravens was there' (no referent of 'there'). (c) '. . . they sounded different' ('they' to refer to a raven). (d) 'But they finally got them all out' (referent of both pronouns could be ravens or pigeons). (e) 'This was the story of the raven that . . . painted his feathers white.' **Question 2** Whilst acknowledging that the lesson or moral of the fable involves an imperative not to behave in a certain way ('don't . . . '), the speaker's response reveals a rather concrete interpretation of the events in the story. There is no evidence that the speaker has inferred a deeper or abstract lesson about human behaviour. Also, the speaker's response reveals a semantic paraphasic error in the form of 'chicken' for 'pigeon'. **Question 3** The three expressions which indicate that the speaker has a rather literal, concrete interpretation of this proverb are 'birds', 'I got hot' and 'drop of rain'. **Question 4** (a) Extensive use of fillers, e.g. '. . . that means that uh, they was a lot more birds'. (b) Extensive repetition, e.g. '. . . there's not a . . . there's not a . . . there's not a, there's not any . . . '. (c) Use of stereotyped expressions, e.g. 'let's see'. (d) Use of pauses, e.g. 'See (6 sec) swallow . . . '. (e) Use of non-specific vocabulary, e.g. 'Or there's more of anything'. **Question 5** The two expressions which reveal some appreciation of this proverb's meaning on the part of the speaker with aphasia are 'they was a lot more birds' and 'Or there's more of anything.'

3.7 Acquired aphasia 2

Question 1 (a) 'she says get your things' (direct reported speech). (b) 'Linda called me and she said she's sick' (indirect reported speech). (c) 'I says my bus is coming at three' (report of Mary's own speech). (d) 'she said she's sick' (affirmative utterance); 'I said no I can't call you early' (negative utterance). (e) 'she says can you come early' (question); 'I says my bus is coming at three' (statement). **Question 2** Mary makes extensive use of the reporting verb 'say' to indicate the use of reported speech (e.g. 'she says can you come early'). None of Ethel's reported speech is introduced by a reporting verb. **Question 3** The omission of a reporting verb like 'says' appears to contribute directly to Barnie's misunderstanding. Instead of uttering 'Barnie says I love bratwurst', Ethel produces only 'I love'. She tries to attribute this utterance to Barnie by pointing to him as she says it. She also points to the bratwurst on the plate. However, these pointing gestures appear not to compensate adequately for Ethel's limited expressive language, with the result that Barnie understands Ethel to be saying that it is she who loves bratwurst. **Question 4** The non-elliptical version of Ethel's final reported speech episode in data set 2 is 'I told you that Barnie loves bratwurst'. This reported speech episode is directed towards the researcher in the adjacent room, and not to Barnie. **Question 5** (a) True. (b) False. (c) True. (d) False. (e) False.

3.7 Acquired aphasia 3

Question 1 In data set 1, the interviewer's utterances are of three types: (1) yes–no questions (e.g. 'Do you do that on purpose?'); (2) grammatical statements which function as yes–no questions (e.g. 'That happens automatically?'); (3) open questions (e.g. 'Why don't you do that?'). Utterance types (1) and (2) place minimal demands on HW's limited expressive language skills. To the extent that the interviewer is aiming to engage HW in conversation, he or she will want to reduce the communicative burden on HW to the best extent possible. It is unsurprising, therefore, that 10 of 13 turns contributed by the interviewer contain utterances of types (1) and (2). Utterance type (3) requires an elaborated response on the part of HW. This is a more challenging type of utterance for HW in view of her limited expressive language skills. The interviewer is aiming to keep utterances of this type to a minimum and, indeed, uses only three in the whole of this data set. **Question 2** (a) The interviewer asks HW 'What do you mean, too fast?' In order to address a question about language meaning, HW must have metalinguistic knowledge. HW produces a competent response to this question by explaining that she cannot search for words when she is talking too fast. (b) HW is able to understand that the referent of *that* in the utterance 'And looking for words, is <u>that</u> difficult too?' is the preceding clause *looking for words*. (c) HW is able to understand that the referent of *that* in the utterance 'Do you do <u>that</u> on purpose?' is HW's earlier description of how she omits certain words. (d) HW mentions her difficulties with writing for the first time in the utterance '... it doesn't come at moment when I write ...'. The novel content of this utterance contributes to topic development when the interviewer uses the issue of writing as the basis of the next question 'When you are writing?' (e) HW displays an understanding of indirect speech acts at the very outset of the exchange when she begins to describe her 'talking problem' in response to the utterance (an indirect request) 'Can you tell me about what are your problems?' **Question 3** (a) HW utters 'Reinier row about <u>I want in the attic</u> Renate no <u>I want in the attic</u>' (underlining indicates direct reported speech). (b) HW utters '... the house fifteen meters width seventeen <u>no seven meters</u>' (underlining indicates self-initiated repair). (c) HW utters 'Ah big <u>one</u> big <u>one</u> behind the house ...' ('one' is a substitute for *garden*); HW comprehends the interviewer's utterance 'That is the oldest <u>one</u> ...' ('one' is a substitute for *child*). (d) HW revises her description of the size of the room from ninety metres to nine metres in response to the interviewer's utterance 'No, that seems very large.' HW was already engaging in self-initiated repair by the time the interviewer produced this utterance, as indicated by her use of 'no' at the end of her preceding turn. (e) HW takes the interviewer's utterance 'But no presents?' to mean 'Do you not exchange presents?' **Question 4** The following utterances were all used by the interviewer and readily understood by HW: 'You don't <u>know</u>'; 'You are <u>glad</u> with it, aren't you?'; 'Were you <u>eager</u> to move?'; 'Yes, you <u>want</u> to plant trees'; 'But, as I <u>understand</u>, you also encounter problems when making a sentence?' The mental state terms, which reflect a combination of cognitive and affective states, are underlined in each utterance. They suggest an intact theory of mind on HW's part. **Question 5** The following utterances were used by HW and contain contradictory information. (1) The interviewer has asked HW to describe her problems: 'Er talking problem yes but forming <u>difficult</u> sentences <u>easy</u> when no <u>easy</u> when first not er <u>difficult</u>

words . . . ' (2) The interviewer has asked HW if she has any plans for Christmas: 'Yes no plans not not Sinterklaas shopsbusiness me purse always empty future no past er'. Contradictory information takes the form of semantically related words (underlined) produced in quick succession. These words are likely to be semantic paraphasias.

3.7 Acquired aphasia 4

Question 1 In data sets 2 and 3, Roy's daughter Di employs the following conversational strategy. Di allows Roy to slowly construct a meaningful utterance over an extended conversational turn. During this turn, Di produces supportive back-channel behaviours such as 'mm' and 'yeah'. Once this turn is completed, Di effectively summarises for Roy what she has taken him to be communicating. Roy then confirms that Di's summary is correct, at which point Di produces a concluding comment such as 'perhaps you can go next year dad'. This is an effective strategy for Di to use with Roy, as it both allows him the conversational time he needs to construct a meaningful utterance, and gives Di the opportunity to check her interpretation of Roy's utterance. **Question 2** (a) Roy can ask questions, e.g. 'two weeks innit' (data set 5). Roy is asking Di if her birthday is in two weeks' time. (b) Roy can produce comments, e.g. 'I know and suddenly [clicks fingers]' (data set 5). Roy is commenting that the time until Di's birthday will pass very quickly. (c) Roy can respond to questions, e.g. 'well yeah eh- because um (0.4) working' (data set 7). Roy is responding that his friends can afford a large mortgage because they are working. (d) Roy can report factual information, e.g. 'me, (0.5) u- ur (0.2) Ascot, no' (data set 2). Roy is reporting the fact that he has never been to Ascot. (e) Roy can express an evaluative judgement, e.g. 'I (0.9) think no, (0.5) er er- (0.7) u- special' (data set 3). Roy is expressing an evaluative judgement when he describes the job of a nursery nurse as being 'special'. **Question 3** Roy uses three linguistic devices to retain his turn. (1) Roy uses fillers such as 'uh' and 'um' particularly in front of pauses, e.g. 'ur (1.4) ah (0.7) twenty or something' (data set 1). (2) Roy prolongs sounds particularly in front of pauses, e.g. 'er er- (0.7) u- special' (data set 3). (3) Roy makes extensive use of level intonation (indicated by a comma), particularly in front of pauses, e.g. 'then, (.) all of a sudden, (1.3)' (data set 1). **Question 4** The three factors which may limit Roy's use of non-verbal communication are as follows. (1) Roy has a dense hemiplegia which affects his right arm. This will make certain gestures difficult or impossible to perform. (2) At least one of Roy's interlocutors, his daughter Di, is a familiar listener. Roy knows that Di can use her background knowledge to interpret his severely agrammatic output in the absence of non-verbal communication. (3) Roy makes extensive use of nouns and adverbs which convey considerable content or meaning. Through linking these words with a number of set phrases such as 'I think' and 'you know', Roy is able to communicate his message quite successfully in the absence of non-verbal communication. **Question 5** (a) Roy can use fixed storytelling phrases, e.g. 'all of a sudden' (data set 1). (b) Roy can use direct reported speech, e.g. 'never mind' (data set 8). Roy is reporting here a standard phrase that speakers use to comfort or reassure someone who is upset. Direct reported speech is taking the place of a verb like 'to comfort' which Roy cannot produce. (c) Roy can interrelate utterances by means of causal relations, e.g. in data set 7, Roy explains that his friends can afford their large mortgage because they are working. (d) Roy can use discourse markers to initiate a narrative episode, e.g. in data set 1, Roy introduces a narrative episode with 'so then'. (e) Roy can use symbolic noise to animate picture description, e.g. in data set 8, Roy produces the symbolic noise 'oooooh' to indicate the distress of the hostess when she discovers the fish has been stolen. The use of symbolic noise does not take the place of a verb which Roy cannot produce, as the use of direct reported speech in (b) above does. In fact, Roy goes on to utter the verb 'crying'.

3.7 Acquired aphasia 5

Question 1 By virtue of asking a question, JJ's husband has effectively selected JJ to be the next speaker. Under most circumstances of this type, speakers would respond to a prolonged silence by attempting a reformulation of their original question. That JJ's husband makes no attempt to reformulate his question might be explained in terms of his knowledge of JJ's language problems. He may be aware, for example, that silences do not indicate that JJ has not understood the question (her eventual response clearly indicates that she has) and that she merely needs time in which to plan her reply. Alternatively, JJ may benefit from some reworking of her husband's lengthy question. In this case, his refusal to undertake a reformulation might be construed as a conversational behaviour that is not facilitative of JJ's attempts to engage in turn-taking. **Question 2** EN appears to be assuming a passive role in the interaction with her male cousin. She mostly produces minimal turns such as 'o:h' and 'aah'. However, on closer examination, it becomes clear that this style of interaction is forced on EN by the conversational behaviour of her cousin. He is particularly insensitive to her attempts to communicate and in most cases completely disregards her turns. This can be seen in the following series of turns by the cousin: 'I don't know whether she was with her . . . 'cause she's got a house . . . down there 'cause he's in the police.' These three turns of the cousin are broken up by two turns from EN, neither of which is picked up by the cousin in his subsequent turn. In effect, the cousin continues his own contribution regardless of what EN is saying. With all of EN's turns simply glossed over by the cousin, EN is reduced to a passive conversational role in the exchange. **Question 3** In data set 3, the researcher gives EN time in which to produce her turn. The researcher then summarises the point which she believes EN has been making. EN confirms on two occasions that the researcher's understanding of what she has been saying is correct. The researcher then contributes a turn which continues the topic first introduced by EN. The researcher's turns pick up on the content of EN's turns and develop it further. There is no attempt by the researcher to gloss over EN's turns as was routine for EN's cousin in data set 2. **Question 4** The researcher in data set 4 is using her conversational turns to conduct a word search with the aim of helping AD retrieve the lexeme 'university'. The word search develops as follows. It is clear from AD's use of 'London' in front of three pauses that the word which AD cannot retrieve must be able to complete the compound 'London _____'. The researcher offers 'London University' as a plausible suggestion. AD's own attempt to say 'London University' is confirmation that the researcher's suggestion is correct. However, three phonemic paraphasias stand in the way of AD's successful production of 'university'. During these paraphasic errors, the researcher utters 'university' which AD then confirms is correct. By means of two facilitative turns, the researcher achieves AD's active participation in a successful word search. **Question 5** (a) *False*: EN's first overlap in data set 2 occurs at the point where her cousin is in the process of completing a clause 'I don't know (overlap starts) whether . . . ' (b) *False*: AD uses only one overlap and its purpose is not to initiate a topic change but to achieve production of a target phrase. (c) *True*: EN uses two overlaps in data set 3 to signal agreement with the current speaker. (d) *False*: There is no evidence in data set 2 that MC is using overlaps to correct EN's linguistic impairments. (e) *True*: In data set 4, the researcher uses an overlap to interrupt AD's phonemic paraphasic errors during his attempt to say 'university'.

3.7   Acquired aphasia 6

Question 1 Ed produces a metalinguistic statement such as 'I can't think of the name of it' or 'What do you call it?' before M feels she has the authority to join Ed in his word search. These forms, particularly the second one, solicit assistance from a conversational partner in the way that fillers and pauses alone do not. **Question 2** The topics of conversation in data sets 1 and 2 are mundane in nature and make a successful guess on M's part quite likely. It is less likely that M will successfully guess the particular medical investigation that Ed has undergone as this is an area where her knowledge is likely to be rather limited. M eventually identifies the particular word that Ed had in mind. However, in order for this to happen, Ed first had to offer additional information. This information is phonological in nature ('srays') and helped M narrow her search down to X-rays. **Question 3** In data set 4, M uses the word which she believes Ed has in mind to complete his utterance. This completion strategy is different from the plausible guesses of data sets 1 to 3 in that M simply appends the word 'okra' onto the end of Ed's incomplete utterance, producing a declarative statement. Ed uses a sound stretch in set 4 ('There's a:::') rather than a metalinguistic statement ('I can't think of the name of it') to indicate his word search in this case. **Question 4** After three unsuccessful attempts to guess the word that Ed has in mind, M indicates through the use of the utterance 'The president or whatever it's called' that the specific word is less important to the further development of the conversation than is the fact that it's someone with the seniority of a president. Ed at first appears unhappy with M's attempt to close down the word search, as he responds with 'Well it, well he's a pres'. But M overlaps Ed's turn with another utterance which indicates that the specific name of the person is less important to the development of the topic of conversation than is his senior role: 'He's the local leader there.' In effect, M is indicating to Ed that she does not need to know the specific name or position of this individual to follow the topic of the conversation, a point which Ed eventually appears to accept. **Question 5** M feels compelled to repeat this particular guess because of the pause of 1.6 seconds between her first suggesting 'Traholi' as the word Ed wanted and Ed responding 'no'. This pause has created uncertainty in M's mind that Ed knows who she is referring to. To address this uncertainty, M repeats this particular guess and expands it to 'Tom Traholi' as a means of helping Ed identify the person she has in mind.

3.7   Acquired aphasia 7

Question 1 Parts (c) and (d). **Question 2** LS in data set 1 has clearly guessed the word 'destinations' that NS is attempting to say. She uses her first turn in the repair sequence to present this word to NS so that he can confirm if it is correct. In data set 2, RB has also clearly guessed the word (probably 'physiotherapy') that JB is attempting to say. However, instead of presenting this word to JB for confirmation, as LS does, RB provides JB with a phonemic cue /f:/ to the word. Already at this early stage of the repair sequence it is apparent that LS is adopting a more facilitative approach to the repair of a trouble source than RB. **Question 3** The three strategies employed by LS to ensure a swift, effortless repair of the trouble source are as follows. (1) When LS presents NS with her 'best guess' for the target word, she does so within the context of a yes–no question which NS can readily confirm. This question type places minimal burden on NS's limited expressive language skills. (2) When NS confirms that LS has identified the correct word, LS uses it in the context of the original utterance that NS was attempting to produce ('we've now got two destinations'). This serves to validate this utterance as a relevant contribution to the conversational exchange. (3) Finally, LS produces a somewhat reflective or philosophical comment to the effect that she and NS are 'just making life complicated' for themselves. This comment helps restore a sense of normalcy to the exchange after the repair has taken place. **Question 4** After receiving a phonemic cue from RB, JB is committed to a series of turns in which he has little option but to offer suggestions or guesses for the identity of the target word. His first guess is 'speech therapy' which he utters as a phonemic paraphasia '/kriʃ/ therapy'. RB indicates that this guess is incorrect, at which point JB offers another alternative in the form of '/ɵu/ therapy'. Although it is not possible to identify the particular type of therapy JB has in mind from this production, RB uses the initial sounds /ɵu/ to reject JB's suggestion (these sounds do not match the phonemic cue that RB provided). After two failed suggestions, JB discontinues this strategy and begins to signal in a more direct way to RB that he needs his assistance (see JB's final turn in the exchange). This sequence positions RB as the knowledgeable, and thus powerful, partner in the exchange. JB assumes the role of an incompetent communicator who must be put through an instructional activity akin to that acted out between teachers and their pupils. **Question 5** JB appears to use the following three expressions to signal to RB that he wants him to say the troublesome word and terminate the protracted repair sequence: (1) 'tryin' to understand that'; (2) 'don't know what it'; (3) 'no remember it now'.

3.7   Acquired aphasia 8

Question 1 (a) Phonemic paraphasia, e.g. /kikiz/ for 'cookies' (data set 2). (b) Circumlocution, e.g. 'falling to the floor' for *overflowing* (data set 2). (c) Word-finding difficulty, e.g. 'near the ... /a/ ... no ... near the ...' (data set 2). (d) Incorrect noun phrase as object of verb, e.g. 'filled the water' for *filled the sink with water* (data set 2). (e) Omission of auxiliary verb, e.g. 'the stool [is] falling down' (data set 3). **Question 2** Picture description makes less cognitive and linguistic demands of BB than a task that requires him to describe his previous work. BB does not need to retrieve events from memory in order to describe a picture which is in front of him. Also, he does not need to organise information in order to describe the Cookie Theft picture. It does not matter if BB reports that the sink is overflowing with water before or after he reports the fact that the mother is drying dishes. **Question 3** (a) Poor use of lexical substitution as a type of cohesive relation, e.g. 'Girl wants one' in data set 2 (it is unclear what 'one' is intended to substitute, particularly given that BB leaves the topic of cookies only to return to it again at the end of his description). (b) Use of personal pronoun in the absence of a preceding referent, e.g. 'we went through to the hospital' in data set 3 (it is unclear what the referent of 'we' is). (c) Reporting of actions in incorrect temporal order, e.g. in data set 2, BB reports that the van was packed *after* reporting that he drove the van to Cambridge. (d) Presence of topic digression, e.g. the introduction of the topic of BB's stroke in data set 3 after his description of his previous work. (e) Conjunctive cohesion markers express only additive and temporal meanings, e.g. 'And the girl is reaching up for the cookies' (additive conjunction in data set 3); 'then we went through to the hospital' (temporal conjunction in data set 3). **Question 4** (a) BB can engage in self-initiated repair, e.g.

'man . . . no . . . woman' (data set 1). (b) BB can foreground the central elements of a scene during picture description, e.g. BB always describes the people present and what they are doing before going on to describe the things (flowers, trees, footpath, etc.) which can be viewed through the kitchen window. (c) BB can use spatial deixis, e.g. 'one bowl is . . . there' where 'there' is being used to locate the bowl on the kitchen top. (d) BB can comprehend indirect speech acts, e.g. BB responds to the indirect request 'Can you tell me anything else?' by continuing his description. (e) BB can use direct reported speech, e.g. it is likely that BB is using 'yes alright' in data set 2 to report the (imagined) words of the boy when the girl is pressing him for a cookie. **Question 5** It is difficult to discern any causal relationship between BB's structural language skills and his pragmatic and discourse skills. Clearly, BB was capable of performing certain pragmatic and discourse functions (e.g. self-initiated repair, comprehension of indirect requests) when his structural language skills were particularly poor at the outset of the study. Also, there is evidence that certain aspects of pragmatics and discourse (e.g. topic maintenance, use of lexical substitution) are problematic when BB's structural language skills displayed considerable improvement during the study. On the basis of this pattern of skills and impairments, we can reasonably conclude that any pragmatic and discourse deficits on BB's part are *not* secondary to his structural language impairments.

3.8 Right-hemisphere language disorder 1

Question 1 (a) Behavioural disturbance, e.g. JB displays poor impulse control in data set 1 when she begins to leave without warning. (b) Behavioural disturbance, e.g. SV displays a lack of motivation when she utters 'I don't care' in data set 2. (c) Emotional disturbance, e.g. SV displays emotional lability in data set 2 when she begins to cry. **Question 2** The adult who makes appropriate use of non-literal language is WM in data sets 4 and 5. This adult makes appropriate use of the idiomatic expressions 'pass muster' (data set 4) and 'as good as gold' (data set 5). **Question 3** In the context of a first-encounter conversation, JB inappropriately begins to talk about food getting stuck in her mouth. This topic would not be inappropriate in the context of conversation with a familiar partner (spouse, etc.) or even a therapist who had previously worked with JB. But it is inappropriate when the conversational partner is someone whom JB has met for the first time. **Question 4** Adult WM uses humour to good effect in data set 5 when she talks about the FBI tapping the lines. This is quite high-level humour in that WM is displaying knowledge of the FBI and the type of covert surveillance this organisation is known to undertake. She then relates this knowledge to her current situation in that she is being recorded during her conversation with ST. This use of humour by WM reveals abstract reasoning skills on her part. **Question 5** The adult who uses a direct speech act when an indirect speech act would be more appropriate in the context is SV in data set 3. SV utters 'Ask me something' when her lack of familiarity with her conversational partner requires the use of an indirect speech act such as 'Would you like to ask me something?' Also, the direct speech act marks an abrupt change of topic from the preceding discussion of SV's friends and their car breakdown. The combination of these features marks out SV's utterance as somewhat impolite in the exchange.

3.8 Right-hemisphere language disorder 2

Question 1 (a) Use of direct reported speech, e.g. 'And I say, "Don't ask me nothing"' (GH, data set 2). (b) Use of ellipsis, e.g. 'Yes, I have [made a good whack at it]' (PT, data set 1). (c) Use of demonstrative pronoun to achieve reference, e.g. 'Look at this' (GH, data set 2). (d) Use of pronominal reference, e.g. 'you'll have to ask your physical therapist that . . . he look at it, he say he didn't like it either' (GH, data set 2). (e) Use of indirect reported speech, e.g. 'He said they usually get this kind . . . ' (GH, data set 2). **Question 2** In data set 1, at the point when DT is attempting to terminate the conversation, PT introduces the topic of foreign travel to Australia. This is particularly inappropriate as the conversational closing sequence has already been completed. In data set 3, CD abandons the topic of his cold to ask his partner what the class is about. The conversational partner in this case indicated through the use of 'oh' that some development of this topic would be appropriate in the context. **Question 3** Adult GH in data set 2 screams and uses language with violent content ('Take somebody and beat they head in'). There is also use of blasphemous language ('God, what's this!?') These verbal and non-verbal behaviours are socially inappropriate in this exchange. Poor impulse control in right-hemisphere damage may account for these behaviours. **Question 4** There is evidence of insensitivity on the part of these adults to the phase of conversation in which they are engaged. Adult PT in data set 1 opens up a new topic of conversation (foreign travel) at the point at which conversational closure has taken place. Also, adult CD in data set 4 appears to be trying to bring the conversation to a premature conclusion when he utters 'How long we got to go this session?' during its maintenance phase. **Question 5** Adult PT in data set 1 appears to misjudge his social relationship to the conversational partner when he says to her 'I'd like to have a drink'. This may merely be a statement to the effect that PT wants to have a drink on his own – there was, after all, previous mention made of alcohol. But DT's response suggests that she reads PT's utterance as an inappropriate invitation to her to join him for a drink. This is indicated by the fact that DT explains to PT that they are expected to be somewhere else. This is then followed by a second attempt by DT to terminate the interaction in the form of the utterance 'so, it's been nice chatting with you, we will have to talk again.'

3.9   Traumatic brain injury 1

Question 1 (a) Use of a personal pronoun in the absence of a referent, e.g. ' . . . go somewhere and, you go . . . ' (no referent for 'you'). (b) Use of an incomplete prepositional phrase, e.g. 'you go and coming through and keep going' (through what?). (c) Use of non-specific lexemes, e.g. 'people', 'things' and 'somewhere'. (d) Use of an incomplete relative clause, e.g. 'who . . . things'. (e) Use of repetitive language, e.g. 'like go somewhere and, you go and coming through and keep going'. **Question 2** (a) Ellipsis, e.g. 'no I haven't [been to a Halloween party where there were really outrageous costumes]'. (b) Self-initiated repair, e.g. 'I've seen- . . . no . . . I've seen people'. **Question 3** SM uses his final conversational turn in data set 2 (1) to summarise what he believes NB has been trying to communicate and (2) to confirm with NB if his understanding is correct. **Question 4** It is not possible for topic development to take place in either of these exchanges. This is because the utterances which NB contributes are so often unclear and uninformative that it is not possible for SM to establish what NB is talking about, and then use that understanding to develop a topic further. In effect, SM appears to be so fully engaged in trying to understand what NB is attempting to communicate that topic development is not a feature of either exchange. **Question 5** Parts (a) and (d). NB protects the pauses within his conversational turns by the use of continuing intonation.

This prosodic feature lets SM know that NB intends to keep talking and that SM should not attempt to take the conversational turn from him.

3.9 Traumatic brain injury 2

Question 1 The speaker with TBI in data set 1 engages in topic perseveration when s/he keeps stating the point that s/he did drawings while listening to 'the music' (presumably, Janis Joplin's music). This perseverative tendency in the early part of the response gives way in the later part of the response to an increasingly abstract and technical (and irrelevant) account of how to do the drawings. **Question 2** In data set 2, the series of three photographs is examining a conventional indirect request (part c). The post-response explanation makes a rather general (and unfounded) statement to the effect that TV watching can be problematic for couples when, in fact, the specific issue is one that the woman is not happy even though she has received the controls she wanted her partner to give her. **Question 3** There is a confabulatory quality to the post-response explanation of the speaker with TBI in data set 3. This speaker reports, for example, that the man in the photographs spent a fortune on his glasses. However, this is an embellishment on the part of the speaker which is completely unsupported by any information in the photographs. The speaker even goes so far as to act out part of an imagined dialogue between the man and woman in the photographs. **Question 4** In data set 4, the series of three photographs is examining an unconventional indirect request (part e). The two features of the post-response explanation which indicate that the speaker with TBI has an intact theory of mind are statements to the effect that the man in the photographs did not take the woman's situation into account (a direct reference to perspective-taking) and that the woman should express her discontent (a reference to an affective state of the woman). **Question 5** The speaker with TBI in data set 1 exhibits perseveration. Perseveration is associated with impaired inhibitory control (part c).

3.9 Traumatic brain injury 3

Question 1 The narrator in data set 2 chooses non-specific words to refer to people and objects in the story. These lexemes are in stark contrast to the specific words used by the narrator in data set 1 to refer to the same people and objects. Several examples are: Mr McDonald (data set 1) – a man (data set 2); his wife (data set 1) – a woman (data set 2); the tenants (data set 1) – everybody (data set 2); all the vegetables and animals (data set 1) – everything (data set 2); diced vegetable stand (data set 1) – something (data set 2). **Question 2** In line 1 of data set 2, the narrator commences by saying 'they had' in the absence of any referent for the pronoun 'they'. He appears to realise his omission when he abandons this utterance in order to introduce 'a man and a woman' (the presumed referent of 'they'). He then resumes his original utterance 'they had . . . a tomato plant' in the knowledge that he has now put a referent in place for 'they'. In line 4 of data set 2, the narrator uses 'there'. Again, he displays awareness that some referent is needed for this expression when he continues the utterance by saying 'in the building'. **Question 3** The narrator in data set 2 uses 'and then' to relate events in temporal terms. However, the temporal meaning of the second of these conjunctions is not appropriate on every occasion of use. For example, the use of 'and then' in the following extract is somewhat anomalous in the absence of further elaboration: 'a man and a woman and a borough and then . . . they had a tomato plant'. The narrator in data set 1 uses a wider range of

225

temporal expressions to relate events including 'as time went by', 'then later on' and 'eventually'. Moreover, these expressions are used appropriately in the context of the particular utterances they are serving to link, e.g. 'had vegetables here there each and everywhere then later on he brought in some animals'. **Question 4** The narrator in data set 2 states that 'everybody got out of the building' before stating that 'they grew all the tomato plants and everything out there in the building'. However, the latter statement should have preceded the former statement, as it was the fact that vegetables and animals were being kept in the apartment which caused the tenants to leave the building. The narrator displays a poor grasp of the causal relationship between these events. The conceptual relationship of causality is clearly problematic to some extent for this narrator. **Question 5** (a) True. (b) True. (c) True. (d) False. (e) True.

3.9   Traumatic brain injury 4

Question 1 The monologic narrative in data set 1 is uninformative for three reasons. Firstly, it makes extensive use of repetitive language. In the space of this short extract, the adult with TBI states no less than five times that someone is 'walking down the stairs'. Secondly, there is also evidence of the use of tautological language in 'the other person is doing what they're doing'. Thirdly, non-specific lexemes such as 'person' and 'someone else' are used to describe the two human characters in the story. **Question 2** In the jointly produced narrative in data set 2, friend EK is asking PF a question to which he already knows the answer. This infelicitous use of a question – it is one of the felicity conditions on asking a question that the questioner does not know the answer – is only permissible in certain contexts. One such context is the classroom where teachers routinely ask pupils questions to which they already know the response. By mimicking this type of instructional context, EK is assuming the role of a teacher in the exchange. By implication, PF must assume the less powerful role of the pupil in the interaction. **Question 3** JS poses a number of questions to MB which are designed to check MB's knowledge state. They include 'Do you know what the Roads and Traffic Authority is?' and 'you know a driving school?' Given that MB has clearly indicated at the outset of the exchange that he has previously been a motorist, JS can reasonably assume an affirmative response to both these questions. By performing these checks of MB's knowledge, JS is assuming a level of power in the exchange which even exceeds that expected of his role as a police officer. **Question 4** JS checks MB's understanding on two occasions by asking 'Right?' On one of these occasions, he adds 'If you can understand that.' These checks – and certainly this last utterance – would probably not have been made of an adult with no brain injury. Nor are these utterances warranted by MB's linguistic performance in the exchange. It is quite clear that MB is a competent language user. He displays good auditory comprehension, can produce intelligible speech and can use syntactically complex utterances. Yet again, this conversational strategy serves to disempower MB as he is being cast in the role of the less competent communicator in the exchange. **Question 5** At the outset of the exchange in data set 3, JS asks MB to confirm his name. In the context of this particular telephone conversation, it is doubtful that MB's name is even relevant – the enquiry is a general one about the steps which need to be taken to get a driving licence back after a car accident. In putting MB through this question–answer sequence, JS is forcing MB to establish his credibility as a competent oral communicator when, in fact, it is clear from the exchange that MB is just such a communicator.

3.10   Dementias 1

Question 1 (a) Semantic paraphasia, e.g. use of 'crows' for *pigeons*. (b) Omission of pronouns, e.g. '... took care of him it, ... got his own food'. (c) Word-finding difficulty, e.g. 'So he went back to his uh (4 seconds)'. (d) Utterance revision, e.g. 'you had now- it was a bird'. (e) Incomplete relative clause, e.g. 'it was uh, raven uh, who was uh'.
Question 2 The adult with Alzheimer's disease in data set 1 succeeds in conveying the following components: a hungry raven saw that the pigeons in the coop had food ('he noticed that ... the crows ... was ... getting something to eat'); he painted his feathers white to look like them ('so he ... got ... painted'); the pigeons realised he was a raven and chased him ('the ... crows ... kinda knocked him out of that game'); the raven then returned to his own kind ('he went back to his own business'). The following story components are omitted altogether: the raven painted himself *white to look like the pigeons*; it was the raven's crowing which revealed his true identity to the pigeons; the ravens chased him also as they did not recognise him with white feathers. **Question 3** In the fable, the raven painted himself in order to obtain more food to eat. So it was the desire to obtain more food that *caused* the raven to paint himself. However, as the adult in data set 1 represents these actions, this causal relationship is effectively reversed, e.g. 'so he ... got ... painted ... figured he could get more, a better deal on that'. A more accurate representation of these events would have been reported as 'he figured he could get more so he got painted'. Also, the story component in which the ravens chased away the duplicitous raven is falsely reported as 'Took care of him'. **Question 4** The adult in data set 2 conveys a general life lesson when he says that 'you can't get anything for nothing'. Moreover, this lesson has some relevance in the context of this particular fable, because the raven is trying to obtain 'free' food or at least food which does not belong to him. But this fable contains a much deeper lesson about the importance of displaying loyalty to one's group or community and the serious consequences (rejection, etc.) of suspending that loyalty in order to achieve a short-term gain. **Question 5** The essence of this proverb's meaning is that the involvement of a large number of people in a project can often compromise the quality of that project and that, on occasion, it is best for a single person to have general oversight and 'responsibility' (to use this adult's own word). The adult with Alzheimer's disease manages to build this meaning incrementally across a series of three utterances. Each of these utterances captures the idea that a better outcome can often be achieved through the involvement of a small number of people, or even just a single person. These utterances are: 'you can't get a whole lot of things done with a whole lot of people'; 'You've got to come up with some kind of a thing that's "doable" and that some people may not be involved in it'; 'you can't have twelve people getting involved with something and somebody's got to do it'.

3.10   Dementias 2

Question 1 Warren's verbosity is evident in the extended nature of each of his conversational turns, while the speech–language pathologist produces somewhat minimal turns such as 'Uh huh?' and 'Oh dear'. Warren is clearly unable to maintain a topic. The speech–language pathologist has asked him a question about his age. However, in addressing this question, he digresses into talk about a calculator and batteries. Warren is also unaware of the needs of his listener when he uses words for which the listener has no referents. This can be seen in the following utterance, in which there are no clear referents for the underlined words: 'So I've added <u>there</u> as well and the years come along and I didn't remember doing either of the first two so I did <u>it</u> again.' **Question 2** (a) Use of pronominal reference, e.g. '... so that guaranteed <u>the calculator</u> was working properly 'cause <u>it</u> kept telling me ...'. (b) Use of lexical substitution, e.g. 'In September as a halfway between the two <u>ages</u> I start saying what the next <u>one</u> is'. (c) Use of direct reported speech, e.g. 'I went "no, I'm not I'm 34"'. (d) Use of presupposition, e.g. '... I didn't remember doing either of the first two so I did it <u>again</u>' ('again' presupposes that Warren had added years to his age *before*). (e) Use of causal connectives to link actions, e.g. 'I didn't remember doing either of the first two <u>so</u> I did it again when I was 32'. **Question 3** Warren produces the utterances 'I've been 34 for the last 3 years' (false utterance) and 'Someone pointed out that I was 34 last year and 33 last year' (contradictory utterance). These utterances violate the Gricean maxim of quality. **Question 4** (a) Warren makes use of mental state language in the following utterances: 'I <u>forgot</u> about it', 'I didn't <u>remember</u> doing either of the first two', and 'I <u>thought</u> "well, it's fairly obvious I'm in it"'. (b) Warren's use of mental state language suggests that he has a theory of mind, at least to some extent. **Question 5** It may appear inconsistent to say that the speaker who is unaware of the needs of his listener (question 1) has a theory of mind (question 4). After all, the speaker who is unaware of the needs of his listener does not *know* what his listener needs to *know* in order to follow the utterances of a speaker. And these knowledge states are none other than the type of mental states which are involved in a speaker having a theory of mind. However, what appears to be an inconsistency can be explained in the following terms. When Warren engages in mental state attribution in the utterances in question 4, he is attributing mental states *to his own mind about the world*. However, when he is attempting to establish the needs of his listener, he is attributing mental states *to his own mind about the mind of his listener*. The former mental state attribution is not as cognitively challenging as the latter mental state attribution, and appears to be within Warren's cognitive capacity. The latter mental state attribution appears to exceed Warren's theory of mind skills, which is what leads to him being somewhat unaware of the needs of his listener.

3.10 Dementias 3

Question 1 (a) The retention of long-term memory, e.g. HP in data set 1 is able to describe how she used to cook for her family. (b) The understanding of abstract concepts, e.g. CD in data set 2 displays an understanding of *nationality* when she describes her husbands as not being American and as 'belonging to other countries'. (c) The use of ellipsis, e.g. 'I used to [cook] when I raised my family' (HP in data set 1); 'kinda think that he wasn't [American]' (CD in data set 2). **Question 2** WP in data set 3 displays a lack of topic relevance when she responds to a question about her favourite restaurant meal by talking about her daughter Sally. The information that WP contributes about her daughter is inconsistent in that WP says that Sally is *and* is not her daughter. **Question 3** *Structural language deficits*. (1) Word-finding difficulty, e.g. 'I went from um-' (data set 6). (2) Utterance reformulation, e.g. 'I get out and I- didn't take me long to change my mind' (data set 6). *Discourse deficits*. (1) Incorrect pronominal reference, e.g. 'kinda think that <u>he</u> wasn't' (use of 'he' in data set 2 when the referent in preceding discourse is both husbands). (2) Use of repetitive language, e.g. repetition of 'I majored first in landing' in data set 6. **Question 4** In data set 6, JK's extended turn displays the following three features which make it particularly difficult to follow. (1) JK uses pronouns with no identifiable referent, e.g. 'I held it' (does 'it' refer to *job* or something else?). (2) JK repeatedly starts utterances only to abandon them, e.g. 'I went from um-'. (3) JK shifts between 'get out' and 'get off' during his extended turn. The meaning of 'get out' is particularly unclear between *getting out* of the marines (as in leaving the job) and *getting out* of ships (as in disembarking during a landing). **Question 5** (a) 'my husband . . . he's sick' (use of 'he' to refer to *husband* in data set 4). (b) 'walking . . . it can be boring' (use of 'it' to refer to *walking* in data set 5). (c) 'he gets around but . . . he can't walk' (use of conjunction 'but' that expresses a meaning of 'contrary to expectation' between these two clauses). (d) 'it can be boring because . . . there are no . . . challenges' (use of conjunction 'because' that expresses a reason why the walking is boring). (e) 'my son is in the army and then . . . my husband . . . he's sick' (use of conjunctions 'and then' which link the clauses that describe family members).

3.10   Dementias 4

Question 1 *Three examples of impaired deixis.* (a) 'She's reading . . . ': Use of 'she' to refer to the man in the picture (data set 1). (b) ' . . . you can walk from there': Client with dementia is unable to establish the referent of 'there' (data set 3, exchange 1). (c) 'Do you want to have a drink now . . . ': Client with dementia is unable to establish the referent of 'you' (data set 3, exchange 2). **Question 2** Checks of utterance interpretation are conducted at the following points in the data sets. (1) 'Where on (pause) on the T.V.?' (data set 2, exchange 1). (2) 'You mean the purchasing power of the Canadian dollar is better than the American?' (data set 2, exchange 2). **Question 3** In early-stage Alzheimer's dementia clients still appear to be capable of checking their understanding of utterance meaning. In middle-stage Alzheimer's dementia the ability to establish the referents of deictic expressions such as 'you' and 'there' is beginning to be disrupted. Both pragmatic–discourse skills require the use of theory of mind (ToM). The hearer who checks his interpretation of a speaker's utterance meaning is attempting to determine if his understanding matches the speaker's communicative intention (a mental state). Equally, to establish the referent of a deictic expression, a hearer must be able to determine a speaker's communicative intention. The preserved ability to conduct checks of utterance meaning in early-stage Alzheimer's dementia (ESAD) combined with an impairment of the ability to establish the referents of deictic expressions in middle-stage Alzheimer's dementia (MSAD) suggest that ToM may be intact in ESAD and impaired in MSAD. **Question 4** The following lexical checks occur in the data sets. (1) ' . . . I want to say 'flag', but it's not a flag . . . ' (data set 1). (2) 'What did Paul call it . . . ' (data set 4, exchange 1). (3) 'What's her name . . . ' (data set 4, exchange 2). **Question 5** Lexical checks occur in these data sets in the presence of word-finding difficulties. These checks require the use of metalinguistic skills – the speaker who is discussing whether to apply the word 'flag' of a pictured object is talking *about* language. The fact that a speaker can still use metalinguistic skills at the same time as he is unable to produce a target word shows that linguistic and metalinguistic skills can be selectively impaired in dementia. In this case, metalinguistic skills are intact while linguistic skills are impaired.

3.10   Dementias 5

Question 1 (a) Direct reported speech, e.g. 'we'll be running around saying "where's this and where's the other?"' (data set 1). (b) Prosody, e.g. use of rising intonation in 'I say "how's ↑things"' (data set 3). (c) Facial expressions, e.g. 'they just go *((face))* I said and I *((face))* for you as well' (data set 3). (d) Body movements, e.g. 'I don't want those *((2 hand brush aside))*' (data set 2). (e) Eye gaze, e.g. use of eye pointing (data set 2). **Question 2** (a) In data set 3, Jacqueline asks Doug 'Is that the Spar shop?', to which he responds 'Yes sorry I don't say do I I keep forgetting at the Spar shop'. (b) In data set 2, Doug says 'I really want that . . . I don't want those . . . ' with 'that' and 'those' referring to entities in the discourse context. (c) In data set 2, Doug utters 'I'll take this one' with 'one' acting as a substitute for *shirt*. (d) In data set 2, Doug utters 'I'm quite happy with em' with 'em' referring back to shirts. (e) In data set 4, Doug utters 'I suppose it has [affected my speech]'. **Question 3** (1) Cognitive ToM: 'I know most of the people there . . . ' (data set 3). (2) Affective ToM: 'I'm quite happy with em . . . ' (data set 2). (3) Cognitive ToM: 'I keep forgetting' (data set 3). (4) Cognitive ToM: 'I really want that' (data set 2). (5) Cognitive ToM: 'you think about (.) what have we got' (data set 1). **Question 4** In data set 1, Doug uses direct reported thought when he says 'you think oh blimey forgot that one . . . ' **Question 5** (1) Data set 1: 'you turn round and walk back to get it'. (2) Data set 1: 'you walking around'. (3) Data set 1: 'what have we got we got to take when we get there'. (4) Data set 2: 'I can look down'. (5) Data set 1: 'we got to go on that ways'.

3.11   Neurodegenerative disorders 1

Question 1 (a) Direct reported speech, e.g. 'Granny looks out of the window and says "Could I help you?"' (data set 1). (b) Demonstrative reference, e.g. 'I didn't understand that' (data set 2). (c) Self-initiated repair, e.g. 'I'll be I'll meet you downstairs' (data set 1). (d) Cohesive conjunction, e.g. 'So he goes in' (data set 1). (e) Anaphoric reference, e.g. 'he dropped a bowling ball down the drainpipe and somehow it got inside him' (data set 2). **Question 2** In data set 1, the speaker uses the pronoun 'she' instead of 'he' to refer to Sylvester the cat ('and she said'). In data set 2, the speaker uses the pronoun 'he' of two potential referents in the utterance 'and he climbed up the drainpipe and he dropped a bowling ball'. The first use of this pronoun refers to the cat, while the second use refers to the bird. **Question 3** In data set 2, the speaker with PD uses mental state language in the utterance 'I didn't understand that'. The use of this language suggests intact theory of mind skills on the part of this speaker. **Question 4** The speaker in data set 1 is using gesture to indicate the spatial location of Granny in the cartoon. The speaker keeps her left hand raised for the duration of the direct reported speech episode between Granny and Sylvester the cat. **Question 5** In the following extract, the speaker starts to report the speech of Sylvester the cat only to abandon it, and then produce direct reported speech on the part of Granny: 'and knocks on the door and says-/ granny looks out the top of the/ window and says/ could I help you'. It appears that the speaker's original communicative intention to report Sylvester's speech is abandoned at this point in the narrative.

3.11   Neurodegenerative disorders 2

Question 1 (a) 'I had a nice one' ('one' is a substitute for *holiday* or *trip*). (b) 'I had never seen the ocean before. It was really beautiful.' (c) 'And so I saw I had never seen the ocean before.' (d) 'Years ago we went down to the Caribbean.' (e) 'And so I saw . . . ' **Question 2** (a) Mental state language, e.g. 'I don't know.' (b) Evaluative language, e.g. 'It

was really beautiful.' (c) Descriptive language, e.g. '. . . we went down to the Caribbean.'
Question 3 The speaker in data set 1 uses repetitive language when he talks about the
beauty of the water and the ocean in the Caribbean. **Question 4** The account of the
scene by the adult in data set 2 amounts to little more than a list of all the objects present.
It is certainly accurate and informative about the explicit content of the picture. However,
this account fails to advance the narrative that the speaker is relating as it does not
integrate these details in a way that will enable a hearer to derive the gist of the story.
Question 5 Part (c) higher-order integration of visual material.

3.12   Central nervous system infections

Question 1 Loss is the overriding theme of D.L.'s spontaneous speech in data sets 1 and
2. D.L. uses the theme of loss in order to organise his personal narrative. He switches
back and forth between past and present temporal frames which relate to his loss of
language and cognitive skills, e.g. 'I lost my language – I'm just kind of waking up – I
lost my concen(tration) – I'm just now concentrating'. **Question 2** The two linguistic
constructions which effectively structure D.L.'s personal narrative are 'I lost . . . ' and
'I'm just . . . '. The function of these constructions is to do more than describe what has
happened to D.L. to this point in time. Through their repetition, these constructions
achieve the organisation of key events in D.L.'s life in a context where a range of cognitive
deficits are likely to compromise narrative organisation. **Question 3** The following
utterances indicate that D.L. has retained some metalinguistic and metacognitive
awareness: (a) 'I lost my language' (data set 1); (b) 'I'm just now concentrated' (data set 2);
(c) 'To interpret what he's doing?' (data set 3). **Question 4** Anomalies in the use of nouns
and pronouns make it difficult to follow the final utterance in D.L.'s picture description.
These anomalies include the use of 'he's asking him' to refer to the girl in the picture
and the use of 'he's a girl' when the correct noun is clearly *boy*. These anomalies make it
difficult for the hearer to establish who D.L. is referring to in this part of the picture
description. **Question 5** (a) D.L. is able to use self-initiated repair, e.g. 'he's a girl I mean
a boy'. (b) D.L. is able to describe prominent objects in the scene, e.g. cookie jar, water,
sink. (c) D.L. is able to describe the goals of the characters, e.g. 'to get the cookies'.
(d) D.L. is able to describe prominent actions in the scene, e.g. 'he's falling'. (e) D.L. is able
to interpret actions in intentional terms, e.g. 'he's asking him to drink'.

Chapter 4: Mental health and pragmatic and discourse disorders

Section A: Short-answer questions

4.1   Schizophrenia

(1) Parts (b) and (e). **(2)** False. **(3)** True. **(4)** Part (c). **(5)** False. **(6)** Social; sarcasm;
prosody; non-literal; flouted; communicative intention; narrative; excessive; relation;
manner; attribution; knowledge; interpretation; proverbs; causal; executive function;
flexibility. **(7)** Part (e). **(8)** Part (d). **(9)** Parts (b), (c) and (e). **(10)** Part (c).

4.2 Bipolar disorder

(**1**) Part (d). (**2**) Parts (a), (b) and (d). (**3**) Parts (b) and (d). (**4**) False. (**5**) True. (**6**) True. (**7**) Prosody; comprehension; depression; syntax; pragmatics; mean length of utterance; paragrammatic; clinical state; lexical–semantic; independent. (**8**) Parts (a) and (d). (**9**) Parts (b) and (c). (**10**) Parts (b) and (d).

4.3 Personality disorder

(**1**) Parts (a) and (c). (**2**) True. (**3**) False. (**4**) Parts (b) and (c). (**5**) Parts (a) and (c). (**6**) True. (**7**) Part (c). (**8**) Parts (b) and (c). (**9**) Part (b). (**10**) Part (c).

4.4 Emotional disturbance in children

(**1**) False. (**2**) False. (**3**) Parts (c) and (d). (**4**) Parts (a), (c) and (d). (**5**) True. (**6**) False. (**7**) Parts (b), (c) and (d). (**8**) Part (b). (**9**) False. (**10**) True.

4.5 Behavioural disorders in children

(**1**) Parts (b) and (e). (**2**) (a) Inattention; (b) hyperactivity; (c) impulsivity; (d) impulsivity; (e) inattention. (**3**) False. (**4**) False. (**5**) Part (a). (**6**) Parts (a) and (c). (**7**) Parts (b) and (d). (**8**) Part (c). (**9**) False. (**10**) False.

Section B: Data analysis exercises

4.6 Schizophrenia 1

Question 1 (a) Scenario B, data set 2. (b) Scenario C, data set 3. (c) Scenario A, data set 3. (d) Scenario B, data set 1. (e) Scenario E, data set 1. **Question 2** (a) Scenario A, data set 2. (b) Scenario C, data set 1. (c) Scenario D, data set 1. (d) Scenario B, data set 3. (e) Scenario A, data set 1. **Question 3** (a) In scenario B, data set 1 there is an elaborative inference from the verb 'knock over' that the vase was *broken*. (b) In scenario A, data set 1 there is a causal inference to the effect that the boy was tired *because* he had been working really hard. (c) In scenario B, data set 2 there is an action inference to the effect that the girl in the scenario had *cooked* the soup. (d) In scenario A, data set 3 there is a mental state inference to the effect that Robert *liked* the tie. (e) In scenario D, data set 1 there is an affective inference to the effect that the wife's annoyance is related to her husband's reading of the newspaper. **Question 4** *Affective ToM*: in scenario D of data set 1, the subject makes an inference about the wife's emotional state of *annoyance*. *Cognitive ToM*: in scenario A of data set 2, the subject draws an inference about the girl's cognitive state, namely, that she does not *want* coffee. **Question 5** The following features suggest semantic impairment on the part of the adults with schizophrenia. (1) Words are used which are not the target word but are close in meaning to the target. Examples include the use of 'book' for *newspaper* (scenario D, data set 1) and 'perplexed' for *annoyed* (scenario A, data set 3). (2) One of the responses contradicts the information in the videotaped scenario. In scenario E of data set 1, the brother is described as being 'too concentrated on his breakfast' when the scenario portrays the brother as 'paying no attention'.

4.6 Schizophrenia 2

Question 1 The two topics which dominate the discourse of the three speakers with schizophrenia are: (1) telepathy and reading the minds of people, e.g. 'I could read their mind' (data set 3), 'I don't know exactly what telepathy means' (data set 1); (2) one's own speech and the speech of others, e.g. 'she is sometimes discourteous in her words' (data set 1), 'I say it out before anything else could happen' (data set 2). **Question 2** The speaker in data set 2 displays relatively good topic development, while the speaker in data set 3 displays almost no topic development at all. The decisive factor in explaining this difference appears to be the participation of the speech and language therapist (Irene) in data set 2. Irene and Yvette are able to develop the content of each other's utterances in their respective turns. For example, Irene takes Yvette's statement 'I'm thinking too fast' as the reason why her utterances have 'to come straight out'. In her turn, Yvette uses Irene's utterance 'it has to come straight out' as the reason why she 'says things that are corrupt'. The lack of a conversational partner in data set 3 may limit topic development. Instead, the speaker with schizophrenia in this data set perseverates on topics such as reading other people's minds (e.g. 'I think I could read people mind') and his or her own verbal behaviour (e.g. 'should I answer should I not answer'). **Question 3** (a) Ability to use ellipsis, e.g. 'they don't [leave you alone]' (data set 1). (b) Ability to use pronouns and possessives to achieve cohesion, e.g. 'But, also my mother has to behave <u>herself</u>, but . . . <u>she</u> is sometimes discourteous in <u>her</u> words and <u>she</u> can be a bit rude' (data set 1). (c) Ability to establish referents of demonstrative pronouns, e.g. 'have you any ideas of how you can help <u>that</u>' (in data set 2, Yvette clearly understands the referent of 'that' in Irene's utterance). (d) Ability to integrate part of prior speaker's turn within current turn, e.g. Yvette integrates part of Irene's utterance ('it has to come straight out') in her utterance 'it has to come straight out and this is what makes me say things that are corrupt' (data set 2). (e) Ability to use mental state language, e.g. 'I don't <u>know</u> exactly what telepathy means. But maybe I <u>believe</u> in it a little' (data set 1). **Question 4** The discourse in data set 3 is difficult to follow for the following reasons. (a) The speaker with schizophrenia uses definite noun phrases such as 'the car' and 'the house' in the absence of any preceding referents. This leads the hearer to ask himself 'what car?' and 'what house?' (b) The speaker with schizophrenia appears to abandon an utterance in order to report people's thoughts ('. . . by in the car sh- *will I see paradise will I not see paradise . . .* '). He then as quickly abandons his report of these thoughts in order to continue his monologue ('*should I not answer I not answer w-* their thought of how . . . '). This suspension of the main discourse, indicated in italics, is not signalled by the speaker. (c) The speaker with schizophrenia uses pronouns and possessives in the absence of clearly established referents of these terms. For example, does the speaker intend the referent of these underlined words to be *people*, which is somewhat non-specific, or does he have some other referent in mind?: '<u>their</u> thought'; '<u>their</u> mind'; '<u>they</u> pass by in the car'; 'I just correct for <u>them</u>'. **Question 5** 'I found that I say certain things which are out of context and em I find that <u>everything I wanted to say</u> I say <u>it</u> out before anything else could happen I say it out and I find that <u>this</u> is the reason – that <u>this</u> is one of the ways why I say those things <u>I'm thinking too fast</u>'. *Anaphoric reference*: '. . . <u>everything I wanted to say</u> I say it out before anything else could happen . . . ' *Cataphoric reference*: . . . I find that this is the reason . . . why I say those things I'm thinking too fast'.

4.6 Schizophrenia 3

Question 1 After an appropriate response to the doctor's initial question, the speaker with schizophrenia pursues a sequence of topics which is characterised by linguistic and other associations between key words and ideas. The speaker's introduction of the topic of his name is somewhat irrelevant as a response to the doctor's question about 'special abilities' and is the start of a chain of topics that is increasingly difficult to follow. After stating that people laugh at his name, and then being unable to clarify this remark for the doctor, the speaker abruptly changes topic to begin talking about people from a certain area. The trigger for this topic change appears to be the fact that people from the area in question have the same name as the speaker's family name. There is then a remark that the speaker's name (this is somewhat unclear) is 'a kind of sacred relic'. When asked by the doctor to clarify this remark, the speaker with schizophrenia shifts the topic again to talk about a town called X which is seen on the news. He then returns to the topic of his name by stating that, if he had a choice, he would rather be known as Marko. When pressed by the doctor about the reason for a name change, the speaker indicates that it would be 'cool' to have this new name. The entire sequence is characterised by a gradual, radial extension of topics. **Question 2** *Referential use of demonstrative pronouns.* (1) 'I have not thought about that' (The speaker with schizophrenia uses 'that' to refer to an issue raised by the doctor in his question. The issue concerns potential harm to the speaker from others.) (2) 'I should not be teased for that' (The speaker with schizophrenia uses 'that' to refer to what appears to be his name which he describes as 'a sacred relic'.) *Use of lexical substitution to achieve cohesion.* (1) 'my family name X-er is one' (The speaker with schizophrenia uses 'one' as a substitute for 'a relic'.) (2) 'since I am one' (The speaker with schizophrenia uses 'one' as a substitute for 'inhabitant of province X'.) **Question 3** *Problematic pronominal reference.* (1) 'I kind of imagine that it is a kind of sacred relic' (Does 'it' refer to the speaker's name or to a location?) (2) 'They are jobless' (Does 'they' refer to people in trades/professions or to something or someone else?) (3) 'they watch it' (Does 'they' refer to some people or to someone else?) **Question 4** *Non-specific words and phrases.* (1) 'and the like' (2) 'and such like that' (3) 'these kind of things' (4) 'I do watch something' (5) 'A group of people can come up with wise things'. **Question 5** *Anaphoric reference:* 'Then some people, well they are stars and the like' (use of 'they' to refer to *some people*). *Ellipsis*: 'I would want to be better educated, but I am not [better educated]' (speaker appropriately omits *better educated*).

4.7 Bipolar disorder 1

Question 1 (a) 'And I said, "Oh my God, these poor kids, you know, their hope has got to be kept alive"' (data set 5). (b) 'She's never really going to go anywhere' (data set 2). (c) 'they would always ask . . . if I was feeling well enough' (data set 1). (d) 'Oh gee, that's really brave. Will you bring me books?' (data set 1). (e) 'She's never going to really be able to accomplish anything' (data set 2). **Question 2** *Cognitive states*: 'I remember that hospitalization' (data set 2); 'I think it was after my sixth hospitalization' (data set 1); 'I began to believe that . . . ' (data set 3). *Affective states*: 'I felt devastated' (data set 2); 'I felt despondent for about two weeks' (data set 5); 'it's so sad' (data set 2). **Question 3** *Temporal expressions*: 'I felt despondent for about two weeks' (data set 5); 'That only lasted for about a year though' (data set 4); 'once I was there like three or four months' (data set 2). *Spatial expressions*: 'I had a long term stay at Eastern County Medical Center' (data set 1); 'they transferred me to the Barrymore Psychiatric Center' (data set 1); 'you would end up back in the hospital' (data set 3). The use of these temporal and spatial expressions suggests that cognitive skills such as memory and visuospatial perception are relatively intact in Kelly. **Question 4** Kelly uses the metaphor of a fire in her account of her recovery from illness. This metaphorical use of language is evident in the utterances: 'there is a fire in me'; 'That just kind of got really ignited'; 'You couldn't even see a spark of life'. **Question 5** The following discourse particles were used extensively by Kelly: 'That just kind of got really ignited, you know, not only in terms of myself' (data set 5); 'I started kind of like that state dependent thing' (data set 3); 'I just said to myself' (data set 5). These particles do not contribute to the truth-conditional content of the utterances in which they appear. However, they appear to function by weakening the force of certain of Kelly's utterances (see 'kind of like' above). On other occasions, their function appears to reflect some uncertainty on Kelly's part as a speaker and her need for reassurance from her addressee (see 'you know' above).

4.7 Bipolar disorder 2

Question 1 Data set 1: 'My life was blown to pieces, and I was not capable of mending it' (anaphoric reference). Data set 3: 'when I was just high I kind of was all those things' (unclear referent). **Question 2** Nancy uses the metaphor of a journey to describe her recovery from bipolar disorder. This metaphorical use of language is evident in the following utterances: 'all recovery means to me is not the kind of journey'; 'I have had a little bit of that nonlinear stuff back and forth, forward steps and back steps'; 'And they don't take anybody who isn't at the end of the road'. **Question 3** (a) 'a medical approach was always taken, and one that I accepted' (data set 4). (b) 'And they always did that' ('that' refers to the corrective actions taken by Nancy's family) (data set 1). (c) 'they knew I was nuts' (data set 3). (d) 'So that's the ending' (data set 5). (e) 'When I say not helped, I mean not significantly [helped]'. **Question 4** The following expressions suggest that Nancy is aware of the maxim of quantity: 'My recovery, in a nutshell, to me was . . . '; 'So very briefly, all recovery means to me . . . '; 'And my experience there, to make a long story short, I would say . . . '. Although Nancy appears to be aware of the need to attend to the quantity maxim, she does not succeed in producing a succinct account of her recovery from bipolar disorder. **Question 5** 'unlike my colleagues in the movement, as we call it' (data set 5); 'it's oversimplifying but not a great oversimplification to say that my manias . . . were extremely severe' (data set 2); 'I was what they call a non-responder to everything' (data set 4).

4.8 Personality disorder

Question 1 (a) 'And so I figure . . . ' (data set 4). (b) 'I ended up at the Betty Ford Center and it took me for a ride' (data set 1). (c) 'Since the new millennium I've lost two brothers' (data set 4). (d) 'my wife contracted cancer . . . she eventually died . . . I ended up at the Betty Ford Center' (data set 1). (e) 'He was just an all around good man, good husband, good grandpa' (data set 2). **Question 2** *Positive agency*: the speaker in the first extract in data set 1 describes positive life experiences which have just happened in the absence of his or her agency. *Negative agency*: the speaker in the second extract in data set 1 describes a series of negative life events over which he or she is characterised as having no control.

Question 3 Both extracts in data set 3 lack narrative coherence but for different reasons. The speaker in the first extract in data set 3 provides insufficient information to orient a hearer to a discrete time and place which would constitute a low point. The speaker in the second extract in data set 3 fails to integrate the described events with the theme of a high point in his or her life. **Question 4** A lack of communion is a feature of the first extract in data set 2, where the speaker is describing a lack of need for attachment or any other relationship with others. A lack of communion fulfilment is a feature of the second extract in data set 2, where the speaker is describing her need for a nurturing relationship with her husband which was subsequently thwarted by his premature death. **Question 5** The dominant theme of the extract in data set 4 is loss. This is manifested in the following utterances: 'my family's starting to die off'; 'I've lost two brothers and a sister'; 'my family is just disappearing'.

4.9   Emotional disturbance in children

Question 1 Mimi's mutism at school is likely to compromise the development of a range of pragmatic language skills. Three such skills are: (1) the use of speech acts – in the absence of spoken communication with her peers, Mimi will not gain experience of making requests of others, declining offers and invitations and soliciting information from others; (2) conversational rules – Mimi will also not gain experience of opening and closing conversations, taking turns with others, avoiding overlaps and dealing with pauses and silence; (3) topic management – Mimi will also not gain experience of selecting conversational topics of interest to her interlocutors, developing and terminating those topics. **Question 2** Although at the age of 9 years Mimi is still displaying significant syntactic and phonological errors, these linguistic deficits are likely to play at best a contributory rather than a causal role in Mimi's mutism. This is consistent with the diagnostic criteria for selective mutism in the fifth edition of the *Diagnostic and Statistical Manual of Mental Disorders*, which require that 'the disturbance is not better explained by a communication disorder' (American Psychiatric Association, 2013). **Question 3** Mimi's interpersonal relationship with her mother is described as being 'particularly enmeshed'. This will have adverse implications for the development of Mimi's pragmatic language skills. To the extent that Mimi's mother is speaking on her behalf, attending to her every need and dealing with other details in her life, Mimi will not be required to develop cognitive and language skills related to managing social relationships and negotiating difficult interpersonal relationships with others. These skills include the ability to attribute mental states (and particularly communicative intentions) to the minds of others (i.e. theory of mind) and the ability to tailor verbal utterances to accommodate the knowledge and mental states of others (i.e. pragmatics). **Question 4** The following are qualitative differences between Mimi's communication skills and the communication skills of children with ASD. (1) Mimi's lack of spoken communication occurs in certain contexts (e.g. at school), while a lack of spoken communication occurs in all contexts in children with ASD. (2) Even as Mimi does not use spoken communication at school, she is able to use gesture and written language. However, gesture and written language are also lacking or impaired in non-verbal children with ASD. (3) Mimi has normal social interaction skills as evidenced by the fact that she has a best friend and a close social relationship to her mother. Mimi's strong social impetus for communication is lacking in children with ASD. **Question 5** Even in the absence of spoken communication in school Mimi is able to make use of gesture and written language to communicate to others.

Speech and language therapists can harness gesture to ensure Mimi's continued development of pragmatic skills, as gestures are as effective as verbal utterances in conveying and interpreting communicative intentions. Teachers can harness Mimi's use of written language to aid the development of her academic skills in areas such as reading and spelling.

4.10 Behavioural disorders in children

Question 1 The two features of data set 1 which reveal Abraham's eagerness to communicate before his utterances have been adequately planned are (1) the repetition of conjunctions such as 'so' and 'then' at the start of Abraham's turns and (2) reformulations of utterances such as when he says 'because I because *when* I' and 'then I then *he*'. The former feature appears to buy Abraham some additional processing time in which to plan his utterance. The latter feature suggests the hurried production of language which is then inaccurate and has to be reformulated. Both features appear to be related to the behavioural characteristic of impulsivity in ADHD. **Question 2** The teacher may have expected Abraham to follow her utterance 'so you just threw it gently' with some type of confirmatory utterance like 'yes' or 'that's right'. Instead, Abraham hurriedly moves on to describe the next action in his story. The behavioural feature of inattention in ADHD may explain Abraham's omission in this case. He is not sufficiently attentive to the conversational expectations that are raised by the teacher's utterance. **Question 3** Adam reports two events – going to his cousin's house and returning home from snow tubing – in the incorrect temporal order. He reports going to his cousin's house *first* even though this happened *after* returning home from snow tubing. Adam's utterance violates the Gricean maxim of manner. **Question 4** The account of snow tubing is unclear for the following reasons. (1) Several words and phrases lack clear referents including personal pronouns (e.g. 'he spins you'), spatial expressions (e.g. 'up there') and directional terms (e.g. 'back up', 'down'). (2) Utterances are often incomplete (e.g. 'they put the hook inside [what?] and then . . .') or are reformulated mid-way (e.g. 'they have a machine that will they have a hooks that will'). (3) Descriptions are vague and use non-specific vocabulary (e.g. 'a little round thing'). **Question 5** (a) Use of direct reported speech, e.g. 'Then I said "look out"' (data set 1). (b) Use of anaphoric reference, e.g. 'you have eight tickets you give one of them' (data set 2). (c) Use of conjunctions that express a causal relationship between events, e.g. 'so he can play with it' (data set 1). (d) Use of conjunctions that express a temporal order between events, e.g. 'they put . . . the hook inside and then . . . it pulls you back up' (data set 2). (e) Comprehension of indirect speech acts, e.g. Adam comprehends the request in 'Can you tell us about snow tubing?' (data set 2).

Chapter 5: Pragmatics and discourse in other disorders and populations

Data analysis exercises

5.1 Early corrective heart surgery

Question 1 (a) James can make appropriate use of ellipsis, e.g. 'When I was three I did [go to the beach and go swimming]'. (b) James's non-verbal communication can contradict utterance meaning, e.g. James shakes his head 'no' in response to the interviewer's question about going to the beach and then goes on to say that he did go to the beach when he was three. (c) James contributes uninformative utterances, e.g. 'I went in the water' is uninformative given that James had previously said he went swimming. (d) James produces a statement of ignorance to foreclose narrative development, e.g. 'I don't know what happened again.' (e) James can provide a temporal context for the events in his narrative, e.g. 'When I was three I did.' **Question 2** (a) A lack of pronominal reference, e.g. 'And then it was it was this . . . ' (no referent for demonstrative pronoun). (b) Unclear semantic–logical links between events, e.g. 'Because that's why it did . . . ' (the causal meaning of this conjunction is inappropriate in this context). **Question 3** The two ways in which George adheres to narrative structure are as follows. (1) George opens his personal narrative with a statement of temporal context ('When I was a little boy . . . '). This statement performs the same function as 'Once upon a time . . . ' in a fictional narrative. (2) George recognises the need to conclude his narrative with some statement to the effect that his story is at an end. In this case, the end of the story *is* the end of the bee: 'that was the end of the bee'. **Question 4** In data set 2, George uses the two conjunctions 'and then' to express a temporal order on events: 'I weh with a bee and then it caught my ear'. Although Darryl in data set 3 uses the simpler conjunction 'and' to relate events, his repetition of this conjunction across several clauses serves to confer a temporal order on the events expressed in those clauses: 'I went by him and he . . . and I hit him and he went "Ahhh".' The hearer assumes Darryl to be adhering to the manner maxim in reporting events in the temporal order in which they occurred. **Question 5** In data set 1, the interviewer repeats part of the child's prior turn when he utters 'When you were three?' This same pattern of repetition occurs twice in data set 3 when the interviewer states 'He went "Ahhh"?' and 'Real hard'. However, the child with ECHS in data set 1 is only able to respond to this repetition by confirming it (he nods 'yes'). However, the typically developing child Darryl in data set 3 is able to use the interviewer's repetition as an opportunity for topic development. Each of the interviewer's repetitions in this data set is followed by the contribution of new information and not by a confirmation of the type used by James in data set 1. In this way, Darryl responds to 'He went "Ahhh"?' with 'Real hard' and to 'Real hard?' with 'With his teeth'.

5.2   Functional illiteracy

Question 1 The following discourse features contribute to the success of the narrative in data set 1. (a) Use of pronominal reference as a form of cohesion, e.g. 'the bear puts a plaster on his tail and the fish the same. They're both swimming along quietly.' (b) Use of direct reported speech, e.g. 'he asks himself "What's that yellow thing?"' (c) Use of indefinite noun phrases to introduce characters into the hearer's discourse representation, e.g. 'There's a bear having a nice quiet swim.' (d) Narrative engages with the cognitive and affective states of the characters, e.g. 'the bear is very pleased' (affective state); 'a big fish . . . wants to gobble them both up' (cognitive state). (e) Several linguistic devices contribute dramatic tension to the narrative. These include repetition (e.g. 'what's going on, what's going on?'), use of adverbs (e.g. 'suddenly') and phrases (e.g. 'with a start'). **Question 2** The adult with functional illiteracy in data set 2 succeeds in reporting all the main events in the story. However, the narrative is nonetheless dull and uninteresting on account of three features. (a) Events are merely juxtaposed, with no causal or temporal relationships expressed between them. (b) The characters lack animation on account of the absence of direct reported speech. (c) There is no report given of how the characters experience the various events in the story. For example, we are not told how the dog feels upon having his tail bitten by the fish. This should be compared with the narrative in data set 3 where we are told that the bear (actually dog) is hurt at having his tail bitten. **Question 3** (a) Use of pronouns with unclear referents, e.g. 'And then suddenly, he hurt . . . ' (does 'he' refer to the fish or to the bear?) (b) Use of cataphoric reference, e.g. 'he has a think, Baby Fish, he has a think'. (c) Use of poor information ordering, e.g. the information we need to establish the referent of 'he' in 'And then suddenly, he hurt . . . ' does not occur until after 'he hurt'. That information is *the fish bites the tail of a little bear*. (d) Use of temporal conjunctions to relate events, e.g. the conjunctions 'and then' are used seven times in this extract to relate events. The excessive use of these conjunctions appears to exclude other relationships (e.g. causality) through which events can be related. (e) Use of anaphoric reference, e.g. 'And then the bear, he bites the tail at the fish'. **Question 4** (a) Definite noun phrases (e.g. 'the tail') are used for the first mention of entities, prompting a hearer to ask 'what tail?' (b) Incomplete information, e.g. 'He sees the tail [of what?]' (c) Pronouns are routinely used in advance of their referents, e.g. 'There he's swimming the little fish'. (d) Repetitive language, e.g. 'he's swimming . . . he's swimming . . . He bites the tail . . . he bites the tail'. (e) Events are not related causally or temporally but are merely juxtaposed, e.g. 'He sees the tail. He's surprised. He bites the tail'. **Question 5** The feature in question is the use of metalinguistic discourse by the narrator. This occurs when the narrator is querying the name (dog/bear/something else) that should be given to one of the main characters in the story. The reason the use of metalinguistic discourse is problematic for narrative development is that it marks a suspension of the primary, narrative discourse.

5.3   Hearing loss

Question 1 (a) Chelsea is able to respond to yes–no questions, e.g. she responds 'no' to the question 'Is it a blouse?' (b) Chelsea is able to express gratitude, e.g. she utters 'Thank you!' (c) Chelsea is able to produce statements, e.g. she is able to communicate that the interviewer received a scarf for her birthday by uttering 'you . . . collar'. (d) Chelsea is able to confirm her understanding of her interlocutor's utterance, e.g. she repeats a single word such as 'Think?' from her interlocutor's utterance to confirm her understanding. (e) Chelsea is able to express mental states, e.g. she utters 'Don't think'. **Question 2** Three examples: (1) 'Think?' (shakes head) (2) 'Book? Don't think.' (3) 'Blouse? No.' This pattern allows Chelsea to indicate her understanding of the interviewer's question and then respond to the question either verbally as in (2) and (3), or non-verbally as in (1). **Question 3** (a) *True*: Chelsea understands the interviewer's utterance 'That is named "turquoise".' (b) *True*: Chelsea understands that 'it' in the utterance 'Is it a blouse?' refers to the gift. (c) *False*: Chelsea understands that 'that' in the utterance 'That is named "turquoise"' refers to the colour of the jewellery. (d) *False*: Chelsea does appreciate that the interviewer is attempting to be humorous when she states that there is no gift after all. (e) *True*: Chelsea communicates a response of 'don't know' when she shakes her head in response to the question 'What do you think it is?' **Question 4** The three non-verbal behaviours of Chelsea which have a communicative function are: (1) she shakes her head; (2) she laughs; and (3) she hugs the interviewer. By shaking her head, Chelsea is communicating that she does not know what the gift is. By laughing, Chelsea is indicating her appreciation of the interviewer's humour. By hugging the interviewer, Chelsea is indicating her gratitude to the interviewer for the gift. Only (3) supplements a verbal response on Chelsea's part, as Chelsea had already verbally indicated her gratitude by uttering 'Thank you!' Both (1) and (2) take the place of verbal responses such as 'Don't know' and 'That's funny', respectively. **Question 5** There is limited opportunity for topic development on Chelsea's part in this exchange. This is on account of two reasons. Firstly, the entire exchange is oriented to the task of unwrapping the gift and trying to guess its identity. Secondly, the interviewer largely controls topic development through her posing of questions to Chelsea which require minimal or one-word responses. Chelsea is thereby restricted in the contribution that she can make to the exchange. However, even within these limitations of the exchange, Chelsea is able to contribute to topic development. When Chelsea utters 'you . . . collar', the interviewer is able to use this utterance as the basis of her own turn, an account of how she (the interviewer) received a scarf for her birthday.

5.4   Augmentative and alternative communication

Question 1 (a) A misunderstands the teacher's question 'How did the clay feel in your hands?' (b) A makes a rolling motion to indicate what she did to the clay in her hands. (c) A fails to maintain topic relevance when she begins to talk about her brother Kevin. (d) A engages in self-initiated repair in 'Not going. Kevin not going.' (e) A produces an under-informative utterance when she fails to say where Kevin is going to. **Question 2** Child S is the only child to make use of discourse cohesion. Even then, S only makes use of a simple form of cohesion in the form of the additive conjunction 'and'. This form of cohesion precludes the expression of causal and temporal relations between events in discourse. **Question 3** (a) Child S in data set 4 creates humour when she adds 'Throw up' to the teacher's utterance 'She ate them up and . . . ' (b) Child S in data set 4 uses discourse deixis in the utterance 'This sentence in my story will be the end.' (c) Child D in data set 3 makes poor communicative use of pointing, as evidenced by the teacher's difficulties in understanding D's pointing to both icons and the photograph. (d) Child S in data set 4 uses pronominal reference appropriately in the utterance 'She ate them up.' The teacher's response indicates that he or she can establish the referents of 'she' and 'them'. (e) Child H in data set 6 makes good communicative use of head nodding. This child is able to use head nodding to both confirm and correct the teacher's interpretation of her message. **Question 4** The teachers use the following types of utterance as a means of accommodating to the limited output of these children. (1) The teachers use utterances which summarise their understanding of what the children are attempting to communicate. These utterances take the form of prosodic questions which only require the child to indicate his agreement or disagreement with a particular understanding, e.g. 'They are going in the door?' (data set 6). (2) The teachers use utterances which cue the production of a target word, e.g. 'And a silly what?' (data set 5). (3) The teachers pose largely yes–no questions ('Did you put something in the pot?' in data set 3), and questions that require only a single-word response ('How did the clay feel in your hands?' in data set 1). **Question 5** In data set 4, the teacher encourages expansion of the child's output by combining two of S.'s utterances in 'She ate them up and . . .'. S is aware of the teacher's expectation that the utterance should be expanded, and achieves this expansion by adding 'Throw up'.

5.5   Aging and the elderly

Question 1 (a) 'bringing the little <u>ones</u> something to eat' (referent of 'ones' (*chicks*) only introduced subsequently). (b) 'the lady's looking at <u>the man</u>' (definite noun phrase used on first mention instead of 'a man'). (c) 'I can't hear and <u>this other one</u> does' (unclear referent). (d) '<u>they</u>'re shaking a plum tree' (no referent). (e) 'a woman's pointing to a little bird drinking up <u>there</u>' (no referent of 'there'). **Question 2** The adult omits the following information from his or her narrative: (1) the man climbs the tree and (2) the branch of the tree breaks. **Question 3** (a) At the end of the narrative, the speaker introduces 'the little birds' again. (b) The speaker uses 'sleeping' to describe the man lying on the ground, and 'police' in place of paramedics or ambulance workers. (c) 'I don't <u>know</u> what the man <u>wants</u> to do with the birds'. (d) 'the lady's looking at the man it must be to, so that . . . I don't know what the man'. (e) '<u>the gentleman</u> fell down <u>he</u> was . . . in the tree'. **Question 4** The speaker is repetitive in his or her description of feeding the birds: 'bringing the little ones something to eat, bringing the chicks something to eat . . . the woman feeding the little birds . . . the little birds can't find anything to eat'. **Question 5** Temporal and causal relations between events are not clearly represented in this narrative. For example, the speaker does not indicate any causal relation between the man's fall and his subsequent removal to hospital. In fact, the latter event is presented somewhat abruptly in 'here he is now in the . . . bed of the hospital'. Temporal relations between events are misrepresented. For example, the narrative reports first that the man fell down and only after that indicates that he was in the tree: 'the gentleman fell down he was in . . . the tree'.

Glossary

acoustic neuroma: a benign tumour that is also known as vestibular schwannoma. Acoustic neuroma is the most commonly occurring tumour in the head and neck. When of sufficient size, it can appear on a CAT or MRI scan, but is often detectable before then using an auditory brainstem response test. Symptoms include hearing loss, tinnitus and imbalance.

aetiology: the medical or other causes of a disorder. Causes may range from organic problems (e.g. neurodegeneration in Alzheimer's disease) through to psychological and behavioural factors (e.g. the communication impairment in selective mutism). Many communication disorders have a mixed aetiology, with organic, psychological and behavioural factors all contributing to the development of these disorders.

agnosia: a condition in which an affected individual is unable to recognise visual stimuli (visual agnosia) or auditory stimuli (auditory agnosia) despite having no sensory impairment (e.g. a patient will have a normal audiogram). If the recognition of spoken words is compromised, a verbal auditory agnosia is diagnosed. If the recognition of environmental sounds is disrupted, a non-verbal auditory agnosia is diagnosed. Verbal auditory agnosia is one of the first presenting signs of Landau–Kleffner syndrome.

agrammatism: a feature of non-fluent aphasia (hence, term 'agrammatic' aphasia) in which the speaker retains content words but omits function words and inflectional morphemes from his or her speech. Verbal output has the appearance of a telegram, e.g. 'Man . . . walk . . . dog' for *The man is walking the dog*.

AIDS dementia complex: also referred to as AIDS-related dementia, AIDS encephalopathy and HIV encephalopathy. The condition is characterised by a progressive deterioration in cognitive function, including language, which is accompanied by motor abnormalities and behavioural changes. The association of cognitive changes with motor and behavioural signs is denoted by the word 'complex'.

Alzheimer's disease: a neurodegenerative disease that is the most frequent cause of dementia. Amyloid plaques and neurofibrillary tangles develop in the brains of AD sufferers.

amyotrophic lateral sclerosis: see *motor neurone disease*.

anomia: the inability of an adult with aphasia to access the spoken names of objects and concepts despite having the articulatory skills to produce these names if they could be retrieved. If this inability occurs alongside normal comprehension and fluent sentence production, then the patient is described as having anomic aphasia.

aphasia (dysphasia): an acquired language disorder in which the expression and/or reception of language (spoken, written and signed) is compromised. Aphasia can be broadly classified as fluent and non-fluent types. Fluent aphasia is further subdivided into Wernicke's, anomic, conduction and transcortical sensory aphasia. Non-fluent aphasia is further subdivided into Broca's and transcortical motor aphasia. A further non-fluent aphasia – global aphasia – is characterised by severe impairment of all language functions.

apraxia (dyspraxia): a motor disorder which can affect speech production (verbal dyspraxia), the movement of limbs (limb dyspraxia), the movement of oral structures (oral dyspraxia), etc. The dominant terms to describe the speech disorder in children and adults are childhood apraxia of speech and apraxia of speech, respectively.

attention deficit hyperactivity disorder: a disorder that is diagnosed on the basis of symptoms of inattention and hyperactivity–impulsivity. There are three main subtypes of ADHD: a combined type; a predominantly inattentive type; a predominantly hyperactive–impulsive type.

augmentative and alternative communication: when spoken communication skills are severely impaired and are unlikely to improve, a type of AAC may be considered for use with a client. AAC may take high- and low-tech forms such as a communication board attached to a client's wheelchair or the use of synthesised speech output.

autism spectrum disorder: a neurodevelopmental disorder in which there are persistent deficits in social communication and social interaction across multiple contexts and restricted, repetitive patterns of behaviour, interests, or activities. Symptoms must be present in the early developmental period and must cause clinically significant impairment in social, occupational, or other important areas of functioning. These deficits must not be better explained by intellectual disability, which frequently occurs alongside autism spectrum disorder.

Babinski sign: the Babinski reflex occurs in children up to 2 years old. When the sole of the foot is firmly stroked, the big toe moves upwards or towards the top surface of the foot and the other toes fan out. As children mature, the reflex disappears. Its presence in an adult is a sign of neurological disorder.

benign Rolandic epilepsy: also known as benign childhood epilepsy with centrotemporal spikes. Benign Rolandic epilepsy is the most common idiopathic focal epilepsy in children. The condition is described as 'benign' because of the absence of neurological deficits, infrequent focal somatosensory or motor seizures which occur predominantly during sleep, reasonable response to medication and spontaneous resolution before 15 to 16 years of age.

bipolar disorder: formerly known as manic depression, this is a psychiatric disorder in which the patient's mood alters between manic episodes (characterised by euphoria, restlessness, poor judgement and risk-taking behaviour), depressive episodes (characterised by depression, anxiety and hopelessness), and episodes of normal mood (known as euthymia).

birth anoxia: a lack of oxygen during the birth process. Anoxia can cause cerebral damage in conditions such as cerebral palsy.

bradykinesia: slowness of movement. Bradykinesia is one of the cardinal manifestations of Parkinson's disease.

cerebral palsy: a neurodevelopmental disorder that results in impairment of gross and fine motor skills, speech production included. Cerebral palsy is caused by a range of factors in the pre-, peri- and post-natal periods which cause damage to the brain's motor centres.

cerebrovascular accident: the medical term for a stroke. CVAs may be caused by a blood clot (embolus) in one of the blood vessels in the brain or leading to the brain (embolic stroke) or by a haemorrhage (haemorrhagic stroke) in one of these vessels.

circumlocution: means literally to talk ('locution') around ('circum') a word. Circumlocutions are used by aphasic speakers when they cannot retrieve a target word and stutterers who are trying to avoid words that will cause them to block.

cochlear implant: a surgically implanted electronic device which is coupled to external components and provides useful hearing to children and adults with severe-to-profound sensorineural hearing loss.

cognitive–communication disorder: the term applied to any communication disorder which is related to cognitive deficits. The language and communication impairments of clients with traumatic brain injury and right-hemisphere damage are described as cognitive–communication disorders.

computerised axial tomography (CAT): a technique in which an X-ray source produces a narrow, fan-shaped beam of X-rays to irradiate a section of the body. On a single rotation of the X-ray source around the body, many different 'snapshots' are taken. These are then reconstructed by a computer into a cross-sectional image of internal organs and tissues for each complete rotation.

conduct disorder: a disorder in which an individual displays a persistent and repetitive pattern of behaviour that violates the basic rights of others or age-appropriate societal norms or rules. Behaviours include aggression to people and animals and destruction of property. The behaviour disturbance causes clinically significant impairment in social, academic or occupational functioning.

context: any aspect of a language user's knowledge, physical environment and social relationships to others may shape the production and interpretation of utterances and form part of their context. These aspects include physical context (e.g. setting of a conversation), social context (e.g. social standing of speaker and hearer), epistemic context (background knowledge of speaker and hearer), and linguistic context (e.g. preceding utterances in a conversation).

conventional implicature: a type of implied meaning that is attached by convention to particular lexical items. For example, the word 'but' in the utterance 'Frank is overweight but healthy' generates an implicature to the effect that it was not expected that Frank would be healthy.

cooperative principle: a principle proposed by Grice to capture certain rational expectations between participants in verbal and non-verbal exchanges. This principle is the basis upon which speakers and hearers can derive implied meanings from utterances in conversation.

Creutzfeldt–Jakob disease: a neurodegenerative disease characterised by spongiform change in the brain, neuronal loss and proliferation of astrocytes (specialised glial cells that contiguously line the entire central nervous system). The disease has sporadic, familial and iatrogenic forms and, more recently, a variant form which is related to BSE in cattle. Affected individuals develop dementia.

cri du chat syndrome: a rare genetic disorder which is associated with a partial deletion on the short arm of chromosome 5. The disorder is characterised by a high-pitched cry in infancy and childhood, from which the syndrome derives its name (literally, 'cry of the cat'). Children with this syndrome present with physical and cognitive problems, including malocclusion, hyper- and hypotonia, delayed motor development, microcephaly, mild-to-profound intellectual disability, a short attention span, and a range of problematic behaviours (e.g. hyperactivity, aggression).

cytomegalovirus: the most common cause of congenital infection in the US. Congenital cytomegalovirus (CMV) infection is the leading cause of sensorineural hearing loss in young children and can also cause significant intellectual disability. CMV is also a common opportunistic infection in individuals with HIV infection.

deixis: linguistic expressions that can be used to 'point' to aspects of spatiotemporal, social and discoursal context. There are five types of deixis: personal, social, temporal, spatial and discourse deixis.

dementia: a deterioration in higher cortical functions (e.g. language, memory) that can be caused by a range of diseases (e.g. vascular disease, Alzheimer's disease), infections (e.g. HIV infection) and lifestyle (e.g. alcohol-related dementia).

derailment: a feature of formal thought disorder in schizophrenia, in which utterances slip or shift from one topic to another without bridging concepts.

Down's syndrome: a chromosomal disorder that results from an extra chromosome 21. This additional chromosome may be found in all cells (trisomy 21), in some cells (mosaic) or attached to another chromosome (translocation). Down's syndrome results in physical problems (e.g. heart defects) and cognitive difficulties (intellectual disability).

dysarthria: a speech disorder that is caused by damage to the central and peripheral nervous systems. Dysarthria can be developmental or acquired in nature and affects articulation, resonation, respiration, phonation and prosody.

dyslexia: a reading impairment which can be found in children (developmental dyslexia) and in adults (acquired dyslexia). There are different types of dyslexia. For example, the individual with deep dyslexia can read words with concrete meanings more easily than words with abstract meanings. In surface dyslexia, which is often found in semantic dementia, the reading of non-words is preserved while the reading of irregular words is impaired.

dysphagia: the term given to a swallowing disorder in children and adults. Dysphagia can arise following a stroke (neurogenic dysphagia), as a result of structural causes (e.g. a tumour), as a complication of surgery (iatrogenic dysphagia) or on account of psychological factors (psychogenic dysphagia). In most cases, the disorder can be managed by dietary and other modifications. When dysphagia is severe, non-oral feeding is instituted as the only safe method of feeding.

echolalia: the repetition of another speaker's utterance either immediately (immediate echolalia) or after several conversational turns (delayed echolalia). Echolalia is found in individuals with autism and in some speakers with aphasia.

electroencephalography (EEG): a non-invasive technique in which the brain's electrical activity is recorded by means of electrodes placed on the scalp. Given that this electrical activity is small – it is measured in microvolts – the signal must be amplified before a resultant trace can be made. Although EEG has good temporal resolution (brain activity can be recorded almost as soon as it happens), the technique cannot locate the source of a signal. Functional MRI (fMRI) has better spatial resolution than EEG.

emotional and behavioural disorder: a disorder in which affected individuals commonly engage in behaviours (e.g. verbal and physical aggression) that negatively influence their ability to negotiate peer and adult relationships and their educational experience.

epidemiology: the study of the prevalence and incidence of a disease or disorder. Prevalence describes the total number of cases of a disease or disorder which exist in a population. Incidence captures the number of newly diagnosed cases of a disease or disorder, typically within a year.

executive dysfunction: executive functions are a group of cognitive skills which are essential to goal-directed behaviour (e.g. planning ability, mental flexibility) and which are believed to be mediated in large part by the brain's frontal lobes. Impairment of these cognitive skills is related to communication difficulties in clients who sustain a traumatic brain injury.

felicity condition: a condition on the appropriate performance of a speech act. Felicity conditions specify who must say and do what and in what circumstances in order for a speech act to be performed felicitously. If these conditions are not met, a speech act is infelicitous.

flight of ideas: a feature of manic discourse in which topical shifts are accompanied by pressured speech (excessive speech produced at a rapid rate) and may include wordplay; rarely found in schizophrenia.

foetal alcohol syndrome: a set of birth defects caused by pre-natal exposure of the foetus to alcohol; characteristics include abnormal facial features, growth deficiencies and central nervous system defects (e.g. intellectual disability); the phenotypic expression of this syndrome is highly variable in accordance with factors such as the amount of alcohol consumed and the duration of exposure.

formal thought disorder: a core symptom of schizophrenia in which there is a disturbance in the logical connections between ideas. Features of formal thought disorder include poverty of (content of) speech, derailment and tangentiality.

fragile X syndrome: the most common inherited form of intellectual disability. It is caused by the fragile X mental retardation 1 (FMR1) gene on the X chromosome and is more commonly seen in males.

frontotemporal dementia: a group of dementias which is associated with a range of neuropathologies including motor neurone disease, corticobasal degeneration, Pick's disease, progressive supranuclear palsy, Alzheimer's disease, Lewy body variant, prion disease and vascular dementia. Frontotemporal dementia includes a behavioural variant, semantic dementia and progressive non-fluent aphasia.

generalised conversational implicature: a type of implied meaning that does not require any special context for its generation. For example, the indefinite article 'a' in 'Bill is meeting a woman this evening' generates an implicature to the effect that the woman Bill is meeting is not his mother, sister, wife, etc.

glossomania: a feature of schizophrenic language, also known as clanging, in which a speaker produces long sequences of utterances in which sound or meaning associations are developed.

hemiplegia: a congenital or acquired condition in which there is paralysis of one side of the body. In a less serious condition known as hemiparesis, one side of the body is weak. Hemiplegia and hemiparesis are found in a number of the clinical groups managed by speech–language pathologists, including children with cerebral palsy and traumatic brain injury and adults with aphasia.

hypernasality: excessive nasal resonance in speech which may be caused by velopharyngeal incompetence; a feature of cleft palate speech and dysarthric speech.

hypotonia: decreased muscle tone. Hypotonia is a feature of some dysarthrias (e.g. flaccid dysarthria) and certain syndromes (e.g. Prader–Willi syndrome).

implicature: a type of implied or implicated meaning that goes beyond what is said by an utterance. Grice recognised the following types of implicature: generalised conversational implicatures (includes scalar implicatures), particularised conversational implicatures and conventional implicatures.

indirect speech act: a speech act can be performed directly (e.g. 'Open the window!') or indirectly (e.g. 'Can you open the window?'). The choice of speech act is determined by politeness considerations, amongst other factors. An indirect speech act is often produced by questioning one of the preparatory conditions on the performance of a speech act (in the case of the above directive, that the hearer *can* undertake the requested action).

intellectual disability: another term for mental retardation or learning disability (the latter is used in the UK). It applies to children and adults with an intelligence quotient (IQ) below 70 such as occurs in a range of syndromes (e.g. Down's syndrome) and other clinical disorders (e.g. autism spectrum disorder).

Landau–Kleffner syndrome: also known as acquired epileptic aphasia or aphasia with convulsive disorder; a rare disorder in which a child's language skills regress, either suddenly or gradually, in the presence of seizures.

Lewy body dementia: a form of dementia which shares clinical and pathological features with both Alzheimer's disease and Parkinson's disease. The condition is caused by the accumulation of Lewy bodies (aggregations of alpha-synuclein protein) inside the nuclei of neurones in certain regions of the brain. In dementia with Lewy bodies, deficits of attention, memory and executive function can be more severe than those found in Parkinson's disease dementia.

magnetic resonance imaging (MRI): a technique that employs a magnetic field and a radiofrequency pulse to create a magnetic resonance image. MRI has advantages over other imaging techniques. It is non-invasive, uses non-ionising radiation and produces high-quality images of soft tissue resolution in any imaging plane.

mania: an abnormal and persistently elevated, expansive or irritable mood. This mood disturbance must be accompanied by other symptoms among which are included inflated self-esteem or grandiosity, psychomotor agitation, flight of ideas and pressure of speech.

maternal rubella: a viral infection which has severe consequences for a developing foetus. Although the rubella virus can affect the foetus at any stage of pregnancy, defects are rarely noted after the 16th week of gestation. The most common defects in the congenital rubella syndrome are hearing loss, intellectual disability, cardiac malformations and eye defects. The hearing loss is profound and sensorineural in nature.

maxim: a proposal of Grice in which four maxims of quality, quantity, relation and manner are used to give effect to the cooperative principle. Maxims can be flouted or not observed in various ways, often with a view to generating implied meanings.

meningitis: a bacterial or viral infection in which there is inflammation of the meninges, the membranes which envelope the brain and spinal cord. Meningitis is a significant cause of developmental and acquired speech, language and hearing disorders.

motor neurone disease: a progressive neurodegenerative disease in which there is a widespread and often rapid deterioration in upper and lower motor neurones. Motor neurone disease (MND) affects all aspects of speech production and eventually swallowing and feeding. There are three types of MND: amyotrophic lateral sclerosis, progressive bulbar palsy and progressive muscular atrophy.

multiple sclerosis: a neurodegenerative disease in which the myelin sheath which envelopes the axons of neurones is destroyed in a process known as demyelination. There are three types of multiple sclerosis: relapsing remitting, primary progressive and secondary progressive. Multiple sclerosis can cause dysarthria and swallowing problems. Increasingly, cognitive and language problems are being identified in this clinical population.

multiple subpial transection: a surgical procedure which is used in the treatment of Landau–Kleffner syndrome. Tangential, or horizontal, intracortical fibres are severed, while the vertical fibre connections of both incoming and outgoing nerve pathways are preserved. The selective disruption of neurones which have horizontal linkages eliminates the capacity of the treated cortex to produce epileptiform activity.

muscular dystrophy: the most common neurological disorder after cerebral palsy to result in developmental dysarthria. All striated muscles, including those of the speech mechanism, atrophy and weaken in this disorder.

mutism: speechlessness, which can have a neurological or behavioural aetiology. Mutism is a feature of many clinical conditions including childhood posterior fossa tumour, traumatic brain injury, dementia and Landau–Kleffner syndrome.

neologism: means literally new ('neo') word ('logism'). Neologisms are found in aphasia and schizophrenia (e.g. a schizophrenic speaker who utters 'geshinker').

otitis media: an infection of the middle ear that is commonly known as 'glue ear'. Otitis media can cause conductive hearing loss and repeated episodes can compromise speech development in children.

Parkinson's disease: a neurodegenerative disease which is caused by the loss of cells that produce dopamine (a neurotransmitter substance) in the substantia nigra of the brain. There are four forms of parkinsonism: idiopathic Parkinson's, multiple system atrophy, progressive supranuclear palsy, and drug-induced parkinsonism. Dysarthria is commonly seen in Parkinson's disease, with reduced vocal intensity a common and early feature of the disorder.

particularised conversational implicature: a type of implied meaning that requires a particular context for its generation. This meaning is recovered through the combined operation of the cooperative principle and maxims.

perseveration: the repetition of a linguistic form (word, phrase, etc.) beyond the point where it is appropriate. Perseveration is a feature of the spoken output of several types of clients with communication disorders, including adults with aphasia and patients with schizophrenia.

pervasive developmental disorder: see *autism spectrum disorder*.

phonemic paraphasia: a language error in which sounds are substituted, added, or rearranged so that the uttered form has a sound resemblance to the target word (e.g. 'buckboard' for *cupboard*); a feature of aphasia in adults.

posterior fossa tumour: the posterior fossa is a small space in the skull which is found near the brainstem and cerebellum. The growth of a tumour in this area can block the flow of cerebrospinal fluid and increase pressure on the brain and spinal cord. Posterior fossa tumours account for half of all brain tumours in children. Mutism, dysarthria and dysphagia are associated with surgery for these tumours.

poverty of content of speech: spoken output which conveys little content or meaning despite being of an acceptable quantity or amount; a feature of schizophrenic language.

poverty of speech: also known as alogia. It describes the substantially reduced verbal output that is a negative symptom of schizophrenia.

Prader–Willi syndrome: a deletion of the long arm of paternal chromosome 15 which is usually associated with mild intellectual disability. Individuals with this syndrome are distinguished by their voracious appetite (hyperphagia). Early, severe hypotonia can cause articulation problems, feeding difficulties and hypernasality due to velopharyngeal insufficiency. Language, particularly expressive language, is generally delayed.

pragmatic language impairment: a successor to the term 'semantic–pragmatic disorder'. It describes a subgroup of children with SLI in which there are marked difficulties with the pragmatics of language.

pressured speech: excessive speech which is produced at a rapid rate and is difficult to interrupt. It is one of the features of speech in hypomania and mania but rarely occurs in schizophrenia.

presupposition: a term used to describe information which is assumed, taken for granted or in the background of an utterance. Presuppositions reduce the amount of information that a speaker must explicitly state and are triggered by certain lexical items and constructions.

primary progressive aphasia: a slowly progressive aphasia which occurs initially in the absence of generalised dementia. As speech and language impairments in primary progressive aphasia (PPA) worsen over time, patients begin to exhibit more of the classical symptoms of dementia. PPA is associated with a number of neuropathologies including Alzheimer's disease, frontotemporal dementia, Lewy body dementia and vascular dementia. Three subtypes of PPA are recognised: non-fluent/agrammatic, logopenic and semantic PPA.

prognosis: the probability or risk of an individual developing a particular state of health (an outcome) over a specific period of time given that individual's clinical and non-clinical profile. An outcome may include an event such as death or a quantity such as disease progression.

progressive non-fluent aphasia: a form of frontotemporal dementia in which a person's ability to produce fluent and grammatically well-formed speech is severely compromised. Agrammatism, effortful, slowed speech output, phonemic paraphasias and articulatory struggle are all present. Patients display difficulty comprehending syntactically complex sentences in the context of spared single-word comprehension and object knowledge. The condition evolves to complete mutism.

proposition: a unit of meaning expressed by a sentence or utterance and which can be true or false. Traditionally, propositional meaning has been studied in semantics. Increasingly, theorists are recognising a role for pragmatic factors in propositional meaning.

psychosis: a condition in which there is a loss of contact with reality, delusions (the holding of false and bizarre beliefs), and hallucinations (the perception of things which do not exist). Psychosis is a feature of several mental illnesses including schizophrenia and bipolar disorder.

right-hemisphere language disorder: stroke-induced and other lesions in the right hemisphere of the brain produce a different pattern of language impairment from that which occurs in left-hemisphere damage; while structural langauage is often intact, significant impairments in pragmatics and discourse can compromise many aspects of communication.

scalar implicature: a type of generalised conversational implicature that is generated by a set of terms which differ in informational strength. For example, the word *some* in the utterance 'The thief stole some of the jewels' generates the implicature that the thief did not steal all the jewels (*some* is semantically weaker than *all*).

schizophrenia: a serious mental illness which is diagnosed on the basis of positive and negative symptoms. Positive symptoms include thought disorder, delusions and hallucinations (mostly auditory). Negative symptoms include affective flattening, poverty of speech, apathy, avolition and social withdrawal.

selective mutism: one of the emotional and behavioural disorders in which an affected child fails to communicate in a specific context (e.g. at school) despite doing so effectively in other contexts (e.g. at home). The failure to communicate is not on account of inadequate speech and language skills, although these may also be present.

semantic dementia: a form of frontotemporal dementia in which there is progressive bilateral degeneration of the temporal lobes. The most pronounced feature of this form of dementia is degradation of semantic knowledge which is evident across all modalities (e.g. written and spoken language) and modes of input and output (e.g. comprehension and expression).

semantic paraphasia: a language error in which a word that is semantically related to the target form is produced (e.g. 'ear' for *eye*); a feature of aphasia in adults.

sensorineural hearing loss: a hearing loss which is related to cochlear damage, impairment of the auditory pathway to the brain and damage of the auditory cortices in the brain; possible causes include infections such as meningitis, trauma and cerebrovascular accidents.

social communication: describes any form of communication the purpose of which is to establish, facilitate or maintain social relationships with others. Social communication depends on a range of linguistic and cognitive skills in the areas of pragmatics, social perception and social cognition.

specific language impairment: a severe developmental language disorder in children. SLI has been described as a diagnosis by exclusion, as language impairment occurs in the absence of hearing loss, craniofacial anomaly or intellectual disability (i.e. a range of factors known to cause language disorder).

speech act: a term used by Austin and later Searle to describe utterances which perform acts or actions. Both Austin and Searle recognised different types of speech acts such as assertives (e.g. statements) and directives (e.g. requests).

stroke: see *cerebrovascular accident*.

Sturge–Weber syndrome: a sporadic, congenital neurocutaneous disorder characterised by a port-wine stain, abnormal capillary venous vessels in the leptomeninges (the inner two meninges – arachnoid membrane and pia mater – which envelop the brain) and choroid (the layer of blood vessels and connective tissue between the white of the eye (sclera) and retina), glaucoma, seizures, stroke and intellectual disability.

stuttering: also known as stammering; a fluency disorder which is characterised by word- and syllable-initial iterations (repetitions) and perseverations (prolongations). Stuttering occurs in developmental, acquired (mostly neurogenic) and psychogenic forms.

theory of mind: the cognitive ability to attribute mental states (e.g. beliefs, knowledge) both to one's own mind and to the minds of others. Theory of mind deficits are a feature of many disorders in which there are significant communication problems including autism spectrum disorder and schizophrenia.

traumatic brain injury: injury caused by an external force. There are two forms of traumatic brain injury: in an open or penetrating head injury, the skull is fractured or otherwise breached by a missile; in a closed head injury, the brain is damaged while the skull remains intact.

velopharyngeal incompetence: the failure of the velopharyngeal port to close adequately during speech production. VPI can be caused by structural anomalies (e.g. a short velum or excessively capacious pharynx) or by neurological impairment (e.g. an immobile velum after a stroke).

weak central coherence: a type of cognitive processing, typically seen in autism, in which there is a preference for parts over wholes. Applied to language, the child with autism may be unable to extract information from context and use it to make a global coherence inference about a character's action in a story.

Williams syndrome: a rare genetic disorder in which there is a deletion of 26 contiguous genes on chromosome 7q11.23. This genetic defect gives rise to intellectual disability and physical anomalies including dysmorphic facial features, elastin arteriopathy, short stature, connective tissue abnormalities and infantile hypercalcemia; the full-scale intelligence quotient is usually in the 50s to 60s with a range of 40–85.

Wolf–Hirschhorn syndrome: a multiple malformation disorder caused by a deletion of a portion of the short arm of chromosome 4. The syndrome is characterised by abnormal craniofacial features, severe intellectual disability, seizures, congenital heart malformations, microcephaly, failure to thrive and prenatal-onset growth retardation.

word-finding difficulty: an expressive language problem in which an individual cannot produce a target word and may substitute a vague term (e.g. thing, stuff) or engage in circumlocution (i.e. talk around the target word); a feature of many communication disorders including aphasia in adults.

References

Adams, C. 2005. 'Social communication intervention for school-age children: rationale and description', *Seminars in Speech and Language* **26**:3, 181–8.

Adler, J. M., Chin, E. D., Kolisetty, A. P. and Oltmanns, T. F. 2012. 'The distinguishing characteristics of narrative identity in adults with features of borderline personality disorder: an empirical investigation', *Journal of Personality Disorders* **26**:4, 498–512.

American Psychiatric Association 2013. *Diagnostic and statistical manual of mental disorders*, Washington, DC: American Psychiatric Association.

Barrett, J. 1998. *Old McDonald had an apartment house*, New York, NY: Atheneum.

Bastiaanse, R. 1995. 'Broca's aphasia: a syntactic and/or a morphological disorder? A case study', *Brain and Language* **48**:1, 1–32.

Beeke, S., Wilkinson, R. and Maxim, J. 2007. 'Individual variation in agrammatism: a single case study of the influence of interaction', *International Journal of Language & Communication Disorders* **42**:6, 629–47.

Biddle, K. R., McCabe, A. and Bliss, L. S. 1996. 'Narrative skills following traumatic brain injury in children and adults', *Journal of Communication Disorders* **29**:6, 447–69.

Bishop, D. V. M. 2003. *The children's communication checklist, version 2 (CCC-2)*, London: Psychological Corporation.

Bishop, D. V. M. and Rosenbloom, L. 1987. 'Classification of childhood language disorders', in W. Yule and M. Rutter (eds), *Language development and disorders*, London: MacKeith Press, 16–41.

Booth, S. and Swabey, D. 1999. 'Group training in communication skills for carers of adults with aphasia', *International Journal of Language & Communication Disorders* **34**:3, 291–309.

Boudreau, D. M. and Chapman, R. S. 2000. 'The relationship between event representation and linguistic skill in narratives of children and adolescents with Down syndrome', *Journal of Speech, Language, and Hearing Research* **43**:5, 1146–59.

Brinton, B. and Fujiki, M. 1994. 'Ability of institutionalized and community-based adults with retardation to respond to questions in an interview context', *Journal of Speech and Hearing Research* **37**:2, 369–77.

Brockway, J. P., Follmer, R. L., Preuss, L. A., Prioleau, C. E., Burrows, G. S., Solsrud, K. A., Cooke, C. N., Greenhoot, J. H. and Howard, J. 1998. 'Memory, simple and complex language, and the temporal lobe', *Brain and Language* **61**:1, 1–29.

Chafe, W. L. 1980. *The pear stories: cognitive, cultural and linguistic aspects of narrative production*, Norwood, NJ: Ablex.

Chaika, E. 1982. 'A unified explanation for the diverse structural deviations reported for adult schizophrenics with disrupted speech', *Journal of Communication Disorders* **15**:3, 167–89.

Chapman, S. B., Gamino, J. F., Cook, L. G., Hanten, G., Li, X. and Levin, H. S. 2006. 'Impaired discourse gist and working memory in children after brain injury', *Brain and Language* **97**:2, 178–88.

Chapman, S. B., Highley, A. P. and Thompson, J. L. 1998. 'Discourse in fluent aphasia and Alzheimer's disease: linguistic and pragmatic considerations', *Journal of Neurolinguistics* **11**:1–2, 55–78.

Colle, L., Angeleri, R., Vallana, M., Sacco, K., Bara, B. G. and Bosco, F. M. 2013. 'Understanding the communicative impairments in schizophrenia: a preliminary study', *Journal of Communication Disorders* **46**:3, 294–308.

Colozzo, P., Gillam, R. B., Wood, M., Schnell, R. D. and Johnston, J. R. 2011. 'Content and form in the narratives of children with specific language impairment', *Journal of Speech, Language and Hearing Research* **54**:6, 1609–27.

Conti-Ramsden, G. and Gunn, M. 1986. 'The development of conversational disability: a case study', *British Journal of Disorders of Communication* **21**:3, 339–51.

Cummings, L. 2005. *Pragmatics: a multidisciplinary perspective*, Edinburgh: Edinburgh University Press.

Cummings, L. 2008. *Clinical linguistics*, Edinburgh: Edinburgh University Press.

Cummings, L. 2009. *Clinical pragmatics*, Cambridge: Cambridge University Press.

Cummings, L. 2011. 'Pragmatic disorders and their social impact', *Pragmatics and Society* **2**:1, 17–36.

Cummings, L. 2012a. 'Pragmatic disorders', in H.-J. Schmid (ed.), *Cognitive pragmatics*, vol. 4 of Handbook of Pragmatics, Berlin and Boston: Walter de Gruyter, 291–315.

Cummings, L. 2012b. 'Establishing diagnostic criteria: the role of clinical pragmatics', *Lodz Papers in Pragmatics* **8**:1, 61–84.

Cummings, L. 2013. 'Clinical pragmatics and theory of mind', in A. Capone, F. Lo Piparo and M. Carapezza (eds), *Perspectives on linguistic pragmatics*, vol. 2 of Perspectives in Pragmatics, Philosophy and Psychology, Dordrecht: Springer, 23–56.

Cummings, L. 2014a. *Pragmatic disorders*, Dordrecht: Springer.

Cummings, L. 2014b. 'Pragmatic disorders and theory of mind', in L. Cummings (ed.), *Cambridge handbook of communication disorders*, Cambridge: Cambridge University Press, 559–77.

Cummings, L. 2014c. *Communication disorders*, Houndmills, Basingstoke: Palgrave Macmillan.

Cummings, L. 2015. 'Pragmatic disorders and social functioning: a lifespan perspective', in J. L. Mey and A. Capone (eds), *Pragmatics, culture and society*, vol. 3 of Perspectives in Pragmatics, Philosophy and Psychology, Dordrecht: Springer.

Dardier, V., Bernicot, J., Delanoë, A., Vanberten, M., Fayada, C., Chevignard, M., Delaye, C., Laurent-Vannier, A. and Dubois, B. 2011. 'Severe traumatic brain injury, frontal lesions, and social aspects of language use: a study of French-speaking adults', *Journal of Communication Disorders* **44**:3, 359–78.

De Renzi, E. and Vignolo, L. A. 1962. 'The Token Test: a sensitive test to detect receptive disturbances in aphasics', *Brain* **85**:4, 665–78.

De Villiers, J., Myers, B. and Stainton, R. J. 2012. 'Differential pragmatic abilities and autism spectrum disorders: the case of pragmatic determinants of literal content', in M. Macaulay and P. Garcés-Conejos (eds), *Pragmatics and context*, Toronto, CA: Antares.

Dewart, H. and Summers, S. 1988. *The pragmatics profile of early communication skills*, Windsor: NFER Nelson.

Dobbinson, S., Perkins, M. R. and Boucher, J. 1998. 'Structural patterns in conversations with a woman who has autism', *Journal of Communication Disorders* **31**:2, 113–34.

Dronkers, N. F., Ludy, C. A. and Redfern, B. B. 1998. 'Pragmatics in the absence of verbal language: descriptions of a severe aphasic and a language-deprived adult', *Journal of Neurolinguistics* **11**:1–2, 179–90.

Duncan, S. 2008. 'Gestural imagery and cohesion in normal and impaired discourse', in I. Wachsmuth, M. Lenzen and G. Knoblich (eds), *Embodied communication in humans and machines*, Oxford: Oxford University Press, 305–28.

Eme, E., Lacroix, A. and Almecija, Y. 2010. 'Oral narrative skills in French adults who are functionally illiterate: linguistic features and discourse organization', *Journal of Speech, Language, and Hearing Research* **53**:5, 1349–71.

Folstein, M., Folstein, S. and McHugh, P. 1975. '"Mini-mental state": a practical method for grading the cognitive state of patients for the clinician', *Journal of Psychiatric Research* **12**:3, 189–98.

Giddan, J. J., Ross, G. J., Sechler, L. L. and Becker, B. R. 1997. 'Selective mutism in elementary school: multidisciplinary interventions', *Language, Speech, and Hearing Services in Schools* **28**:2, 127–33.

Goodglass, H., Kaplan, E. and Barresi, B. 2001. *Boston diagnostic aphasia examination*, Baltimore: Lippincott Williams & Wilkins.

Gross, R. G., Ash, S., McMillan, C. T., Gunawardena, D., Powers, C., Libon, D. J., Moore, P., Liang, T.-W. and Grossman, M. 2010. 'Impaired information integration contributes to communication difficulty in corticobasal syndrome', *Cognitive and Behavioral Neurology* **23**:1, 1–7.

Hella, P., Niemi, J., Hintikka, J., Otsa, L., Tirkkonen, J.-M. and Koponen, H. 2013. 'Disordered semantic activation in disorganized discourse in schizophrenia: a new pragma-linguistic tool for structure and meaning reconstruction', *International Journal of Language & Communication Disorders* **48**:3, 320–8.

Hemphill, L., Uccelli, P., Winner, K., Chang, C.-J. and Bellinger, D. 2002. 'Narrative discourse in young children with histories of early corrective heart surgery', *Journal of Speech, Language, and Hearing Research* **45**:2, 318–31.

Hengst, J. A., Frame, S. R., Neuman-Stritzel, T. and Gannaway, R. 2005. 'Using others' words: conversational use of reported speech by individuals with aphasia and their communication partners', *Journal of Speech, Language, and Hearing Research* **48**:1, 137–56.

Huber, W., Poeck, K., Weniger, D. and Willmes, K. 1983. *Der Aachener Aphasie Test (AAT)*, Göttingen, Germany: Hogrefe.

Illes, J. 1989. 'Neurolinguistic features of spontaneous language production dissociate three forms of neurodegenerative disease: Alzheimer's, Huntington's, and Parkinson's', *Brain and Language* **37**:4, 628–42.

Jones, E. V. 1986. 'Building the foundations for sentence production in a non-fluent aphasic', *British Journal of Disorders of Communication* **21**:1, 63–82.

Jorgensen, M. and Togher, L. 2009. 'Narrative after traumatic brain injury: a comparison of monologic and jointly-produced discourse', *Brain Injury* **23**:9, 727–40.

Juncos-Rabadán, O., Pereiro, A. X. and Rodríguez, M. S. 2005. 'Narrative speech in aging: quantity, information content, and cohesion', *Brain and Language* **95**:3, 423–34.

Kennedy, M. R. T. 2000. 'Topic scenes in conversations with adults with right-hemisphere brain damage', *American Journal of Speech–Language Pathology* **9**:1, 72–86.

Kertesz, A. 1979 [1982]. *Western Aphasia Battery*, New York: Grune & Stratton.

Kindell, J., Sage, K., Keady, J. and Wilkinson, R. 2013. 'Adapting to conversation with semantic dementia: using enactment as a compensatory strategy in everyday social interaction', *International Journal of Language & Communication Disorders* **48**:5, 497–507.

Korkman, M., Kirk, U. and Kemp, S. 1998. *NEPSY: a developmental neuropsychological assessment*, San Antonio, TX: The Psychological Corporation.

Laws, G. and Bishop, D. V. M. 2004. 'Pragmatic language impairment and social deficits in Williams syndrome: a comparison with Down's syndrome and specific language impairment', *International Journal of Language & Communication Disorders* **39**:1, 45–64.

Lê, K., Coelho, C., Mozeiko, J. and Grafman, J. 2011. 'Measuring goodness of story narratives', *Journal of Speech, Language, and Hearing Research* **54**:1, 118–26.

Leinonen, E. and Letts, C. 1997. 'Why pragmatic impairment? A case study in the comprehension of inferential meaning', *European Journal of Disorders of Communication* **32**:2s, 35–51.

Liles, B. Z. 1987. 'Episode organization and cohesive conjunctions in narratives of children with and without language disorder', *Journal of Speech and Hearing Research* **30**:2, 185–96.

Loukusa, S., Leinonen, E., Jussila, K., Mattila, M.-L., Ryder, N., Ebeling, H. and Moilanen, I. 2007. 'Answering contextually demanding questions: pragmatic errors produced by children with Asperger syndrome or high-functioning autism', *Journal of Communication Disorders* **40**:5, 357–81.

Lovett, M. W., Dennis, M. and Newman, J. E. 1986. 'Making reference: the cohesive use of pronouns in the narrative discourse of hemidecorticate adolescents', *Brain and Language* **29**:2, 224–51.

Mancini, M. A. and Rogers, R. 2007. 'Narratives of recovery from serious psychiatric disabilities: a critical discourse analysis', *Critical Approaches to Discourse Analysis Across Disciplines* **1**:2, 35–50.

Mayer, M. 1969. *Frog, where are you?*, New York: Dial Press.

Mayer, M. 1974. *Frog goes to dinner*, New York: Dial Press.

McCabe, P. J., Sheard, C. and Code, C. 2008. 'Communication impairment in the AIDS dementia complex (ADC): a case report', *Journal of Communication Disorders* **41**:3, 203–22.

McTear, M. F. 1985. 'Pragmatic disorders: a case study of conversational disability', *British Journal of Disorders of Communication* **20**:2, 129–42.

Mentis, M., Briggs-Whittaker, J. and Gramigna, G. D. 1995. 'Discourse topic management in senile dementia of the Alzheimer's type', *Journal of Speech and Hearing Research* **38**:5, 1054–66.

Mentis, M. and Prutting, C. A. 1991. 'Analysis of topic as illustrated in a head-injured and a normal adult', *Journal of Speech and Hearing Research* **34**:3, 583–95.

Moseley, M. J. 1990. 'Mother–child interaction with preschool language-delayed children: structuring conversations', *Journal of Communication Disorders* **23**:3, 187–203.

Most, T., Shina-August, E. and Meilijson, S. 2010. 'Pragmatic abilities of children with hearing loss using cochlear implants or hearing aids compared to hearing children', *Journal of Deaf Studies and Deaf Education* **15**:4, 422–37.

Murdoch, B. E. and Chenery, H. J. 1990. 'Latent aphasia and flaccid dysarthria associated with subcortical and brainstem calcification 20 years post-radiotherapy', *Journal of Neurolinguistics* **5**:1, 55–73.

Oelschlaeger, M. L. and Damico, J. S. 2000. 'Partnership in conversation: a study of word search strategies', *Journal of Communication Disorders* **33**:3, 205–25.

Ogar, J. M., Baldo, J. V., Wilson, S. M., Brambati, S. M., Miller, B. L., Dronkers, N. F. and Gorno-Tempini, M. L. 2011. 'Semantic dementia and persisting Wernicke's aphasia: linguistic and anatomical profiles', *Brain and Language* **117**:1, 28–33.

Orange, J. B., Lubinski, R. B. and Higginbotham, D. J. 1996. 'Conversational repair by individuals with dementia of the Alzheimer's type', *Journal of Speech and Hearing Research* **39**:4, 881–95.

Paradis, M. 1987. *The assessment of bilingual aphasia*, Hillsdale, NJ: Lawrence Erlbaum.

Peets, K. F. 2009. 'Profiles of dysfluency and errors in classroom discourse among children with language impairment', *Journal of Communication Disorders* **42**:2, 136–54.

Perkins, L. 1995. 'Applying conversation analysis to aphasia: clinical implications and analytic issues', *European Journal of Disorders of Communication* **30**:3, 372–83.

Perlini, C., Marini, A., Garzitto, M., Isola, M., Cerruti, S., Marinelli, V., Rambaldelli, G., Ferro, A., Tomelleri, L., Dusi, N., Bellani, M., Tansella, M., Fabbro, F. and Brambilla, P. 2012. 'Linguistic production and syntactic comprehension in schizophrenia and bipolar disorder', *Acta Psychiatrica Scandinavica* **126**:5, 363–76.

Phelps-Terasaki, D. and Phelps-Gunn, T. 2007. *Test of pragmatic language: 2*, Austin, TX: Pro-Ed.

Prud'hommeaux, E. and Rouhizadeh, M. 2012. 'Automatic detection of pragmatic deficits in children with autism', *Proceedings of the 3rd Workshop on Child, Computer and Interaction (WOCCI, 2012)*, Portland, OR: ISCA.

Prutting, C. A. and Kirchner, D. M. 1987. 'A clinical appraisal of the pragmatic aspects of language', *Journal of Speech and Hearing Disorders* **52**:2, 105–19.

Radanovic, M., Nunes, P. V., Forlenza, O. V., Braga Ladeira, R. and Gattaz, W. F. 2013. 'Cognitive–linguistic deficits in euthymic elderly patients with bipolar disorder', *Journal of Affective Disorders* **150**:2, 691–4.

Rapin, I. and Allen, D. A. 1983. 'Developmental language disorders: nosologic considerations', in U. Kirk (ed.), *Neuropsychology of language, reading and spelling*, New York: Academic Press, 155–84.

Raven, J. C. 1956. *Coloured progressive matrices, sets A, Ab*, London: BHK Levis & Co.

Rinaldi, W. 2000. 'Pragmatic comprehension in secondary school-aged students with specific developmental language disorder', *International Journal of Language & Communication Disorders* **35**:1, 1–29.

Rollins, P. R., Pan, B. A., Conti-Ramsden, G. and Snow, C. E. 1994. 'Communicative skills in children with specific language impairments: a comparison with their language-matched siblings', *Journal of Communication Disorders* **27**:2, 189–206.

Sahlén, B. and Nettelbladt, U. 1993. 'Context and comprehension: a neurolinguistic and interactional approach to the understanding of semantic–pragmatic disorder', *European Journal of Disorders of Communication* **28**:2, 117–40.

Semel, E., Wiig, E. H. and Secord, W. A. 2003. *Clinical Evaluation of Language Fundamentals*, fourth edition (CELF-4), Toronto, Canada: The Psychological Corporation.

Smith Doody, R., Hrachovy, R. A. and Feher, E. P. 1992. 'Recurrent fluent aphasia associated with a seizure focus', *Brain and Language* **42**:4, 419–30.

Solomon, O. 2004. 'Narrative introductions: discourse competence of children with autistic spectrum disorders', *Discourse Studies* **6**:2, 253–76.

Soto, G. and Hartmann, E. 2006. 'Analysis of narratives produced by four children who use augmentative and alternative communication', *Journal of Communication Disorders* **39**:6, 456–80.

Stirling, L., Barrington, G., Douglas, S. and Delves, K. 2009. 'Analysis of perspective management and reported interaction in story retellings by children with ASD and typically developing children', *Electronic Journal of Applied Psychology: Innovations in Autism* **5**:1, 31–38.

Strong, C. 1998. *Strong narrative assessment procedure*, Eau Claire: Thinking Publications.

Thagard, E. K., Hilsmier, A. S. and Easterbrooks, S. R. 2011. 'Pragmatic language in deaf and hard of hearing students: correlation with success in general education', *American Annals of the Deaf* **155**:5, 526–34.

Togher, L. 2001. 'Discourse sampling in the 21st century', *Journal of Communication Disorders* **34**:1–2, 131–50.

Tompkins, V. and Farrar, M. J. 2011. 'Mothers' autobiographical memory and book narratives with children with specific language impairment', *Journal of Communication Disorders* **44**:1, 1–22.

Walsh, I. P. 2008. 'Whose voice is it anyway? Hushing and hearing "voices" in speech and language therapy interactions with people with chronic schizophrenia', *International Journal of Language & Communication Disorders* **43**:S1, 81–95.

Wechsler, D. 1981. *Wechsler adult intelligence scale: revised*, New York: Psychological Corporation.

Index

academic (under-)achievement, 7, 165, 182, 183, 186
accommodation, 196
acute lymphoblastic leukaemia, 31, 32
aetiology, 7, 10, 18, 36, 95, 242, 248
affective
    flattening, 158, 160, 250
    state, 90, 104, 169, 176
aggression, 244, 245
aging, 196
agrammatism, 31, 115, 242, 249
alcohol, 18, 22, 127, 129, 156, 246
alogia, 156, 158, 249; *see also* poverty of speech
Alzheimer's disease, 2, 6, 9, 16, 103, 139, 242, 245, 246, 247, 249
ambiguity, 6, 49, 50, 161
amyotrophic lateral sclerosis (ALS), 106, 242, 248; *see also* motor neurone disease
anaphoric reference, 150, 151, 153, 172, 174, 180, 184, 190, 197; *see also* cataphoric reference
anomia, 15, 107, 242; *see also* word-finding difficulty
antipsychotic medication, 166, 172
anxiety, 157, 243
aphasia, 3, 7, 16, 30, 92, 95, 96, 97, 98, 99, 101, 106, 107, 110, 112, 115, 118, 122, 141, 153, 157, 242, 245, 246, 248, 250, 251
    agrammatic, 8, 98, 242, 249
    anomic, 133, 242
    battery, 141, 143
    Broca's, 112, 124, 242
    conduction, 242
    epileptic, 103, 247
    fluent, 97, 108, 109, 110, 242
    global, 242
    non-fluent, 2, 16, 97, 98, 103, 104, 242, 246, 249
    transcortical motor, 242
    Wernicke's, 242
Asperger's syndrome, 26, 67, 72; *see also* autism spectrum disorder
astrocytoma, 30, 32; *see also* brain tumour
atrophy, 91, 248
attention, 14, 19, 21, 28, 29, 31, 58, 106, 107, 133, 154, 167, 187, 196, 244, 247
    deficit hyperactivity disorder, 8, 10, 22, 156, 165, 183, 243
augmentative and alternative communication, 26, 186, 192, 243

Austin, J. L., 250
autism spectrum disorder, 1, 2, 3, 5, 8, 9, 10, 14, 15, 18, 19, 22, 24, 25, 30, 41, 64, 67, 69, 70, 72, 73, 74, 75, 78, 79, 157, 164, 165, 183, 243, 245, 247, 251
avolition, 158, 250

bipolar disorder, 107, 156, 160, 174, 177, 243, 249
body movement, 24, 56, 150, 192, 195
bradykinesia, 152, 243
brain tumour, 10, 30, 32, 91, 95, 248

cataphoric reference, 172, 190; *see also* anaphoric reference
central nervous system, 106, 153, 196, 244, 246
cerebral palsy, 23, 193, 243, 246, 248
cerebrovascular accident, 2, 9, 95, 97, 99, 115, 243, 250; *see also* stroke
chemotherapy, 18, 31, 32
childhood cancer, 18, 30, 31, 91
chorea, 152
circumlocution, 39, 123, 125, 158, 244, 251
circumstantiality, 162
classroom discourse, 183
cocaine, 18, 156
cochlear implant, 191, 244
cognition, 162, 250
cognitive flexibility, 71
cognitive–communication disorder, 3, 95, 96, 244
cohesion, 11, 20, 28, 62, 67, 75, 83, 85, 89, 126, 150, 153, 157, 171, 174, 179, 180, 195, 196
cohesive device, 5, 39, 59, 135, 144
collocation, 5
communication
    disorder, 3, 157, 242, 248, 251
    skills training, 122
communicative
    intention, 6, 10, 12, 16, 19, 25, 152, 159
    partner, 110, 115
conduct disorder, 156, 162, 165, 166, 244
congenital heart disease, 187
content unit, 135
context, 1, 4, 6, 10, 11, 49, 105, 137, 152, 159, 161, 170, 188, 244, 245, 246, 248, 251
conversation
    analysis, 8, 20, 97
    first-encounter, 126, 128, 129, 130
    telephone, 137, 138

conversational
  discourse, 137
  exchange, 2, 5, 20, 33, 42, 44, 54, 76, 78, 79, 102,
    111, 112, 114, 115, 117, 145, 158, 162, 166,
    170, 181
  floor, 132
  partner, 118, 120, 123, 126, 130, 145
  strategy, 117, 139
cooperative principle, 244, 247, 248
corticobasal syndrome, 152
cranial irradiation/radiotherapy, 18, 25, 30, 32
Creutzfeldt–Jakob disease, 103, 244; see also dementia
cri du chat syndrome, 23, 244
cytomegalovirus, 18, 245

decoding, 6, 98, 102, 163
default interpretation, 44
deixis, 4, 5, 64, 85, 89, 109, 126, 144, 146, 160, 195,
    245
delusion, 158, 249, 250; see also schizophrenia
dementia, 95, 96, 103, 105, 108, 144, 145, 146, 152,
    245, 249
  AIDS dementia complex, 8, 103, 141, 242
  alcohol-related, 156, 245; see also Korsakoff's
    syndrome
  Alzheimer, 2, 6, 9, 16, 103, 143, 145, 242
  frontal lobe, 104
  frontotemporal, 8, 10, 103, 147, 246, 249, 250
  Lewy body, 105, 247, 249
  Parkinson's disease, 17, 247
  semantic, 103, 150, 245, 246, 250
  vascular, 10, 108, 246, 249
demyelination, 101, 105, 248; see also multiple sclerosis
depression, 157, 158, 160, 164, 175, 178, 243
derailment, 245, 246
developmental
  language disorder, 19, 20, 36, 49, 250
  period, 2, 243
Diagnostic and Statistical Manual of Mental
    Disorders, 156
dialect, 64
disambiguation, 97
discourse
  analysis, 1, 96, 174
  particle, 176
disempowerment/empowerment, 137, 179
dopamine, 105, 248; see also Parkinson's disease
Down's syndrome, 2, 8, 18, 23, 59, 60, 61, 62, 245,
    247
dysarthria, 16, 27, 30, 92, 141, 192, 245, 246, 248
dyslexia, 147, 245
dysphagia, 27, 31, 245, 248
dystonia, 152

early corrective heart surgery, 186
echolalia, 25, 27, 28, 39, 44, 97, 123, 245
education, 127, 133, 143, 181, 183

egocentric discourse, 9, 99, 162, 166
ellipsis, 4, 36, 39, 44, 64, 66, 67, 85, 89, 99, 112, 130,
    132, 144, 150, 171, 174, 179, 188
emotion, 73, 162
emotional
  and behavioural disorder, 156, 165, 245, 250
  state, 160
encephalitis, 95, 106, 153; see also herpes simplex
ependymoma, 32; see also brain tumour
epidemiology, 245
epilepsy, 8, 10, 18, 28, 91, 95, 101
  frontal lobe, 29
  Rolandic, 30, 108, 243
  temporal lobe, 28, 29, 89
euphoria, 160, 243
euthymia, 160, 243
evaluative language, 153, 163, 165, 180
executive
  dysfunction, 19, 102, 246
  function, 7, 14, 19, 21, 24, 27, 96, 99, 102, 106,
    133, 142, 156, 161, 166, 246, 247
eye, 247, 250
  contact, 15
  gaze, 147

facial expression, 14, 24, 149, 164, 169
felicity condition, 246
figurative language, 26, 31, 164
filler, 29, 58, 60, 122
flight of ideas, 28, 158, 160, 161, 246, 247
foetal alcohol syndrome, 24, 246
formal thought disorder, 245, 246; see also
    schizophrenia
fragile X syndrome, 8, 17, 18, 23, 24, 246
friendship, 179
frontal lobe, 29, 102, 112, 133, 246

genetic syndrome, 7, 10, 18, 22, 23
gesture, 6, 14, 16, 17, 24, 26, 56, 152, 164, 166, 168,
    173, 181
glioma, 30, 32; see also brain tumour
global coherence/connectedness, 135, 152, 162, 251
glossomania, 25, 28, 123, 158, 246; see also
    schizophrenia
grammar, 14, 18, 39, 135, 136, 163
grandiosity, 160, 177, 247
Grice, H. P., 5, 64, 142, 158, 166, 184, 244, 247

hallucination, 157, 158, 249, 250; see also
    schizophrenia
head injury, 10, 16, 81, 83, 95, 131, 251; see also
    traumatic brain injury
hearing, 22, 36, 44, 51, 56, 244
  aid, 191
  conductive, 248
  loss, 59, 186, 191, 242, 247, 250
  sensorineural loss, 15, 22, 191, 244, 245, 250

hemiparesis, 126, 246
hemiplegia, 16, 27, 92, 115, 120, 124, 126, 246
hemispherectomy, 85, 87
herpes simplex
    encephalitis, 107
    virus, 106
HIV infection, 245
homonymy, 50
human immunodeficiency virus (HIV), 18, 106
humour, 2, 16, 17, 22, 26, 32, 128, 158, 192, 195; *see also* joke
Huntington's disease, 95, 96, 103, 105, 106, 152, 153
hydrocephalus, 21, 31, 107
hyperactivity, 8, 10, 22, 156, 165, 183, 243, 244
hypomania, 249

idiom, 50, 100
illiteracy, 186, 189, 190
illocutionary force, 1, 11, 26, 97, 159
imagination, 20, 22
implicature, 1, 2, 7, 10, 64, 73, 97, 159, 166, 169, 247
    conventional, 244, 247
    conversational, 161, 246, 247, 248, 250
    scalar, 247, 250
impulsive behaviour, 157
impulsivity, 160, 165, 243
inattention, 165, 243
incarceration, 157
inference, 12, 14, 27, 36, 40, 42, 62, 90, 95, 98, 99, 100, 102, 169, 251
    bridging, 41, 98
    elaborative, 12, 169
    mental state, 12, 169
    pragmatic, 169
    textual, 12
inferential comprehension, 27
information
    management, 11, 103
    processing, 83, 85, 133
informativeness, 62, 105, 131
inhibition, 133
intellectual
    disability, 2, 9, 17, 18, 20, 22, 41, 62, 64, 74, 83, 157, 191, 243, 244, 245, 246, 247, 249, 250, 251
    functioning, 30, 42, 56, 85, 91, 108, 156, 165
intelligence quotient (IQ), 247, 251
interruption, 152, 165
intonation, 6, 76, 115, 131, 147
irony, 18, 27, 64, 105, 166, 169; *see also* sarcasm

joke, 9, 16, 17, 77, 173; *see also* humour

Korsakoff's syndrome, 103, 156; *see also* dementia

Landau–Kleffner syndrome, 18, 28, 30, 108, 242, 247, 248
language

acquisition, 16, 21, 22
development, 54, 72
signed, 1, 191, 242
spoken, 1, 170, 191, 242, 250
written, 1, 164, 189, 242, 250
left hemisphere, 16, 85, 95, 110, 112, 122
    damage, 97
lesion, 95, 249
lexical
    reiteration, 5
    retrieval deficit, 28, 83, 118; *see also* word-finding difficulty
linguistics, 1, 20
literacy, 192
lobectomy, 90
local coherence/connectedness, 135, 152
logical form, 10, 41, 73
logopenic progressive aphasia, 249; *see also* dementia, primary progressive aphasia

magnetic resonance imaging (MRI), 247
mania, 160, 161, 175, 177, 247, 249
maxim, 28, 142, 166, 184
    manner, 5, 158
    quality, 5, 64
    quantity, 5, 64, 158, 169, 179
    relation, 5, 64, 158
mean length of utterance (MLU), 56, 57, 59, 60, 74
medulloblastoma, 30, 32; *see also* brain tumour
memory, 28, 83, 90, 106, 245, 247
    autobiographical, 51, 52, 163
    episodic, 29, 133, 153, 161
    immediate, 83
    long-term, 93, 144
    semantic, 147
    verbal, 154
    working, 14, 27, 83, 135
meningitis, 10, 15, 18, 22, 24, 95, 106, 247, 250
mental
    flexibility, 19, 102, 106, 133, 135, 246
    functioning, 143, 157
    health, 147, 156, 157, 164, 174, 177, 178
    state, 12, 19, 20, 25, 27, 58, 71, 73, 87, 89, 102, 159, 164, 169, 192, 251
    status, 153, 172
mental state language, 115, 142, 150, 151, 153, 162, 164, 172, 176, 179, 195, 197
mentalising, 163, 164, 165; *see also* theory of mind
metalinguistic knowledge, 114
metaphor, 17, 64, 73, 100, 106, 158, 176, 179
metapragmatic knowledge, 133
morphology, 161
morphosyntax, 20, 51
motor
    development, 20, 244
    neurone disease, 96, 105, 246, 247; *see also* amyotrophic lateral sclerosis

multiple sclerosis, 95, 105, 106, 248
mutism, 30, 181, 182, 248, 249
myelin, 248

naming, 28, 92, 143, 153, 154
narrative
    coherence, 162, 179, 181
    development, 11, 188, 190
    discourse, 4, 26, 27, 83, 85, 87, 89, 96, 106, 137,
        162, 163, 193
    fictional, 89
    introduction, 67, 71
    oral, 189
    personal, 8, 11, 15, 20, 22, 154, 158, 187
    production, 18, 44, 51, 59, 67, 81, 93, 196
    spoken, 1, 5, 10, 16, 17, 27, 96
    summary, 83, 84, 85
    written, 11, 102, 164, 165
negative symptom, 158, 249, 250; *see also*
        schizophrenia
neologism, 27, 39, 99, 123, 154, 248
neoplasm, 7, 18, 25, 95
neurodegenerative
    disease, 99, 242, 244, 247, 248
    disorder, 105, 152
neurodevelopment, 18, 29, 156
neurodevelopmental disorder, 18, 243
neurologist, 17, 191
neurosurgery, 32
non-literal language, 1, 2, 9, 15, 16, 18, 25, 49, 51,
        99, 128, 159, 164, 166
non-verbal communication, 14, 20, 24, 117

obsessive–compulsive disorder, 164
occupational functioning, 7, 9, 162, 244
otitis media, 37, 56, 248
overlap, 65, 68, 76, 81, 118, 120, 147, 170, 172, 184

Parkinson's disease, 10, 95, 103, 105, 150, 152, 243,
        247, 248
pause, 39, 81, 117, 122, 132
perinatal period, 36, 243
perseveration, 27, 38, 39, 102, 133, 135, 163, 248,
        250
personality disorder, 156, 162
    antisocial, 162
    borderline, 162, 179
    schizotypal, 162
perspective-taking, 25, 164; *see also* theory of mind
phonemic
    cue, 92, 123
    paraphasia, 25, 92, 125, 248, 249
phonetics, 93
phonology, 16, 19, 42, 93, 104, 164
planning, 19, 29, 83, 85, 102, 135, 158, 246
pointing, 24, 54, 97, 164, 195
politeness, 102, 105, 126, 247

positive symptom, 158, 250; *see also* schizophrenia
posterior fossa tumour, 30, 32, 91, 248; *see also* brain
        tumour
postnatal period, 18, 36, 243
post-traumatic stress disorder, 164
poverty of content of speech, 246, 249
poverty of speech, 156, 246, 249, 250; *see also* alogia
Prader–Willi syndrome, 23, 24, 246, 249
pragmatic
    assessment, 7, 13, 14, 19, 20, 22, 24, 28, 31, 96
    competence, 58, 64, 174
    development, 51
    enrichment, 73
    intervention, 20, 96
pragmatic language impairment, 8, 16, 18, 32, 97,
        249
pragmatics, 1, 2, 5, 12, 17, 18, 24, 25, 26, 30, 32, 49,
        66, 67, 93, 95, 101, 105, 130, 133, 142, 156,
        157, 159, 186, 249, 250
prenatal period, 36, 156, 243
pressure of speech, 247
presupposition, 1, 5, 6, 19, 36, 73, 91, 142, 159, 160,
        166, 249
primary progressive aphasia, 104, 249; *see also*
        dementia
prison, 157, 186
problem solving, 29
procedural discourse, 102
profanity, 103
progressive non-fluent aphasia, 103, 104, 246, 249; *see
        also* dementia
progressive supranuclear palsy, 246, 248
pronominal reference, 9, 85, 87, 89, 97, 130, 142,
        151, 160, 174, 188, 195
pronoun reversal, 25, 42, 44
prosody, 99, 149, 160, 245
proverb, 100, 108, 139
psychiatrist, 8, 96, 156, 172, 176, 178
psychiatry, 156, 174
psychologist, 19, 26, 96, 156, 164
psychosis, 27, 30, 172, 249

quantifier, 6, 65, 97

radiotherapy, 31, 32, 91
reading, 16, 104, 154, 161, 182, 186, 193, 194, 245
reasoning, 83, 91, 107
referent, 4, 48, 62, 67, 108, 109, 126, 132, 159, 192
referential communication, 103
rehabilitation, 16, 31, 96, 126, 131, 172
repair, 18, 29, 48, 59, 67, 101, 104, 109, 114, 122,
        126, 132, 144, 151, 153, 155, 187, 195; *see also*
        trouble source
repetitive language, 6, 8, 15, 82, 105, 132, 197
reported speech, 48, 59, 64, 89, 110, 111, 114, 117,
        126, 130, 142, 149, 150, 151, 163, 176, 184
request for clarification, 64, 67

right hemisphere, 2, 16, 85, 95, 126, 249
  damage, 128
rubella, 18, 23, 36, 247

sarcasm, 12, 16, 17; *see also* irony
schema, 52
schizophrenia, 3, 5, 8, 9, 10, 15, 19, 95, 156, 166,
  245, 246, 248, 249, 250, 251
Searle, J. R., 250
seizure, 29, 30, 85, 108; *see also* epilepsy
selective mutism, 156, 163, 181, 242, 250
self-esteem, 157, 247
semantic
  cue, 15
  field, 14, 25, 163
  impairment, 170
  knowledge, 39, 91, 98, 250
  paraphasia, 38, 39, 92, 140, 158, 160, 250
  system, 149
semantic–pragmatic disorder, 20, 36, 38, 249
semantics, 1, 21, 93, 124, 249
set shifting, 96
silence, 119
social
  cognition, 250
  communication, 20, 22, 25, 156, 163, 243, 250
  context, 105, 244
  integration, 96
  interaction, 14, 25, 157, 243
  isolation, 157
  perception, 250
  relationship, 102, 130, 244, 250
  withdrawal, 250
social anxiety disorder, 163, 164
specific language impairment, 3, 16, 18, 21, 23, 45,
  51, 58, 74, 250
speech act, 1, 2, 3, 5, 6, 8, 14, 16, 17, 18, 20, 21, 23,
  26, 27, 28, 36, 55, 99, 114, 126, 128, 134, 135,
  159, 166, 181, 184, 246, 247, 250
speech and language therapist, 8, 13, 19, 23, 39, 95,
  96, 98, 105, 147, 156, 160, 164, 170, 183
speech and language therapy, 16, 17, 121, 124, 156,
  157, 164
speech–language pathologist, 19, 32, 54, 141, 143,
  191, 246
speech–language pathology, 156
stereotyped
  conversation, 23
  utterance, 24
story
  component, 135, 137, 141
  generation, 107, 108, 139
  grammar, 14, 18, 135
  telling, 6, 7, 17, 32, 96, 98, 110, 115, 117, 150,
    163, 164

stroke, 2, 16, 95, 118, 124, 127, 243, 245, 249, 250,
  251; *see also* cerebrovascular accident
Sturge–Weber syndrome, 85, 87, 250
stuttering, 157, 250
substance use disorder, 16, 156
substantia nigra, 248; *see also* Parkinson's disease
substitution, 5, 67, 114, 126, 142, 150, 153, 160, 174,
  179
swallowing, 245, 248
syntax, 1, 16, 19, 21, 27, 29, 39, 42, 93, 95, 98, 104,
  124, 164, 165
syphilis, 106
systemic functional linguistics, 20

tangentiality, 246
teasing, 17, 26, 166
teratogen, 18, 24
theory of mind, 7, 19, 20, 25, 58, 71, 72, 73, 83, 85,
  91, 99, 100, 102, 106, 135, 146, 150, 157, 159,
  166, 170, 251
topic
  development, 98, 103, 104, 114, 132, 164, 171,
    192
  digression, 126, 134
  exchange, 56
  initiation, 103
  management, 8, 18, 20, 25, 103, 131, 142, 164,
    174
  preseveration, 38, 39
  relevance, 104, 144, 174, 195
  termination, 104
toxoplasmosis, 18, 107
transition relevance place, 15
traumatic brain injury, 1, 2, 3, 6, 8, 9, 14, 15, 19, 22,
  27, 28, 81, 82, 83, 84, 95, 96, 101, 131, 133,
  244, 246, 248, 251; *see also* head injury
trouble source, 122, 123; *see also* repair
turn-taking, 14, 16, 20, 22, 23, 104, 105, 118, 157,
  164, 181

utterance interpretation, 10, 20, 93, 95, 146

verbosity, 21
vision, 44, 192
visual impairment, 59, 186
vocabulary, 13, 39, 48, 54, 56, 105, 162, 163, 165
vocational functioning, 96

weak central coherence, 85, 251
what is said, 247; *see also* Grice
Williams syndrome, 8, 15, 18, 23, 251
word-finding difficulty, 25, 89, 123, 125, 140, 251; *see
  also* lexical retrieval deficit
world knowledge, 12, 38, 40, 41, 91, 98, 100, 169
writing, 154, 186